Fodor's

Bed & Breakfasts, Country Inns, and Other Weekend Pleasures

THE SOUTH

Fodor's Travel Publications, Inc.
New York • London • Toronto

ISBN 0-679-02150-7

First Edition

**Fodor's Bed & Breakfasts, Country Inns,
and Other Weekend Pleasures: The South**

Editor: Conrad Little Paulus, with Amanda Jacobs
Art Director: Fabrizio La Rocca
Cartographer: David Lindroth
Illustrator: Alida Beck, Karl Tanner
Design: Rochelle Udell and Fabrizio La Rocca
Cover Photograph: H. Mark Weidman (Two Meeting Street, Charleston, SC)

Special Sales

MANUFACTURED IN THE UNITED STATES OF AMERICA
10 9 8 7 6 5 4 3 2 1

Contributors

Mitzi Gammon, who lives in Atlanta, contributed our Georgia chapter

Sylvia Higginbotham, who wrote our chapter on Mississippi, is a freelance writer based in Columbus, in that state. She writes business and travel articles and is the principal in a communications company that prepares sales and PR materials.

The chapter of Alabama was contributed by **Henrietta MacGuire,** associate editor of *Montgomery Magazine,* who has done freelance writing for a newspaper in Costa Rica. She was ably assisted by **Mickey Ingalls.**

Real-live Southerner **Honey Naylor,** author of our Louisiana chapter, is a freelance writer whose features have appeared in *Travel & Leisure, New Orleans Magazine, USA Today,* and other national publications. She is also a contributor to *Fodor's Bermuda* and *Fodor's New Orleans.*

Susan Spano, who lives in Connecticut, contributed the chapter on Virginia. She writes about travel for the *New York Times, New Woman,* and *British Heritage* and reviews books for *New York Newsday, Kirkus,* and the *Bloomsbury Review.*

Carol Timblin, author of our North and South Carolina chapters, won first place in the Lowell Thomas Travel Journalism Competition and the Discover America Award in 1988. She lives in Charlotte, North Carolina, and writes a weekly travel feature for the Charlotte *Leader.*

Contents

Foreword

While every care has been taken to ensure the accuracy of the information in this guide, the passage of time will always bring change, and, consequently, the publisher cannot accept responsibility for errors that may occur.

All prices and listings are based on information supplied to us at press time. Details may change, however, and the prudent traveler will avoid inconvenience by calling ahead.

Fodor's wants to hear about your travel experiences, both pleasant and unpleasant. When an inn or B&B fails to live up to its billing, let us know and we will investigate the complaint and revise our entries where the facts warrant it.

Send your letters to the editors of Fodor's Travel Publications, 201 E. 50th Street, New York, NY 10022.

Introduction

Fodor's Bed & Breakfasts, Country Inns, and Other Weekend Pleasures *is a complete weekend planner that tells you not just where to stay but how to enjoy yourself when you get there. We describe the B&Bs and country inns, of course, but we also help you organize trips around them, with information on everything from parks to beaches to antiques stores—as well as nightlife and memorable places to dine. We also include names and addresses of B&B reservation services, should properties we recommend be full or should you be inspired to go in search of additional places on your own. Reviews are divided by state and, within each state, by region.*

All inns are not created equal, and age in itself is no guarantee of good taste, quality, or charm. We therefore avoid the directory approach, preferring instead to discriminate—recommending the very best for travelers with different interests, budgets, and sensibilities.

It's a sad commentary on other B&B guides today that we feel obliged to tell you our reviewers visited every property in person, and that it is they, not the innkeepers, who wrote the reviews. No one paid a fee or promised to sell or promote the book, in order to be included in it. Fodor's has no stake in anything but the truth: A dark room with peeling wallpaper is not called quaint or atmospheric, it's called run-down; a gutted 18th-century barn with motel units at either end is called a gutted 18th-century barn with motel units at either end, not a historic inn.

Is there a difference between a B&B and a country inn? Not really, not any more; the public has blurred the distinction—hence our decision to include both in the title.

There was a time when the B&B experience meant an extra room in someone's home, often with paper-thin walls and a shared bathroom full of bobby pins and used cotton balls.

But no longer; Laura Ashley has come to town with her matching prints, and some B&Bs are as elegant as the country's most venerable inns. The only distinction that seems to hold is that a B&B was built as a private home and an inn was built for paying guests. Most B&Bs, but not all, serve breakfast, and some serve dinner, too; most inns have full-service restaurants. B&Bs tend to be run by their owners, creating a homey, family feeling (which can be anathema to those who relish privacy), while inns are often run by managers; but the reverse is true, too. B&Bs can cost more than inns, or less. B&Bs tend to be smaller, with fewer rooms, but not always. The truth is that many B&Bs are called so only to circumvent local zoning laws.

What all places in this guide—B&Bs or country inns—offer is the promise of a unique experience. Each is one of a kind, and each exudes a sense of time and place. All are destinations in themselves—not just places to put your head at night, but an integral part of a weekend escape.

So trust us, the way you'd trust a knowledgeable, well-traveled friend. And have a wonderful weekend!

***

A word about the service material in this guide:

A second address in parentheses is a mailing address that differs from the actual address of the property. A double room is for two people, regardless of the size or type of beds; if you're looking for twin beds or a king- or queen-size bed, be sure to ask.

Rates are for two in the high season, and include breakfast; ask about special packages and off-season discounts. Mandatory state taxes are extra. Most places leave tipping to the discretion of the visitor, but some add a service charge to the bill; if the issue concerns you, inquire when you make your reservation, not when you check out.

What we call a restaurant serves meals other than breakfast and is usually open to the general public. Inns listed as MAP (Modified American Plan) require guests to pay for two meals, usually breakfast and dinner. The requirement is usually enforced during the high season, but an inn may waive it if it is otherwise unable to fill all its rooms.

B&Bs don't have phones or TVs in rooms unless otherwise noted. Pools and bicycles are free; "bike rentals" are not. Properties are open year-round, unless otherwise noted.

Michael Spring
Editorial Director

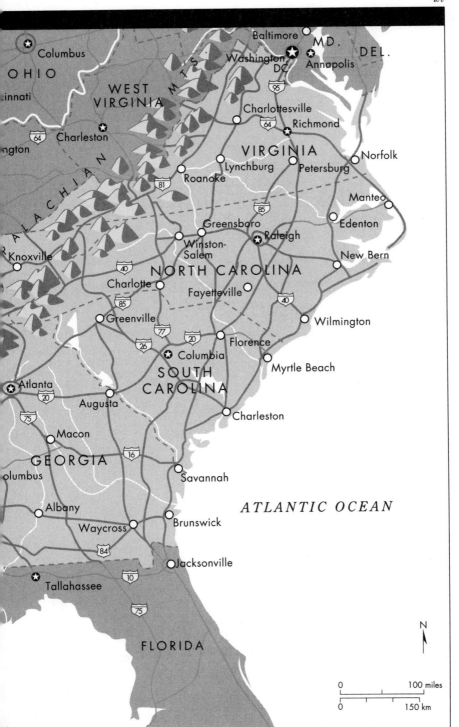

Special Features at a Glance

Name of Property	Accessible for Disabled	Antiques	On the Water	Good Value	Car Not Necessary	Full Meal Service	Historic Building	
ALABAMA								
Blue Shadows		✓		✓				
The Colonel's Rest				✓				
Grace Hall		✓		✓	✓		✓	
The Guest House	✓				✓		✓	
Hill-Ware-Dowdell House							✓	
Mentone Inn				✓				
Merschon Court		✓			✓		✓	
Noble House		✓		✓			✓	
The Plantation House		✓		✓			✓	
Oakwood		✓		✓	✓		✓	
Red Bluff Cottage		✓		✓				
Roses and Lace		✓		✓			✓	
Rutherford Johnson House		✓					✓	
Wood Avenue Inn		✓		✓			✓	
GEORGIA								
Ansley Inn	✓	✓		✓	✓		✓	
Ballastone Inn	✓	✓			✓		✓	
The Black Swan Inn		✓		✓				
The Brady Inn	✓					✓	✓	
Brunswick Manor	✓	✓			✓		✓	
Captain's Quarters Bed & Breakfast Inn	✓	✓		✓			✓	
The 1842 Inn	✓	✓		✓	✓		✓	
Evans House Bed & Breakfast	✓	✓		✓	✓		✓	

Romantic Hideaway	Luxurious	Pets Allowed	No Smoking Indoors	Good Place for Families	Near Arts Festivals	Beach Nearby	Cross-Country Ski Trail	Golf Within 5 Miles	Fitness Facilities	Good Biking Terrain	Skiing	Horseback Riding	Tennis	Swimming on Premises	Conference Facilities
✓			✓	✓			✓			✓				✓	
✓		✓		✓	✓		✓	✓		✓				✓	✓
✓	✓		✓		✓			✓		✓					
			✓		✓			✓		✓					✓
										✓					
✓			✓	✓	✓		✓	✓		✓	✓				
			✓		✓			✓		✓				✓	
✓	✓		✓		✓			✓		✓					
✓			✓	✓				✓		✓					
			✓	✓				✓		✓					
✓	✓		✓	✓	✓			✓		✓					
✓		✓	✓	✓						✓					
		✓	✓	✓	✓					✓					
✓			✓	✓	✓			✓		✓					
✓	✓				✓			✓	✓				✓	✓	✓
✓	✓		✓		✓	✓		✓		✓			✓		
✓	✓				✓			✓		✓			✓		
				✓	✓			✓		✓					
✓	✓	✓	✓	✓	✓	✓		✓		✓		✓	✓		
✓	✓		✓		✓					✓			✓		
	✓			✓	✓			✓		✓			✓		
	✓		✓		✓			✓		✓		✓			

Name of Property	Accessible for Disabled	Antiques	On the Water	Good Value	Car Not Necessary	Full Meal Service	Historic Building	
The Gastonian	✓	✓		✓	✓		✓	
Glen-Ella Springs Hotel	✓	✓		✓		✓		
The Gordon-Lee Mansion		✓					✓	
Greyfield Inn		✓	✓	✓	✓	✓	✓	
Magnolia Place Inn	✓	✓		✓		✓	✓	
Merriwood Country Inn	✓					✓	✓	
Morris Manor	✓	✓					✓	
Olde Harbour Inn	✓		✓	✓	✓		✓	
Open Gates	✓	✓		✓		✓	✓	
The Pittman House		✓		✓				
A Place Away		✓		✓			✓	
Pulaski Square Inn	✓	✓			✓		✓	
Rivendell	✓		✓	✓		✓		
Rose Manor Guest House	✓	✓		✓			✓	
Statesboro Inn	✓	✓		✓		✓	✓	
Stoneleigh Bed and Breakfast						✓		
Susina Plantation Inn		✓				✓	✓	
The Tate House	✓	✓		✓			✓	
The Veranda		✓		✓		✓	✓	
Victorian Village	✓	✓			✓		✓	
The York House								
LOUISIANA								
A la Bonne Veillée		✓		✓			✓	
Barrow House		✓					✓	

Romantic Hideaway	Luxurious	Pets Allowed	No Smoking Indoors	Good Place for Families	Near Arts Festivals	Beach Nearby	Cross-Country Ski Trail	Golf Within 5 Miles	Fitness Facilities	Good Biking Terrain	Skiing	Horseback Riding	Tennis	Swimming on Premises	Conference Facilities
✓	✓		✓		✓	✓		✓		✓			✓		
✓	✓			✓				✓				✓		✓	
	✓			✓									✓		
✓				✓		✓				✓					
✓					✓					✓					
✓				✓						✓			✓		
	✓			✓	✓					✓					
					✓	✓	✓	✓		✓			✓		
✓						✓				✓			✓	✓	
		✓		✓	✓					✓					
					✓	✓				✓					
✓	✓				✓	✓		✓		✓			✓		
✓	✓		✓	✓	✓			✓		✓		✓		✓	✓
✓					✓	✓		✓		✓			✓	✓	
	✓			✓						✓					
			✓					✓		✓					
✓	✓	✓	✓		✓			✓		✓		✓	✓	✓	
✓	✓			✓	✓			✓		✓		✓	✓	✓	✓
✓					✓			✓		✓		✓			
					✓			✓		✓			✓		
				✓				✓			✓	✓			
✓				✓		✓				✓					
					✓					✓					

Name of Property	Accessible for Disabled	Antiques	On the Water	Good Value	Car Not Necessary	Full Meal Service	Historic Building
Bois des Chênes	✓	✓					✓
Chrétien Point Plantation		✓		✓			✓
Cloutier Townhouse		✓			✓		✓
Cornstalk Hotel		✓			✓		
Cottage Plantation		✓		✓			✓
Fleur-de-Lis	✓						
Hotel Maison de Ville and Audubon Cottages		✓			✓	✓	✓
Hotel Villa Convento					✓		
Jefferson House		✓	✓				
Josephine Guest House		✓			✓		✓
Lafitte Guest House		✓			✓		✓
Lamothe House		✓			✓		✓
Loyd's Hall	✓	✓		✓			
Madewood Plantation		✓		✓			✓
Melrose Mansion		✓			✓		
Milbank		✓		✓		✓	✓
Mouton Manor Inn							
Nottoway		✓				✓	✓
Old Castillo Hotel/Place d'Evangeline		✓	✓			✓	✓
Ormond Plantation		✓					✓
Plantation Bell	✓	✓					
River Run Plantation		✓	✓				
St. Charles Guest House					✓		
Soniat House	✓	✓		✓	✓		✓
Sully Mansion					✓		✓

Romantic Hideaway	Luxurious	Pets Allowed	No Smoking Indoors	Good Place for Families	Near Arts Festivals	Beach Nearby	Cross-Country Ski Trail	Golf Within 5 Miles	Fitness Facilities	Good Biking Terrain	Skiing	Horseback Riding	Tennis	Swimming on Premises	Conference Facilities
✓	✓	✓	✓		✓			✓							
✓	✓	✓	✓							✓			✓	✓	✓
	✓				✓			✓	✓						
	✓				✓			✓	✓						
✓			✓		✓		✓	✓	✓						✓
					✓			✓	✓						
✓	✓				✓			✓	✓					✓	✓
				✓	✓			✓	✓						
	✓				✓			✓	✓						
	✓	✓	✓		✓			✓	✓						
✓					✓			✓	✓						✓
✓	✓				✓			✓	✓						✓
✓			✓	✓	✓		✓		✓					✓	
✓	✓		✓				✓		✓						
✓	✓		✓		✓		✓		✓			✓		✓	✓
	✓		✓		✓			✓	✓						
✓		✓	✓		✓			✓	✓						
	✓		✓						✓					✓	
				✓					✓						
			✓						✓						✓
			✓						✓						
			✓	✓					✓					✓	
			✓		✓			✓	✓					✓	
✓	✓				✓			✓	✓	✓					✓
					✓			✓	✓						

Name of Property	Accessible for Disabled	Antiques	On the Water	Good Value	Car Not Necessary	Full Meal Service	Historic Building	
Ti'Frère's House		✓						
Terrell House		✓			✓		✓	
William and Mary Ackel House		✓					✓	
MISSISSIPPI								
The Amzi Love House		✓		✓		✓	✓	
Anchuca		✓		✓		✓	✓	
Balfour House		✓		✓		✓	✓	
The Briars	✓	✓	✓	✓		✓	✓	
The Burn	✓	✓		✓		✓		
Cedar Grove	✓	✓	✓	✓		✓	✓	
The Corners		✓	✓	✓		✓	✓	
Duff Green House	✓	✓		✓		✓	✓	
Dunleith		✓		✓		✓		
French Camp Academy Bed and Breakfast		✓		✓		✓	✓	
The General's Quarters B&B		✓				✓	✓	
Governor Holmes House		✓		✓		✓	✓	
Ivy Guest House	✓	✓		✓		✓	✓	
The Hamill House		✓		✓		✓		
Hamilton Hall		✓		✓		✓	✓	
Hamilton Place		✓		✓		✓	✓	
Hope Farm		✓		✓		✓	✓	
The Isom Place		✓		✓		✓	✓	
Lansdowne		✓		✓		✓	✓	
Lincoln, Ltd.		✓		✓				

Romantic Hideaway	Luxurious	Pets Allowed	No Smoking Indoors	Good Place for Families	Near Arts Festivals	Beach Nearby	Cross-Country Ski Trail	Golf Within 5 Miles	Fitness Facilities	Good Biking Terrain	Skiing	Horseback Riding	Tennis	Swimming on Premises	Conference Facilities
	✓	✓	✓		✓			✓		✓					
	✓				✓			✓		✓					
			✓					✓		✓					
✓				✓				✓		✓					
✓			✓		✓					✓				✓	
✓	✓		✓		✓					✓					
✓	✓		✓	✓	✓					✓				✓	
✓	✓		✓	✓	✓					✓				✓	
✓	✓		✓	✓	✓					✓				✓	
✓			✓		✓					✓					
✓		✓	✓	✓	✓					✓				✓	
	✓		✓		✓			✓		✓					
✓		✓	✓	✓						✓					
✓				✓						✓					
✓			✓		✓			✓		✓					
✓	✓	✓	✓	✓	✓			✓		✓					✓
			✓	✓	✓					✓					
	✓		✓	✓	✓					✓					
✓	✓		✓	✓						✓				✓	
✓			✓	✓	✓			✓		✓					
			✓							✓					
✓			✓		✓					✓					
✓			✓	✓	✓					✓					

Name of Property	Accessible for Disabled	Antiques	On the Water	Good Value	Car Not Necessary	Full Meal Service	Historic Building	
Linden	✓	✓		✓		✓	✓	
Millsaps Bule House		✓		✓		✓	✓	
Monmouth	✓	✓		✓		✓	✓	
Mount Repose		✓		✓		✓	✓	
Natchez Eola Hotel	✓	✓		✓		✓		
Oak Square	✓	✓		✓		✓	✓	
Oliver-Britt House		✓		✓		✓	✓	
Pleasant Hill		✓		✓		✓		
Ravenna		✓		✓		✓	✓	
Redbudd Inn		✓		✓		✓	✓	
Red Creek Colonial Inn		✓		✓		✓	✓	
Stanton Hall		✓		✓		✓	✓	
Tally House		✓		✓		✓	✓	
NORTH CAROLINA								
The Arrowhead Inn		✓		✓			✓	
The Blooming Garden Inn		✓						
Catherine's Inn on Orange		✓		✓	✓		✓	
Cedar Crest Inn		✓					✓	
The 1868 Stewart-Marsh House		✓		✓	✓		✓	
Eseeola Lodge	✓					✓		
The Fearrington House	✓	✓				✓		
The Figurehead Bed and Breakfast			✓					
The Five Star Guest House		✓		✓				
Granville Queen Inn	✓				✓			

Romantic Hideaway	Luxurious	Pets Allowed	No Smoking Indoors	Good Place for Families	Near Arts Festivals	Beach Nearby	Cross-Country Ski Trail	Golf Within 5 Miles	Fitness Facilities	Good Biking Terrain	Skiing	Horseback Riding	Tennis	Swimming on Premises	Conference Facilities
✓			✓		✓			✓		✓					
✓	✓		✓		✓			✓		✓					✓
✓	✓		✓		✓			✓		✓					
✓	✓		✓	✓	✓					✓					
✓	✓	✓	✓	✓	✓			✓		✓					✓
✓				✓	✓					✓					
		✓		✓						✓					
✓	✓		✓	✓	✓			✓		✓					
			✓	✓	✓			✓		✓					
✓			✓	✓						✓					
✓			✓	✓	✓	✓		✓		✓					
✓	✓		✓		✓					✓					
			✓		✓					✓					
		✓						✓		✓					
	✓		✓					✓							
						✓		✓		✓					
	✓							✓							
			✓					✓		✓					
✓	✓			✓			✓	✓		✓			✓	✓	
✓	✓							✓		✓			✓	✓	
✓						✓				✓					
						✓		✓		✓					
✓	✓		✓					✓		✓					

Name of Property	Accessible for Disabled	Antiques	On the Water	Good Value	Car Not Necessary	Full Meal Service	Historic Building
Greystone Inn	✓		✓			✓	✓
Harmony House Inn		✓		✓	✓		✓
The Homeplace		✓					
The Inn at Taylor House		✓					
The Island Inn			✓	✓		✓	
The King's Arms Inn		✓			✓		✓
Langdon House		✓			✓		✓
The Lodge on Lake Lure			✓				
The Magnolia Inn					✓	✓	✓
New Berne House		✓			✓		
Pilot Knob Inn		✓					✓
The Pine Crest Inn						✓	✓
The Randolph House		✓		✓		✓	✓
The Tranquil House Inn	✓		✓		✓		
The Trestle House Inn				✓			
The Waverly Inn		✓		✓	✓		
SOUTH CAROLINA							
Annie's Inn		✓		✓			✓
The Belmont Inn	✓				✓	✓	✓
The Briar Patch		✓		✓			
Brustman House				✓			
Chesterfield Inn			✓	✓		✓	
The Constantine House		✓					
Elliott House Inn	✓					✓	✓

Romantic Hideaway	Luxurious	Pets Allowed	No Smoking Indoors	Good Place for Families	Near Arts Festivals	Beach Nearby	Cross-Country Ski Trail	Golf Within 5 Miles	Fitness Facilities	Good Biking Terrain	Skiing	Horseback Riding	Tennis	Swimming on Premises	Conference Facilities
✓	✓						✓	✓	✓	✓		✓	✓		
	✓							✓		✓					
			✓					✓							
✓	✓		✓												
				✓		✓				✓				✓	
				✓				✓		✓					
			✓							✓					
✓						✓		✓							
✓	✓							✓						✓	
		✓						✓		✓					
✓	✓							✓						✓	
✓	✓						✓	✓					✓		✓
			✓					✓							
	✓			✓		✓		✓		✓					
								✓	✓						
			✓		✓			✓							
			✓					✓						✓	
		✓		✓											✓
			✓					✓		✓			✓		
			✓			✓		✓		✓					
				✓				✓		✓				✓	
								✓							
		✓		✓	✓	✓				✓					

Name of Property	Accessible for Disabled	Antiques	On the Water	Good Value	Car Not Necessary	Full Meal Service	Historic Building	
Five-Thirty Prince Street Bed & Breakfast		✓		✓	✓			
Guest Quarters, Riverfront Apartments			✓		✓			
Guilds Inn						✓		
Hollie Berries Inn Bed and Breakfast		✓		✓				
The Inn on the Square	✓					✓		
Kings Courtyard Inn					✓		✓	
Maison DuPré		✓			✓		✓	
Rhett House Inn		✓			✓	✓	✓	
The Sea View Inn			✓			✓		
Serendipity, An Inn				✓				
The Shaw House		✓		✓				
Two Meeting Street		✓			✓		✓	
Two Sons Inn			✓		✓			
The Willcox Inn	✓				✓	✓		
TENNESSEE								
Big Spring Inn		✓				✓	✓	
Blue Mountain Mist Country Inn	✓	✓						
Buckhorn Inn	✓	✓					✓	
Edgeworth Inn	✓	✓					✓	
Hachland Hill Dining Inn	✓	✓				✓	✓	
Hale Springs Inn						✓	✓	
Highland Place		✓					✓	
Lynchburg Bed and Breakfast		✓					✓	
Magnolia Manor		✓				✓	✓	

Romantic Hideaway	Luxurious	Pets Allowed	No Smoking Indoors	Good Place for Families	Near Arts Festivals	Beach Nearby	Cross-Country Ski Trail	Golf Within 5 Miles	Fitness Facilities	Good Biking Terrain	Skiing	Horseback Riding	Tennis	Swimming on Premises	Conference Facilities
			✓					✓		✓					
								✓		✓					
		✓			✓										
		✓		✓				✓							
				✓				✓						✓	✓
				✓		✓				✓					✓
			✓			✓									
	✓		✓							✓					
				✓		✓		✓		✓					
				✓		✓		✓		✓				✓	
								✓		✓					
	✓		✓			✓				✓					
			✓							✓					
	✓		✓					✓		✓					
✓	✓	✓	✓		✓		✓	✓		✓	✓		✓	✓	✓
✓	✓		✓		✓		✓	✓		✓	✓				✓
✓					✓		✓	✓		✓	✓	✓			✓
✓	✓		✓		✓		✓	✓		✓			✓	✓	✓
✓		✓	✓	✓			✓	✓		✓			✓		✓
	✓			✓				✓							
	✓		✓					✓							
✓				✓						✓					
✓	✓		✓												

Name of Property	Accessible for Disabled	Antiques	On the Water	Good Value	Car Not Necessary	Full Meal Service	Historic Building
McEwen Farm Log Cabin Bed & Breakfast		✓					✓
Milk and Honey Country Hideaway		✓			·		
Monthaven Bed & Breakfast	✓	✓				✓	✓
Old Cowan Plantation	✓	✓					✓
The Peach Tree Inn		✓	✓			✓	
River Road Inn		✓	✓				✓
Seaton Springs Inn		✓	✓			✓	✓
Von-Bryan Inn		✓				✓	
The Wren's Nest Inn		✓					✓
VIRGINIA							
Applewood		✓					
The Ashby Inn		✓					✓
The Bailiwick Inn	✓	✓					✓
Belle Grae Inn	✓	✓				✓	✓
Brookside		✓					✓
Caledonia Farm		✓					✓
The Channel Bass Inn		✓					
Clifton		✓					✓
Colonial Capital		✓					
The Conyers House		✓					✓
Edgewood		✓					✓
Fassifern		✓					✓
Fort Lewis Lodge			✓	✓		✓	
Fountain Hall	✓	✓		✓			

Romantic Hideaway	Luxurious	Pets Allowed	No Smoking Indoors	Good Place for Families	Near Arts Festivals	Beach Nearby	Cross-Country Ski Trail	Golf Within 5 Miles	Fitness Facilities	Good Biking Terrain	Skiing	Horseback Riding	Tennis	Swimming on Premises	Conference Facilities
✓			✓	✓	✓		✓			✓		✓			
✓	✓		✓		✓		✓	✓		✓	✓	✓			
✓		✓	✓	✓	✓		✓			✓					
✓	✓		✓	✓	✓			✓		✓					
✓			✓	✓	✓					✓					
✓		✓	✓	✓	✓		✓	✓		✓	✓		✓	✓	
✓	✓		✓	✓	✓		✓			✓	✓				
✓	✓		✓		✓		✓							✓	✓
✓	✓			✓	✓			✓	✓	✓			✓		
			✓	✓											
✓							✓			✓		✓			
✓	✓		✓		✓										
								✓	✓				✓		✓
✓	✓		✓							✓		✓			
✓			✓				✓			✓		✓			✓
✓	✓					✓				✓					
✓	✓									✓			✓	✓	
✓		✓					✓			✓		✓			
✓										✓				✓	
			✓									✓			
✓				✓			✓			✓				✓	✓

Name of Property	Accessible for Disabled	Antiques	On the Water	Good Value	Car Not Necessary	Full Meal Service	Historic Building
The Garden and the Sea		✓					✓
High Meadows		✓					✓
The Inn at Gristmill Square		✓					✓
The Inn at Little Washington		✓				✓	
The Inn at Narrow Passage		✓	✓				✓
Jordan Hollow Farm						✓	✓
Joshua Wilton House		✓					✓
L'Auberge Provençale		✓					✓
Liberty Rose		✓					
Mayhurst		✓					✓
Miss Molly's		✓	✓	✓			✓
The Morrison House	✓				✓	✓	
The Norris House		✓					✓
North Bend Plantation		✓	✓	✓			✓
Oak Spring Farm and Vineyard		✓		✓			✓
Pickett's Harbor		✓	✓	✓			
The Pink House		✓					✓
Prospect Hill		✓					✓
The Red Fox Inn		✓				✓	✓
Sea Gate							
The Shadows		✓					✓
The Silver Thatch Inn		✓					✓
Sycamore Hill							
Thornrose House		✓		✓			
Trillium House							

Romantic Hideaway	Luxurious	Pets Allowed	No Smoking Indoors	Good Place for Families	Near Arts Festivals	Beach Nearby	Cross-Country Ski Trail	Golf Within 5 Miles	Fitness Facilities	Good Biking Terrain	Skiing	Horseback Riding	Tennis	Swimming on Premises	Conference Facilities
✓	✓					✓									
✓	✓	✓	✓							✓					
		✓						✓				✓	✓		
✓	✓									✓		✓			
✓				✓			✓				✓			✓	✓
✓				✓			✓			✓	✓	✓			
	✓										✓				
✓	✓						✓					✓			
✓			✓							✓					
✓		✓								✓					
				✓		✓									
✓	✓				✓			✓							
✓			✓												
				✓						✓					
✓			✓												
✓			✓				✓			✓				✓	
✓					✓					✓					
✓	✓								✓					✓	✓
	✓									✓					
					✓					✓					
✓			✓	✓						✓					
✓			✓										✓		
✓												✓			
			✓					✓					✓		
							✓	✓	✓		✓	✓	✓	✓	

Name of Property	Accessible for Disabled	Antiques	On the Water	Good Value	Car Not Necessary	Full Meal Service	Historic Building	
200 South Street		✓						
Woodstock Hall		✓					✓	
The Year of the Horse			✓					

Romantic Hideaway	Luxurious	Pets Allowed	No Smoking Indoors	Good Place for Families	Near Arts Festivals	Beach Nearby	Cross-Country Ski Trail	Golf Within 5 Miles	Fitness Facilities	Good Biking Terrain	Skiing	Horseback Riding	Tennis	Swimming on Premises	Conference Facilities
	✓														
✓			✓							✓					
				✓		✓									

Virginia

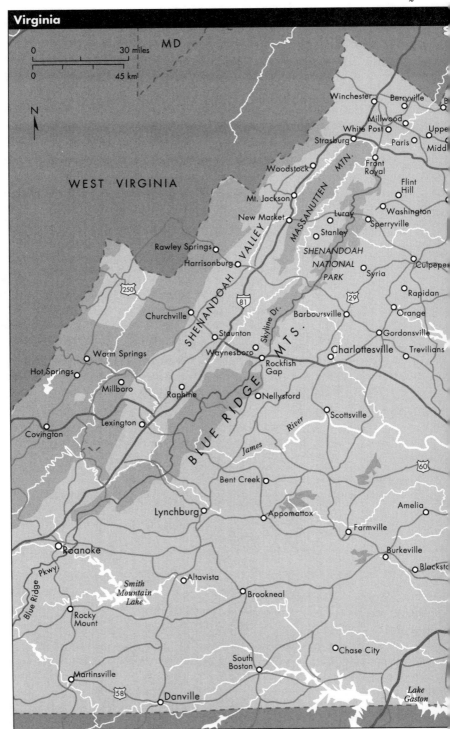

Northern Virginia

Think of northern Virginia as the Colonists' prize. Given the hostile Indians and mosquito-infested swamps they encountered around Jamestown, it's sometimes hard to fathom why they bothered to stay on in North America at all; but wander farther up the rivers into the verdant fields and rolling hills of northern Virginia, and the reasons become clear.

The region nurtured great numbers of American revolutionaries, and almost half the battles of the Civil War were waged in this countryside. Nowadays, though, it's refugees from Washington's bureaucratic wars who are claiming their rewards in northern Virginia. With the District's shiny office parks and shopping malls encroaching from the east, development is being tenuously held at bay.

The fast track to this Eden west of D.C. is Route 66 (except on Friday and Sunday afternoons), but cognoscenti opt for Route 50, which in an easy hour of driving puts you in Middleburg, the capital of hunt country. This discreet town breathes—and caters to—old money, with a collection of upscale galleries, antiques stores, and gun shops, with names like Dominion Saddlery, The Chronicle of the Horse, and Thoroughbreds. Hunt season in Loudoun, Fauquier, Clarke, and Rappahannock counties begins in late October with an opening meet, peaks around Thanksgiving, and continues into March, provided the ground doesn't freeze. Experienced riders can join in, but most content themselves with watching the colorful proceedings. To follow the hunt, keeping in sight of the horses, a map is helpful, but, frankly, most hunt country visitors prefer to spend their time window-shopping at Middleburg real-estate offices and driving Loudoun County's back roads. (Route 734 from Aldie to Bluemont is highly recommended, provided you're on the alert for careering Maseratis and BMWs.)

Northeast of Middleburg lies Leesburg, founded about 1760, which remained in Federal hands during the Civil War and thus retains much of its Colonial architecture. Leesburg's spruced-up storefronts and row houses are now restaurants and shops. South and west of Leesburg, a 30-mile corridor between the hamlets of Flint Hill and Syria makes for peak auto idling, too. Here the Blue Ridge asserts itself on the horizon as the roads wind up into the foothills. Fauquier County offers horseback riding in Shenandoah National Park, and all across the countryside, wineries such as Prince Michel and Dominion are flourishing.

At the southern border of the area sits Fredericksburg, boyhood stomping ground of George Washington, and hotly contested during the Civil War. Between 1862 and 1864, the battles at Chancellorsville, Wilderness, Spotsylvania Court House, and just south of Fredericksburg itself resulted in more than 17,000 casualties. On almost any fair weekend costumed Civil War re-enactors loiter on Fredericksburg's streets or down by the Rappahannock River.

Alexandria, a mere 10-minute drive from Washington, D.C., was surveyed in the late 1740s by a lad named George Washington. Tobacco was shipped from here to the smoky coffeehouses of London, and dissident Scots rankling over the Act of Union with England flocked here (which explains Alexandria's continuing fascination with things Scottish). A walk along Alexandria's shady lanes takes you by handsome brick houses built in the late 1700s and offers peeks into mazelike courtyards. Shoppers will find present-day Alexandria as mercantile as ever; there's an arts-and-crafts center on the historic waterfront and restaurants aplenty, including venerable Gadsby's Tavern (tel. 703/548–1288), which has dispensed spirits and victuals since 1772.

Places to Go, Sights to See

Alexandria. The *Alexandria Archaeology Museum* (tel. 703/383–4399) preserves the Colonial treasures hidden beneath the paving stones of Old Town. *Carlyle House* (tel. 703/549–2997), built in 1753 by a Scottish merchant, is considered by some the true birthplace of the Revolution, because it was here that British General Braddock conceived of a Colonial taxation scheme that resulted in the detested Stamp Act. Parishioners of *Christ Church* (tel. 703/549–1450) included George Washington and Robert E. Lee. *Gadsby's Tavern Museum* (tel. 703/838–4242) is next door to the tavern where five U.S. presidents signed the register. New York's Metropolitan Museum made off with its tavern doorway, then returned it in 1949.

Gunston Hall (15 mi south of Alexandria, tel. 703/550–9220), the Georgian mansion of George Mason, author of the first Virginia constitution and Virginia Declaration of Rights, was built around 1755, with a Palladian parlor and Chinese-inspired dining room.

Historic Fredericksburg. Pick up a brochure at the Visitor Center (706 Caroline St.) for a self-guided tour. Sights include the *James Monroe Museum* (tel. 703/899–4559); the *Mary Washington House* (tel. 703/373–1569), bought by a dutiful son for his retired mother; the *Silversmith* (tel. 703/373–5646); *Hugh Mercer Apothecary* (tel. 703/373–3362); and *Rising Sun Tavern* (tel. 703/371–1494).

Kenmore (tel. 703/373–3381). This Colonial mansion near Fredericksburg was the home of George Washington's sister, Betty. Its dining room is "one of the 100 most beautiful rooms in America."

Manassas National Battlefield Park (tel. 703/361–1865) was the scene of the First and Second Battles of Manassas, during which the Confederacy lost 11,000 men and the Union 17,000. This is where General Thomas J. Jackson's nickname was coined, when a soldier cried, "There stands Jackson like a stone wall! Rally behind the Virginians!"

Morven Park (tel. 703/777–2414) is a handsome Greek Revival mansion near Leesburg, built by a governor of Maryland, lived in by a governor of Virginia, and now a private trust. It has a carriage museum and frequent special events, including an annual steeplechase.

Mount Vernon (tel. 703/780–2000). George Washington's Mount Vernon is 10 miles south of Alexandria. In its owner's words, "No estate in United America is more pleasantly situated than this." The museum holds Jean-Antoine Houdon's bust of Washington, many period antiques, and the first president's sunglasses and sword.

Oatlands (near Leesburg, tel. 703/777–3174), a Classical Revival mansion, was built in 1803 by George Carter, grandson of the Williamsburg planter

"King" Carter. Its terraced formal gardens are considered some of the most distinguished in the state.

Trinity Church, west of Middleburg, in the hamlet of Upperville, is one of the most beautiful Episcopal churches in America, the style being adapted from French country stone churches of the 12th and 13th centuries.

Waterford, a village north of Leesburg so reminiscent of rural England that it could tug at the heart of any Anglophile, is, from one end to the other, a National Historic Site.

White's Ferry. The historic ferry across the Potomac at the edge of Leesburg, the 15-car tugboat *General Jubal Early* (tel. 301/349–5200), runs daily 5 AM–11 PM. The fare is $4 round-trip ($2.25 one way).

Restaurants

Bleu Rock Inn, on Route 211 between Washington and Sperryville (tel. 703/987–3190), serves nouveau French and American cuisine and has five rooms for rent. **Davis Street Ordinary,** in an old brick hardware store in Culpeper (tel. 703/825–3909), has a fireplace and a grand piano and serves classic American fare. At **4 and 20 Blackbirds,** in Flint Hill (tel. 703/675–1111), all the pastry is baked on the premises. **Jordan's,** on Market Street in Leesburg (tel. 703/777–1471), serves contemporary American food. In Alexandria, try the intimate **Le Refuge** (tel. 703/548–4661) for excellent and reasonable French food; **Tavola** (tel. 703/683–9070) for nouvelle Italian cooking; and the **Union Street Public House** (tel. 703/548–1785) for hamburgers, soups, and Virginia Native, a wonderful local beer.

Tourist Information

Alexandria Convention and Visitors Bureau (221 King St., Alexandria, VA 22314, tel. 703/838–4200). **Fairfax County Convention and Visitors Bureau** (8300 Boone Blvd., Suite 450, Tysons Corner, Vienna, VA 22182, tel. 703/790–3329). **Fredericksburg Visitors Center** (706 Caroline St., Fredericksburg, VA 22401, tel. 703/373–1776). **Loudoun County Conference and Visitors Center** (108-D South St., SE, Market Station, Leesburg, VA 22075, tel. 703/777–0519). **Virginia Division of Tourism** (1021 E. Cary St., Richmond, VA 23219, tel. 804/786–4484). **Winchester Visitors Center** (1360 S. Pleasant Valley Rd., Winchester, VA 22601, tel. 703/662–4118).

Reservation Services

Bed & Breakfast Guild of Rappahannock (Rte. 1, Box 2080, Flint Hill, VA 22627). **Blue Ridge Bed & Breakfast Reservation Service** (Rocks & Rills, Rte. 2, Box 3895, Berryville, VA 22611, tel. 703/955–1246). **Princely Bed & Breakfast Reservation Service** (819 Prince St., Alexandria, VA 22314, tel. 703/683–2159).

The Ashby Inn

West of Middleburg and Upperville along Route 50, the turnoff for minuscule Paris comes upon you suddenly; half the travelers looking for this hamlet in a hollow below the road probably miss it completely and end up crossing Ashby Gap or the Shenandoah River—not bad detours except that they delay your arrival at The Ashby Inn. The inn has the air of a way station in the wilderness where you'd be happy enough for a slab of overcooked prime rib. Instead, armed with reservations and a somewhat loose grip on your billfold, you're treated to some of rural Virginia's most sophisticated food, prepared by chef Eric Stamer and masterminded by innkeeper Roma Sherman. The menu is changed nightly, though some Ashby favorites, like sautéed mixed mushrooms, duckling braised with turnips, and profiteroles stuffed with homemade honey vanilla ice cream, routinely reappear. Dinner runs about $70 for two.

Perhaps the only danger in staying at the inn is that dinner will leave you too blissfully comatose to appreciate your room. Guest rooms are furnished with an authentic spareness that is a calming contrast to the rich food. Quilts, blanket chests, rag and antique rugs, four-poster and cannonball beds set the country tone, though in every case the views are the chief enhancement. As morning light shines through the windows, you'll spy the garden, the Blue

Ridge foothills, lowing cows, and other pastoral delights. Guests book many months ahead to stay in the Fan Room, which has two skylights and a glorious fan window opening onto a private balcony. Others find contentment in the dormer rooms, tucked under the green tin roof.

Roma and her husband, John, are generally too busy during dinner to chat, but at breakfast—eggs cooked to order, Virginia cured bacon, fried apples, and succulent muffins—you might get to know your hosts. Roma left advertising for innkeeping, and John, once a House Ways and Means Committee staffer, still writes political speeches between stints as The Ashby Inn's maître d'.

Nearby, there are vineyards to tour, hiking trails, antiques markets, and, of course, the Middleburg hunt scene. Many come to The Ashby Inn only to dine and bed down, returning refreshed to the metropolis next day, tempted to chuck it all and open an inn in some spot as idyllic as this.

Address: *Rte. 1, Box 2A, Paris, VA 22130, tel. 703/592–3900.*
Accommodations: *4 double rooms with baths, 2 doubles with sinks share a bath, 4 suites.*
Amenities: *Restaurant, air-conditioning; phones, fireplaces, porches, and TV in suites.*
Rates: *$80–$175; full breakfast. AE, MC, V.*
Restrictions: *No pets.*

The Conyers House

I f you want to climb Old Rag, make the scene at the meeting of the Rappahannock Hunt, have a group of companionable dogs lead you to a swimming hole (which a local church also uses for River Jordan–style baptisms), or go hill-hopping on horseback, The Conyers House will suit you like a pair of jodhpurs. No inn in northern Virginia is more remote; it lies on a narrow country road southwest of Sperryville and shouldn't be attempted in the dark without directions. This is part of its charm—but only a part.

The innkeepers, Norman and Sandra Cartwright-Brown, are responsible for the rest, for The Conyers House is a very personal place, stuffed with family mementos and curios the two have collected in their wanderings. In the Bartholomew Conyers guest room, there's a stuffed zebra head and a Texas bed with—since everything's big in Texas—7-foot posts. Jarring, you might wonder? Surprisingly not. One imagines that Sandra Cartwright-Brown could design a miniature golf course and still have it turn out tasteful.

She and Norman bought the house as a summer retreat from their Chevy Chase home. Built as a general store in 1810, it had a house added in 1815 and became a hippie commune in the 1970s. The beige frame structure sits on the side of Walden Mountain. There are seven porches and 10 working fire-places, seven of which are in the bedrooms. In addition to the six rooms in the main building, there's Springhouse Cottage and Hill House out back, where pets are allowed, not to mention a stall for your horse.

With prior arrangement, Sandra and Norman serve a six-course dinner in the gigantic dining room with such entrées as trout; medallions of veal with cider, Calvados, and cream; and charcoal-grilled salmon. The $62.50 price per person includes four wines, tax, and service. They can also direct you to wonderful local restaurants.

The Conyers House has an air of un-stuffy, slightly gone-to-seed ele-gance. It's the kind of place where you can appear for breakfast in jeans, disappear for the day canoe-ing on the Shenandoah, and return confident of being invited to sip a preprandial sherry.

Address: *Rte. 1, Box 157, Slate Mills Rd., Sperryville, VA 22740, tel. 703/987-8025, fax 703/987-8709.*
Accommodations: *7 double rooms with baths, 1 suite.*
Amenities: *Air-conditioning; TV/ VCR in common areas and suite; TV/VCR in Springhouse and Hill House; double whirlpool bath in Hill House; riding arranged.*
Rates: *$90–$195; full breakfast, af-ternoon tea. No credit cards.*
Restrictions: *No smoking in bed-rooms, 2-night minimum Oct.– mid-Nov. and on holiday weekends.*

The Inn at Little Washington

I n 1978 Patrick O'Connell, master chef at The Inn at Little Washington, and his partner, Reinhardt Lynch, opened a restaurant that grew into a legend, in a village of 150 in the eastern foothills of the Blue Ridge.

From the outside, the three-story white frame building looks like any quiet Southern hotel; only the Chinese Chippendale balustrade on the second-floor porch suggests the decorative fantasy within. The sumptuous interior is the work of British designer Joyce Evans, who has designed theatrical sets and rooms in English royal houses. The settees in the inn bear as many as 13 elegantly mismatched pillows each; the garden, with crab apple trees, fountain, and fish pond, cries out to be used as a backdrop in *The Importance of Being Earnest.* One bedroom has a bed with a bold plaid spread, shaded by a floral-print half-canopy—and, amazingly, the mélange works. And in the slate-floored dining room with Robert Morris wallpaper, a fabric-swathed ceiling makes guests feel like pashas romantically sequestered in a tent. A building across the street was recently converted into The Guest House, with two new rooms.

Much has been written about Chef O'Connell's food, all of it giddily rhapsodic. The menu itself, which changes nightly, makes compelling reading, and the five course dinner costs $88 per person on Saturday, $68 weekdays, not including drinks or wine from the extensive list.

Clearly the inn, with its staff of 60, is a place for indulgence, and anyone unwilling to succumb to it—both psychologically and financially— should opt for humbler digs. But judging from the waiting list, there are many unabashed hedonists out there (among them famous faces, who add juice to the already electric atmosphere in the dining rooms). Be sure to come with a sense of fun, as the star in a real-life theater piece with fantastical trappings, *grâce à* O'Connell and Lynch.

Address: *Middle and Main Sts., Washington, VA 22747, tel. 703/675–3800, fax 703/675–3100.*
Accommodations: *9 double rooms with baths, 3 suites.*
Amenities: *Restaurant, 24-hour room service, air-conditioning and phones in rooms, whirlpool baths and separate double showers in suites.*
Rates: *$290–$490; Continental breakfast. MC, V.*
Restrictions: *No pets, closed Tues. except in Oct. and May.*

The Bailiwick Inn

Anne and Ray Smith named their Greek Revival town house The Bailiwick because it stands across the street from the historic Fairfax County Courthouse. This location, at the intersection of two major arteries for western D.C. suburbs, makes The Bailiwick prime for business travelers. The oldest portion of the house was constructed shortly after the courthouse, and the building's redbrick and green-shuttered 18th-century look has been retained. Inside you'll find carefully crafted reproduction furnishings; in the Lee Room, the bedspread's pattern comes from the White House of the Confederacy. The founding fathers would feel at home in these surroundings, though they'd marvel at the 1990s bathrooms. Don't miss Ray's Robert E. Lee eggs in mush-room sauce, or the whimsical portraits in the front parlor, depicting the Smiths as 18th-century innkeepers (Georgene Cecula assists them nowadays). The Bailiwick holds murder-mystery weekends and invites the public to Sunday tea.

Address: *4023 Chain Bridge Rd., Fairfax, VA 22030, tel. 703/691-2266 or 800/366-7666, fax 703/934-2112.*
Accommodations: *13 double rooms with baths, 1 suite.*
Amenities: *Air-conditioning, whirlpool tubs in 2 rooms, fireplaces in 4 rooms, 1 room accessible to wheelchairs.*
Rates: *$95–$175; full breakfast, afternoon tea. AE, MC, V.*
Restrictions: *No smoking indoors, no pets.*

Brookside

Even if Carol and Gary Konkel weren't such nice people, you would still like Brookside. This intimate bed-and-breakfast, right beside Spout Run and the historic Burwell Morgan Mill, was built in two stages in the 1780s by the grandson of Williamsburg's "King" Carter. It's a frame house, with a bay added in the late 1800s by a Victorian builder who thought an extra touch would improve the classic facade; fortunately he didn't do much damage. The Konkels have an antiques shop in the rear and opened the B&B as a showplace for such treasures as a mid-1800s schoolmaster's desk, miniature silhouettes, and everywhere horses—Carol's personal passion. The guest rooms have high feather beds, bed hangings, and working fireplaces; as a special bonus, Carol lays out antique nighties for ladies to wear. There's a housekeeping suite in the Old Toll House cabin that once taxed traffic over Burwell's Spout Run. Antiquing and biking are occupations of choice here; Millwood's major industry is antiques.

Address: *Millwood, VA 22646, tel. 703/837-1780.*
Accommodations: *3 double rooms with baths, 1 suite.*
Amenities: *Air-conditioning, turndown service, conference room.*
Rates: *$95–$125; full breakfast. MC, V.*
Restrictions: *No smoking indoors, no pets.*

Caledonia Farm

Before opening his Blue Ridge farmhouse to guests, Bill Irwin went to some 250 bed-and-breakfasts. Caledonia Farm, built of fieldstone in 1812, is now a landmark on the National Register. On a clear day, you can see the Skyline Drive from it, and you can walk out the door and be atop The Peak (2,925 ft) in a little over two hours. There are two rooms on the second floor of the main house, and a suite occupies the old summer kitchen. Hessian soldiers who stayed after the Revolutionary War did much of the handsome carpentry, and 32-foot beams run the length of the house. The historic and natural setting are the keynotes here—not luxury (for instance, the bathrooms, while adequate, look to be vintage 1965). Bill is a host full of bonhomie and advice on exploring nearby caves and vineyards, hiking, cross-country skiing, and dining at the excellent local restaurants. An enthusiastic environmentalist, he has fought to keep a high-voltage cable out of the Fodderstack Valley.

Address: *Rte. 1, Box 2080, Flint Hill, VA 22627, tel. 703/675-3693.*
Accommodations: *2 double rooms share 1 bath, 1 suite.*
Amenities: *Air-conditioning, TV/ VCR in common area, fireplaces in rooms, small conference room; bicycles, hayrides.*
Rates: *$70-$100 (50% surcharge Sat.); full breakfast. No credit cards.*
Restrictions: *No smoking indoors, no pets, 2-night minimum in Oct. and on holiday weekends.*

Fountain Hall

Fountain Hall, a baby-blue Colonial Revival mansion, is surrounded by boxwood bushes and reached by a long brick walkway. Steve Walker, the owner, opened it as a bed-and-breakfast out of sympathy for business travelers, whose tales of loneliness and displacement he had listened to as night manager at a hotel in Niagara Falls. Here Steve and his wife, Kathi, their baby, and their yellow Lab, Oscar, provide business people temporarily stationed in Culpeper with a place to put down their briefcases and feel cared for. Fountain Hall isn't plush—though a few of its bathrooms do have whirlpools—but it offers what many travelers deem essential: phones in every room, parlor TV and VCR, and comfortable corners for entertaining guests. Downtown Culpeper is just a few blocks away, with the Davis Street Ordinary, its solitary hot spot, and the Amtrak station (where the Walkers will meet guests).

Address: *609 S. East St., Culpeper, VA 22701, tel. 703/825-8200.*
Accommodations: *5 double rooms with baths.*
Amenities: *Air-conditioning, phones in rooms, TVs and VCR in common areas.*
Rates: *$65-$95; Continental breakfast. AE, D, MC, V.*
Restrictions: *No smoking indoors, no pets, 2-night minimum on Oct. weekends.*

L'Auberge Provençale

Along with The Inn at Little Washington, northern Virginia holds yet another culinary shining star—L'Auberge Provençale is owned and operated by a fourth-generation chef from Avignon, who learned his art from his family. Behind the wide industrial stove in his jampacked kitchen, Alain Borel nightly concocts delicacies; he is renowned for his gourmet breakfasts, which have been known to include freshly baked croissants and lobster claws with tarragon maple syrup. The inn occupies a Victorianized 1750s stone house that looks a little like Appomattox Court House. However, the feeling inside is all Provençale, with modern French prints; shelves of wine (only a few of the 200 varieties on the wine list); and carved Spanish carousel animals that are for sale. There are two additions, but we liked the chambers (with fireplaces) in the main house best, reached by a polished staircase lined with curious reed birds. L'Auberge Provençale is a family-run inn, which, even more than the menu and decor, gives it its authentic French character.

Address: *Box 119, White Post, VA 22663, tel. 703/837–1375, fax 703/837–2004.*
Accommodations: *9 doubles with baths, 1 suite.*
Amenities: *Restaurant, air-conditioning.*
Rates: *$120–$200; full breakfast. AE, DC, MC, V.*
Restrictions: *No pets.*

The Morrison House

A Scottish flag snaps in the breeze above the white-pillared portico of The Morrison House, bespeaking the heritage of the owner, a Washington real estate developer and world traveler. Robert E. Morrison built the five-story Federal-style building in 1985, under the eye of a curator from the Smithsonian. It is constructed of red brick laid in Flemish bond and has arched windows and a small fountained garden at the foot of the entryway. Little luxuries abound, including state-of-the-art marble bathrooms, triple-sheeting on the high four-poster beds, afternoon tea, and a bag of Virginia peanuts in every room. All 45 guest rooms are different, decorated with camelback sofas, Chippendale-style chairs, swagged draperies, and a few fireplaces (which, alas, don't work). The Morrison House is a short walk from the King's Street metro; guests can park in the lot beneath the hotel and explore the District and Old Town Alexandria unhampered by the area's byzantine parking regulations and one-way streets.

Address: *116 S. Alfred St., Alexandria, VA 22314, tel. 703/838–8000 or 800/367–0800, fax 703/684–6283.*
Accommodations: *42 double rooms with baths, 3 suites.*
Amenities: *Restaurant, room service, air-conditioning, TV/VCR, videotape library, turn-down service, phones in rooms.*
Rates: *$130–$385; full breakfast. AE, DC, MC, V.*
Restrictions: *No pets.*

The Norris House

One Norris House regular returns every August to work his way through Brodie's biography of Thomas Jefferson; even after he finishes it he'll no doubt find reason to come back to this Federal-style inn in the center of Leesburg. Two celebrated early-19th-century builders, the Norris brothers, are responsible for the portico with turned spindles, the Adam-style mantel in the ethereal Blue Parlor, and shiny wild-cherry bookcases in the Music Room. Nowadays, Pam and Don McMurray set the pleasant tone at The Norris House. Their inn is an airy, relaxed, and civilized place, with unpainted wideboard floors, samplers, lace canopies, and fresh flowers.

On Sunday mornings, the *Washington Post* is likely to be strewn across the sofa in the library, while classical music plays in the background. And should you plan a wedding in the rear garden, Don will plant perennials in your chosen colors (given notification in the fall).

Address: *108 Loudoun St. SW, Leesburg, VA 22075, tel. 703/777–1806.*
Accommodations: *6 double rooms share 3 baths.*
Amenities: *Air-conditioning. Cable TV and guest phones in library and kitchen.*
Rates: *$70–$112; full breakfast. V, MC.*
Restrictions: *No smoking indoors, no pets.*

The Pink House

The Pink House lies at a crossroads in the wee village of Waterford, founded in 1733 by Quakers. The town resisted embroilment in the Revolution, but joined the Union during the Civil War, when Confederate troops laid waste their rolling Loudoun County farms. Today the whole 1,400-acre town is a National Historic Landmark, special among such places because modern development hasn't touched its periphery. This Brigadoon is accessible by bike path from Alexandria or by car via Routes 7, 9, and 662. The Pink House is owned by Chuck and Marie Anderson, who love opera, books, theater, and long, cozy chats. The prettiest of its two homey, cluttered guest rooms, called the Opera Suite, features 18th-century antiques, a whirlpool bath,

a TV with VCR, a baby grand piano, and a folk-arty mural depicting Waterford notables attending a gala at the Met. Both suites have fireplaces and private entrances and open onto the Waterford fields, where walking is encouraged. Marie's breakfasts include Irish soda bread, but for lunch or dinner you'll have to drive to Leesburg (20 minutes away), as the village puts itself out for tourists only during the October Waterford Crafts Fair.

Address: *Waterford, VA 22190, tel. 703/882–3453.*
Accommodations: *2 suites.*
Amenities: *Private outdoor sitting areas.*
Rates: *$90; full breakfast, afternoon tea. No credit cards.*
Restrictions: *No pets.*

The Red Fox Inn

The Red Fox has always been at the center of things in Middleburg. In fact, it predates the town, for the attractive yellow fieldstone structure was built by Joseph Chinn in 1728 at the halfway point on the road from Alexandria to Winchester. During the Civil War it served as the meeting place for General J.E.B. Stuart and Colonel John Mosby, and as a Confederate field hospital (indeed, the Tap Room's bar was an operating table). Today The Red Fox is still an inn, whose busy restaurant packs crowds into seven dining rooms on the first and second floors. Given the tourist traffic, we suggest overnighters opt for rooms in annexes called the Stray Fox Inn and McConnell House, which lie about a half block off Route 50. In the Stray Fox, ask for the palatial Belmont Suite, or the snugger but equally attractive Hulbert Room, which has a fireplace. All the rooms are individually done in 18th-century antiques, with canopy beds and four-posters, and a *Washington Post* is delivered to your door with breakfast. Just across the courtyard is Red Fox Fine Art, owned by the innkeeper, F. Turner Reuter.

Address: *Rte. 50, Box 385, Middleburg, VA 22117, tel. 703/687–6301, 800/223–1728, or 202/478–1808 in DC, fax 703/687–3338.*
Accommodations: *12 double rooms with baths, 7 suites.*
Amenities: *Restaurant, TV and phones in rooms.*
Rates: *$125–$225; Continental breakfast. AE, D, DC, MC, V.*
Restrictions: *No pets.*

Sycamore Hill

Get out your cameras, please, for the serious photo opportunities at Sycamore Hill, a ranch-style house seemingly dropped from the sky onto the crest of Menefee Mountain. As you wind up the mile-long approach from town, you begin to doubt there could possibly be a lodging at the end of the road. Fear not. Eventually the forest gives way to Kerri Wagner's extensive gardens, and finally you arrive at the Virginia fieldstone house wrapped by a 65-foot veranda. The view from this spot is the raison d'être of Sycamore Hill—there's Old Rag to the right, Tiger Valley, and Red Oak Mountain. And the 52 acres are a certified wildlife sanctuary. All the guest rooms face south, so you'll open your eyes to the Blue Ridge in the morning. Two are on the ends of the house and have triple exposure, and all are done in contemporary style, with blond floors, many plants, and pale blues and greens. Kerri Wagner is a cheerful hostess who treats her guests like friends, aided by a shaggy white mop of a dog named Molly Bean, and her husband, Steve, an artist whose fascinating magazine covers line the walls.

Address: *Rte. 1, Box 978, Washington, VA 22747, tel. 703/675–3046.*
Accommodations: *3 double rooms with baths.*
Amenities: *Air-conditioning, TV and fireplace in common area.*
Rates: *$95–$120; full breakfast. MC, V.*
Restrictions: *No smoking indoors, no pets, 3-night minimum in Oct. and on holiday weekends.*

The Eastern Shore

Most people think of the long peninsula east of the Chesapeake Bay as territory claimed by the states of Maryland and Delaware. Indeed, the most developed and touristy parts of Delmarva are; but if you look closely at a map you'll see a boundary line with the word Virginia *printed beneath. The border lies about 75 miles north of the peninsula's tip, and in between is Virginia's very own toehold on the Eastern Shore, encompassing two counties— Northampton and Accomack—with a combined population close to that of Charlottesville. The area was settled in the 1600s, by English Colonists; visited by vacationers (who made the trip by ferryboat) in the 19th century; and surveyed by the railroad, which reached the peninsular terminus, at Cape Charles, in about 1885. Several decades ago the peninsula was bisected by a highway, Route 13, which brought some—but not many—1950s-style motels and drive-in restaurants. Off Route 13, however, the Eastern Shore lives and looks the way it did around the turn of the century—no quaint restored villages or swishy resorts. True back-roaders will like it immensely—providing they understand in advance a few basic facts.*

Above all, Virginia's Eastern Shore is not a beach haven, except for the stellar sandy stretches at its northeast corner lying within the Chincoteague National Wildlife Refuge. On the bay side, tidal creeks and marshes predominate. Seaside, a string of barrier islands has kept beaches from forming at the shoreline. The islands themselves either are privately owned or, like the islands of Cobb, Smith, and Hog, are provinces of the Nature Conservancy's Virginia Coast Reserve (tel. 804/442-3049). To reach them you'll need to charter a boat, or sign up for one of the VCR's infrequent island trips. There are spring and fall boat tours, led by trained naturalists.

Nor are there any cities of note on Virginia's Eastern Shore, with the possible exceptions of Chincoteague, whose meager population swells in peak summer months but otherwise figures at about 3,500; and Cape Charles, which thrived during ferry and railroad days but now has only a cranking cement factory to keep it from becoming comatose. County maps show many other towns (with colorful names such as Temperanceville, Birds Nest, and Oyster), but these are really only crossroads with, if you're lucky, a general store. East of Route 13, skinny local arteries such as Routes 679 and 600 reach these villages and the architectural contradictions that surround them. The Virginia peninsula has its own unique building style, followed for hundreds of years: "chain" houses made of frame, consisting, when the pattern holds, of big house, little house, colonnade, and kitchen linked in a row. You can glimpse a good example, the privately owned Holly Brook Plantation, on the west side of Route 13, 8 miles south of Nassawadox.

The town of Chincoteague lies on 8-mile-long Chincoteague Island (not to be confused with the island holding the wildlife refuge, Assateague Island, to which it provides access via a bridge) and exists almost wholly to cater to tourists, with motels, restaurants, and shops. It is atmospherically similar to other Atlantic beach resorts in Maryland and Delaware, but its low-lying, marshy location brings septic and mosquito problems. Nonetheless, it has one attraction that will probably never cease drawing crowds: the legendary Pony Penning event, held in late July. The miniature horses swim the channel between Assateague and Chincoteague, where they are corraled and auctioned off, usually for about $600 each. This roundup began in 1924, though it was made nationally famous by Marguerite Henry's Misty of Chincoteague *in 1947. Misty herself was a real pony; her mortal remains are taxidermically preserved at the Chincoteague Miniature Pony Farm (tel. 804/336–3066).*

Places to Go, Sights to See

Accomac, a particularly pretty town and the seat of Accomack County, is one of two villages on the Eastern Shore (the other is Eastville) with an 18th-century debtors' prison. The Victorian clerk's office on the west side of the courthouse green holds records dating to 1663.

Accomack Vineyards (tel. 804/442–2110). This peninsula winery near the town of Painter completed its first pressing in 1986. Wines produced and sold here include chardonnay, Riesling, merlot, and cabernet sauvignon. Tours are available by arrangement.

Cape Charles, a place decidedly in the slow lane, was by 1953 abandoned by the passenger railroad and ferry service that made the town boom briefly around the turn of the century, then—to hammer the nails into its coffin— was bypassed by Route 5. Today most of its 136 acres constitute a historic district, though an unusual one because the houses date from the first quarter of this century. A walking tour takes you past two Sears-catalogue homes built in the mid-1920s, the pleasant bayside boardwalk, and a wonderful Art Deco moviehouse. Some will feel that industrial works to the south mar the townscape, though at these you can watch freight trains being loaded onto barges that take them across the mouth of the bay to Norfolk. In all, it's a funky, beyond-the-pale sort of place that attracts more and more refugees from northern metropolises, who are finding that they can still buy property in Cape Charles for a song.

Chesapeake Bay Bridge-Tunnel. This 17-mile engineering marvel links the peninsula with Norfolk and Virginia Beach. Completed in 1964, after costing taxpayers $400 million in concrete and steel, it has brought the Eastern Shore into the Virginia fold only to a degree, largely due to the hefty $10 toll—which, as some peninsula dwellers see it, keeps the Navy riffraff out. To support its mammoth span, islands were built, where there are scenic stopping places, a fishing area, and a snack bar; and to accommodate Chesapeake Bay ship traffic, the two-lane bridge gives way to two tunnels, one more than a mile long. The trip is either awesome, unsettling, or soporific, depending on the soundness of your stomach and nerves.

Chincoteague National Wildlife Center (tel. 804/336–6122). Despite the surfboarders and sun worshipers headed toward its long stretch of Atlantic beach, the refuge exists first and foremost for the benefit of birds, snakes, ponies, rare Delmarva gray squirrels, and Sika deer. Many of the species preserved in this veritable Noah's Ark are visible from a 6-mile loop drive that winds through forests and marshes. There's a visitor center, a lighthouse (built 1866), a crabbing ridge, and a fishing area—but no restaurants, camping, or bonfires. In season the refuge sponsors fishing expeditions, evening cruises, and a wildlife safari, which takes nature lovers along back roads where they can observe the intimate habits of the famed Chincoteague feral ponies.

Custis Tombs. The Custises were Eastern Shore gentry who married into the Lee and Washington clans. At this walled gravesite 6 miles north of the Bay Bridge-Tunnel on Route 644 you'll find the grave of John Custis, known chiefly for his legendarily chilly marriage to Frances.

Eyre Hall, the peninsula's handsomest and most historic plantation, was built in 1733, on land granted to the owners in 1662. The brick-and-frame house near the bay is open only during Garden Week, but its grounds, with ancient plantings, flowering shrubs, and venerable trees, can be visited year-round. Turn west 1½ miles north of Cheriton.

Hopkins & Bro. General Store (tel. 804/787–8220). This 1842 country store–cum–restaurant at Onancock's town dock is a Virginia Historic Landmark, with a companionable bar and a menu featuring such shore inevitables as crab cakes and seafood salad.

Kerr Place (tel. 804/787–8012), on the outskirts of Onancock, is a distinguished brick mansion built in 1799. Housed within are the collections of the Eastern Shore of Virginia Historical Society, including costumes, portraits, and furnishings.

NASA Goddard Flight Center and Wallops Flight Facility Visitor Center (tel. 804/824–2298). The first rocket was launched, in 1945, at this 6,000-acre NASA enclave (encompassing Wallops Island and areas surrounding Chincoteague). The visitor center, which is the only part of the complex open to visitors, displays space suits, moon rocks, and scale models of satellites and space probes. On the first Saturday of every month NASA conducts model-rocket launches on the grounds.

Pear Valley is the peninsula's oldest house, built in 1672. This one-room cottage with a chimney and loft is owned by the Association for the Preservation of Virginia Antiquities, though currently it is unrestored. It can be seen from Route 689, near Johnstown.

Refuge Waterfowl and Oyster Museums (tel. 804/336–5800 and 804/336–6117, respectively). These two tiny museums are neighbors on Piney Island (barely an island really, as it's only tenuously separated from Chincoteague, by skinny Eel Creek). The Waterfowl Museum has a collection of hand-crafted decoys, and the Oyster Museum tells the life story of the bivalve and how generations of watermen have pursued it.

Tangier Island. To reach this tiny island, stuck like a buoy in the middle of Chesapeake Bay, catch the *Captain Eulice*, at Onancock harbor (tel. 804/787–8220), sailing June–September at 10 and returning at 3. A livestock-grazing range before the Revolution, Tangier is now home to approximately 900 souls—most of them named Crockett, Parks, Thomas, and Pruitt—whose speech is Elizabethan cockney, barely changed since the first settlers moved in. It's an insular place, devoted to seafood harvesting and Methodism, with one main street, too narrow for cars, and the *Chesapeake House* (tel. 804/891–2331), whose reputation for family-style shellfish feasts has spread far and wide. Slightly less renowned is *Double-Six* (tel. 804/891–

2410), a local haunt once featured in *National Geographic* because it serves hot oyster sandwiches.

Wachapreague. This sleepy village on the Atlantic side of the peninsula once held a 30-room hotel and attracted vacationers from as far away as New York City. But the hotel burned down, leaving only the 340-odd permanent residents, along with a carnival ground that still lights up in late July. It remains a fishing mecca, with charter boats tied up to its dock; flounder is the prized catch.

Restaurants

Chincoteague is the one place for fancy dining on Virginia's Eastern Shore. Its culinary star is **The Channel Bass Inn** (tel. 804/336–6148; *see* below), where an ex–classical guitarist, James Hanretta, serves 20 guests each night, by reservation only (you give your credit-card number at the time you book). Recently a French restaurant opened in the area (in New Church, just south of the Maryland state line), called **The Garden and the Sea** (tel. 804/824–0672). It's a pleasant spot indeed, offering haute and nouvelle French cuisine. It's also a bed-and-breakfast (*see* below).

Seafood is on the menu at local family spots like **E.L. Willis & Co.** (Willis Wharf, tel. 804/442–4225), the **Trawler** (Exmore, tel. 804/442–2092), **Wright's** (north of Atlantic, tel. 804/824–4012), and **Rebecca's** (Cape Charles, tel. 804/331–3879). *See* also Hopkins & Bro. General Store, above. On Friday several churches serve homemade fare: soul food at Wachapreague's **Grace Methodist Church** and ham and chicken salad at **St. James Episcopal** in Accomac.

Tourist Information

Chincoteague Chamber of Commerce (Box 258, Chincoteague, VA 23336, tel. 804/336–6161). **Eastern Shore of Virginia Tourism Commission** (Box R, Melfa, VA 23410, tel. 804/787–2460). **Virginia Division of Tourism** (1021 E. Cary St., Richmond, VA 23219, tel. 804/786–4484).

Reservation Services

Amanda's Bed & Breakfast Reservation Service (1428 Park Ave., Baltimore, MD 21217, tel. 301/225–0001). **Bed & Breakfast of Tidewater Virginia Reservation Service** (Box 3343, Norfolk, VA 23514, tel. 804/627–9409). **Inns of the Eastern Shore** (1500 Hambrooks Blvd., Cambridge, MD 21613, tel. 301/228–0575).

The Channel Bass Inn

The Channel Bass occupies a pale-lemon building constructed in the 1880s—making it one of Chincoteague's oldest—and added onto in the 1920s, resulting in an untroubled asymmetry and a kind of appealing architectural buxomness. But the inn's design style, its history, even its proximity to Chincoteague National Seashore, are all eclipsed by another feature: its restaurant.

Jim Hanretta, who is both innkeeper and chef, opened The Channel Bass 20 years ago, and since then its culinary reputation has spread. The restaurant is known for its unusual recipes, invented on the premises by Jim, who learned his craft in Barcelona. Here you'll find local seafood brightened with Spanish and Basque sauces, beef tenderloin in a Peruvian marinade, and backfin crab medallions with chorizos. Jim cooks every dish all alone in his compact kitchen, which is why only 20 people can be served each night; dining here is a little like hiring yourself a private chef. The dining room is intimate (just seven tables wide), with windows providing views of the romantically lit garden in back. Wedgwood china, silver, and linen napkins are de rigueur. Of course you will pay dearly for the Channel Bass dining experience, with the average four-course meal ringing in at approximately $75 for one person, not including drinks. A green salad costs $12, and wines can be astronomical (Jim has a private reserve list topped off with an $800 bottle of 1966 Château Lafite Rothschild).

The nine guest rooms, on the second and third floors, are luxurious, with original art on the walls, plump picture books on the coffee tables, triple-sheeted beds, Neutrogena toiletries, and Egyptian-cotton towels. But they do not demonstrate the same unique sense of personality the restaurant does; rather, they are immensely comfortable neutral zones.

By arrangement, Jim holds special three-day cooking vacations, which include dinners and rooms, as well as hands-on lessons in the kitchen, during which some of The Channel Bass's secrets are revealed.

Address: *100 Church St., Chincoteague, VA 23336, tel. 804/336–6148.*
Accommodations: *7 double rooms with baths, 2 suites.*
Amenities: *Restaurant, air-conditioning, turndown service.*
Rates: *$108–$217; breakfast extra. AE, DC, MC, V.*
Restrictions: *No pets, 3-night minimum during Pony Penning, 2-night minimum on weekends, closed Dec. 20–Jan. 20.*

Pickett's Harbor

To begin with, you'll need a county map to help you find Pickett's Harbor. It lies 4 miles north of the Bridge-Tunnel and 2 miles west of Route 13—on the bay side of the peninsula, which thins decidedly as it nears land's end. The road to this isolated bed-and-breakfast winds past sweet-potato fields, through a grove of trees, and crunches underneath your tires, since it's made of oyster shells. Eventually the house, owned by Sara and Cooke Goffigan, appears on the left. Built of beige frame and brick, it is a free interpretation of the Eastern Shore style, comprising big house, little house, and littler house still—like schoolchildren lined up by height. Though she's a teacher rather than an architect, Sara designed the home in 1976; it wasn't hard, she claims.

Hard or not, the result is temperately graceful. Cedar trees, loblolly pines, dogwood, and sea grass surround it. Its front yard is a 17-acre stretch of private beach, frequented by deer and horseshoe crabs. What about jellyfish, we asked straightaway, knowing that the gelatinous creatures known locally as nettles make most Chesapeake Bay beaches unswimmable. As Sara explains, Pickett's Harbor is so close to the mouth of the bay that the gentle laving action of the waves keeps the nettles away. So here you'll find a rare thing indeed, at least for this part of Virginia's Eastern Shore—a sandy beach all your own, complete with dunes and the eerie wrecks of several World War II Liberty ships offshore.

Nor is the inside of the house a disappointment. It's furnished with antiques and family items and has blue wainscoting, high ceilings, and flooring made of rafters taken from a 200-year-old barn on the James River. The one downstairs bedroom has a four-poster bed, easy chairs, and an exceptional water view, but the upstairs rooms are pretty too, especially those beneath the dormers.

Before heading off to school on weekdays Sara serves breakfast, which routinely features sweet-potato biscuits, thinly sliced Virginia ham, and popovers. Before she goes, though, see if you can get her to talk about her family, an Eastern Shore clan that came to the area shortly after Captain John Smith explored the peninsula, in the early 1600s.

Address: *Box 97AA, Cape Charles, VA 23310, tel. 804/331-2212.*
Accommodations: *2 double rooms with baths, 4 doubles share 2 baths.*
Amenities: *Air-conditioning, TV in common areas.*
Rates: *$65-$85; full breakfast. No credit cards.*
Restrictions: *Smoking only on porch, no pets, 2-night minimum on holiday weekends.*

The Garden and the Sea

Victoria Olian and Jack Betz, former Washingtonians, bought old Bloxom's Tavern, built around 1800 in the hamlet of New Church, and straightaway began doing what they like best—cooking French-inspired meals. The menu routinely contains one or two prix-fixe dinners and à la carte specialties such as baked salmon in pastry and grilled duck breast with cassis. The prices are high, but not exorbitant, and the dining room is an airily pretty place. Overnight guests can take their leisure in the downstairs sitting room, furnished with an Edwardian mahogany and satinwood buffet. At present, there are just two guest rooms, decorated in nouvelle-Victorian style, with ballooning fabrics and French furniture. The one called Chantilly holds a wicker sleigh bed and ceiling fan; both rooms have luxurious baths with bidets. Jack and Victoria's next project is to remodel the oldest house in New Church, which they moved to the garden behind the inn, for more guest rooms.

Address: *Box 275, New Church, VA 23415, tel. 804/824–0672.*
Accommodations: *2 double rooms with baths.*
Amenities: *Restaurant, air-conditioning.*
Rates: *$80–$105; full breakfast. AE, D, DC, MC, V.*
Restrictions: *Smoking in common rooms only, no pets, 2-night minimum summer weekends, 3-night minimum during Pony Penning Week, closed Nov.–Mar.*

Miss Molly's

This lodging is owned by Jim and Priscilla Stam; it was built in the second half of the 19th century. Miss Molly's is distinguished by Marguerite Henry's having stayed here while writing *Misty.* "One night I brought a tiny live seahorse into the room," she wrote, "and set him in front of a window in a glass of water. In the morning when I awoke those pure white curtains were 'appliquéd' all over with . . . baby seahorses which had hatched in the night from the father's pouch." Somehow, that episode describes Miss Molly's to a T; its back faces the channel still plied by fishing boats, and inside, the furnishings are Victorian—including a fascinating John Rogers Civil War statuette. Marguerite Henry's room is perhaps the best, with blue wallpaper and a three-window bay.

Address: *113 N. Main St., Chincoteague, VA 23336, tel. 804/336–6686.*
Accommodations: *5 double rooms with baths, 2 doubles share 1 bath.*
Amenities: *Air-conditioning, TV in common room, refrigerator; beach towels.*
Rates: *$69–$115; full breakfast, afternoon tea. No credit cards.*
Restrictions: *Smoking in public areas only, no pets, 2-night minimum on weekends, 3-night minimum on holiday weekends, 4-night minimum during Pony Penning, closed Dec.–Mar.*

Sea Gate

J im Wells and Chris Bannon, both formerly of New York City (as are so many recent arrivals to the town), have laughingly taken to calling Cape Charles "the Cape." The Sea Gate was built in 1913; it's a rotund pink frame house a block from the water, on one of the town's prettiest residential streets. There's a wide porch out front and a grand piano in the entryway; the residents are Albert the cat, Chris, Jim, and Chris's elderly mother. The furnishings are comfortable but hardly rare; rather, it's the relaxed tone of the place that's so winning. Generally guests sit up late talking in the living room—about 1930s musicals, Tahitian islands, real estate, anything. The next morning at breakfast the conversation picks up as if it had never ended. Then it's off to explore Cape Charles (which will take you all of an hour), followed by a visit to the beach, afternoon tea, and phenomenal sunset-watching. Then dinner at the only restaurant in town (Rebecca's), more talk. . . . Call it the Cape Charles warp.

Address: *9 Tazewell Ave., Cape Charles, VA 23310, tel. 804/331–2206.*
Accommodations: *1 double room with bath, 2 doubles with half baths and 1 double with sink share 1 hall bath.*
Amenities: *Air-conditioning, TV in rooms.*
Rates: *$60–$75; full breakfast, afternoon tea. No credit cards.*
Restrictions: *Smoking in public areas only, no pets, 2-night minimum on holiday weekends.*

The Year of the Horse

E very year one man comes to The Year of the Horse just to crab, spending his days with a pot and pole on the 100-foot pier overlooking Chincoteague Sound. Not for him the pristine beaches of the refuge; he's got to keep after those crustaceans, so that he can return home with a full ice chest. For those similarly inclined, The Year of the Horse is an excellent retreat, occupying a summer house built in the 1920s, whose garage once stabled Misty's colt, Cloudy. Carl Bond has surrounded it with Florida-style lawn ornaments—pink flamingos and the like—and filled its sitting rooms with a weird assortment of collectibles, including a rocking camel, a fedora-decked hat rack, a Buddha, and a Victorian fainting couch. Three guest rooms look out on the bay; they have private decks but unhappily are furnished motel style. In addition, there's a two-bedroom apartment. Carl is a tall, lanky man, soft-spoken and just plain nice; when guests don't finish the cinnamon rolls at breakfast, he takes the leftovers out to the school-bus stop and distributes them to the kids.

Address: *600 S. Main St., Chincoteague, VA 23336, tel. 804/336–3221.*
Accommodations: *3 double rooms with baths, 1 suite.*
Amenities: *Air-conditioning, kitchen in 1 double, cable TV; dock.*
Rates: *$55–$95; Continental breakfast. D, MC, V.*
Restrictions: *No pets, 2-night minimum on weekends, 3-night minimum on holidays, closed Dec.–Jan.*

Williamsburg and the Peninsula

"Down in Virginia there is a little old-fashioned city called Williamsburg. It stands on the ridge of the peninsula that separates the James and York Rivers." This is how The City of Once Upon a Time, *a children's book written by Gilchrist Waring in 1946, opens.* That book and The Official Guide to Colonial Williamsburg *are two of the best introductions to the legendary city, which is visited by some 1 million people every year.*

As both books explain, Williamsburg was the capital of Virginia between 1699 and 1780, when the colony was immense, extending west to the Mississippi River. A planned city like Annapolis, Maryland, and a thriving business center serving the farms and tobacco plantations between the rivers, it was an unarguably beautiful place and still is. In 1926 the rector at Williamsburg's Bruton Parish Church persuaded John D. Rockefeller to restore the town, and the continuing project has resulted in a living-history museum of 173 acres, a mile long and half a mile wide, holding 88 restored and 50 reconstructed buildings and surrounded by a 3,000-acre "greenbelt." The restoration has become a pattern for similar endeavors nationwide. As a modern city Williamsburg doesn't really exist, except as suburbs that grew up in the 1930s, when the restoration crews moved in. There are outlying malls and commercial strips, which woo travelers with shopping opportunities at bargain emporiums like the Williamsburg Pottery Factory and Soap and Candle Company and at Merchant's Square, which adjoins the historic district but should not be confused with it, despite the square's look of authenticity.

Once you've located Colonial Williamsburg proper, you can simply wander in and soak up the atmosphere, perhaps slaking your thirst on a cup of cider, peddled streetside, or you can stop at the visitor center (tel. 804/220–7645 daily

8:30–5), which lies off the Colonial Parkway (the National Park artery that connects Jamestown, Williamsburg, and Yorktown), to view a 35-minute film and buy passes that entitle you to enter the buildings and ride the fleet of shuttle buses that link the top sights.

Williamsburg is not the oldest English settlement in the United States. That title is held by nearby Jamestown, where a sea-weary party of 104 men and boys aboard the Sarah Constant, Godspeed, *and* Discovery *landed in 1607 and hung on, despite hostile Indians, disease bred in nearby swamps, and chaos engendered by the fear that they'd been forgotten by suppliers across the Atlantic. Today Jamestown Island, the site of a national park, is a much more rustic place than civil Williamsburg.*

It is entirely understandable that visitors to the area should feel overwhelmed. Besides Jamestown and Williamsburg there's nearby Yorktown to explore (the scene of the last battle of the Revolution and the surrender of General Cornwallis) and scores of plantations along the James River (among them Carter's Grove and the brilliant chain of privately owned historic houses off Route 5) that should not be missed. Charles City County, which hugs the river between Richmond and Williamsburg, is truly a place apart. The same handful of families have owned and farmed its plantations since the 17th century and have stoically kept development out. So a drive along Route 5, which offers access to all the historic homes, makes a scenic trip indeed.

Finally, the thing to keep in mind about Williamsburg's bed-and-breakfasts is that none of them lies within the historic district; indeed, none of them occupies a historic house, though a number of them are exceedingly fine places to stay. Those intent on booking accommodations in a bona fide Colonial structure with a historic pedigree should contact the Williamsburg Inn (tel. 804/229–1000 or 800/447–

8679). It manages 85 rooms located in taverns and houses in the restored district.

Places to Go, Sights to See

Abby Aldrich Rockefeller Folk Art Center (tel. 804/220–7670) has nine galleries filled with 125 delightful paintings, carvings, and household items created by talented but untrained American artists, including Edward Hicks's painting *Peaceable Kingdom.* Closed for renovations, it is scheduled to reopen in mid-1992.

Berkeley (tel. 804/829–6018), the Harrison family home, occupies the spot where settlers celebrated the first Thanksgiving, in 1619. The house, perfectly Georgian in style, was built in 1726 and later lived in by President William Henry Harrison, of Tippecanoe fame. It is surrounded by 10 acres of formal boxwood gardens, and you can dine in its Coach House Tavern.

Busch Gardens/The Old Country (off Rte. 60, tel. 804/253–3350). This theme park re-creates things German, French, Italian, and English and offers rides on such curiosities as the "Loch Ness Monster," "Roman Rapids," and "Big Bad Wolf."

Carter's Grove (tel. 804/220–7645), an 18th-century plantation 8 miles east of the historic district, was built in 1750 by a grandson of the Colonial tobacco tycoon Robert "King" Carter and renovated and enlarged in 1928. Before Carter Grove was built, the site was the administrative center for a plantation syndicate called the Society of Martin's Hundred, whose palisaded fort and company compound were recently discovered by archaeologists and partially reconstructed.

The College of William and Mary, the second-oldest college in the United States, was founded in 1693 by charter from King William and Queen Mary of England. Its centerpiece, the Wren Building, begun in 1695, is thought to have been influenced by Christopher Wren.

Colonial Williamsburg (tel. 804/229–1000). In the restored district, some of the most interesting historic buildings are the *Capitol,* where Patrick Henry delivered his famous speech; *Bruton Parish Church;* and the handsome *Governor's Palace,* with its stable, kitchen, exquisite gardens, and working wheelwright's shop. The *Courthouse* in *Market Square,* fronted by pillories and stocks, and the octagonal *Magazine and Guardhouse,* where Redcoats parade and muskets are cleaned, loaded, and discharged, are two of the town's original structures. Along Duke of Gloucester Street are the *Printing Office, Mary Stith's Music School,* the *James Anderson Blacksmith Shop,* and *Golden Ball Silversmith's.* Crafts shops in the historic district include *Prentis Store,* for pottery, baskets, soaps, pipes, and tools; the *Post Office,* for books, prints, maps, stationery, and sealing wax; and *Raleigh Tavern Bake Shop,* for gingerbread and tarts.

DeWitt Wallace Decorative Arts Gallery (tel. 804/220–7724 or 804/220–7645), a modern museum behind the Public Hospital in Williamsburg, contains 8,000 examples of English and American furniture, ceramics, textiles, and costumes primarily from the 17th and 18th centuries.

Jamestown National Historic Site (5 miles west of Williamsburg, tel. 804/229–1733) is an island, which is why the colonists selected it as a settlement site in 1607. It was to prove a bad choice; in one year alone nine-tenths of the settlers died of starvation, violence, or disease, and the capitol there burned four times before it was relocated to Williamsburg. Today Jamestown is an atmospheric ghost town, where you'll find a visitor center, a museum, paths leading through the ruins of "James Cittie," a scenic loop drive, and Glasshouse, where craftspeople demonstrate one of Virginia's first industries, glassblowing.

Jamestown Settlement (adjacent to the National Historic Site, tel. 804/229–1607), run by the state of Virginia, is an outdoor re-creation of Jamestown village, with reproductions of James Fort, a Powhatan Indian village, and the 110-foot *Sarah Constant.*

The Mariner's Museum (Newport News, tel. 804/595–0368). Here maritime history is documented, from the Indian dugout canoe and Chesapeake workboats to modern shipbuilding at Newport News.

NASA Visitors Center (near Hampton, tel. 804/864–6000). Test your knowledge of aerospace on a computer game; see the *Apollo 12* Command Module and a 4-billion-year-old rock collected on the moon. Exhibits at the center document flight from the Wright brothers onward.

Shirley Plantation (on the James River off Rte. 5, tel. 804/829–5121 or 800/232–1613). Surmounted by a hand-carved pineapple finial, once a landmark for riverboats, this Georgian plantation house has been owned by 10 generations of Hills and Carters (Anne Carter was the mother of Robert E. Lee). Shirley was founded six years after the settlers arrived in Jamestown, and the house was built in 1723. Especially noteworthy are its three-story "flying" staircase, which appears completely unsupported, and the Queen Anne forecourt.

The War Memorial Museum of Virginia (Newport News, tel. 804/247–8523) displays a collection of 60,000 artifacts from all of America's wars, including the Vietnam conflict.

Water Country, U.S.A. (Rte. 199, off I–65, east of town, tel. 804/229–9300) offers 40 acres of water rides, pools, slides, and shows, including the U.S. High Diving Team. Closed mid-September–early May.

Westover (tel. 804/795–2882). Seat of the Byrd family and considered one of the finest Georgian plantations in the United States, Westover lies on the James River (off Rte. 5). Its spectacular grounds are open daily, though the house can be seen only in the spring, during Virginia's Garden Week.

Yorktown Battlefield National Historic Site (tel. 804/898–3400). Here Washington laid siege to Cornwallis's army, and in 1781 the British surrendered in the (restored) Moore House. English, French, and American breastworks still line the battlefield, and it's a good idea to stop first at the visitor center to view the dioramas and rent a taped tour. The Yorktown Victory Monument commemorates the French, who provided decisive help in winning the battle.

Restaurants

When hunger overtakes you, you'll find several Colonial taverns (tel. 804/229–2141) scattered around Williamsburg's historic district, among them the **King's Arms, Christiana Campbell's, Shields,** and **Chownings.** These serve such traditional fare as prime rib, game pie, Sally Lunn (slightly sweet raised bread), and peanut soup. For formal dining there's the award-winning **Regency Room,** at the Williamsburg Inn (tel. 804/229–2141), and the **Trellis** (tel. 804/229–8610), in Merchant's Square. The **Old Chickahominy House** (Jamestown Rd., tel. 804/229–4689) is noted for its Brunswick stew; west of town, **Pierce's** (Rochambeau Rd., tel. 804/565–2955), just off I–64, has good barbecue, and at **Indian Fields** (Rte. 5, tel. 804/829–5004) the menu includes such Tidewater delicacies as Virginia ham in pineapple-raisin sauce, and scallops in puff pastry.

Tourist Information

Colonial National Historical Park (Jamestown–Yorktown) (Box 210, Yorktown, VA 23690, tel. 804/898–3400). **Colonial Williamsburg Foundation** (Box 1776, Williamsburg, VA 23187, tel. 804/229–1000). **Jamestown-Yorktown Foundation** (Drawer JF, Williamsburg, VA 23187, tel. 804/253–4838). **Virginia Division of Tourism** (1021 E. Cary St., Richmond, VA 23219, tel. 804/786–4484). **Virginia Peninsula Tourism** (8 San Jose Dr., Suite 3B, Newport News, VA 23606, tel. 804/873–0092). **Virginia Plantation Country** (201-D Randolph Sq., Hopewell, VA 23860, tel. 804/541–2206). **Williamsburg Area Convention & Visitors Bureau** (Box GB, Williamsburg, VA 23187, tel. 804/253–0192 or 800/368–6511).

Reservation Services

Bensonhouse of Williamsburg (2036 Monument Ave., Richmond, VA 23220, tel. 804/648–7560). **Travel Tree Reservation Service** (Box 838, Williamsburg, VA 23187, tel. 804/253–1571 or 800/989–1571 weekdays 6–9 PM).

Edgewood

Ridgely Copland of North Bend Plantation (*see* below) and Dot Boulware of Edgewood (just down Route 5, and approximately a half hour from Colonial Williamsburg) are dear friends, but they're as different as, well, the Federal and Victorian styles. Says frothy Dot in her liquid Southern accent, "I have to tell you, I am a romantic." Nonetheless, before she and her husband, Julian, bought Edgewood Plantation, just over 10 years ago, she didn't care a bit for Victoriana. Fortunately tastes change, and when she became the mistress of an 1850s carpenter Gothic house she began collecting Victorian antiques like a woman possessed.

Dot's 14-room house, visible from Route 5, looks on the inside like Miss Haversham's dining room, minus the cobwebs. It is full to bursting with old dolls, antique corsets and lingerie, lace curtains and pillows, love seats, baby carriages, stuffed steamer trunks, mighty canopied beds, highboys, Confederate caps . . . the list goes on and on. At Christmastime she personally decorates 17 trees and festoons the banister of the graceful three-story staircase with bows. Clearly, more is more at Dot Boulware's Edgewood.

In her hands, Victoriana is thoroughly feminine, even though in one chamber, the Civil War Room, she's tried to cater to the opposite sex, decorating with intimate details of men's 19th-century apparel. Large people of either sex will have a hard time moving freely in this wildly crowded bed-and-breakfast, and the commonest reason men book a room is as a special treat for their mates. Lizzie's Room, the favorite, has a king-size pencil-post canopy bed and a private bath. The room enshrines the memory of a teenager who, Dot says, died of a broken heart when her beau failed to return from the Civil War; her name is scratched on the window.

Breakfast is served in the dining room by candlelight. Outside there's an unrestored mill house dating from 1725, an antiques shop, a gazebo, and a swimming pool with a hot tub. Edgewood is centrally located for touring the Charles City County plantations and is down the road from the area's best restaurant, Indian Fields.

Address: *Charles City, VA 23030, tel. 804/829–2962.*
Accommodations: *3 double rooms with baths, 4 doubles share 2 baths.*
Amenities: *Air-conditioning; swimming pool, hot tub.*
Rates: *$95–$145; full breakfast. MC, V.*
Restrictions: *No pets.*

Liberty Rose

Bed-and-breakfast keepers in Williamsburg are in something of a bind. Because all the historic buildings in town are owned by either the Williamsburg Foundation or the College of William and Mary, they can't offer travelers authentic Colonial accommodations. Some have Colonial-style decoration anyway, but others, like Sandy and Brad Hirz, owners of the Liberty Rose, have come up with different, imaginative solutions to the dilemma.

Understand first that Sandy and Brad are a tremendously romantic story. They were just friends when Sandy decided to leave the West Coast to open a B&B in Williamsburg. Brad was helping Sandy house-hunt when they looked at a 1920s white clapboard and brick home a mile west of the restored district (on the road to Jamestown), and Sandy bought it in five minutes. Then Brad started seriously courting her, but it was Sandy, and not the B&B, who inspired him. Now they're a devoted married couple who run Williamsburg's most romantic B&B, decorated à la nouvelle Victorian with turn-of-the-century touches.

Sandy, a former interior designer, has a special talent for fabrics and is responsible for the handsome tie-back curtains, many-layered bed coverings, and plush canopies. The patterns are 19th-century reproductions. Brad has held up his end of the business by managing remodeling de-

tails. The bathrooms are particularly attractive: One has a floor taken from a plantation in Gloucester, a comfortable claw-foot tub, and an amazing freestanding, glass-sided shower. Old black-faced dolls and Noah's Ark carvings are tucked away in corners, and the furnishings are a copacetic mix of 18th- and 19th-century reproductions and antiques. Sandy's next project is to come out with a Liberty Rose catalogue.

Liberty Rose sits on a densely wooded hilltop, and the lake on the William and Mary campus is a pretty walk away. It is definitely not Colonial, but then the Colonial style isn't that romantic—which is, above all, the tone pursued and achieved at Liberty Rose.

Address: *1022 Jamestown Rd., Williamsburg, VA 23185, tel. 804/253–1260.*
Accommodations: *2 double rooms with baths, 2 suites.*
Amenities: *Air-conditioning, TV/VCR in suites, fireplace in 1 suite.*
Rates: *$95–$165; full breakfast. MC, V.*
Restrictions: *No smoking indoors, no pets.*

North Bend Plantation

R outinely, a stay at this Charles City County plantation begins with a tour of the house and grounds conducted by Ridgely Copland, a farmer's wife and a nurse (several years ago named Virginia nurse of the year). Along the way Ridgely points out Union breastworks from 1864, wild asparagus, herds of deer, a swamp, and the wide James River. At some point during the trip she might stop and repeat the question she asks herself just about every day: "What lucky girl lives here?" The answer is Ridgely, of course, and, for a spell, her bed-and-breakfast guests.

Few other Virginia bed-and-breakfasts are so strikingly authentic, and North Bend is a working plantation. The Coplands are salt-of-the-earth people striving to keep their acreage intact in the face of modern agriculture dilemmas, and a stay here leaves visitors with a sense of reawakened admiration for that very American institution, the family farm.

North Bend, on the National Register and also a Virginia Historic Landmark, is a fine example of the Academic Greek Revival style, a wide, white frame structure with a red roof and a slender chimney at each corner. Built in 1819, with a classic two-over-two layout, large center hall, and Federal mantels and stair carvings, it was remodeled in 1853 from Asher Benjamin designs.

But beyond its architectural distinctions, North Bend is drenched in history. Its premier guest bedroom contains a walnut desk used by the Union general Philip Sheridan, complete with his labels on the pigeonholes. His map was found in one of its drawers; a copy is framed on the wall of the billiard room. Above all, though, at North Bend history means family. George Copland is the great-great-great-nephew of William Henry Harrison, who, Ridgely laughingly reminds guests, served as president for just 30 days. Family heirlooms are everywhere, as is Ridgely's collection of Civil War first editions, which make fascinating bedtime reading.

As you might expect, North Bend is not a luxurious place. Only the suite has a private bath, and there are no quaint touches in evidence—no down comforters, bubble bath, or sachets. There's just North Bend, its history, and the extraordinarily kind owners.

Address: *12200 Weyanoke Rd., Charles City, VA 23030, tel. 804/829–5176 (after 5:30).*
Accommodations: *2 double rooms share 1 bath, 1 suite.*
Amenities: *Air-conditioning; swimming pool.*
Rates: *$75–$95; full breakfast. No credit cards.*
Restrictions: *Smoking only in sun room, no pets, closed Dec. 25.*

Applewood

pplewood, so named because its owner collects things with an apple theme (ceramic apples, apple prints, even a copy of John Cheever's *The World of Apples*), is a spotlessly tidy bed-and-breakfast on Richmond Road, about four blocks from the historic district. Like other houses in the area, it was built in the late 1920s by a Colonial Williamsburg restorer, who added many of the kinds of details he'd been working on in the historic area: The house has a Flemish-bond brick exterior, a handsome 18th-century-style portal, and dentil crown moldings in the interior—and the trim is painted in those milky blues and greens that are so common in Williamsburg. One suite has a canopy bed, a fireplace, a private breakfast area and private entrance, and a convertible sofa bed—a fine choice for families with children. The Golden Pippin Room sleeps four, one in a trundle bed. Innkeeper Fred Strout serves afternoon tea and breakfast, including, of course, apple muffins.

Address: *605 Richmond Rd., Williamsburg, VA 23185, tel. 804/229–0205 or 800/899–2753.*
Accommodations: *3 double rooms with baths, 1 suite.*
Amenities: *Air-conditioning, TV in parlor.*
Rates: *$65–$100; full breakfast, afternoon tea. MC, V.*
Restrictions: *No smoking indoors, no pets, 2-night minimum on holiday weekends and during special events.*

Colonial Capital

he Colonial Capital, a frame three-story house painted lime-sherbet green, is within walking distance of the historic district, Merchant's Square, and the College of William and Mary; in fact, it's across the street from both Cary Field and the Alumni House. The exceedingly nice innkeepers, Phil and Barbara Craig, are a retired stockbroker and a university administrator who moved to Williamsburg after 25 years in North Carolina. The Colonial's five rooms are named after Tidewater-area rivers. Second-floor Potomac contains a bed-and-breakfast rarity—a queen-size waterbed, which Phil says makes converts out of travelers who normally wouldn't go near one. Prettiest, though, is Pamlico, with dormer windows and a white-canopied bed. Downstairs, there's a large living room with a fireplace and access to a sun porch, where the Craigs keep games, books, and puzzles. And, perhaps best of all, the Colonial Capital has parking in the rear for guests, which could otherwise prove a serious problem in teeming Williamsburg.

Address: *501 Richmond Rd., Williamsburg, VA 23185, tel. 804/229–0233 or 800/776–0570.*
Accommodations: *4 double rooms with baths, 1 suite.*
Amenities: *Air-conditioning, cable TV/VCR in guest parlor, phones on each floor; bicycles, parking.*
Rates: *$85–$125; full breakfast, afternoon refreshments. MC, V.*
Restrictions: *Smoking only in guest parlor, no pets, 2-night minimum, on weekends Apr.–Dec.*

Around Charlottesville

Few cities in this country are so deeply devoted to—one might say, so in love with—a single man as is Virginia's piedmont capital, Charlottesville. On a farm east of town (in the present-day hamlet of Shadwell) Thomas Jefferson, the third president of the United States, was born; and on a mountaintop overlooking a countryside Jefferson himself considered Edenic, he built his home. We have all seen Monticello, for it appears on one side of the nickel, though its minted image hardly does it justice. The breathtakingly beautiful edifice, constructed on architectural principles that would change the face of America, is a house that reveals volumes about the man who built and lived in it.

For instance, in the terraced vegetable gardens (restored according to Jefferson's Garden Book*), he introduced the tomato to North America and raised 19 types of English peas, his favorite food. (Mr. Jefferson, as he is called around here, attributed his long life—he lived to be 83—to his vegetarian diet.) Here he built a glass-enclosed pavilion, where he came to read, write, and watch his garden grow. Most of the 20,000 letters he wrote were penned in his study in a reclining chair with a revolving desk (he had rheumatism and worked from a semirecumbent position). Jefferson was also a collector; the parlor walls are lined with portraits of friends, like Washington and Monroe, and the east entrance hall displays mastodon bones and a buffalo head brought from the West by Lewis and Clark.*

"Architecture," wrote Jefferson, "is my delight and putting up and pulling down one of my favorite pastimes." Originally he built Monticello in 1779 as an American Palladian villa, but after seeing the work of Boullée and Ledoux in France, he returned to Monticello with a head full of new ideas—above all, about its dome—and an aversion to grand staircases, which he believed took up too

much room. Today the full effect is best seen from the flower gardens on the west side.

Another reason for Charlottesville's love affair with Jefferson lies at the western end of town—the University of Virginia. If Monticello is a taste of Jeffersonian style, the school's rotunda and colonnade are the banquet. Jefferson began designing the university buildings at the age of 74; in 1976 the American Institute of Architects voted them the most outstanding achievement in American architecture. The rotunda was inspired by the Pantheon in Rome, but the dual colonnade that extends from it, intended as both dwelling place and study center for students and faculty, is all Jefferson's own. Students still inhabit the colonnade rooms, amid fireplaces, porches, and rocking chairs.

Charlottesville today has its shopping malls and fast-food strips, not to mention a serious parking problem. Downtown has been converted into a pedestrian mall where shoppers find intriguing stores, such as Paula Lewis Quilts and the Rubaiyat, for women's clothes.

Charlottesville lies in the piedmont, the Blue Ridge foothills, and the driving here is fun and scenic. Highway 20, called the Constitution Route, takes travelers past Montpelier (James Madison's home) in Orange, 25 miles north of Charlottesville, and south past Michie Tavern, Ash Lawn (where James Monroe lived), and Scottsville. This village on the James River, once the seat of Albemarle County, is rich in Revolutionary and Civil War history. It's a favorite spot for canoe and inner-tube trips. Twenty miles to the west the Blue Ridge rises, with access to the Skyline Drive or the Blue Ridge Parkway at Rockfish Gap.

Places to Go, Sights to See

Ash Lawn (tel. 804/293–9539), just down the road from Monticello, is the restored home of James Monroe, whose mountaintop site (selected by Jefferson) offers views of Monticello's dome. Monroe built the vernacular Federal-style structure in 1799 and a complementary addition in 1816.

A Victorian wing was contributed in 1880. Ash Lawn is a working, 550-acre farm where sheep and peacocks roam. Summertime brings an opera festival and a July 4th Colonial crafts festival.

Barboursville Vineyards (north of Charlottesville, tel. 703/832–3824) produces pinot noir, chardonnay, merlot, and cabernet sauvignon wines, among others. Tastings are held daily from 10 to 4, and tours on Saturday from 10 to 5. Here you can also explore the ruins of Governor James Barbour's plantation home. The Jefferson Wine Grape Growers Society (tel. 804/296–4188) distributes a brochure on other area vineyards, including Simeon, Chermont, Oakencroft, and Autumn Hill.

Court Square, in downtown Charlottesville, is the locus of Albemarle County government, with a courthouse built between 1803 and 1867. In the 18th century a meetinghouse occupied the site, and it was here that Jefferson worshiped. The square also holds an impressive equestrian statue of Stonewall Jackson.

Michie Tavern (tel. 804/977–1234). This tavern, dating from 1765, was moved to its present location on the road to Monticello in the 1920s. With its ceaseless crowds and general store, many visitors find it too commercial. The cafeteria-style restaurant serves historic fast food—fried chicken, black-eyed peas, stewed tomatoes, and the like. The adjacent Meadow Run Grist Mill houses the Virginia Wine Museum.

Monticello (tel. 804/295–8181) lies about a mile southeast of the intersection of Routes 64 and 20. The tour, which ascends Mr. Jefferson's "little mountain" by shuttle bus, lasts about half an hour and is extremely rewarding. Afterward visitors are free to roam the gardens, view the hidden dependencies, and make a pilgrimage to the great man's grave. The museum shop is worth a stop, if only for its extensive collection of books by and about Jefferson. Near the shuttle-bus station you'll also find a sandwich shop and the Thomas Jefferson Center for Historic Plants, which sells seedlings of some of the exotic varieties Jefferson cultivated. Note that Monticello is best taken in before the tour buses arrive around 11 AM. At the visitor center 400 artifacts and pieces of Jeffersoniana are on permanent display. The film *Thomas Jefferson: The Pursuit of Liberty* is shown daily at 11 and 2.

Montpelier (south of Orange, tel. 703/672–2728) was the home of James Madison, Jr., who was president after Jefferson and before Monroe. Known as the Father of the Constitution, he is credited with seeing America through the War of 1812. He and his wife, Dolley, lived here from 1797 to 1836, followed by William du Pont, Sr., who bought the house in 1901 and transferred it to the National Trust. The Montpelier Hunt Race takes place here on the first Saturday in November. The tour of the estate leads visitors over the 2,700-acre grounds, through the 55-room house, and past Madison's grave.

Rapidan. This village about 5 miles northeast of Orange is bisected by the Rapidan River and holds the *Waddell Memorial Presbyterian Church,* an architectural hymn in Carpenter Gothic. Nearby you'll also find the *Riverside*

Winery (tel. 703/672–4673) and *Marmont Orchards* (tel. 703/672–2730), where, in season, you can pick your own peaches, plums, and nectarines.

Scottsville sits on the James River and is where Lafayette made a successful stand against General Cornwallis in 1781. In the village are 32 Federal-style buildings and the locks of the *James River Kanawha Canal*, which were a target for 10,000 bluecoats under General Sheridan during the Civil War. Nearby you'll find the *James River Runners* (tel. 804/286–2338), where you can rent tubes, rafts, and canoes.

1740 House (tel. 804/977–1740), an antiques store located near Ivy, west of Charlottesville on Route 250, is known for its museum-quality 18th- and 19th-century furniture.

University of Virginia (tel. 804/924–1019). Tours leave the rotunda several times daily (except during holidays and exams). It's just as enjoyable to wander the grounds on your own. Inside the rotunda stands Alexander Galt's statue of Jefferson, which students saved from the fire of 1895.

Restaurants

Charlottesville's restaurant scene is surprisingly cosmopolitan. **Duner's** (tel. 804/293–8352) is favored for French and nouvelle American cuisine, and the **Blue Ridge Brewing Company** (tel. 804/977–0017), owned in part by a grandson of William Faulkner, for its riotous atmosphere. At any of these and other city eateries you may find a celebrity at a table nearby. Among those who've relocated to the lush countryside around Charlottesville are Sissy Spacek and Jessica Lange. Gordonsville has a pleasant restaurant, the **Toliver House** (tel. 703/832–3485).

Tourist Information

Charlottesville/Albemarle Visitors Bureau (Box 161, Charlottesville, VA 22902, tel. 804/293–6789). **Orange County Visitors Bureau** (Box 133, Orange, VA 22960, tel. 703/672–1653). **Virginia Division of Tourism** (1021 E. Cary St., Richmond, VA 23219, tel. 804/786–4484).

Reservation Services

Guesthouses Bed & Breakfast, Inc. (Box 5737, Charlottesville, VA 22905, tel. 804/979–7264) is a reservation service run by Mary Hill Caperton, which can arrange entrée to private houses otherwise closed to the public. The oldest service of its kind, Guesthouses handles such properties as an estate that was the home of Thomas Jefferson's nephew and ward, a Japanese house with a tennis court and a sunken tub, a Blue Ridge farm with a spring-fed pond, a 200-year-old log cabin, and an antebellum cottage that was part of the original Jefferson plantation.

High Meadows

High Meadows, in Scottsville, is above all a bed-and-breakfast inn done by hand. The hands in question are those of Peter Sushka, a retired submariner; his wife, Mary Jae Abbitt, an analyst for the Securities and Exchange Commission; and their innkeeper, Don Currence.

In this unique B&B, Federal and late-Victorian architecture exist side by side, now happily joined by a longitudinal hall. However, it wasn't always so. The Italianate front section was built in 1882 by Peter White, who intended to level the older house several paces behind it. But bearing in mind her growing family, his wife refused to give up the old place, built in 1830, and for a time a plank between the two was the tenuous connector that kept the marriage intact. Today High Meadows is on the National Register and Virginia Trust.

Peter and Mary Jae have decorated the place with great originality, keeping intact the stylistic integrity of each section. They've also used fabrics imaginatively on the bed hangings and windows. Of the three guest rooms in the Federal section and five in the Victorian, who can say which you'd prefer? Fairview, in the 1880s portion, is the quintessential bride's room, with a fireplace, flowing bed drapery, a three-window alcove, and a claw-foot tub. The Virginia suite, upstairs in the Federal section, has stenciled walls lined with antique stuffed animals, a fireplace, and rafters across the ceiling. In the Patrick Henry common sitting room, there's an ornate gold-leaf mirror in front of which the Revolutionary leader said, "Give me liberty or give me death."

Breakfast, served in the downstairs dining room, consists of Sushka specialties like cranberry-almond muffins and ham-and-egg cups laced with tomatoes and Gruyère cheese. Peter also takes a novel approach to the afternoon and evening meals. By arrangement he'll provide you with reasonably priced gourmet baskets stuffed with wine and ramekins of hot food, to eat in your room or on the terrace. How did a former submarine officer learn to cook? During stints underwater, of course, when there was nothing else to do.

Address: *Rte. 4, Box 6, Scottsville, VA 24590, tel. 804/286-2218.*
Accommodations: *5 double rooms with baths, 2 suites.*
Amenities: *Restaurant, air-conditioning in 5 rooms, fireplaces in 3 rooms and 2 common areas.*
Rates: *$85–$130; full breakfast, evening wine and hors d'oeuvres. MC, V.*
Restrictions: *No smoking indoors, pets permitted only in ground-level rooms by arrangement.*

Prospect Hill

For elegance and luxury, Prospect Hill runs second only to the famous Inn at Little Washington. That, added to its architecturally noteworthy setting, makes staying here something worth filling your piggy bank for. Prospect Hill lies east of Charlottesville, in the 14-square-mile Greensprings National Historic District. It is the oldest continuously occupied frame manor house in Virginia. But except for the obligatory dependencies and impressive boxwood hedges, Prospect Hill doesn't look like a plantation, because it was rebuilt in the Victorian era, when a columned facade and decorative cornices were added. The innkeepers have painted it lemony yellow.

There are five nicely furnished rooms in the main house, but the big treat is to stay in one of the six refurbished dependencies. Sanco Pansy's Cottage, about 100 feet away from the manor, is special. It has a sitting room and a whirlpool tub for two. The Carriage House, lit by four Palladian windows, provides views of ponies in the meadow nibbling the green Virginia turf. Surrounded by such *luxe, calme, et volupté*, it's strange to consider that in the last century, the dependencies were filled with hams, ice blocks, and livestock.

Dinner at the inn is a marvelous production, not so much because of the cuisine (French-inspired and well above average) as for the ceremony. You begin with complimentary wine and cider served a half hour before supper—outdoors in good weather. Next, the dinner bell rings, and in you file to hear the menu recited by innkeeper Bill Sheehan or his son, Michael. (Michael looks like a college halfback, but thanks to his delightful mama, Mireille, his French is impeccable.) Then comes grace, delivered so earnestly that it could bring an atheist to God, and five courses.

Breakfast is hot and brought to your dependency on a tray. You could take it in the dining room, but why spoil the fun? In your dependency, you can eat in a whirlpool tub. This really splendid inn is a class act that hasn't become too smoothly professional. You're bound to meet the gregarious innkeepers and appreciate the way they have put their stamp on Prospect Hill.

Address: *Rte. 3, Box 430, Trevilians, VA 23093, tel. 703/967–0844 or 800/277–0844, fax 703/967–0102.*
Accommodations: *5 double rooms with baths in main house, 5 doubles with baths and 3 suites in dependencies.*
Amenities: *Restaurant, air-conditioning, fireplaces in 12 guest rooms, whirlpools in 5 rooms; pool, 1 meeting room.*
Rates: *$120–$180; full breakfast and afternoon tea. MC, V.*
Restrictions: *No pets.*

Clifton

Thomas Randolph, the builder of Clifton and a governor of Virginia, didn't have it easy. Would you want Thomas Jefferson for a father-in-law? Steven and Donna Boehmfeldt, the live-in managers, say that Jefferson didn't much care for his son-in-law, which may explain why Randolph didn't adopt Jeffersonian neoclassicism for his house. This white frame, six-columned manse is handsome, nevertheless. It's owned by a Washington lawyer who seems to prefer the lived-in look to a museum ambience (with grounds that aren't quite up to Garden Club standards), but here the bathrooms win the prize; one contains a full-scale wood sculpture of an erotically reclining nude, and all have windows and shining white tiles. In the main house, rooms 2, 4, and 6 are especially attractive. Two dependencies on the back lawn contain three more suites, which have been renovated Malibu style. At Clifton guests are left pretty much to their own devices, which might include a swim in the lap pool, an inner-tube float on the secluded lake, tennis, or biking along back roads.

Address: *Rte. 13, Box 26, Charlottesville, VA 22901, tel. 804/971–1800.*
Accommodations: *6 double rooms with baths, 3 suites.*
Amenities: *Air-conditioning and fireplaces in guest rooms; lap pool, tennis court.*
Rates: *$148–$178; full breakfast. MC, V.*
Restrictions: *No smoking indoors, no pets.*

Mayhurst

The first glimpse of Mayhurst is as heady as a sip of champagne. You wind up a little hillock south of Orange (leaving behind distractions like shopping centers) and there she lies, for this extravagantly playful, white Italianate villa built in 1860 is surely female. Mayhurst's roofline is bracketed and gabled, her four faces beautified with arched windows, porticoes, and bays; above the architectural fantasy is perched a gazebo, making her look for all the world like a Victorian lady in lacy undies and a hat. The interior, which doesn't quite live up to the facade, does have an unusual oval staircase, with radial treads that squeak resistantly as you climb. Of the six guest chambers in the main house, we liked the Victorian Room best, for its floor-to-12-foot-ceiling window bank, bedstead with 10-foot posts, marble mantel, and claw-foot tub. Mayhurst is surrounded by 36 acres on which lie a pond and a cottage (which we found oppressively dark). It could use a touch of restoration, but it is a remarkable house; some will find it the Victorian mansion of their dreams.

Address: *Box 707, Orange, VA 22960, tel. 703/672–5597.*
Accommodations: *5 double rooms with baths, 1 suite, 1 cottage suite.*
Amenities: *Air-conditioning; fireplaces in 4 guest rooms and suites.*
Rates: *$125–$165; full breakfast. MC, V.*
Restrictions: *No smoking indoors, 2-night minimum on holidays and Oct. weekends.*

The Shadows

Though it's surrounded by cedars and adjoins a cemetery, The Shadows is anything but melancholy. Pat and Barbara Loffredo have filled their 1913 farmhouse just up the road from Montpelier with a cheerful collection of country Victorian antiques. Prize pieces are a wryly funny hunt board carved with a brace of dead birds; an old pump organ; numerous claw-foot tubs; and Maxfield Parrish prints wherever the eye rests. The house is what Barbara calls Gustav Stickley Craftsman style—a modified bungalow of wood and fieldstone. It has dark oak floors and windowsills around which lace curtains flutter. The four guest rooms have standard Victorian trappings (kept spotlessly neat). All the tangibles here are pleasant enough, but Pat and Barbara put The Shadows over the mark. They're refugees from New York, where Pat was a policeman, and their joy in their newfound home is infectious. The two of them delight in coddling guests, overwhelming them at breakfast, laying open their library, and sending them on their way with a hug. Who ever said New Yorkers are unfriendly?

Address: *14291 Constitution Hwy., Orange, VA 22960, tel. 703/672-5057.*
Accommodations: *4 double rooms with baths, 2 cottage suites.*
Amenities: *Air-conditioning.*
Rates: *$70–$100; full breakfast. No credit cards.*
Restrictions: *No smoking, no pets, 2-night minimum May and Oct. and Montpelier race weekends.*

The Silver Thatch Inn

The Silver Thatch, north of Charlottesville off Route 29, was formerly called the Hollymead. The oldest part of its semicircle of connected buildings is log, built by Hessian prisoners during the Revolution. The whole compound has been renovated by owners Joe and Mickey Geller, and it has a new, immaculately kept look. The Gellers also pay close and imaginative attention to the restaurant. Mickey and her chef, Janet Henry, have brought a savvy kind of cuisine to Charlottesville; entrées like grilled veal chops bear tangily vibrant vegetable sauces. In the summer they serve an antipasto plate, cappuccino is available at breakfast, and their wine list has received an award of excellence from the *Wine Spectator*. The Gellers have done a nice job with the guest rooms, too, which all have quilts, down comforters, and antiques; some have fireplaces. The four cottage rooms surpass those in the main house because of their sparkling new bathrooms. Guests may use a pool and tennis courts nearby.

Address: *3001 Hollymead Dr., Charlottesville, VA 22901, tel. 804/978-4686.*
Accommodations: *7 double rooms with baths.*
Amenities: *Restaurant, air-conditioning, cable TV.*
Rates: *$105–$125; Continental breakfast. MC, V.*
Restrictions: *No smoking, no pets, 2-night minimum on weekends Apr.–June and Sept.–Nov., closed Dec. 23–Jan. 7 and first 2 weeks in Aug.*

200 South Street

This popular small hotel in downtown Charlottesville is across the street from and next door to two trendy eateries, Memory and Company and South Street, the latter known for its seafood. The complex consists of two Victorian homes built between 1850 and 1900, which were restored by a team of Charlottesville businessmen. It was a good idea to paint them yellow, which cheers up South Street considerably, and to fill them with English and Belgian antiques including capacious armoires and lace-canopied four-posters. The walls are lined with displays of contemporary art and a much more interesting collection of historic Holsinger photographs. All the rooms are inviting and immaculately renovated, and some of them contain such luxuries as whirlpool baths and fireplaces. We preferred the 10 rooms and suite in No. 200 to those in the neighboring cottage, because there's a parlor there; train tracks in back make a front room desirable. Breakfast is brought to your door on a tray, and in the afternoon, tea and wine are served in the sitting room.

Address: *200 South St., Charlottesville, VA 22901, tel. 804/979–0200.*
Accommodations: *17 double rooms with baths, 3 suites.*
Amenities: *Air-conditioning, TV in 3rd-floor lounge, phones in rooms, turndown service.*
Rates: *$85–$160; Continental breakfast. AE, MC, V.*
Restrictions: *No pets, 2-night minimum on weekends Apr.–May and Sept.–Oct.*

Woodstock Hall

This Colonial way station has two distinctions: It's one of the least altered historic structures in the area, and owners Clarence and Mary Ann Elder also own the 1740 House antiques shop in Ivy. This explains the fine period furnishings and the careful renovation. The Woodstock stands on a hill near Charlottesville, a prim, mustard yellow beacon in excellent biking country. Inside you'll find a case full of artifacts unearthed during the restoration, fireplaces in all rooms, burnished-wood floors, case locks on the doors, much of the original window glass, and a copy of Poe's *The Tale of the Ragged Mountains*—because the poet's stay here inspired him to write it. In the main house, one snug and particularly pleasant room is called the Duc Liancourt Room, and a suite in the old detached kitchen contains two fireplaces and a rather short antique canopy bed. The resident innkeepers keep the place shining and serve breakfast, but they don't assert a sense of personality. It is still a good choice for those who want to visit Charlottesville but stay in the country.

Address: *RR 637, Ivy (Rte. 3, Box 40, Charlottesville, VA 22901), tel. 804/293–8977.*
Accommodations: *3 double rooms with baths, 1 suite.*
Amenities: *Air-conditioning, TV in rooms.*
Rates: *$95–$130; full breakfast, afternoon tea. No credit cards.*
Restrictions: *No smoking, no pets, 3-night minimum on graduation and parents' weekends.*

The Blue Ridge/ Shenandoah Valley

The standard way to see the Blue Ridge Mountains is to pile into a car on a weekend in October and drive south from Front Royal along the Skyline Drive. If you do this, bumper-to-bumper traffic could keep you from covering the full 105-mile course, your feet may only touch ground at rest stops and scenic overlooks, and you probably won't get past Rockfish Gap (just east of Waynesboro), where the drive becomes the equally (some would claim more) splendid Blue Ridge Parkway. Above all, you'll have only the foggiest idea of the landscape at Virginia's western border, markedly different from the rest of the state, a kind of continental precursor to the West.

In geographical terms the Blue Ridge is the eastern wall of the wide Shenandoah Valley, which is retained at the other side by the Allegheny Mountains. Down the middle of the valley, bisecting it for some 50 miles, rises another mini-mountain range called Massanutten Mountain, even though, cuplike, it holds a pretty valley of its own. The Shenandoah River, which runs through the valley, divides north of Massanutten—to further confuse the issue—into a North and South Fork, which in reality lie east and west of Massanutten.

Once you've got the geography down you can plot a more informed assault on the mountains and valley by crossing the ridge along such strategic and scenic routes as Highways 211, 33, and especially 56, an untrammeled two-laner that's a favorite even of view-jaded locals. These paths lead into the central and southern sections of the Shenandoah Valley, bypassing the tourist traps (or have you a yen to visit petting zoos and reptile parks?) clustered around Front Royal.

This is not to say you should skip the national park. It holds the heights of the Blue Ridge in a 100-mile strip from Front Royal to Waynesboro and provides nonpareil views of the Virginia piedmont to the east and splendid Shenandoah Valley to the west. To the park come fishermen to catch the crafty brook trout, and hikers, who find meanders aplenty, including a 95-mile stretch of the Appalachian Trail and 500 miles of park-maintained paths. The unanimous favorite among walkers is the route up Old Rag Mountain, at 3,268 feet, but even a short stroll from a trailhead on the Skyline Drive brings visitors within viewing range of the park's wildlife: 200 species of birds, chipmunks, salamanders, timber rattlesnakes, white-tailed deer, bobcats, and black bears. Spring and fall are peak seasons for nature lovers. In May the green of new foliage moves up the ridge at a rate of 100 feet a day, with clouds of wild pink azaleas providing contrast. Fall colors are at their most vivid between October 10 and 25, when migrating hawks join the human leaf-gazers to take in the display.

Once over the ridge and in the valley (Shenandoah means "daughter of the stars" in an Indian dialect), there are better ways to take in the countryside than by zooming north or south along I–81. Route 11 parallels the superhighway in a delightfully labyrinthine fashion, providing access to big-name sights such as the New Market Battlefield and Luray Caverns, and running through small towns, including Woodstock, Edinburg, Mt. Jackson, and Steele's Tavern, where roadside produce stands, flea markets, and local-history museums further delay your progress.

The towns of Staunton and Lexington are Shenandoah gems that will interest lovers of famous men. Staunton, as hilly as Rome, was Woodrow Wilson's home, though it also boasts the pretty campus of the Mary Baldwin College, the Virginia Institute for the Deaf and Blind, and the Museum of American Frontier Culture. Lexington lives and breathes for Stonewall Jackson and for Robert E. Lee, who was named president of Washington and Lee University after the Civil War ended. Next door to the Washington and Lee campus is the Virginia Military Institute, founded in 1839, where Jackson taught natural philosophy before bedeviling Union armies as a Confederate general.

West along winding country roads from Staunton and Lexington lies a countryside often neglected by valley visitors. Routes 33, 250, and 39 lead to the Appalachian plateau and West Virginia, bordered by the thick foliage of the George Washington National Forest. Every 10 miles or so the roads cross rocky waterways—such as that lovely trio of rivers, the Bullpasture, Cowpasture, and Calfpasture—providing excellent spots for wading and picnicking. Most of the towns in this area are no more than crossroads, with the exception of Hot Springs, site of The Homestead, a 15,000-acre resort that's a Virginia institution. The town at the gates of The Homestead has a pleasant collection of arts-and-crafts shops, gourmet delis, and restaurants.

Places to Go, Sights to See

Belle Grove (1 mi south of Middletown, tel. 703/869–2028), one of the few stately homes in the Shenandoah Valley, was built of local limestone in 1794, with four chimneys and Tuscan porticoes thought to have been added at the urging of Thomas Jefferson. It suffered greatly in 1864, when Confederate forces launched an attack on a Union Army headquartered at the mansion.

Blue Ridge Parkway (Box 453, Asheville, NC 28002). President Franklin Roosevelt was so taken with the Shenandoah National Park when he visited it in 1933 that he authorized a national parkway to connect it to the Great Smoky Mountains, nearly 500 miles away. The resulting scenic highway was finally completed in 1987. Favorite stopping points are the *James River Wayside, Peaks of Otter* (a valley with a 24-acre lake tucked between Sharp and Flat Top mountains), and photogenic *Mabry Mill.*

The Chessie Natural Trail is a hiking and walking path linking Lexington with the nearby town of Buena Vista.

Goshen Pass is a 3-mile gap in the mountains carved by the Maury River, off Route 39 about 20 miles northwest of Lexington. When the wild rhododendrons bloom in May, this is one of the loveliest spots in Virginia, with facilities for tubing, swimming, canoeing, fishing, and hiking.

Luray Caverns (tel. 703/743–6551) are famed for the "stalacpipe organ," which gets played on hour-long cave tours. The place is kitschy but fun, though cave aficionados prefer Skyline Caverns, near Front Royal (tel. 703/635–4545 or 800/635–4599), by virtue of their flowerlike mineral encrustations known as anthrodites. Further reaches of the valley's underground world can be surveyed at Grand, Shenandoah, Endless, and Dixie caverns.

Massanutten offers downhill skiing on 11 slopes, one with a 1,150-foot vertical drop. The Massanutten ski resort (tel. 703/289–9441) also has facilities for golf, tennis, and indoor swimming.

Museum of American Frontier Culture (Staunton, tel. 703/332–7850). This museum compound includes four farmsteads (reminiscent of those that early Shenandoah Valley settlers left behind in England, Ireland, and Germany), where costumed staff members demonstrate the ways in which 18th- and 19th-century farmers planted their fields, harvested, and tended to domestic chores.

Natural Bridge (Natural Bridge, tel. 800/336–5727 or 800/533–1410 in VA). Thomas Jefferson was so impressed by this 215-foot-high, 90-foot-long rock span that he bought it, in 1774. Before the discovery of vaster natural bridges in Utah, it was high on America's great-sights list. In recent decades it's been degraded by commercialism and is now the focus of a hokey light show and the site of a wax museum. There are also caverns here.

Natural Chimneys (tel. 703/350–2510). These 120-foot rock formations just south of Harrisonburg are the backdrop for two jousting tournaments held every August since 1821. There's a campground, a pool, a picnic area, and nature trails.

New Market Battlefield (tel. 703/740–3101). Of all Civil War memorials, this is one of the most affecting, for in the last year of the Civil War 247 cadets from the Virginia Military Institute were sent here to a "baptism of fire." Though some in the battalion were just 15, the VMI boys became heroes that day. The Hall of Valor museum commemorates them.

Shenandoah National Park (Luray, tel. 703/999–2229), 302 square miles in area and encompassing 60 peaks ranging from 3,000 to 4,000 feet high, offers hope to anyone who cares about the wilderness. By 1900 the thin-soiled land that now comprises much of the park had been farmed out, the forest had been denuded, and the animals had gone to happier hunting grounds. In 1926 the Congress and the State of Virginia united in the formation of the park, which in following decades gradually blossomed once again. A movie shown at the Byrd Visitors Center at Big Meadows tells the story of the park's regeneration. Brochures that will guide you to its more than 70 scenic overlooks, 500 miles of hiking trails, and lodges are available here and at the Dickey Ridge Visitor Center, near Front Royal (open May–

early Nov.) and at Byrd Visitor Center at Big Meadows (closed mid-week Jan.–Feb.).

Shenandoah River Floating. The lazily meandering river offers opportunities for mostly gentle canoe and raft rides, with a little fishing, swimming, and inner-tubing thrown in. One good outfitter is the *Downriver Canoe Company* (Bentonville, tel. 703/635–5526), which will put you in for sallies on the South Fork, provide equipment, and pick you up, most likely waterlogged, afterward.

Skyline Drive, the park's 105-mile crown jewel, built in the 1930s by the Civilian Conservation Corps, runs past Marys Rock Tunnel, the Pinnacles, Little Stony Man Cliffs, and other landmarks. There are two busy restaurants along the way, at Skyland and Big Meadows, the former remaining open after November 1. The Park Service keeps the drive open all year, though you should check before attempting the trip in snow and other adverse conditions.

Statler Brothers Complex (tel. 703/885–7297). Staunton loves the Statlers, because the four country musicians are local boys. A converted elementary school showcases artifacts from their career, and every Fourth of July they give a wildly popular "Happy Birthday, America" concert in Gypsy Hill Park.

Stonewall Jackson House (tel. 703/463–2552). In the heart of Lexington (and just up the street from the visitor center), this trim brick two-story is where Major Thomas Jackson, a philosophy professor at VMI, lived with his wife before he rode away to lead the men in gray. General Jackson died at the Battle of Chancellorsville at the age of 39.

Strasburg Emporium (tel. 703/465–3711) is a 60-square-foot grab bag for antiques collectors, who reach in and generally come up with fun junk and occasionally a treasure. Auctions are held occasionally.

Theater at Lime Kiln (Lexington, tel. 703/463–3074). Set in an abandoned lime quarry, this stage for a professional company of actors has been called the most unusual theater setting in the United States. The Memorial Day–Labor Day schedule includes concerts on Sunday.

Virginia Horse Center (tel. 703/463–7060) is a multimillion-dollar equestrian complex on 400 acres just northwest of Lexington, with four barns, 480 stalls, a 1,000-seat grandstand, regulation dressage areas, horse trails, and cross-country courses. A large indoor arena and two more barns are under way. Its calendar includes such events as the Bonnie Blue National, the U.S. Pony Club Regional Rally, and the Virginia Horse Trials.

Virginia Military Institute (Lexington, tel. 703/464–7207) was founded in 1839 as the nation's first state-supported military school. Uniformed cadets conduct tours of the campus, which, except for the anomalous Stick Victorian admissions building, is an austere and blocky Gothic Revival fortress. With any luck you'll catch the cadets drilling on the parade grounds and at the *George C. Marshall Museum* steal a peek at the Nobel Prize of this VMI alumnus and at the Academy Award won by Frank McCarthy, another alumnus, producer of the movie *Patton.*

Virginia School for the Deaf and Blind. A walk down Staunton's graceful Beverley Street leads past the school's handsome main building, whose Greek Revival facade and columned portico were inspired by the architectural principles of Thomas Jefferson.

Washington and Lee University (Lexington, tel. 703/463–8768) was founded in 1749, subsidized by George Washington when the institution was near bankruptcy in 1796, and presided over by Robert E. Lee in the late 1860s. An extraordinary front colonnade and the *Lee Museum and Chapel,* beneath which the general is buried, are its most noteworthy sights.

Wintergreen (tel. 804/325–2200 or 800/325–2200). This 11,000-acre, privately owned resort lies on the eastern flanks of the Blue Ridge, 43 miles southwest of Charlottesville. It has two 18-hole golf courses, 10 ski slopes, an equestrian center, one indoor and five outdoor swimming pools, 25 tennis courts, restaurants, lounges, shopping centers, condos perched mountainside, and an acclaimed nature program. Wintergreen's annual Spring Wildflower Symposium is a big event.

Woodrow Wilson Birthplace (tel. 703/885–0897), an imposing, white Greek Revival home in the prettiest residential section of Staunton, and the museum next door display lots of Wilson memorabilia, including his spiffy Pierce Arrow limousine.

Tourist Information

Front Royal Chamber of Commerce and Visitors Center (414 Main St., Box 568, Front Royal, VA 22630, tel. 703/635–3185). **Harrisonburg–Rockingham Chamber of Commerce** (800 Country Club Rd., Harrisonburg, VA 22801, tel. 703/434–3862). **Jefferson National Forest Information Center** (Box 10, Natural Bridge Station, VA 24579, tel. 703/291–2188). **Lexington Visitors Bureau** (102 E. Washington St., Lexington, VA 24450, tel. 703/463–3777). **Rockfish Gap Regional Information Center** (301 W. Main St., Waynesboro, VA 22980, tel. 703/943–5187). **Shenandoah Valley Travel Association** (Box 1040, New Market, VA 22844, tel. 703/740–3132). **Staunton Tourism** (Box 58, Staunton, VA 24401–0034, tel. 703/885–2839). **Virginia Division of Tourism** (Box 798, Richmond, VA 23206–0798, tel. 804/786–4484).

Reservation Services

Bed & Breakfasts of the Historic Shenandoah Valley (402 N. Main St., Woodstock, VA 22664, tel. 703/459–8241). **Blue Ridge Bed & Breakfast Reservation Service** (Rock & Rills, Rte. 2, Box 3895, Berryville, VA 22611, tel. 703/955–1246). **Historic Country Inns of Lexington** handles the 43 rooms of three Lexington houses (11 N. Main St., Lexington, VA 24450, tel. 703/463–2044).

Jordan Hollow Farm

As anyone who's traveled much in rural America knows, farms aren't always the idyllic-looking places city folk fantasize about. However, Jordan Hollow, a working horse farm set in its own little valley beneath Hawksbill Mountain (on the western side of the Blue Ridge), comes as close to the ideal as possible. It's surrounded by 45 acres of fields and meadows where some 25 horses graze, one can only assume in deep contentment. The passel of cats who have the run of the place also have it good—they sleep on the porch on top of an electric blanket!

Marly and Jetze (pronounced Yetsuh) Beers are the proprietors, and they're a handsome, outdoorsy couple; Marly's blonde, and Jetze strikingly tall and dramatically bearded. They met in Liberia, where she was working for AID and he represented a Dutch marine-engineering firm. When they opened Jordan Hollow as an inn about 10 years ago, their first customers were Peace Corps volunteers in training. Today, though, 80 percent of the visitors are family groups with a passion for horseback riding. Every day, several equestrian groups leave the farm to wander over the foothills; youngsters go on pony rides. And when Marly gets a break from her cooking duties, she might be prevailed upon to hitch up the pony cart. Jetze's forte is keeping things jovial at the Watering Trough, a lounge and game room several paces from the barn.

The main section of the inn is in a white clapboard farmhouse fronted by a galleried porch. Portions of this structure were built of log around 1790, and in two dining rooms the rough wood and chinking is still visible. Breakfast and dinner are served here and in two other dining rooms. No meals are included in the room rates.

There is one low-ceilinged and slightly dark guest room in the main house, 16 more in the motellike Arbor View lodge, and four upscale rooms in a new log building called Mare Meadow Lodge. These are carpeted and have fireplaces, quilts and matching curtains, cedar furniture, and whirlpool baths.

Address: *Rte. 626 (RR 2, Box 375), Stanley, VA 22851, tel. 703/778-2209 or 703/778-2285.*
Accommodations: *20 double rooms with baths, 1 suite.*
Amenities: *Restaurant, air-conditioning; TV in suite, Mare Meadow Lodge, and lounge; phones in rooms; horseback riding, 1 large or 2 small conference rooms.*
Rates: *$78–$130; breakfast extra. DC, MC, V.*
Restrictions: *No pets.*

Trillium House

You've got to hand it to Ed and Betty Dinwiddie. To them, building a bed-and-breakfast on the grounds of the Wintergreen resort may have seemed the most natural thing in the world; after all, their family had vacationed there for years. But to skiers, refugees from the Blue Ridge Parkway, wildflower enthusiasts, and all-around mountain devotees, the idea was a stroke of genius. The simple fact that Trillium House lies across the road from the gargantuan sports complex, with its indoor pool, tennis courts, ski slopes, hiking trails, golf course, and stables, should give you a clue as to the kinds of activities available.

From Wintergreen's gate, a roller-coasterish road brings you 2½ miles to the doorstep of Trillium House. The beige frame building fronted by a porch and a Palladian window, surrounded by trees and stylish condominiums owned by Wintergreen residents, was built in 1983. You enter the Great Room, which is two stories high, near a staircase at the side leading to a loft library. The front sitting area has a wood-burning stove, above which hang several organ pipes; by the front door, a canister holds a collection of walking sticks. Breakfast is served in the dining rooms, with views of the backyard gazebo, and on Friday and Saturday, dinners are cooked by chef Ellen, who formerly worked in one of Wintergreen's restaurants.

The 12 guest rooms at Trillium House lie in two wings off the Great Room. Their architectural tone is slightly motelish, but decorative touches add some personality—here a quilt or a framed picture that could only have been created by one of the Dinwiddie brood, there a writing desk from The Homestead or a bed with a lace canopy.

The odds are that you'll spend most of your stay here pursuing varieties of R&R on the resort or ensconced in the Great Room, chatting with other guests or Ed and Betty, who manage to seem amazingly relaxed despite their demanding housekeeping duties. The single disappointment is that Trillium House doesn't have mountain views; if that's what you're after, you'll have to grab a stick and walk.

Address: *Box 280, Nellysford, VA 22958, tel. 804/325-9126 or 800/325-9126, fax 804/325-1099.*
Accommodations: *10 double rooms with baths, 2 suites.*
Amenities: *Dinner served Fri. and Sat. by reservation, air-conditioning, TV/VCR in sitting room with videocassette library; stables.*
Rates: *$80–$150; full buffet breakfast. MC, V.*
Restrictions: *No smoking in dining room, no pets.*

Belle Grae Inn

The Belle Grae is a classic small-town hotel occupying an old Victorian house and several surrounding buildings five minutes from Staunton's downtown. On your arrival, you'll be met by Bellboy, a sanguine boxer who, according to owner Michael Organ, works for biscuits. The Old Inn, built ca. 1860, has a wide porch offering views of Betsy Belle and Mary Grae, two of the town's many hillocks. Its eight bedrooms have high ceilings and are decorated with amiable Victorian antiques, and downstairs there are two restaurants—one fancy, in Staunton terms, and the other a bistro bar lined with windows. The suites in the Townhouse, adjoining the bistro, are Belle Grae's top-of-the-line, for their upscale decor and such amenities as fireplaces, phones, and cable TV.

Varied accommodations are also available in Jefferson House, in the Bungalow, near the hotel's terrace garden, and in the Bishop's Study. But best of all is the earnest tone at the Belle Grae, a place that's trying hard to be the best Staunton has to offer, and succeeding, if quirkily.

Address: *515 W. Frederick St., Staunton, VA 24401, tel. 703/886–5151.*
Accommodations: *10 double rooms with baths, 8 suites, 1 apartment.*
Amenities: *Restaurant, bistro, fireplaces in 10 rooms and 3 common areas, air-conditioning, cable TV and phones in 11 rooms.*
Rates: *$65–$125; full breakfast. AE, DC, MC, V.*
Restrictions: *No smoking in Jefferson House, no pets.*

Fassifern

Think of it. There are 96,000 horses in Virginia. If you want to buy or show one of them, the place to do it is at the Virginia Horse Center, just north of Lexington. And if you make the trip, you'll be glad to know there's one of the Shenandoah Valley's prettiest bed-and-breakfasts just a trot down the road. The place is called Fassifern, after the Scottish ancestral home of its builder, who erected this three-story, beige brick farmhouse in 1867. It's owned by Francis Smith and managed by her animated daughter, Ann Carol Perry, who keeps three horses of her own, named Sonny, Sinner, and Pye, in the pasture. There's no particular history connected to Fassifern; it's just a lovely country place with a pond, towering maple trees, and an old icehouse

that's been converted into two extra guest rooms. We liked the Colonel's Quarters best because of its wide plank floors and pasture views. In the main house, three more guest rooms are furnished with Victorian armoires, Oriental rugs, and crystal chandeliers. Ann Carol is fun; she likes to gab and can help you plan your Lexington sightseeing.

Address: *Rte. 39W (RR 5, Box 87), Lexington, VA 24450, tel. 703/463–1013.*
Accommodations: *6 double rooms with baths.*
Amenities: *Air-conditioning.*
Rates: *$65–$82; Continental breakfast. AE, MC, V.*
Restrictions: *No smoking, no pets; closed Thanksgiving, Christmas, and New Year's Day.*

The Inn at Narrow Passage

Pack your inner tubes, gang, and your swimming togs and fishing rods; they will all prove useful at The Inn at Narrow Passage, which sits right above the North Fork of the Shenandoah River. Ed Markel, owner of the inn, will kindly put you in about a mile south, and from there it's a 3½-hour float home. Most likely when you return there will be a fire crackling away in the log sitting room in the oldest section of the inn. It was built as a way station on the Wilderness Trail (now Route 11) around 1740, and the Markels meticulously restored it, but guests still claim that you can see daylight through the chinks. There are three guest rooms on the second floor of this section, and nine more in wings built in 1985. The latter are nice, but motelish; we preferred the old rooms by a long shot. They have handmade hinges, tongue-and-groove pine walls, and a lovely hammer dulcimer at the top of the steps. When the valley is blanketed in snow, the inn is a cozy place with a total of 10 working fireplaces. There's skiing at Bryce Mountain a half hour away, and plenty of hiking, too.

Address: *Rte. 11S, Woodstock, VA 22664, tel. 703/459-8000.*
Accommodations: *10 double rooms with baths, 2 doubles share a bath.*
Amenities: *Air-conditioning, TV in sitting room, 1 conference room.*
Rates: *$55–$85; full breakfast. MC, V.*
Restrictions: *No smoking in guest rooms, no pets, 2-night minimum Oct. and holiday and fall weekends.*

Joshua Wilton House

Harrisonburg, a commercial center and the site of James Madison University, is not a markedly handsome town. In it, the Joshua Wilton House strikes the highest note—it's a lovingly renovated and luxuriously equipped mauve, lavender, and pink Queen Anne cottage with triple-decker bays and a turret. It is said that it was the first house in the valley to get electricity, and when the lights went on people came from outlying farms to witness the miracle. You enter by way of a front door surrounded by leaded glass and through a foyer with a gleaming parquet floor, a chandelier, and bushy potted ferns. Throughout the four downstairs dining rooms you'll find painted mantels and pictures by the Shenandoah Valley Watercolor Associates. The guest chambers are really lovely, particularly Room 5, with its four-poster bed and white wing chairs, and Room 4, which has a three-window alcove in the turret and a canopy bed. The owners, Roberta and Craig Moore, live on the premises. Fancy dinners and breakfasts, perhaps with crab-and-cheese omelets, are available.

Address: *412 S. Main St., Harrisonburg, VA 22801, tel. 703/434-4464.*
Accommodations: *5 double rooms with baths.*
Amenities: *Restaurant, bar, air-conditioning, phones in rooms, fireplace in 1 room.*
Rates: *$85–$95; full breakfast. AE, MC, V.*
Restrictions: *Smoking in bar only, no pets.*

Oak Spring Farm and Vineyard

We saw Oak Spring Farm while it was still being renovated, but even then all signs were good. To begin with, the proprietors, Jim and Pat Tichenor, restored and operated nearby Fassifern before selling it to its present owners—clearly, they have an eye for properties that fix up well. Oak Spring is a two-story farmhouse whose sections were built in 1826 and 1840. While deep in plaster and paint, the Tichenors discovered walls in the ell made of oak planks stacked up like pancakes—an architectural point that will make Oak Spring a shoo-in for the National Register of Historic Places. The three guest rooms are on the second floor, and are filled with fine antiques; we liked the Regency Room best, because a window by its claw-foot tub provides pastoral views while you soak. The farm is surrounded by 40 acres planted in hay and alfalfa, a pasture where 20 burros graze, and 5 acres of grapes. Oak Spring Farm is a good out-of-town headquarters for exploring nearby Lexington, and an excellent spot to lay over during trips on the Blue Ridge Parkway.

Address: *RR 1, Box 356, Raphine, VA 24472, tel. 703/377–2398.*
Accommodations: *3 double rooms with baths.*
Amenities: *Air-conditioning, fireplace in guest living room.*
Rates: *$55–$65; Continental breakfast. MC, V.*
Restrictions: *No smoking, no pets, 2-night minimum on parents' and graduation weekends.*

Thornrose House

Proprietors Ray and Carolyn Hoaster are admirers of English bed-and-breakfasts and have fashioned Thornrose along those lines, offering strong English tea and grilled tomatoes at breakfast, cramming the place with heavy Victorian antiques, and presiding over it all with true British conviviality. The house is pretty enough, with upstairs bedrooms named Canterbury, Windemere, and Yorkshire; but Ray and Carolyn are far and away its most attractive features. He was with the Air Force band; she's an exchanteuse—and occasionally the two of them still hold forth at Staunton's Belle Grae Inn. They're full of quirky ideas, like Victorian Sampler weekends, when Thornrose House rings with music-hall songs and guests play whist. Ray has a large collection of videocassettes. The house is across the street from bucolic Gypsy Hill Park, with its pool, tennis courts, and golf course, and where the July 4th Statler Brothers concerts are held.

Address: *531 Thornrose Ave., Staunton, VA 24401, tel. 703/885–7026.*
Accommodations: *3 double rooms with baths.*
Amenities: *Air-conditioning in rooms, fireplace, cable TV/VCR, and grand piano in guest sitting room.*
Rates: *$40–$60; full breakfast. No credit cards.*
Restrictions: *No smoking, no pets, 2-night minimum on Oct. and graduation weekends, 3-night minimum on July 4.*

Off the Beaten Track

Fort Lewis Lodge

On a 3,200-acre farm in the Allegheny Mountains, John and Caryl Cowden raise Angus cattle, soybeans, and corn. The beautiful Cowpasture River deepens into a swimming hole nearby, and Tower Hill Mountain looms above, traversed by paths and logging roads. Below the manor house there's a dining hall in an old mill, and a lodge. The Cowdens began by catering to bow hunters in pursuit of deer, wild turkey, and the occasional black bear, then opened their lodge to summertime rusticators. They arrange camping trips for guests, with dinner delivered to a shelter, where bedding is laid out. The common rooms contain stuffed bears, raccoons, and red fox—all Allegheny Highland species. The lodge rooms are exceptionally comfortable, with locally made headboards and spreads and curtains from the Sears and Spiegel catalogues. There's a laundry room, and a stone hearth in the gathering room. A converted silo with three bedrooms provides views of the countryside and nothing else. All you'll find at Fort Lewis Lodge are fields, rivers, mountains, forests, and Cowden hospitality.

Address: *HCR3, Box 21A, Millboro, VA 24460, tel. 703/925-2314.*
Accommodations: *7 double rooms with baths, 6 doubles share 3 baths, 1 suite.*
Amenities: *TV/VCR in game room, meeting room; guided hunting.*
Rates: *$110-$125 MAP. MC, V.*
Restrictions: *No smoking in bedrooms, no pets, closed Jan.-Mar.*

The Inn at Gristmill Square

Bath County in western Virginia covers 540 bumpy square miles inhabited by just 5,000 souls, and it hasn't got a single stoplight. Warm Springs, the county seat, has a post office, a courthouse, and an inn— and that's about all. Still, The Inn at Gristmill Square, occupying restored mill buildings, blacksmith shop, and hardware store, is reason enough to visit this quintessentially peaceful spot. Its Waterwheel Restaurant is one of the area's best places to sup, with a chef trained at the Culinary Institute of America and a cool subterranean wine cellar. A pebbled courtyard separates the restaurant and country store from one bank of rooms, and across the lane there's an inn annex, called the Steel House, a small swimming pool, and tennis courts. The Miller House, up the road, has rooms named Oat, Barley, Rye, and Wheat, which we liked best. Janice McWilliams and her son, Bruce, are the able proprietors, former owners of an inn in Vermont. They serve breakfast and the *Richmond Times Dispatch* in a picnic basket at your door.

Address: *Box 359, Warm Springs, VA 24484, tel. 703/839-2231.*
Accommodations: *12 double rooms with baths, 2 apartments.*
Amenities: *Restaurant, cable TV and phones in rooms, air-conditioning in Miller House, fireplaces in 7 guest rooms; swimming pool, sauna, 3 tennis courts, store.*
Rates: *$90-$125; Continental breakfast. MC, V.*
Restrictions: *No pets.*

North Carolina

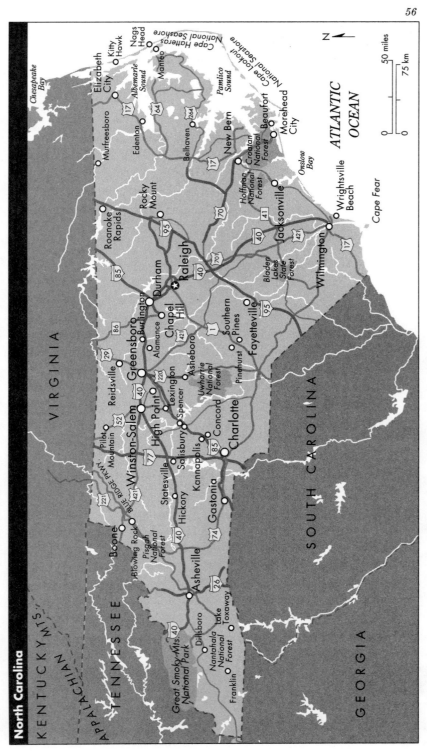

North Carolina

The Outer Banks and Albemarle Region

The northern part of the North Carolina coast, a region of broad bays, meandering rivers, and shallow inlets protected by a chain of barrier islands, was settled very early. Long before Plymouth Rock, earlier than Jamestown, English colonists came in 1584, lived for a time on Roanoke Island, and disappeared mysteriously in 1591. For 100 years or more, the Indians and the dunes were left mostly undisturbed, and the shifting shoals garnered their annual harvest of shipwrecks. A few towns were founded, a Colonial capital was established, and farming and fishing flourished. In this mild and mannerly land much remains the same.

The old character of the Outer Banks is most evident on Ocracoke Island and in fishing villages like Wanchese and Hatteras. The descendants of early settlers of these isolated places speak their own dialect of Elizabethan English, and the wild ponies that roam the Shackleford Banks are another reminder of a bygone era.

On the 130 miles of barrier islands that stretch from Cape Lookout to the Virginia line, large areas are protected as national seashores, which helps preserve the marshes, dunes, rare plants, birds, and aquatic life. Although fishing is still the main industry in some of the small villages, tourism has taken hold in others. In summer, the ferries and bridge from the mainland are loaded with cars bound for Ocracoke, Kill Devil Hills, Nags Head, and Manteo. And only when school starts do the towns and villages return to their normal, quiet pace.

Today the image of the coastal region is changing as more people take up residence and its popularity as a travel destination grows. Tourists visit the historic houses in Edenton and Beaufort; flashes of bright nylon on the backs of windsurfers and hang gliders are seen in Nags Head and

*Kill Devil Hills; the charter boats and head boats leave
daily for deep-sea fishing. And in the northernmost part of
the Outer Banks, where exclusive hunting clubs once
flourished, posh residential communities are taking shape.
Even with all the changes, though, the area still has that
uncrowded, laid-back, old-sneakers feel. The ocean view
remains unobstructed, the roads aren't lined with tacky
neon signs, and people don't dress to go out to dinner.
Though you can swim or fish, sail or dive, the Outer Banks
is one of the great places on Earth to do nothing.*

Places to Go, Sights to See

Wright Brothers National Memorial. The Visitor Center at Kill Devil Hills
(tel. 919/441–7430) has on display a replica of the plane that the two bicycle
mechanics from Ohio, Wilbur and Orville Wright, used in their first
successful flight on December 17, 1903; National Park Service rangers give
interpretive talks on the historic event. The aviators' four takeoffs and
landings are marked on the grassy strip outside.

Roanoke Island. During the summer, historical interpretations and guided
tours are given at the *Elizabeth II State Historic Site* (tel. 919/473–1144),
a replica of a 16th-century sailing vessel, harbored in Shallowbag Bay in
downtown *Manteo*. The town, which has a New England look to it, is fun to
explore. You can buy a walking-tour guide at Manteo Booksellers. *The Lost
Colony* (tel. 919/473–1144), an outdoor drama, has reenacted each summer
since 1937 the story of the first colonists, who mysteriously disappeared
when some of their party returned to England for supplies. In summer,
performances are given nightly and backstage tours in the afternoon. Also
on Roanoke Island are the *Fort Raleigh National Historic Site* (tel.
919/473–2111), a reconstruction of what's thought to be the first colonists'
fort; the *Elizabethan Gardens* (tel. 919/473–3234), with walking trails amid
period plantings; and the *North Carolina Aquarium* (Airport Rd., tel. 919/
473–3494), which offers exhibits, tours, and expeditions to coastal habitats.

Cape Hatteras Lighthouse, 205 feet high, is the tallest lighthouse in
America. Exhibits in the Visitor Center (tel. 919/995–4474) explain the flora
and fauna of the Cape Hatteras National Seashore and show graphically how
the ocean is fast encroaching on the lighthouse—you'd better see it soon.

Ocracoke Island, ideal for walking and bicycling, is accessible only by ferry
and has a quiet village of shops, inns, and restaurants.

Beaufort. Founded in 1713, North Carolina's third-oldest town has more than
100 historic houses, a complex of restored Colonial buildings, the *North*

Carolina Maritime Museum (315 Front St., tel. 919/728–7317), and
a waterfront lined with antiques shops and restaurants.

Several towns on the mainland side of Albemarle Sound compose the historic
Albemarle Region, whose primary attraction is **Edenton.** Here, in 1774,
a rebellion against the Crown took place that is known as the Edenton Tea
Party. The first provincial capital of North Carolina, dating to 1685, Edenton
has many historic buildings; four of them can be seen on a walking tour run
by Historic Edenton (tel. 919/482–3663) that leaves from the 1782 Barker
House on South Broad Street. You'll see *St. Paul's Episcopal Church* (built
between 1736 and 1760); the *Cupola House* (1725), a Jacobean wood building;
the Georgian *Chowan County Courthouse* on the village green; the *Barker
House;* and the waterfront on Albemarle Sound.

Beaches. Most of the Outer Banks' 130 miles of unspoiled beaches are part
of the national seashores and are ideal for a variety of water sports.
Lifeguards are stationed at Coquina Beach, Salvo, Cape Hatteras, Frisco, and
Ocracoke in the Cape Hatteras National Seashore; many motels and hotels
also have lifeguards.

Restaurants

The **Sanderling Inn and Restaurant** (Rte. 12, Duck, tel. 919/261–4111)
serves gourmet Continental and Southern regional dishes in an elegantly
restored lifesaving station on the oceanfront. **Etheridge's Seafood
Restaurant** (U.S. 158 bypass, tel. 919/441–2645) is one of the best in Kill
Devil Hills, whereas **Kelly's Outer Banks Restaurant & Tavern** (U.S. 158
bypass, tel. 919/441–4116) is the place to go for fish in Nags Head. The
Weeping Radish Brewery and Restaurant (U.S. 64/264, Kill Devil Hills, tel.
919/473–1157) serves Bavarian-style cuisine and Holpen beer, made on site.
The **Elizabethan Dinner Theatre** (U.S. 64/24, Manteo, tel. 800/346–2466)
puts on five-course Renaissance dinner shows on certain days from June
through late October. In Edenton, **Caroline's** (Broad St., tel. 919/482–2711)
offers gourmet made-from-scratch dishes.

Tourist Information

Dare County Tourist Bureau (Box 399, Manteo, NC 27954, tel. 919/473–
2138). **Historic Albemarle Tour, Inc.** (Box 759, Edenton, NC 27932, tel.
919/482–7325). **North Carolina Coast Host** (Box 5044, Station 1, Wilmington,
NC 28403, tel. 919/395–4012). **Outer Banks Chamber of Commerce** (Box
1757, Kill Devil Hills, NC 27948, tel. 919/441–8144).

Reservation Service

North Carolina Bed & Breakfast Assn. (Box 1077, Asheville, NC 28802, tel.
919/592–2634).

Granville Queen Inn

Guests get to live out their fantasies at this bed-and-breakfast inn in the heart of Edenton. The ornate sign with its elaborate crown is the first clue to what's inside, and the bright pink paint on the neoclassic 1907 house sends a message that this isn't your ordinary Colonial with 18th-century furniture. Californians Greg Haden and Marilyn Miller traveled the continent looking for a place to put their imaginations and talents to work, and they have created a place where the rich and famous might hang their hats.

The first thing you encounter after entering the front door is a sculpture of a pair of cranes, their feet planted in a square white marble fountain and their heads pointed upward to a dark ceiling made of plaster squares hand-molded with cupid faces and then gilded. There's a formal dining room with a crystal chandelier; a side porch sporting white wicker, glass-top tables, and ceiling fans has been enclosed as another eating area.

Each of the guest rooms provides an ambience you might find by taking a trip to a foreign country or stepping into the pages of a storybook. In the Egyptian Room, the most exotic and most requested, guests go to sleep under a leopard coverlet, watched over by two black sphinxes flanking a pair of thronelike chairs draped with the same sheer gold-shot fabric that's at the windows. The marble bathroom has a double tub with brass cobra-handle faucets. The bath of the Queen's Cottage, with its 19th-century French country decor, features a three-seater toilet (two of the lids are just for effect). The Captain's Quarters is furnished in dark mahogany, with a decorated, lacquered dinghy suspended over the bed. The Queen Victorianna Room, often requested by women business travelers, is outfitted in white eyelet.

Dining at the Granville Queen also is a memorable experience. Greg and Marilyn serve a five-course gourmet breakfast that includes grilled chicken breast or filet mignon with eggs and potatoes. In the afternoon they hold wine tastings.

Address: *108 S. Granville St., Edenton, NC 27932, tel. 919/482–5296, fax 919/482–4319.*
Accommodations: *9 double rooms with baths, some with gas-log fireplaces.*
Amenities: *Air-conditioning; cable TV, VCRs, and phones in rooms.*
Rates: *$85–$95; full breakfast and wine tasting. MC, V.*
Restrictions: *No smoking, no pets.*

The Island Inn

History has been made at this establishment, the oldest inn on the Outer Banks, which sits at the edge of the village of Ocracoke overlooking Silver Lake. Built in 1901 of timbers from an old ship, the inn served as an Odd Fellows Lodge, public school, and officers' club before becoming an inn in 1945.

The lobby and most of the guest rooms have a casual, well-worn appearance, though they are immaculately kept. People have such a good time at the inn they don't care that there's no five-star luxury here; they do find good food and very caring, hospitable hosts. Bob and Cee Touhey, formerly of Winston-Salem, gave up their careers in marketing and teaching to buy the inn and are renovating it in stages, beginning with air-conditioning, new wiring, and other basics.

The best rooms in the house, offering panoramic views of the water, are in the Crow's Nest, but you must climb steep stairs to get there. A motellike annex was added in 1982, and two cottages are also for rent. The dining room is the oldest restaurant on the Outer Banks and certainly the most charming, with its low-beamed ceiling, antique tables, and old china. Chef Chester Lynn learned to cook at the knee of his mother, who worked here for many years, and today he carries on the food traditions she started. (A native

of Ocracoke, he speaks with that Elizabethan tinge.) House specials are crab cakes, clam chowder, homemade pies, and herring roe with scrambled eggs, grits, biscuits, or toast. The Touheys' winter special has gone over quite well; one couple decided to tie the knot before their scheduled wedding date to take advantage of the two nights' lodging, two breakfasts, and a dinner, for $120 per couple.

The village of Ocracoke is on the remote island of the same name, which is accessible only by ferry. The laid-back, casual atmosphere of the place makes it seem a little like Cape Cod. The famous pirate Blackbeard was killed on the island, close to where the Ocracoke Lighthouse now stands. The inn has a resident ghost named Godfrey, a friendly former innkeeper who has never been actually seen but who sometimes leaves things out of place.

Address: *Lighthouse Rd., Rte. 12, Ocracoke, NC 27960, tel. 919/928–4351.*
Accommodations: *35 double rooms with baths.*
Amenities: *Restaurant, individual air-conditioning units; pool.*
Rates: *$40–$90 Memorial Day–Labor Day, $30–$65 rest of year; cottages off-season $70–$80. MC, V.*
Restrictions: *No pets.*

Langdon House

angdon House, a block from the Beaufort waterfront and across the street from the Old Burying Ground, is just about as old as that historic cemetery. It's built of hand-hewn heart-pine timbers, put together with hand-forged nails, and owner Jimm Prest is fairly sure the ballast-stone foundation was laid in 1733. (The cemetery was deeded to the town in 1731.)

A Colonial/Federal-style house with a Bahamian roofline, Langdon House is painted white with dark green shutters and has upstairs and downstairs porches across the front. The floor plan is very simple, with a central hall and stairway running down the middle, a parlor on the left side, a bedroom to the right (the largest and sunniest), and three to the rear. All the rooms have queen-size beds (with no headboards but with lots of comfy pillows) and are named for different guests. The dining room, upstairs over the parlor, resembles an 18th-century tavern, with an Edwardian oak table that takes up most of the room. The kitchen is also upstairs—an arrangement already in place when Prest renovated the house in 1985. (Neighbors helped him get the roof on just before a major storm hit.)

Langdon House is furnished with an assortment of antiques, some on loan from local residents. The parlor contains an Estes pump organ, an 1840s Empire secretary, and other treasures—all furniture that is friendly and familiar, not museum pieces you wouldn't dare touch.

The house stands on its own merits, but Jimm Prest really makes it come alive. Formerly an employee of Coca-Cola, he's a giant of a fellow who meets his guests with a big smile and a cordial welcome at the front door. Before you've barely made it across the threshold, he's offering you some iced tea with mint leaves from his herb garden and giving you tips on places to eat and things to do in Beaufort; he will even arrange special excursions.

Prest encourages his guests to sleep late and will cook a full breakfast for them anytime after 7:30 AM. The main dish is usually too-pretty-to-eat orange-pecan waffles or omelets. Prest says he's not in the business of just renting rooms; he prefers to think he's practicing the fine art of innkeeping.

Address: *135 Craven St., Beaufort, NC 28516, tel. 919/728–5499.*
Accommodations: *4 double rooms with baths.*
Amenities: *Air-conditioning, guest phone; bicycles, fishing rods, ice chests, and beach baskets with towels and suntan lotion.*
Rates: *$88–$120; full breakfast and refreshments. No credit cards.*
Restrictions: *No smoking indoors, no pets, 2-night minimum on summer weekends and holidays.*

The Tranquil House Inn

This inn, on Manteo's waterfront in the heart of the village, looks old but was built in 1988. It combines the architecture of the old Roanoke Hotel with the name and reputation for hospitality of another local inn that flourished in the first half of this century. Both have since disappeared from the scene.

The inn is a three-story, gray shingled building with a green roof, overlooking Shallowbag Bay. Guests sit and watch the goings and comings on the waterfront from long verandas and from decks atop the gables on the third floor. The small, functional lobby with its registration desk is in the center of the building, and off to the side is a cozy library with a fireplace that is a congregating place for guests. Breakfast is served here, in the guest rooms, or on the verandas and decks. Guests have access to the kitchen after breakfast, so if you want to whip up a sandwich for lunch (from your own fixings, of course) you may do so. As you might expect, guests find it easy to get acquainted here, and couples often team up for dinner or for day trips.

The bedrooms have pine floors and are decorated with bright floral wallpapers. The furnishings are all pine reproductions, with king and queen beds, canopies and four-posters, double beds, and sleep sofas. Porta-cribs and cots are available. Guests are greeted with complimentary wine

and fresh flowers upon arrival. Two suites have galley kitchens, and the third-floor rooms have refrigerators. Packages in conjunction with Clara's Restaurant are available.

Because the inn is right in the middle of everything, you can leave your car, walk to the local shops and restaurants, and stroll around the quaint seaside village. You can also use the inn's bicycles for getting around town.

Address: *405 Queen Elizabeth St. (Box 2045), Manteo, NC 28054, tel. 919/473-1404 or 800/458-7069, fax 919/473-1772.*
Accommodations: *26 double rooms with baths, 2 housekeeping suites.*
Amenities: *Air-conditioning, cable TV, and phones in rooms; bicycles, gas grill.*
Rates: *$89–$139; Continental breakfast, wine. AE, DC, MC, V.*
Restrictions: *No pets; 2-night minimum on summer weekends, 3-night minimums on holiday weekends.*

The Figurehead Bed and Breakfast

Patterned after the lifesaving stations that once lined the Outer Banks, The Figurehead is on Albemarle Sound, a 10-minute walk to the ocean. Innkeeper Ann Ianni has used sea and sand and natural and nautical themes to create the casual, relaxed atmosphere of this three-level seaside inn. She even had a figurehead made for the house and named it Jenny Lind, after the Swedish opera star who took America by storm.

Guests gather for conversation around the fireplace in the Keeping Room or relax in the hammock swings and the rocking chairs on the porch (a great place for sunsets). Each of the guest rooms is on a different level of the house, offering ultra privacy. Osprey Watch upstairs (ideal for honeymooners) is decorated in wicker and has its own private sun deck and whirlpool.

Address: *417 Helga St., Milepost 55, Kill Devil Hills, NC 27948, tel. 919/441-6929.*
Accommodations: *3 double rooms with baths.*
Amenities: *Air-conditioning, cable TV in rooms, phones and ceiling fans in Sea One and Osprey Watch rooms, TV/VCR in common area, newspapers; bicycles.*
Rates: *$95-$110; Continental breakfast. MC, V.*
Restrictions: *No smoking in bedrooms, no pets; June–Labor Day 2-night minimum on weekends, 3-night minimum on holiday weekends.*

The Trestle House Inn

The late "Papa Joe" Crisanti, who ran the Osprey Hotel in Manasquan, New Jersey, entertained his family and friends at this lakeside retreat. The Cape Cod brick-veneer house has been maintained as he left it and is now a bed-and-breakfast inn. The inside looks rustic, with exposed beams milled from railroad trestles, knotty-pine paneling, wagon-wheel chandeliers, massive stone fireplaces, and handmade furniture.

One of the spacious guest rooms is on the basement level, as is the large den, which has a fireplace, a billiard table, and a shuffleboard court and is ideal for meetings and retreats. Watching the Canada geese and other wildlife on the lake is a favorite pastime with guests, who can also fish, go rowboating, picnic, and hike around the property or play golf and tennis at the Chowan Country Club. Rich and Fran Oliver serve a bountiful breakfast of dishes like egg rarebit, cheese soufflé, and baked French toast.

Address: *Soundside Rd., Rte. 4, Box 370, Edenton, NC 27932, tel. 919/482-2282.*
Accommodations: *4 double rooms with baths.*
Amenities: *Air-conditioning, cable TV, rowing machine, exercise bike, steam bath, meeting room, cookout room.*
Rates: *$60; full breakfast. AE, MC, V.*
Restrictions: *No smoking in public areas, no pets.*

Wilmington and the Cape Fear Coast

Unlike the Outer Banks region, where the treacherous coastline and fragile barrier islands have restricted development, the Cape Fear River and Wilmington area blossomed into a commercial port early on, shipping cotton in its heyday. It is still North Carolina's largest port, and the river hums with traffic. The Henrietta II *paddle wheeler, a replica of the boats that used to ply the river, has become a familiar sight in recent years, and the completion of Interstate 40 from Raleigh not only strengthens the port but also brings more visitors to the coast.*

Like many seaports along the South Atlantic coast, Wilmington remains picturesque and charming. Here church spires and historic buildings outnumber skyscrapers, but the city is far from asleep. The downtown has been rejuvenated, the arts have returned to the restored Thalian Hall, and Dino De Laurentiis's studio, the Carolina Film Corporation, has made moviemaking an everyday occurrence.

In the northern part of this region, at the confluence of the Trent and Neuse rivers, lies New Bern, a quiet town that served for a time as North Carolina's Colonial capital. Today its Tryon Palace Restoration is one of the major tourist attractions in the state. Visitors flock to seaside cottages strewn along the coast between Wilmington and Morehead City. They are also drawn to the area south of Wilmington, to the family beaches, resort islands, golf links, historic forts, and old plantation houses between Wilmington and the South Carolina line.

Places to Go, Sights to See

Wilmington
The **Burgwin-Wright House** (224 Market St., tel. 919/762–0570), built in 1770 on the foundation of an early jail, is open for tours.

Some of Wilmington's best restaurants and most interesting shops are in **Chandler's Wharf,** a restored warehouse district at Water and Ann streets on the waterfront, and in the **Cotton Exchange,** the building at 321 Front Street that dates to pre–Civil War times.

New Hanover County Museum of the Lower Cape Fear (814 Market St., tel. 919/341–4350) traces the natural and social history of the region and includes an exhibit on some famous Wilmingtonians—among them Michael Jordan, David Brinkley, Charles Kuralt, Charlie Daniels, Sammy Davis Jr., Mary Baker Eddy, Anna McNeill Whistler, and President Woodrow Wilson.

The restored **Thalian Hall** (102 N. 3rd St., tel. 919/763–3398), built in 1858 for performances by such greats as Buffalo Bill, John Philip Sousa, General Tom Thumb, Lillian Russell, and Oscar Wilde, is the site today of plays and concerts.

The **USS** *North Carolina* **Battleship Memorial** (tel. 919/762–1829), moored in Wilmington Harbor, took part in every major naval offensive in the Pacific during World War II and has been restored as a museum. An orientation film prepares visitors for the two-hour self-guided tour, and a narrated tape is available for rent. On summer evenings "The Immortal Showboat," a 70-minute sound-and-light spectacular staged on board, dazzles audiences seated in grandstands across from the ship's bow.

Wilmington Railroad Museum (Red Cross and Water Sts., tel. 919/763–2634), a part of the Coastline Center Convention Complex, highlights the history of the Wilmington and Weldon Railroad from 1840 to the present. Visitors may board the steam locomotive and caboose.

The **Zebulon Latimer House** (126 N. 3rd St., tel. 919/762–0492), an Italianate structure built in 1852, is also open for tours.

Sightseeing tours. Bob Jenkins of *Wilmington Adventure Tours* (tel. 919/763–1785) will give you the inside story on the city during his animated walking tour. Or you can get acquainted with Wilmington with *Sightseeing Tours by Horse Drawn Carriage* (tel. 919/251–8889). Captain Carl Marshburn conducts river tours and dinner excursions aboard the paddle wheeler *Henrietta II* (tel. 919/343–1611).

Brunswick Town State Historic Site (tel. 919/371–6613), on Route 133 south of Wilmington, is an excavated early Colonial town that is open for self-guided tours.

Fort Fisher State Historic Site (Kure Beach, tel. 919/458–5538), the largest earthwork fortification in the South during the Civil War, has exhibits of war relics and artifacts from sunken blockade-runners. The *North Carolina Aquarium* (tel. 919/458–8257), also at Fort Fisher, has a 20,000-gallon shark tank, a touch pool, and a whale exhibit, among others.

Beaches. *Wrightsville Beach,* about 7 miles from Wilmington, appeals to families. *Carolina* and *Kure,* 20 miles south, are other options. *Bald Head*

Island, where people gather to watch the hatching of loggerhead turtles each year, is accessible only by passenger ferry (no cars are permitted).

Poplar Grove Historic Plantation (tel. 919/686–9989), about 15 miles north of Wilmington, was the Foy family home from 1850 until 1980, when it was opened to visitors for tours, crafts demonstrations, and hayrides. There's also a petting zoo, a country store, and a restaurant that serves home-cooked meals.

New Bern

The **Tryon Palace Restoration** complex (610 Pollock St., tel. 919/638–1560) includes the reconstructed *palace of Governor William Tryon* (1770s), the *John Wright Stanley House* (ca. 1783), the *Dixon-Stevenson House* (ca. 1826), and *New Bern Academy* (ca. 1764). Throughout the year many special events are staged, and costumed guides give tours of the palace, which is elaborately decorated during the Christmas holidays and is the site of historical interpretations by actors in summer.

The New Bern Civil War Museum (301 Metcalf St., tel. 919/633–2818), a private collection, has the most complete display of 19th-century firearms, other weapons, and accoutrements on the East Coast.

Restaurants

In Wilmington, **The Pilot House** (tel. 919/343–0200) in Chandler's Wharf serves excellent, fresh seafood; **Ferrovia's** on Nutt Street (tel. 919/763–6677) is known for its outstanding medallions of filet mignon and sautéed fillet of flounder; and the dining room of the **Carolina Film Corporation** on North 23rd Street (tel. 919/353–3500) is a good place to eat lunch and maybe catch a glimpse of the stars.

Tourist Information

Cape Fear Coast Convention and Visitors Bureau (24 N. 3rd St., Wilmington, NC 28401, tel. 919/341–4030 or 800/222–4757). **North Carolina Coast Host** (Box 5044, Station 1, Wilmington, NC 28403, tel. 919/395–4012).

Reservation Service

North Carolina Bed & Breakfast Assn. (Box 1077, Asheville, NC 28802, tel. 919/592–2634).

Harmony House Inn

This 7,000-square-foot Greek Revival house in New Bern's historic district was built in the early 1850s, used as offices and apartments, and enlarged three times before becoming an inn in 1985. Once it was even sawed in half and a large addition built. The unusual house has two front doors, two parallel hallways down the middle, and 12 unused fireplaces. The inviting front porch has rocking chairs and a swing.

During the Civil War the house was occupied by Company K of the 45th Massachusetts Regiment, who posed for a formal picture with the house in 1863. In the parlor, framed pages from *Harper's Weekly* depict the Battle of New Bern, which occurred in the same year; Union troops occupied the town for the duration of the war.

Innkeepers Buzz and Diane Hansen, who moved here from Illinois after he retired from the paper industry, bought Harmony House and furnished it with family pieces, handcrafted local furniture, and antiques. There's an 1875 pump organ (a challenge to play) and a 400-year-old Italian clock. The soft pastel colors of the walls set off the canopy beds and colorful quilts. Needlepoint pictures and such family memorabilia as Buzz's father's christening dress also add interest.

Breakfast is a time for socializing in the formal dining room, where the Hansens lay out a different hot dish on the Empire sideboard each day: pancakes stuffed with cottage cheese, quiche, Scotch eggs, ham Strata, or bacon and eggs, plus fruit and homemade granola. There's also fresh-ground coffee and sometimes sundaes for dessert in the evening.

The Hansens are the kind of hosts who are careful not to intrude on their guests' privacy, but they are always available to answer questions about local attractions and restaurants. The place could pass a white-glove inspection any day, and it is a favorite overnight stop for bike tours from all over the country.

Address: *215 Pollock St., New Bern, NC 28560, tel. 919/636–3810.*
Accommodations: *9 double rooms with baths.*
Amenities: *Air-conditioning, ceiling fans, cable TV in rooms.*
Rates: *$55; full breakfast and complimentary drinks. AE, MC, V.*
Restrictions: *Smoking in guest rooms only, no pets.*

The King's Arms Inn

You pay only half the room rate if you can beat David and Diana Parks at tennis. And if you can play a guitar, David will join you in a jam session. The Parkses moved to New Bern from Nashville, where David worked for a music company, and he still writes music and plays at local restaurants. He'll also arrange sailing, boating, hunting, fishing, and biking excursions for guests, plus tee times, court dates, and day trips.

When the Parkses bought The King's Arms in 1986 they had to do very little to it. It was already a thriving business, named after a Colonial tavern frequented by members of the First Continental Congress when visiting Tryon Palace. The Federal-style frame house, with a small balcony over the entrance, was built in 1848 by John Alexander Meadows, and a "bellcast" (bell-shaped) mansard roof with gabled dormers was added in 1895. It has a late-Victorian stairway and much of its original woodwork, and it is on the National Register of Historic Places.

The inn seems very much like a hotel, except that the Parkses give it a personal touch, serving cold lemonade or hot cider to guests on arrival, depending on the season. Except for the small reception area in the central hall, the inn has no room indoors where guests can mingle, a distinct disadvantage. The rear porch with its white wicker furniture is appealing in good weather. The bedrooms are luxurious havens furnished in period pieces, including some canopy beds. Cribs and cots are provided for children, who are welcome to use the backyard playground equipment. A morning newspaper and a Continental breakfast that includes Diana's homemade breads are delivered to the rooms. (She makes banana and zucchini breads, blueberry and apple streusel, and lemon-ginger and sweet potato muffins.) Business travelers seem to love the privacy and convenience that King's Arms offers.

Address: *212 Pollock St., New Bern, NC 28560, tel. 919/638–4409.*
Accommodations: *9 double rooms with baths.*
Amenities: *Air-conditioning, cable TV, complimentary newspaper.*
Rates: *$75; Continental breakfast and beverages. AE, MC, V.*
Restrictions: *Smoking on porch only, no pets.*

New Berne House

Y ou can spend a weekend trying to figure out whodunit at
this in-town inn, a Colonial Revival house built in 1923. The inn has
a resident ghost—the wife of Elijah
Taylor, who built the house for his
son John. Owners Joel and Shan Wil-
kins present their guests with the
"crime" at a reception on Friday evening, and after intense brainstorm-
ing and clue-searching, the guilty
party is finally revealed after dinner
on Saturday. Shan invents the script
in short-story form, and the clues
are found on a scavenger hunt that
takes participants all over town. The
event also includes a special praline-
waffle or spiced-apple-crepe breakfast with ham or bacon, as well as
afternoon tea. Though the Wilkinses
now live in Roanoke, Virginia, they
are always hosts at the mystery
weekends. David and Gena Hawkins
are the full-time innkeepers.

In addition to the mystery weekends
(given in fall, winter, and spring),
New Berne House offers sailing
packages, complete with a picnic
lunch and tickets to Tryon Palace.
Golf and tennis at special rates can
be arranged at the Greenbrier Country Club. When the palace is all
dressed up for Christmas or spring,
the inn gets into the spirit, too, with
its own decorations. At other times,
guests are content to take in the
sights of the town and then relax in
the hammock under the magnolia
tree or take a ride on the bicycle-
built-for-two. Afternoon tea is

a weekend tradition, and evening
snacks and beverages are always
available. The inn caters to businesspeople during the week. Small pets
are welcome, if the innkeeper is
given advance notice.

Guest rooms are furnished with antiques and attic treasures, which
give the place a homey feel. Room
No. 5, often preferred by honeymooners, features pink pickled
floors, and a claw-foot tub. Room 6
contains a brass bed that was res-
cued from a burning brothel in Pres-
cott, Arizona—many guests want to
sleep in that bed.

The inn is within walking distance of
Tryon Palace and other historic sites,
but its location on New Bern's busy
main thoroughfare is something of
a detraction.

Address: *709 Broad St., New Bern,
NC 28560, tel. 919/636–2250 or
800/842–7688.*
Accommodations: *7 double rooms
with baths.*
Amenities: *Air-conditioning, ceiling
fans, complimentary newspaper;
free airport transportation upon
request; bicycle-built-for-two.*
Rates: *$75; full breakfast. AE, D,
MC, V.*
Restrictions: *No smoking indoors.*

Catherine's Inn on Orange

Catherine Ackiss has put her decorating talents and professional expertise to work in restoring and marketing this inn in the historic district. She and her husband, Walter, a chemist, renovated the building themselves, adding several bathrooms, then opened it in 1989. Built in 1875, the two-story Italianate frame structure, painted Williamsburg blue, is surrounded by a picket fence. It has hardwood floors; slate fireplaces in every room; four-poster, brass, and canopy beds; and some claw-foot tubs. The twin room, painted dark purple, is striking; the king room, popular with honeymooners, has a private porch. Many of the furnishings and decorations belong to the family, including Catherine's mother's grand piano.

Catherine does just about everything around the inn, though when Walter's in town, he makes his special pancakes with orange or blueberry syrup. They're served with homemade sausage on family silver and china. There's a well-stocked guest refrigerator and a library upstairs.

Address: *410 Orange St., Wilmington, NC 28401, tel. 919/251–0863 or 800/476–0723.*
Accommodations: *3 double rooms with baths.*
Amenities: *Air-conditioning, ceiling fans; phones in rooms, cable TV in library, turn-down service.*
Rates: *$60; full breakfast, complimentary drinks. AE, MC, V.*
Restrictions: *Smoking only in downstairs public rooms, no pets.*

The Five Star Guest House

This aptly named bed-and-breakfast in the historic district of Wilmington sparkles and shines; any inspector would surely give it five stars. Built in 1907 in neoclassic style, the house was a residence for many years before becoming an inn in 1986 (the intercom system to the butler's pantry still works). Harvey and Ann Crowther, after rearing five children, retired from their jobs in New Jersey, bought the house in 1987, and became innkeepers.

Turn-of-the-century antiques, lace curtains, several fireplaces, and balloon shades carry out a Victorian theme. Rich, mellow wood paneling and trim distinguish the parlor, formal dining room, and foyer with its staircase. Room No. 1, with a brass double bed and claw-foot tub, is the most popular; No. 2 has two iron beds covered with hand-crocheted spreads. In the dining room, the Crowthers serve breakfasts of fruit, eggs, French toast, pancakes, or muffins and rolls; jams and jellies; and coffee and teas.

Address: *14 N. 7th St., Wilmington, NC 28401, tel. 919/763–7581.*
Accommodations: *3 double rooms with baths.*
Amenities: *Air-conditioning, ceiling fans, phones in rooms.*
Rates: *$60–$75; full breakfast and complimentary drinks. AE, D, MC, V.*
Restrictions: *No smoking in dining room, no pets.*

The Piedmont

Between the mountains and the coastal plain of North Carolina lies a region of rolling hills, large rivers, and lakes. John Lawson called it in his journal (published in 1709) "the finest part of Carolina." In the 1700s, the Piedmont, populated by Indian tribes and teeming with game and fish, was the western frontier. Today, with its interstate crossroads and the large cities, the area, long devoted to commerce, is beginning to be recognized for its travel appeal. People riding the interstates on their way north, south, or west are likely to spend some time in the Piedmont.

The region is rich in historic attractions and in museums of history, art, science, transportation, tobacco, furniture, and textiles. You can spend an entire day exploring the Moravian settlements of Old Salem and Bethabara near Winston-Salem; retrace Revolutionary War battles at Kings Mountain, Guilford Courthouse, and Alamance; or visit the Civil War site at Bentonville. You can see animals from around the world at the North Carolina Zoological Park in Asheboro; enjoy opera, Shakespeare, and concerts; and see government at work in Raleigh, the state capital.

Busloads of travelers shop for clothing, furniture, and household goods at large outlet centers along the interstates in Burlington ("Outlet Capital of the World"), Greensboro, High Point, Winston-Salem, Hickory, Kannapolis, and Charlotte. Antiques are also hot, with entire towns like Waxhaw and Pineville devoted to buying and selling them. Philip Morris, R. J. Reynolds Tobacco, Fieldcrest-Cannon, and Stroh offer tours of their plants. Long recognized for its handmade pottery, the sandy, pine-treed area called the Sandhills has several dozen shops where you can buy utilitarian and decorative pieces.

If you like to play golf or tennis, you'll think you've died and gone to heaven in North Carolina. The state prides itself on its golf courses, its tennis facilities are increasing, and croquet is making a comeback. The craze for basketball is contagious in the Tarheel State. The Charlotte Hornets have broken all attendance records, and everyone knows about the Durham Bulls. NASCAR racing is also popular. Carowinds theme park on the South Carolina line has hair-raising rides, and the state's parks and lakes offer other recreation, as well as natural beauty.

Places to Go, Sights to See

Charlotte. *Discovery Place* (301 N. Tryon St., tel. 704/372–6261), one of the top 10 science museums in the country, offers hands-on and rotating exhibits; it has aquariums, a rain forest, and a brand-new Omnimax theater. The *Mint Museum of Art* (2730 Randolph Rd., tel. 704/337–2000), built in 1837 as a U.S. mint, was moved to its present location in 1936. It has an outstanding collection of pre-Columbian pottery and attracts such prestigious traveling exhibits as "Ramesses the Great."

Durham. *Duke Chapel* (tel. 919/684–2572), a Gothic structure patterned after a European cathedral, was built in 1924 as the focal point of Duke University. Free organ concerts are given regularly. At the *Duke Homestead and Tobacco Museum* (2828 Homestead Rd., tel. 919/477–5498), the mid-19th-century home of Washington Duke, tobacco barns, an original factory, and a museum are open for tours. The complex is a National Historic Landmark.

Furniture Discovery Center (101 W. Green Dr., High Point, tel. 919/884–5255). Opened in 1991 in a renovated warehouse near hundreds of showrooms, this unique museum is devoted entirely to furniture production.

Reed Gold Mine (off U.S. 601 at Rte. 200, 10 mi east of Charlotte, tel. 704/786–8337) is where America's first gold, a nugget weighing 17 pounds, was found in 1799. Visitors get to explore the mine, pan for gold, and learn about the mining process in the museum.

Spencer Shops–North Carolina Transportation Museum (411 S. Salisbury Ave., Spencer, tel. 704/636–2889), in the old railroad repair shops, traces the history of transportation from Indian days through the heyday of railroading to the present. A restored steam train takes visitors on a short loop tour.

State Capitol (Capitol Sq., Raleigh, tel. 919/733–4994). Completed in 1840 and restored in 1976, this old building once housed all the functions of state government. The Capitol Area Visitor Center (301 N. Blount St., tel. 919/733–

3456) conducts free guided tours daily, which cover the contemporary State
Legislative Building, the executive mansion, and other government buildings.

Winston-Salem. *Old Salem* (600 S. Main St., tel. 919/721–7300), a restored
Moravian village dating to the 1700s, comprises 60 buildings where visitors
can see Colonial life relived through cooking, gardening, and the making of
pewter, candles, furniture, and cloth. During the Christmas season there are
candlelight teas and worship services. The *Museum of Early Southern
Decorative Arts* (tel. 919/721–7360) has rooms reconstructed from Southern
houses, with furnishings by Southern makers.

Golf Courses. More than three dozen golf resorts, among them **Pinehurst
Resort and Country Club** (tel. 919/295–6811), **Pine Needles** (tel. 919/692–
7111), and **Mid-Pines Resort** (tel. 919/692–2114), are located in the North
Carolina Sandhills. (Some courses are open only to guests at the resort; some
are open to the public.) **Southern Pines** is home to the PGA/World Golf Hall
of Fame (tel. 919/295–6651), a museum on the history of golf.

Restaurants

North Carolina's best hickory-smoked pork barbecue is served with red slaw
and hush puppies at **Lexington Barbecue** (I–85 Business, tel. 919/249–9814)
in Lexington. (World leaders sampled it at the Williamsburg summit meeting
several years ago.) **The Lamplighter** (1065 E. Morehead St., tel. 704/372–
5343) in Charlotte serves gourmet cuisine in the elegant atmosphere of
a house in the old Dilworth neighborhood. Authentic food of the 18th century
is offered at the **Salem Tavern** (736 S. Main St., tel. 919/748–8585) in Old
Salem. **The Angus Barn, Ltd.** (U.S. 70, tel. 919/787–3505) in Raleigh is
famous for its steaks and ribs. At the **Colmant House** in Pilot Mountain
(Main St., tel. 919/368–2823), John and Sue Colmant, formerly of New
Orleans, serve wonderful Cajun fare at dinner Thursday through Sunday.

Tourist Information

Charlotte Convention & Visitors Bureau (229 N. Church St., Charlotte, NC
28202, tel. 704/371–8700 or 800/231–4636). **Durham Convention & Visitors
Bureau** (Box 3536, Durham, NC 27702, tel. 919/687–0288). **Greensboro Area
Convention & Visitors Bureau** (220 S. Eugene St., Greensboro, NC 27401,
tel. 919/274–2282 or 800/344–2282). **High Point Convention & Visitors
Bureau** (Box 2273, High Point, NC 27261, tel. 919/884–5255). **Pinehurst Area
Convention & Visitors Bureau** (Box 2270, Southern Pines, NC 28387, tel.
919/692–3330 or 800/346–5362). **Raleigh Convention and Visitors Bureau**
(Box 1879, Raleigh, NC 27602, tel. 919/834–5900 or 800/849–8499). **Winston-
Salem Convention & Visitors Bureau** (Box 1408, Winston-Salem, NC 27102-
1408, tel. 919/725–2361 or 800/331–7018).

Reservation Service

North Carolina Bed & Breakfast Assn. (Box 1077, Asheville, NC 28802, tel. 919/636–5553). **Charlotte B&B** (1700–2 Delane Ave., Charlotte, NC 28211, tel. 704/366–0979).

The Arrowhead Inn

Seven miles outside Durham on Roxboro Road you come to a large stone arrowhead at Mason Road. The monument, designating an old Indian trading path, has been there since the Depression, but today it's a well-known landmark for the inn that bears its name.

The manor house was built about 1775 on a 2,000-acre land grant purchased from Joseph Brittain, and for more than 100 years, slaves worked the land. The original house had four rooms—two upstairs and two down—but several were added over the years. Situated on 4 acres, it is a two-story Colonial-style house with brick chimneys and tall Doric columns that support the long front porch. The house is painted white with black shutters. The boxwood, magnolias, and flower beds around it are about 150 years old, and more than 40 species of birds live on the property.

After a succession of owners, Jerry and Barbara Ryan bought the house in 1985 and turned it into a bed-and-breakfast, winning an award from the Durham Historic Preservation Society for adaptive reuse. Jerry had worked as a publisher of business magazines, and Barbara, a former editor and ghostwriter, continues to write magazine articles. In addition to the accommodations in the main house and the carriage house, there's the brand-new Land Grant Cabin, which is popular with families

and couples. The guest rooms are decorated with an assortment of antiques and collectibles from the Colonial period through the Victorian.

The Ryans have perfected the art of innkeeping, and their daughter Cathy has joined them in the business. They greet arriving guests with complimentary refreshments and are always available in the evening when everyone gathers in the keeping room to work puzzles, read, or talk. Breakfast is the highlight of the day at the Arrowhead, with juice, fruit, eggs, bacon or sausage, and homemade muffins and breads.

Jerry and Barbara teach a course in innkeeping at nearby Duke University, and were primary organizers of the North Carolina Bed and Breakfast Association. Barbara runs an annual meeting of innkeepers and B&B owners from across the Southeast.

Address: *106 Mason Rd., Durham, NC 27712, tel. 919/477-8430.*
Accommodations: *6 double rooms with baths, 1 suite, 1 cabin.*
Amenities: *Air-conditioning, ceiling fans in public rooms, TV in keeping room and Brittain suite, phones in some rooms, guest refrigerator; pets boarded.*
Rates: *$55–$125; full breakfast. AE, DC, MC, V.*
Restrictions: *No smoking in guest rooms.*

The Blooming Garden Inn

Like a butterfly unfolding from its cocoon, a blooming garden has replaced the heaps of junk and garbage that once occupied this lot in the Holloway Historic District of Durham. Inside the yellow 1892 Victorian house, the fabrics, wallpaper, and paint are in rainbow hues, and outrageously whimsical accent pieces produce smiles. Then you meet Frank and Dolly Pokrass and understand why the house makes such a strong statement. Dolly is an exuberant hostess who's in love with the inn and her family and wants to share her life with her guests. Frank, the quiet, intellectual one, is happy to remain in the background and applaud his wife.

Innkeeping is new to the couple, though caring for people is not. Dolly, a nurse by profession, ran an antiques shop in nearby Hillsborough for several years; Frank is a retired medical sociologist. After 2½ years of backbreaking work rectifying 30 years of neglect—scraping paint, tearing out layers of carpet, and hauling away truckloads of garbage—they opened the inn in 1990.

The house has nine fireplaces (only one is used now) and the original beveled, leaded, and stained glass. The reception area is a five-sided room with doors leading into the formal dining room, library, parlor, hallway, and a guest room. Dolly has a small gift shop in one corner of the dining room, where breakfast is

served. Such delights as walnut crepes with ricotta cheese and warm raspberry sauce, and ginger waffles with whipped cream are common; and then there's also juice, fresh fruit, and home-ground coffee.

Each guest room is named according to its colors—Ivy (dark green with cherry accents), Tiffany (stained glass), Moroccan (dark green, gold, and red), Morning Glory Suite (purple, mauve, and pink), and Scandinavian Luxury Suite (blue and white). In the Morning Glory Suite, Dolly has used starched linen tablecloths trimmed with eyelet lace as curtains. Fresh flowers from the garden adorn each room.

Address: *513 Holloway St., Durham, NC 27701, tel. 919/687–0801.*
Accommodations: *3 double rooms with baths, 2 suites with whirlpool baths.*
Amenities: *Air-conditioning, ceiling fans, cable TV in library and 1 suite, guest refrigerator.*
Rates: *$75–$125; full breakfast. AE, MC, V.*
Restrictions: *Smoking on verandas only, no pets.*

The Fearrington House

If you didn't know better, you'd think a click of the heels had transported you to the Cotswolds of England when you find yourself in this bucolic setting. Actually, you'll be in the middle of Fearrington Village, a 200-year-old farm that's being made into a residential community just off U.S. 15–501 between Chapel Hill and Pittsboro. The village consists of the inn and private homes, a restaurant (in the former farmhouse), a bank, post office, pottery, jewelry store, bookstore, dress shop, and garden shop.

Fearrington is the creation of R. B. and Jenny Fitch, who studied inns and restaurants all over Europe before they began the 1,100-acre project in 1974. The ultraprivate guest rooms are clustered around a charming courtyard with a central fountain and look out over the gardens and the pasture, where Galloway cows and Tunis sheep graze. The rooms are furnished in English pine that matches the flooring from a London workhouse; they are complemented by polished floral print fabrics and dried arrangements. The luxurious bathrooms have towel warmers. Jenny has had a hand in decorating just about every building in the village, and she helps the chef plan meals for the restaurant. She's quite an accomplished chef herself and has produced a cookbook.

Guests gather for breakfast and afternoon wine in the Garden Room; dinner is served in the restaurant, a formal affair with salmon-colored walls and stenciled floors. Most guests eat lunch in the Market Café or go for a picnic, which can be ordered from the deli. Often requested entrées in the restaurant include sautéed scallops with lemon-garlic butter and toasted almonds, Carolina crab cakes with mustard mayonnaise, and beef tenderloin with a merlot and peppercorn sauce.

One of the most pleasant things about the Fearrington is its low-key country atmosphere. You won't be subjected to a schedule here, but you might try a round of croquet or ride one of the bikes to the swimming pool and tennis courts. Of course, there are plenty of diversions nearby—the Morehead Planetarium at Chapel Hill, Duke Chapel, and the Duke Homestead. The inn is affiliated with Relais & Chateaux.

Address: *Fearrington Village Center, U.S. 15–501, Pittsboro, NC 27312, tel. 919/542–4000 or 800/334–5475, fax 919/542–4202.*
Accommodations: *5 double rooms with baths, 9 suites.*
Amenities: *Restaurant, air-conditioning; TVs and phones in rooms; pool, tennis courts, croquet, bicycles; kennels for pets.*
Rates: *$125–$295; Continental breakfast and drinks. MC, V.*
Restrictions: *No smoking in guest rooms.*

The Homeplace

The Homeplace, a well-preserved remnant of the past, has somehow survived modern development in the bustling Sunbelt city of Charlotte. The almond-colored house, on 2½ wooded acres with profuse plantings of flowers, sits at the corner of a busy intersection. If it were not in this particular location, you might mistake it for the Walton Place.

Frank and Peggy Darien had admired the 1902 country Victorian farmhouse for several years before the chance arose in 1984 for them to buy it and turn it into a bed-and-breakfast. Frank took early retirement from his accounting job, and the inn is now their full-time occupation. They furnished the house in Victorian period pieces (including a mohair sofa in the parlor), quilts, cross-stitch pictures, and family memorabilia. Peggy made all the curtains. The most cherished artwork in the house consists of the naive paintings of West Virginia scenes that Peggy's father did during the last years of his life. The Victorian Lady Room, done in mauve and green, was planned around a cross-stitch picture made by their daughter Debra Moye. The largest room in the inn, it has a four-poster rice bed and a day bed. The blue and white English Garden Room overlooks the garden and the gazebo. The Country Cottage Room downstairs has an antique oak bed and

dresser, ruffled ecru curtains, braided rugs, and its own entrance.

The Dariens, who live on the property, are great believers in practicing Southern hospitality. Upon arrival, guests get a complete tour of the house and are offered refreshments (which are available at any hour of the day). Breakfast, the highlight of any visit, might be poached pears with raspberry sauce, scrambled dill eggs with cheese sauce, or waffles and cinnamon cream.

Address: *5901 Sardis Rd., Charlotte, NC 28270, tel. 704/365–1936.*
Accommodations: *3 double rooms with baths.*
Amenities: *Air-conditioning, ceiling fans in both upstairs rooms, irons and ironing boards in each room, cable TV and guest phone in common areas.*
Rates: *$78; full breakfast. AE, MC, V.*
Restrictions: *No smoking indoors, no pets, 2-night minimum on holiday weekends.*

Pilot Knob Inn

The two-story log tobacco barns that dot the rural landscape of Piedmont North Carolina aren't usually very elegant or luxurious. But at the Pilot Knob Inn, they take on a different appearance as a one-of-a-kind bed-and-breakfast. The property adjoins Pilot Mountain State Park, and the knob that crowns the 1,500-foot mountain is within close view. (If the names ring a bell, it's because they inspired the place names in Andy Griffith's mythical Mayberry.)

Five small barns and a slave cabin, all at least 100 years old, were moved to the 50-acre wooded site by innkeeper Jim Rouse, who added decks and porches to the barns, while keeping their rustic look, and enlarged the slave cabin for himself. Jim's father, Don, who is also involved in the operation, can always find something that needs fixing or changing. Norman Ross, his silent business partner from Chicago, owns the collection of 6,000 records in the library. The barns are furnished in a mix of 18th-century reproductions, Southern primitive, and country English antiques, in addition to Oriental and dhurrie rugs. Each has a whirlpool tub for two and a fireplace and is equipped with such amenities as bathrobes, hair driers, fresh fruit, and flowers. Some of the barns have massive "Paul Bunyan" beds, handmade of juniper logs by a local craftsman. The common room, downstairs in the bilevel central barn—where guests gather to read, listen to music, and watch videos—features a 300-year-old Italian marble fireplace, a William and Mary loveseat, and a coffee table made of parquet flooring from Versailles (really!). There's a dry sauna and a pool, and a 6-acre lake and gazebo are ideal for fishing.

Most people who come here like the privacy and isolation of the inn, though it's minutes away from Winston-Salem and the Blue Ridge Parkway. Each of the barns is set off by itself in the woods on the side of a hill—it's the perfect place to commune with nature, slow down to a standstill, and rekindle romance. Guests usually get together at breakfast, which is served in the central barn and prepared by Jim's mother, Pat, who he says can do anything. Her specialties are chocolate-chip sour-cream coffee cake, sausage biscuits, poached pears, and a peach and cream-cheese concoction called Peach Pilot—all served with fresh berries in season.

Address: *Box 1280, Pilot Mountain, NC 27041, tel. 919/325–2502.*
Accommodations: *5 cabins with baths, fireplaces, whirlpools.*
Amenities: *Air-conditioning, TV and phones in rooms, sauna; pool.*
Rates: *$85–$105; Continental breakfast. MC, V.*
Restrictions: *Smoking only in cabins, no pets, BYOB, 2-night minimum in Oct. and on holidays.*

The 1868 Stewart-Marsh House

After vacationing in the South for years and apprenticing in innkeeping in Massachusetts, Gerry and Chuck Webster, from Pennsylvania, found a Federal-style house in Salisbury's historic district to turn into a bed-and-breakfast when they retired. The renovation work was long and tedious, but now the Websters are heavily involved in historic preservation and even conduct tours of the area.

The house has heart-pine flooring and is filled with antiques, including a baker's cabinet from the 1700s. One of the cheerful guest rooms has twin beds and is done in aqua tones; the other has a double four-poster and is accented in red. An intimate sitting area with books houses the Websters' bell collection. Guests take refreshments in the pine-paneled library or on the screened porch. Breakfast might include such hot entrées as Baked Sandwich, made with layers of cheese, ham, and chicken.

Address: *220 S. Ellis St., Salisbury, NC 28144, tel. 704/633–6841.*
Accommodations: *2 double rooms with baths.*
Amenities: *Air-conditioning, ceiling fans; cable TV in library, guest phone.*
Rates: *$45–$50; full breakfast. MC, V.*
Restrictions: *No smoking indoors, no pets, 2-night minimum on holiday weekends.*

The Magnolia Inn

Even if you're perfectly neutral about pink, you'll either love it or hate it after a stay at The Magnolia Inn, in the New England–style village of Pinehurst. Built in 1896, the house was renovated in 1990, and every room sparkles with some shade of pink—a far cry from the days when golf buddies hung out here, scarring the floors with their cleats. It's now on the National Register of Historic Places.

Under owners Ned Darby and Jan Gripentrog, the inn still caters to golfers; it has package arrangements with several clubs, including the prestigious Pinehurst. The outdoor pool and wraparound porches are a welcome sight after several rounds. The guest rooms are furnished in a turn-of-the-century Victorian style, with brass beds and wicker. The original bathroom fixtures and claw-foot tubs have been refinished to their former luster. Chef Troy Brindle and Lucille Falk serve unforgettable food.

Address: *Magnolia and Chinquapin Rds. (Box 818), Pinehurst, NC 28374, tel. 919/295–6900 or 800/526–5562.*
Accommodations: *12 double rooms with baths.*
Amenities: *Restaurant, pub, air-conditioning, cable TV in pub, pay phone; pool.*
Rates: *$105; full breakfast. MC, V.*
Restrictions: *No smoking in guest rooms, no pets, 2-night minimum on spring and fall weekends.*

The Mountains

*Western North Carolina is blessed with two major ranges
in the Southern Appalachian chain: the Blue Ridge
Mountains, extending from Virginia, and the Great
Smokies, called Shaconage ("place of blue smoke") by the
Indians. The gentle foothills of both ranges crest into peaks
of blue and purple grandeur, many over 5,000 feet high.
Grandfather Mountain, near Linville, is said to be a billion
years old. Mt. Mitchell, at 6,684 feet, is the highest point
east of the Mississippi.*

*The Cherokees lived in these mountains for thousands of
years before the arrival of Scotch-Irish farmers and
enterprising lumberjacks in the mid-1800s. Later, Georgia
and Carolina lowlanders, seeking to escape the scorching
summer heat, established retreats at Flat Rock,
Hendersonville, Highlands, Linville, and Blowing Rock.
Around the turn of the century, George Vanderbilt and
Edwin Wiley Grove fashioned their dreams into fabulous
estates at Asheville and invited their friends to breathe the
pure mountain air amid incredible beauty. In the past 25
years, the region has become a magnet for skiers and
golfers, and resort communities like Linville Ridge, Elk
River, Fairfield, Chetola, and Etowah Valley have sprung
up.*

*Today there's year-round recreation, not only for the silk-
stocking set but also for anyone who loves the outdoors.
You can camp, hunt, and fish in the Great Smoky
Mountains National Park, dig for rubies in Franklin, ride
a steam train through the Nantahala Gorge, join
thousands of other rubberneckers during leaf season on the
Blue Ridge Parkway, and shoot the rapids on the French
Broad. You can play golf and tennis at posh resorts like
the Hound Ears Club and schuss through white powder at
Ski Beech and Sugar Mountain. You can attend plays at
Burnsville's Parkway Playhouse, listen to classical music*

at the Brevard Music Festival, watch European folk dancers at Folkmoot, or learn to clog (the native dance) at the Stompin' Ground. You can stay in century-old log cabins at Cataloochee Ranch or live it up at the luxurious Grove Park Inn and Country Club. You can dine on rainbow trout and vinegar pie at Jarrett House in Dillsboro or have a seven-course gourmet dinner at Eseeola Lodge.

Most people like the high drama of the mountains' four seasons. Many fall in love and decide to sink in deeper roots: Look at the preserved cabins, A-frames, and million-dollar second homes that dot the hillsides. When Rand McNally rated Brevard and Asheville among the most desirable places to live in America, residents were not surprised.

Places to Go, Sights to See

Biltmore (tel. 704/255–1770 or 800/543–2961). The best times to see the fabulous 12,000-acre George C. Vanderbilt estate at Asheville are April and May, when the gardens are in bloom, and December, when the 250-room mansion is decorated for Christmas as it would have been in 1895. A modern winery is housed in the former dairy, where you can see the entire process and sample some of the products.

The Blue Ridge Mountain Frescoes (tel. 919/982–3076). In the 1970s, North Carolina artist Ben Long painted these frescoes of New Testament scenes in two abandoned churches (now restored) in Glendale Springs and Beaver Creek, near West Jefferson.

Blue Ridge Parkway. Thousands of Americans travel this famous crestline highway every year from its beginning at Front Royal, Virginia, to its terminus near Great Smoky Mountains National Park and the Cherokee Indian Reservation. It is dotted with scenic overlooks, mountain cabins, and markers that explain the history and natural phenomena of the area.

Connemara (1928 Little River Rd., tel. 704/693–4178). During the final years of his life, Lincoln biographer and poet Carl Sandburg lived at this Flat Rock estate with his wife, Lilian, who raised champion goats. The National Park Service gives daily tours.

Great Smoky Mountains National Park (tel. 615/436–1200 or 615/436–5615). The most visited park in America straddles the North Carolina–Tennessee border and offers a wealth of outdoor activities amid its 517,368 acres. There are more than 800 miles of hiking and riding trails and 16 summits higher than 6,000 feet.

Great Smoky Mountains Railway (Sylva, tel. 704/586–8811 or 800/872–4681). Excursion trains traverse the route through rock tunnels and along river gorges between Dillsboro, Bryson City, and Nantahala. Travelers can ride in coach, caboose, or "Kodak" (open) cars. In Spring 1992 a steam locomotive will be put in service from Dillsboro to Bryson City.

Thomas Wolfe Memorial (48 Spruce St., tel. 704/253–8304). The famous writer's mother operated a boarding house at this dwelling in downtown Asheville. Now a state historic site, it is open for tours.

Mountains

Grandfather Mountain (tel. 704/733–2013 or 800/468–7325) is a must. Known for its rocky profile that resembles an old man, it stands 5,964 feet tall and has a mile-high swinging bridge; hiking trails; an "environmental habitat" for bear, deer, and other animals; and a nature center with a restaurant and movie theater. **Mt. Mitchell** (Blue Ridge Pkwy., tel. 704/675–4611)—at 6,684 feet, the highest point east of the Mississippi River—is surrounded by a large state park, with camping and hiking, an observation lounge, tower, and museum. In the heart of Great Smoky Mountains National Park is **Clingmans Dome** (6,643 feet), whose peak is actually in Tennessee.

Restaurants

You can make an evening of dining at **Gabrielle's** (tel. 704/252–7313), in the Richmond Hill Inn in Asheville; at **The Market Place on Wall Street** (tel. 704/252–4162), also in Asheville; or at the **Eseeola Lodge** in Linville (tel. 704/733–4311). Another option is **Heidi's** (Banner Elk, tel. 704/898–5020), which serves authentic Swiss cuisine, or the **Jarrett House** (Haywood St., Dillsboro, tel. 704/586–9964), for fried trout and good country food.

Tourist Information

Asheville Convention and Visitors Bureau (151 Haywood St., Box 1011, Asheville, NC 28802, tel. 800/257–1300 or 800/548–1300 in NC). **North Carolina High Country Host** (701 Blowing Rock Rd., Boone, NC 28607, tel. 704/264–1299 or 800/438–7500).

Reservation Service

North Carolina Bed & Breakfast Assn. (Box 1077, Asheville, NC 28802, tel. 919/592–2634).

Cedar Crest Inn

The Cedar Crest Inn, its yellow paint and high-pitched roof exuding warmth and cheer, sits on a hill overlooking Biltmore Village. Though you would never guess it, the Victorian inn has close ties to Vanderbilt's 250-room French chateau. Built in 1891 by the craftsmen who worked on the famous mansion, Cedar Crest has the same hand-carved mantels, beveled glass, and other fine detailing found in Biltmore.

Innkeepers Jack and Barbara McEwan, former residents of Racine, Wisconsin, looked for a year and a half before finding Cedar Crest, which in 1930 had been converted into a guest house. The McEwans restored it in 1984, removing 13 layers of wallpaper and adding several bathrooms. Barbara did the decorating herself, using family heirlooms and antiques and filling in with pieces found at estate sales; Jack drew upon the management skills he had learned as a hotelier; and the McEwans' grown-up children, all talented musicians, found themselves entertaining guests at afternoon tea.

Each room in the house has its own Victorian character, accomplished with lace and silk fabrics, soft colors, and wallpapers. The Queen Anne Room, which has shirred fabric on the ceiling, is a favorite; another is the Garden Room, with a brass bed, mosquito netting, and white linen bedding. Honeymooners and anniversary couples love the guest cottage.

Visitors enjoy gathering around the fire in the parlor; in the formal dining room, where the McEwans serve breakfast; or in the study, which has a coffee table made from a Washington, D.C., street grating. Depending on the season, iced tea, lemonade, pressed cider, hot chocolate, or wassail is served in the parlor or library. When the weather is warm, guests often team up for badminton or croquet; otherwise, they like to stay indoors reading or playing cards and board games. In addition to visiting the Biltmore estate, guests can explore the sights and shops in the village, including All Souls Episcopal Church, which George Vanderbilt had built in 1896 for his daughter's wedding.

Address: *674 Biltmore Ave., Asheville, NC 28803, tel. 704/252–1389.*
Accommodations: *8 double rooms with baths, 2 doubles share a bath, 1 housekeeping cottage.*
Amenities: *Air-conditioning, phones in rooms, cable TV in study.*
Rates: *$65–$150; Continental breakfast, refreshments. AE, D, MC, V.*
Restrictions: *Smoking only in the study, no pets, 2-night minimum on weekends and holidays.*

Eseeola Lodge

I t's hard to miss the rustic lodge, with its stone arches and bark siding, behind the manicured hemlock hedges of Linville. For more than 100 years there has been an inn in this resort village at the base of Grandfather Mountain, and the same families have been coming here for generations. The inn is owned by Linville Country Club members, many of whom have homes in the area.

The present building dates only to 1936, but it's on the National Register of Historic Places. The chestnut paneling used throughout is rare now because of the blight that hit the chestnut trees several decades ago. The first Eseeola Inn, built in 1891, was known for its Fourth of July celebrations in the early days, when lathered-hog races, ox races, and speeches by silver-tongued orators were in vogue. Things are a bit more genteel these days. Guests are likely to either get together for a game of golf on the nearby Donald Ross course or play bridge in the game room. Or they drive across Grandfather Mountain's Linn Cove Viaduct or spread a picnic in McRae Meadows, site of a large annual Scottish clan gathering.

In recent years, all the guest rooms at Eseeola have been redecorated with bright wallpapers and draperies and the bathrooms upgraded with marble and oak vanities. Guests are welcomed with fresh flowers and a fruit basket, and Godiva chocolates are placed on pillows when beds are turned down in the evening. The staff-guest ratio is 2:1.

Food always gets top billing here, and during the summer growing season, chef John Hofland uses local vegetables and fruit. Entrées include grilled Norwegian salmon in lemon tarragon butter, medallions of veal with Alaskan crab legs and red pepper hollandaise, and baked breast of capon stuffed with mushrooms and shallots with *sauce cassis*. The popular Thursday night seafood buffet always draws a crowd.

Address: *Linville, NC 28646, tel. 704/733-4311.*
Accommodations: *29 double rooms with baths.*
Amenities: *Restaurant, air-conditioning, ceiling fans, turndown service; cable TV and phones in rooms; pool, golf, tennis, croquet, children's recreation program.*
Rates: *$190–$250; full breakfast and dinner. MC, V.*
Restrictions: *No pets, closed mid-Oct.–mid-May.*

Greystone Inn

I n the early 1900s, the rich arrived in their private rail cars to vacation at secluded Lake Toxaway. Modern travelers head for the Greystone Inn, a Swiss-style mansion on 3,000 acres that's on the National Register of Historic Places. Built in 1915, the house was converted to an inn in 1985 by Tim Lovelace, a retired financial consultant, who later added Hillmont, a 12-room annex.

Each room has a personality of its own: The Astor Room in Hillmont features cathedral ceilings, a private deck overlooking the lake, a fireplace with gas logs, and a huge bathroom with a whirlpool and separate glass shower. The black floral-print fabric used in the draperies and bedspreads contrasts with the mauve walls. The Firestone Room (formerly the kitchen) still has a 10-foot wood-burning cookstove, a stone fireplace, and exposed beams. The baronial Presidential Suite, in the former library, has 25-foot ceilings, a huge stone fireplace, and a sleeping loft.

In the new dining facility, open only to guests, vast windows frame the mountains and the lake. Chef Winslow Jones serves his "old-line, classical cuisine" (with some nouvelle dishes) to rave reviews.

Greystone guests can play tennis and golf at the adjoining Lake Toxaway Country Club and go swimming, waterskiing, windsurfing, sailing, and canoeing on the lake. Many guests hike or ride horses (from a nearby livery stable) to Mills Creek Falls or Deep Ford Falls, several miles away, for a picnic. Rainy days are devoted to bridge and reading.

After tea, a social highlight of the day, Tim conducts animated lake tours on the *Mountain Lily II.* Everyone gathers in the library lounge for hors d'oeuvres and cocktails before dinner. (Guests bring their own alcohol because the county is dry.)

Greystone must provide a perfect backdrop for romance, because honeymooners keep coming back for anniversaries year after year.

Address: *Box 6, Lake Toxaway, NC 28747, tel. 704/966–4700 or 800/824–5766, fax 704/862–5689.*
Accommodations: *33 double rooms with baths and whirlpools.*
Amenities: *Air-conditioning, ceiling fans; fireplaces, balconies, cable TV, and phones in rooms; turndown service; morning newspaper; airport transportation available.*
Rates: *$180–$300; full breakfast, dinner, afternoon tea, hors d'oeuvres, setups, and all sports except golf. AE, MC, V.*
Restrictions: *No pets, BYOB, 2-night minimum on weekends, closed late Nov.–early May.*

The Pine Crest Inn

J ennifer and Jeremy Wainwright, owners of this inn nestled under the pines, in the hunt country, are originally from England. Although relatively new to innkeeping, they have traveled enough to know what guests expect and appreciate. Good beds, excellent food, peace and quiet, lots of books, and stuffed teddy bears are but a few of the components of their success.

In 1990 the Wainwrights bought the 10-building complex. They refurbished more than half the rooms, retaining their charm and architectural integrity, and left some unchanged in order to offer a wide range of rates.

Pine Crest was established in 1917 by Carter Brown, a local horseman who was instrumental in making Tryon a riding and fox-hunting center. The main inn, a two-story green-and-white frame building, is on the National Register of Historic Places. The lobby is decorated in rich, dark fabrics, leather, brass, wood, and pictures of hunting; the lounge is called, appropriately, the Fox and Hounds Bar. Among the small buildings around the main inn are a one-room log cabin, a three-bedroom stone cottage, and a two-bedroom woodcutter's cottage, all dating from the time the inn was built.

Many of the rooms at The Pine Crest sport a Ralph Lauren or English-cottage look. Sporting prints,

fluffy comforters, hardwood floors, and wood-burning fireplaces give the guest rooms a welcoming, comfortable feeling. Swayback Cottage and Woodcutter Cottage offer the ultimate in privacy; F. Scott Fitzgerald stayed in Swayback in 1930.

Meals at the inn are something to write home about. Chef Bill Squires is famous for his rack of lamb, grilled mountain trout, roast duck, and Maryland crab cakes, served in the tavernlike dining room. (He'll even prepare a picnic lunch if you request it the evening before.) Because of its proximity to the Foothills Equestrian Nature Center and its affiliation with the Tryon Country Club, Pine Crest offers a full array of recreational and social activities—from golf and tennis to tailgating at the annual Block House Steeplechase.

Address: *Pine Crest La., Tryon, NC 28782, tel. 704/859–9135 or 800/633–3001, fax 704/859–9135.*
Accommodations: *30 double rooms with baths, 1 housekeeping cottage.*
Amenities: *Restaurant, air-conditioning, ceiling fans in some rooms; cable TV and phones in all rooms, fireplaces in most rooms.*
Rates: *$85–$400; full breakfast. DC, MC, V.*
Restrictions: *No pets, 2-night minimum on steeplechase weekend and 3-night minimum at Thanksgiving, closed the first 3 weeks of Jan.*

The Inn at Taylor House

In a green mountain valley dotted with grazing Charolais cattle and Christmas trees, this inn, built in 1911 and looking as fresh as the daisies, is still an attention-grabber. Passing motorists stop to ask if there is a vacancy at the white house with wraparound porches. There is also a two-bedroom cottage in the woods, ideal for families.

Roland Schwab, a fifth-generation innkeeper who graduated from École Hôtelière de Lausanne, keeps the inn with his wife, Chip. He also runs Hedgerose Heights restaurant in Atlanta, where Chip used to operate the Truffles Cooking School. The Schwabs opened the inn in 1987, filled it with their eclectic antiques, Oriental rugs, and art, and turned the old smokehouse into a gift shop.

Guests sleep under duvets and then sit down to pancakes with fresh blueberries or homemade Swiss birchermuesli. Valle Crucis has one of the hottest attractions around—the Mast general store—more than 100 years old and still going strong.

Address: *Hwy. 194, Box 713, Valle Crucis, NC 28691, tel. 704/963-5581.*
Accommodations: *7 double rooms with baths, 1 housekeeping cottage.*
Amenities: *Air-conditioning on third floor, ceiling fans in rooms.*
Rates: *$85–$135, full breakfast; cottage $85–$110, no breakfast. MC, V.*
Restrictions: *No smoking indoors, no pets, 2-night minimum on weekends, closed Jan.–Mar.*

The Lodge on Lake Lure

This lakeside mountain lodge provided R&R for North Carolina highway patrolmen in the '30s and '40s and housed an Air Force squadron and a religious group before it was renovated. Texans Robin and Jack Stanier jumped at the property when they were scouting for inns in 1989; he had worked in the oil industry, she in steel. Though they've had little experience, they love what they do, especially the afternoons on the veranda or the deck on the lake.

Robin's breakfast is served on the sun porch, to the strains of recorded dulcimer music. The Staniers provide books, magazines, and games, and there is plenty of space outside, to be by yourself. The big lobby has a beamed cathedral ceiling, fireplace, and piano. Chestnut paneling tends to make the guest rooms a little dark, but the light-colored spreads, framed pictures, and accent pieces add warmth.

Address: *Rte. 1, Box 529-A, Lake Lure, NC 28746, tel. 704/625-2789.*
Accommodations: *10 double rooms with baths, 1 suite.*
Amenities: *Air-conditioning in suite, ceiling fans; cable TV in den, pay phone; boats and canoes.*
Rates: *$65–$100; full breakfast. AE, MC, V.*
Restrictions: *No smoking indoors, no pets, 2-night minimum on weekends, 2- or 3-night minimum on holidays, closed Jan.–Feb.*

The Randolph House

When Ruth Randolph Adams and her husband, Bill, retired from their professions in Atlanta in 1970, they wanted to share their Bryson City family home with others. Ruth had inherited the house, a 12-gable mansion built as an inn in 1895. Now on the National Register of Historic Places, The Randolph House contains the original furnishings and dishes, and guests sleep on the same beds that have been in the family for years.

Ruth's Southern gourmet cooking is acclaimed far and wide, and guests return year after year for her country breakfasts, fresh vegetables, and homemade cobblers and breads. The inn accepts nonguests for dinner if they make reservations. Bill, a nat-

ural with people, enjoys his role as host. Guests take leisurely walks, rock on the stone-pillared veranda, or hike in the Great Smoky Mountains National Park.

Address: *Fryemont Rd., Box 816, Bryson City, NC 28713, tel. 704/488-3472 or (Nov.–mid-Apr.) 404/938-2268.*
Accommodations: *3 double rooms with baths, 4 doubles share 2 baths.*
Amenities: *Restaurant, air-conditioning in 3 rooms, window fans.*
Rates: *$65–$80; full breakfast ($100–$120 MAP). AE, MC, V.*
Restrictions: *No smoking indoors, no pets, 2-night minimum on holiday weekends and during Oct., closed Nov.–mid-Apr.*

The Waverly Inn

Hendersonville's oldest inn, next door to the visitor center on North Main Street, has been serving guests for more than nine decades and is on the National Register of Historic Places. The present owners, John and Diane Shiery, have breathed new life into the old place, putting into practice all the skills and knowledge they acquired in the Atlanta hotel industry and staging special murder-mystery weekends, wine tastings, and romance packages.

The three-story inn, bordered with lavish flower beds, sparkles and glistens with fresh paint, and inside it's luxuriously furnished with antiques and family treasures. The guest rooms, named for native plants and flowers, have four-poster canopy and

brass beds, and bathrooms have claw-foot tubs and pedestal sinks. The Mountain Magnolia Suite has a king-size canopy bed and a six-foot claw-foot tub. Complimentary refreshments are available around the clock, and John's cooked-to-order breakfasts get rave reviews.

Address: *783 N. Main St., Hendersonville, NC 28792, tel. 704/693-9193 or 800/537-8195.*
Accommodations: *13 double rooms with baths.*
Amenities: *Air-conditioning, ceiling fans in most rooms; cable TV in parlor and 2 guest rooms.*
Rates: *$69–$125; full breakfast. AE, D, MC, V.*
Restrictions: *No smoking in dining room, no pets, 2-night minimum on holidays.*

South Carolina

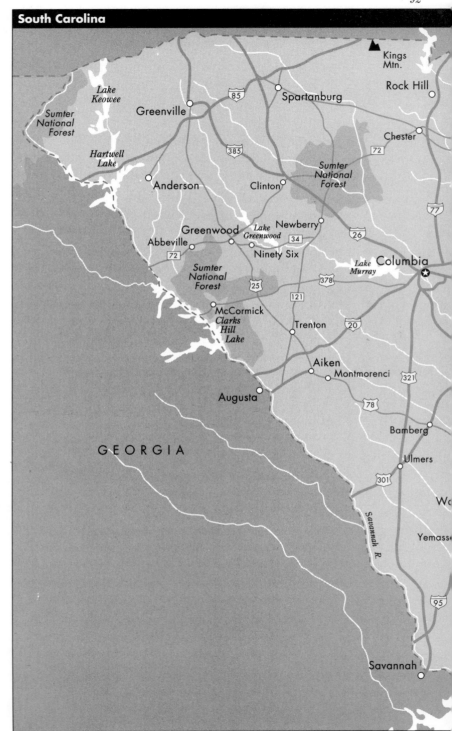

South Carolina

Kings
Mtn.

Rock Hill

Lake
Keowee

Spartanburg

85

Sumter
National
Forest

Greenville

Chester

72

385

Hartwell
Lake

77

Sumter
National
Forest

Anderson

Clinton

Newberry

Greenwood

Lake
Greenwood

34

26

Columbia

Abbeville

Lake
Murray

72

Ninety Six

Sumter
National
Forest

378

Trenton

20

25

121

McCormick
Clarks
Hill
Lake

Aiken

Montmorenci

321

Augusta

78

GEORGIA

Bamberg

Ulmers

301

Wa

Yemasse

Savannah R.

95

Savannah

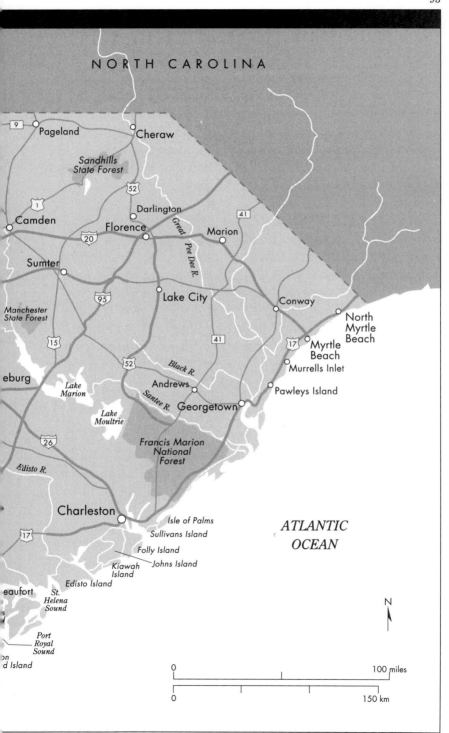

NORTH CAROLINA

9 Pageland

Cheraw

Sandhills
State Forest

52

1 Darlington

Camden 41

20 Florence Marion

Sumter

Manchester
State Forest

95 Lake City

Conway

15 North
Myrtle
Beach

52 41

17 Myrtle
Beach

Black R. Murrells Inlet

eburg Lake
Marion Andrews

Santee R. Pawleys Island

Lake
Moultrie Georgetown

26

Francis Marion
National
Forest

Edisto R.

Charleston Isle of Palms

ATLANTIC
OCEAN

17 Sullivans Island

Folly Island

Kiawah Johns Island
Island

Edisto Island

eaufort St.
Helena
Sound N

Port
Royal
Sound

d Island

0   100 miles

0   150 km

Myrtle Beach and the Grand Strand

The extended necklace that is the Grand Strand begins at Little River on the North Carolina border and reaches about 60 miles south to Georgetown, a Colonial settlement of the 1500s. The jewels dotting the Strand from end to end—glitzy, neon, and natural at the same time—are the oceanside condos and hotels, golf courses, tennis courts, water parks, amusement centers, shops, and restaurants.

Myrtle Beach, the largest town on the Strand, is comparable to Miami Beach in the '50s, with high-rise hotels, nightclubs, upscale restaurants, and bumper-to-bumper traffic. No longer is the tide of tourism tied to the golden days between Memorial Day and Labor Day; it is a year-round flood. Though the region still draws many visitors from the Carolinas, it has become a mecca for Canadians and midwesterners, who think nothing of a little nippy weather in November. The beach is the area's biggest attraction, with miles and miles of sugary sand. After Hurricane Hugo in 1989, the sand was replenished, and the beach is in better condition than before.

The Grand Strand, also famous for golf courses (78 and growing) and tennis courts (about 200), has the distinction of being the "Miniature Golf Capital of the World," with at least 45 courses, each new one more outrageous than the last. (Be sure to see Hawaiian Rumble in North Myrtle Beach, with its 45-foot mountain that rumbles, lets off vapors, and erupts fire every 20 minutes.) The Strand is also a great place for fishing, particularly in fall, and fishermen vie for cash prizes in contests like the Arthur Smith King Mackerel Tournament, one of the world's largest. Shoppers flock to beachwear/souvenir shops, outlet centers like Waccamaw Pottery, and the new Barefoot Landing, a shopping center built over marshland and water in North Myrtle Beach.

Places to Go, Sights to See

Myrtle Beach. The *Myrtle Beach Pavilion* (9th Ave. N and Ocean Blvd., tel. 803/448–6456), a cluster of amusements, shops, and restaurants, is the heart of the Grand Strand. It has a pipe organ with figures that move, an antique merry-go-round, and Big Eli, the Ferris wheel. *Ripley's Believe It or Not Museum* (N. Ocean Blvd. at 9th Ave., tel. 803/448–2331) has more than 500 oddities. *Myrtle Beach National Wax Museum* (1000 N. Ocean Blvd., tel. 803/448–9921) displays animated wax figures of renown.

Murrells Inlet. At *Brookgreen Gardens* (U.S. 17S, tel. 803/237–4218), a sculpture garden and wildlife zoo, more than 400 works by the likes of Augustus Saint-Gaudens, Daniel Chester French, and Frederic Remington are displayed amid formal English landscaping. *Huntington Beach State Park* (U.S. 17S, tel. 803/237–4440), a natural area south of town, where alligators and other wildlife now live, was once a private estate. Besides camping, fishing, hiking, and beachcombing, you can tour Atalaya, the Moorish-style house.

Pawley's Island, south of Murrells Inlet, originally a summer retreat of wealthy rice planters, is one of the last vestiges of the old days along the Grand Strand. Scattered amid the marsh and dunes are elegantly shabby cottages and a handful of inns—places where going barefoot is still okay. The 4-mile island, steeped in legend and tradition, is said to be haunted. Today the island is famous for its hand-tied hammocks.

Georgetown has a historic district dating to 1729, where time has stood still; there are more than 50 early buildings and sites. The area was settled by the Spanish in 1526, claimed by the English 200 years later, and by the mid-1800s was the rice-producing capital of America. Today it is famous for ghost-busting tours of old haunts and for *Ghosts of the Coast,* a theatrical production staged at the Strand Theatre on Front Street every other summer. On a self-guided tour of the town (information at the Chamber of Commerce, 102 Broad St., tel. 803/546–8437), you'll see the *Harbor Walk,* a boardwalk lined with shops, galleries, and restaurants along the waterfront; the *Rice Museum* (Front and Screven Sts., tel. 803/546–7423), for the history of rice and indigo production; the *1721 Prince George Winyah Episcopal Church* (232 Broad St.); the *Kaminski House Museum* (1003 Front St., tel. 803/546–7706), a restored seafarers' house of around 1760; and the 1775 *Man-Doyle House* (528 Front St., tel. 803/546–4612).

The **Bellefield Nature Center,** (U.S. 17N, tel. 803/546–4623), a field station for botanical and marine research, has aquariums, terrariums, and a saltwater touch tank. Guided tours of its 1,300-acre wildlife refuge are conducted weekly, and excursions go up the Waccamaw River.

Hopsewee Plantation (off U.S. 17S, 12 mi south of Georgetown, tel. 803/543–7891), a 1740 rice plantation, is now open for tours.

At **Hampton Plantation State Park** (off U.S. 17S, 15 mi south of Georgetown, tel. 803/546–9361) you can tour the mansion, rice fields, and grounds.

Restaurants

On the Strand seafood is king. At the clusters of restaurants in Calabash, just across the North Carolina line, and in Murrells Inlet, where the fishing boats come in, it is served any way you like it, but the most popular is "Calabash-style," lightly battered and deep-fried. At Myrtle Beach's north end, where U.S. 17 divides, is Restaurant Row. **The Sea Captain's House** (3002 N. Ocean Blvd., Myrtle Beach, tel. 803/448–8082), in a former bed-and-breakfast on the ocean, has the best fresh seafood on the Grand Strand. **Marina Raw Bar** (U.S. 17, North Myrtle Beach, tel. 803/249–3972), a casual eatery, offers fresh oysters, clams, and other seafood. **Shooter's Waterfront Café U.S.A.** (1201 U.S. 17N, North Myrtle Beach, tel. 803/249–4847) offers seafood and sandwiches in a high-key, beachy atmosphere. **Peaches** (900 N. Ocean Blvd., Myrtle Beach, tel. 803/448–7424) has the best hamburgers and hot dogs in the area. For elegant dining, try two restaurants side by side on Restaurant Row: **Chesapeake House** (tel. 803/449–3231) and **Chestnut Hill** (tel. 803/449–3984). Also on Restaurant Row, **Slug's Rib** (tel. 803/449–6419) has the best beef in town and **Nakato's** (tel. 803/449–4433) cooks your food tableside with great flourish. **The Seafood Hut** in Calabash (tel. 919/579–6723) doesn't look like much, but its deep-fried seafood is delicious. **Oliver's Lodge** (U.S. 17 Business, Murrells Inlet, tel. 803/651–2963), in an old sea captain's house, has good seafood and a unique atmosphere.

Nightlife

Southern Country Nights (U.S. 17 Business, Surfside Beach, tel. 803/294–4444), **The Dixie Jubilee** (U.S. 17 Business, North Myrtle Beach, tel. 803/294–4444) and **The Carolina Opry** (82nd Ave., N. Myrtle Beach, tel. 803/238–8888) are live shows held in newly flourishing music halls. Dolly Parton's *Dixie Stampede* music show (U.S. 17N and U.S. 17 Bypass, Myrtle Beach, tel. 803/497–9700) will open July 4, 1992. A dance club called **Studebaker's** (U.S. 17 at 21st Ave. N, tel. 803/448–9747) is the place in Myrtle Beach to shag and listen to beach music. In North Myrtle Beach people go to **Duck's** (229 Main St., tel. 803/249–3858), **Harold's** (2301 N. Ocean Blvd., tel. 803/249–5601), and **The Spanish Galleon** (100 Main St., tel. 803/249–2874). Shagging contests are popular, and every spring and fall thousands attend the Society of Stranders reunion in Myrtle Beach.

Tourist Information

Georgetown County Chamber of Commerce and Information Center (U.S. 17, Box 1776, Georgetown, SC 29442, tel. 803/546–8436). **Myrtle Beach Area Chamber of Commerce and Information Center** (1301 N. Kings Hwy., Box 2115, Myrtle Beach, SC 29578–2115, tel. 803/626–7444 or 800/356–3016, ext. 132). **Pawley's Island Chamber of Commerce** (U.S. 17, Box 569, Pawley's Island, SC 29585, tel. 803/237–1921 or 800/777–7705).

Chesterfield Inn

To stay at the Chesterfield Inn, built more than half a century ago, is to get a sense of Myrtle Beach in the old days. (The inn's motel rooms, though they have oceanfront balconies, don't have the same authenticity.)

The long, three-story brick building facing the ocean appeals to the type of beachcombers who enjoy being with family and friends—the ones who aren't looking for bright lights and glamour. The lobby, with a fireplace, has changed very little over the years and is the perfect place for reading, playing board games, and working puzzles. Guests sit on the verandas to catch the ocean breezes and play on the grassy area between the inn and the beach.

The history of the Chesterfield Inn dates to 1936, when the Chapman family and some friends bought an existing house and opened it to guests. The Chapmans bought out the others and in 1947, after the end of World War II, built the present inn, adding the motel block of rooms about 25 years ago. The inn is now run by a Chapman nephew, Clay Brittain, his wife, Pat, and their two sons. The inn was instantly popular, being the second hotel on the beach to have private baths and phones. By today's standards, the guest rooms, with their varied, old-fashioned furnishings, are simple and plain, but that doesn't deter the families who

have been coming here for five generations. The rooms all have two double beds, and the ones in the main inn are wallpapered.

The food is good at the Chesterfield, and most guests choose the Modified American Plan. Meals are served family style on starched white tablecloths in the paneled dining room overlooking the ocean, where guests of an artistic bent often display their work. The dining room is open to the public; the weekly menu features beef, poultry, pork, and a different variety of fish each evening. Breakfast is one of the best bargains on the beach.

Address: *700 N. Ocean Blvd., Box 218, Myrtle Beach, SC 29578, tel. 803/448-3177, fax 803/626-4736.*
Accommodations: *31 double rooms with baths in old section, 26 doubles with baths in new section (6 with kitchenettes).*
Amenities: *Air-conditioning, cable TV, phones in rooms; pool, shuffleboard.*
Rates: *$66–$91; breakfast extra (MAP $98–$122). AE, D, DC, MC, V.*
Restrictions: *No pets, closed Dec.–Jan.*

Five-Thirty Prince Street Bed & Breakfast

This bed-and-breakfast in the heart of Georgetown's historic district is filled with surprises. Built around the 1920s and restored by owner Nancy Bazemore in 1989, the house explodes with color and eclectic decor. The shocking-pink parlor with its white woodwork makes a brilliant backdrop for the lemon-colored print sofas. The forest-green ceiling of the formal dining room is covered with white latticework. The guest rooms, which tend to be a little more subdued, are furnished with a mixture of antiques and painted furniture, and scattered throughout the house are the innkeeper's special touches, including original contemporary and folk art.

Nancy Bazemore herself isn't a stereotypical Southern gal. She grew up in Philadelphia and has lived in New York; Greenville, South Carolina; and Atlanta. In Atlanta, she worked for the chamber of commerce and rented out one guest room in her home through a bed-and-breakfast agency. She decided to open up the Georgetown inn on a whim and confesses to having no master plan when it comes to running a B&B. Her love of meeting people, entertaining, and the exchange of ideas makes her a natural, however, and her yen for spontaneity keeps her operation fresh and fun. Now settled into the Georgetown community, she's involved in downtown revitalization, and entertains friends a lot.

Arriving guests are usually welcomed with complimentary cocktails, while Nancy briefs them on sights to see and places to go in historic Georgetown. The B&B is just a block off Front Street and Harbor Walk, the center of waterfront restaurants, museums, art galleries, and shops.

The rocker-lined front porch, the wicker-filled sun room, and the private garden patio at Five-Thirty are great places to socialize or enjoy a few quiet moments. One of the guest rooms also has a private deck.

Nancy prepares a full breakfast for her guests that features hot entrées, homemade breads, and gourmet coffees. Some of her specialties are eggs Caracan—a mixture of eggs, dried beef, scallions, cheese, and tomatoes—and French toast made with raisin bread stuffed with cream cheese.

Address: *530 Prince St., Georgetown, SC 29940, tel. 803/527–1114.*
Accommodations: *2 double rooms with baths, 1 double with 1/2 bath and use of a hall bath.*
Amenities: *Air-conditioning, ceiling fans, fireplaces in bedrooms.*
Rates: *$60; full breakfast. No credit cards.*
Restrictions: *No smoking indoors.*

The Sea View Inn

In the morning you can put your feet on the lye-washed hardwood floor and rush to the window to catch a breath of the fresh air that filters through the starched curtains. You might wander out to drink your early morning coffee on the big screened-in porch while Gomez the resident parrot entertains you, or you may take it into the living room, where there's always a fire on cool days. This is the seaside as it was meant to be—unadulterated by air-conditioning, neon, and such citified comforts as wall-to-wall carpeting. Built in the 1930s, The Sea View is a no-frills two-story beachside boardinghouse with long porches, which does, however, have a six-room air-conditioned cottage on the marsh.

Page Oberlin, who once ran a large restaurant, took over as innkeeper about 15 years ago. A stay at her seaside inn, which she calls a "barefoot paradise," though certainly not for everyone, is a very special experience (in high season, the minimum stay is a week). Don't expect any programming here, unless you're attending one of the annual painting workshops or wellness retreats (which feature meditation, yoga, massage, health foods, and guest speakers). Meals, served family style—with grits, gumbo, crab salad, pecan pie, and oyster pie—are really the only scheduled events. The time is yours—to read, collect shells, walk on the beach, or just do nothing. This is life on Pawley's Island.

Each guest room has pickled cypress walls and is simply furnished with a dresser, a double bed and a twin, covered with handmade bedspreads from Guatemala, and artwork from the spring show. Each room has a half-bath; showers are down the hall (and also outside for ocean swimmers). All the rooms have a view of the ocean or the marsh, and the design of the building always guarantees a cross breeze. Your program for getting your life in order won't be disturbed here; though the inn has a well-stocked library, the tube is nonexistent, and there's only one phone. There are sailing, golf, and tennis nearby, plus arts-and-crafts shops. And you can always go ghost hunting among the moss-draped live oaks; you might encounter Alice, searching for her engagement ring in the marshes, or the Gray Man, who warns people about approaching storms.

Address: *Pawley's Island, SC 29585, tel. 803/237-4253.*
Accommodations: *Main house: 14 rooms with 1/2 baths; cottage: 4 doubles with 1/2 baths, 1 double and 1 single share 1 bath.*
Amenities: *Air-conditioning in cottage.*
Rates: *$130–$150 American Plan. No credit cards.*
Restrictions: *No pets; 1 week minimum June–Aug. 21, 2-night minimum May and Aug. 21–Oct.; closed Nov.–Apr.*

Brustman House

This Colonial-style house in a quiet neighborhood two blocks from the ocean in Myrtle Beach is a little out of the ordinary. Innkeeping is a new venture for the Brustmans, who, with their daughters Brandy and May, try to offer their guests an experience in keeping with their philosophy of health, wholeness, and well-being.

Wendell, who works in human resources and produces film and video documentaries, has provided the house with Scandinavian furniture from a store he once owned in their native Minnesota. Goose-down comforters are used on all the beds. Mina's specialty is cooking, and the breakfast menu includes dishes like Tunisian baked eggs, crepes, pancakes, and omelets. Afterward, guests like to take a picnic basket to the beach, play ping-pong, or ride bicycles around the neighborhood. Lemonade is served in the afternoon; the evenings are devoted to reading, playing the piano, watching television, and socializing.

Address: *400 25th Ave., Myrtle Beach, SC 29577, tel. 803/448–7699.*
Accommodations: *3 double rooms with baths.*
Amenities: *Air-conditioning; use of bicycles.*
Rates: *$50–$60; full breakfast. No credit cards.*
Restrictions: *No smoking indoors, no pets, closed Dec.–Jan.*

Guest Quarters, Riverfront Apartments

Have you ever wondered what it might be like to sleep over a shop? You should try the Riverfront Apartments, which were opened in 1989 in an old store building on Georgetown's waterfront, convenient to other shops, restaurants, and historic attractions.

The two apartments are similar in layout: Each has a living room, a dining room, a bedroom, and a balcony overlooking the Sampit River. One has a kitchenette and a shower; the other has a fully equipped kitchen and a tub/shower; both are furnished in a contemporary style with everything you need for housekeeping. Overnight guests may dock boats at the 40-foot finger pier for a small fee.

In case you don't want to cook, Thomas' Café, in the neighborhood, offers a full Southern breakfast and all the trimmings for $2.50, or you can pick up some delicious croissants to go with your coffee at the Kudzu Bakery across the street.

Address: *707 Front St., Georgetown, SC 29440, tel. 803/527–6944.*
Accommodations: *2 housekeeping apartments.*
Amenities: *Air-conditioning, ceiling fans, cable TV, phones.*
Rates: *$55–$75; no breakfast. No credit cards.*
Restrictions: *No pets, 2-night minimum.*

Serendipity, An Inn

The name fits. This small inn two blocks from the beach is a serendipitous find—its Spanish style looks a little different from your run-of-the-mill beach motel, and its owners really care about their guests.

Cos and Ellen Ficarra, from New York, try hard to make everyone's stay memorable, and the setting they have created is part of their hospitality.

Cos, a professional builder, gutted and reconfigured the building in 1984; then Ellen went to work, filling the rooms with antiques and collectibles. Each room is tied to a particular period in history, for example, the Roaring '20s room, outfitted in Art Deco. Guests gravitate to the Garden Room, the gathering place for breakfast and conversation.

Address: *407 71st Ave. N, Myrtle Beach, SC 29572, tel. 803/449–5268.* **Accommodations:** *10 double rooms with baths, 2 housekeeping suites.* **Amenities:** *Air-conditioning; color TV and refrigerators in rooms; pool, ping-pong, shuffleboard.* **Rates:** *$62–$82; Continental breakfast. AE, D, MC, V.* **Restrictions:** *No smoking in breakfast room, no pets, closed Dec.–Feb.*

The Shaw House

Mary Shaw is the epitome of the Southern hostess— attentive, generous, and respectful of privacy. She makes heart-shaped biscuits for honeymooners and puts chocolate kisses on pillows at night. She and her husband, Joe, old hands at running a bed-and-breakfast, grew up in South Carolina, where entertaining is constant and the instinct for hospitality almost a sixth sense. Joe is a retired chemical engineer; Mary has been a homemaker. The Shaws receive guests warmly, with a complimentary drink, and are ready to help with dinner reservations.

Every inch of the 1974 Colonial-style house is inviting—from the rocker-lined porch to the den overlooking the marsh and the big wooden swing outdoors. The house is furnished in family antiques, with loving touches everywhere. The most requested of the guest rooms has a four-poster rice bed, a petticoat mirror, and antique sofas upholstered in white. A typical breakfast might feature quiche, French toast and hot orange sauce, or hot cinnamon apples.

Address: *8 Cypress Ct., Georgetown, SC 29440, tel. 803/546–9663.* **Accommodations:** *3 double rooms with baths.* **Amenities:** *Air-conditioning, cable TV in rooms, phones in common areas.* **Rates:** *$50; full breakfast. No credit cards.* **Restrictions:** *No smoking indoors, no pets.*

Charleston and the Low Country

At first glimpse, historic Charleston and Beaufort (the state's second-oldest town), in South Carolina's storied Low Country, appear stopped in time. But make no mistake: Both cities bustle with 20th-century purpose, past and present meshing gently.

Founded in 1670 by eight English lord-proprietors and named for Charles II, Charleston has over the centuries endured the Civil War, fires, earthquakes, and hurricanes—the latest, Hurricane Hugo, occurred in 1989, though little damage is still evident.

Mariners still use Charleston's church spires to find their way to port. Along the Battery (pronounced Bah-try in Charlestonese), handsome balconied mansions line the point of a narrow peninsula bounded by the Ashley and Cooper rivers. Here one of the nation's largest historic districts preserves scores of house museums, churches, private houses, and commercial and municipal buildings. During the spring and fall historic house tours, you can get a glimpse of the past, as you're welcomed into the homes and gardens of the sixth- or seventh-generation descendants of the original owners. In late May and early June, Charleston is host for the international Spoleto Festival USA, founded in 1977 by Gian Carlo Menotti, featuring concerts, dance, theater, and the visual arts.

In this mild climate, you can play golf virtually year-round, at public courses like Patriots Point, Charleston Municipal, and Shadowmoss, as well as at some resort courses on a space-available basis, including Wild Dunes on the Isle of Palms and those at Kiawah Island. Public beaches are open from mid-April through most of October; there's surf fishing at most of them and deep-sea fishing charters at Charleston Marina and on John's Island.

From Charleston, U.S. 17 south winds through the heart of the Low Country, where seaside islands are separated from the mainland by extensive salt marshes and meandering estuaries. Rivers with lyrical Indian names like Edisto, Ashepoo, Combahee, Coosaw, and Coosawatchie flow through the coastal plains and empty into the Atlantic Ocean. Indigo and rice were once the mainstays of this region; then came Sea Island cotton, followed by produce crops. Now Beaufort and the nearby towns are centers of the oyster, shrimp, and crab industry.

Once called "the wealthiest, most aristocratic, and cultivated town of its size in America," Beaufort was established about 1710. The handsome mansions of wealthy planters and merchants still line its streets, contributing to a delightful 19th-century ambience. As word has spread, increasing numbers of vacationers have begun to visit serene, sunny Beaufort, and many of them have chosen to settle here, as have personnel from nearby military bases, making Beaufort something of a retirement center.

Places to Go, Sights to See

Beaufort
Beaufort Museum (713 Craven St., tel. 803/525–7471). Housed in a 1795 neo-Gothic arsenal, the museum displays prehistoric relics, Indian pottery, Revolutionary and Civil War artifacts, and regional decorative arts. At **Old Point**, part of Beaufort's 304-acre historic district, a National Historic Landmark, some of the many private antebellum houses are open during the spring and fall house-and-garden tours. Two outstanding ones are the **George Elliott House** (1001 Bay St., 803/524–8450), a Greek Revival mansion of 1840, and the **John Mark Verdier House** (801 Bay St., tel. 803/524–6334), an Adams-style mansion of 1790, where the Marquis de Lafayette was entertained in 1825. The **War Memorial Building Museum** (Parris Island U.S. Marine Corps Recruit Depot, tel. 803/525–2111) has collections of vintage uniforms, photographs, and weapons. Visitors may watch actual recruit training on guided or self-guided tours.

Charleston
Charleston Museum (360 Meeting St., tel. 803/722–2996). The nation's oldest municipal museum (1733), now in a handsome contemporary $6 million building, features South Carolina decorative arts, along with natural history, archaeology, and ornithology exhibits.

Charles Towne Landing State Park (1500 Old Towne Rd., tel. 803/556–4450).
The idyllic 663-acre site of the original "Charles Towne" settlement has
replica fortifications, a reconstructed village, beautiful English gardens with
bicycle trails and walkways, a large animal park, a hands-on museum about
the coastal region, and a replica of a 17th-century trading vessel.

The **Dock Street Theatre** (135 Church St., tel. 803/723–5648) combines
a reconstructed early Georgian playhouse and the Planters Hotel (ca. 1809),
built around the ruins of the nation's first theater building.

Fort Sumter National Monument (Charleston Harbor; accessible only by
boat from Municipal Marina, 17 Lockwood Blvd., tel. 803/722–1691).
Confederate forces captured this massive fort on April 13, 1861, after
a 34-hour siege, and its occupation became a symbol of southern resistance
until the end of the Civil War in 1865. The magnificently restored National
Park Service site offers historic displays and dioramas, plus guided tours.

Gibbes Museum of Art (135 Meeting St., tel. 803/722–3706). The notable
American art collection includes 18th- and 19th-century portraits of
Carolinians and more than 300 exquisitely detailed miniature portraits.

Market Hall (188 Meeting St., tel. 803/723–1541). Home of a Confederate
museum run by the Daughters of the Confederacy, this 1841 building was
modeled after the Temple of Nike in Athens. The adjacent **Old City Market**
contains restaurants and shops, along with old-time vegetable and fruit
vendors, a bustling flea market, and the Mt. Pleasant craftswomen who are
so famous for their handmade sweet-grass baskets.

Patriots Point Naval and Maritime Museum (US 17N, tel. 803/884–2727 or
800/327–5723). Here you can board the aircraft carrier *Yorktown*, the nuclear
merchant ship *Savannah*, the World War II submarine *Clamagore*, the cutter
Ingham, and the destroyer *Laffey.*

Charleston's historic houses date from the early 1700s and represent
a variety of architectural styles. **Drayton Hall** (Ashley River Rd., tel.
803/766–0188), built in 1738–42, is considered the nation's finest example of
Georgian Palladian architecture; the **Heyward-Washington House** (87 Church
St., tel. 803/722–0354), a 1772 building, has the city's only restored 18th-
century kitchen that's open to visitors. The **Joseph Manigault House** (350
Meeting St., 803/723–2926) is the city's first Adam-style residence. The
Nathaniel Russell House (51 Meeting St., tel. 803/723–1623) is headquarters
of the Historic Charleston Foundation.

From late March into April, Charleston's formal gardens explode with
azaleas, camellias, daffodils, wisteria, and dogwood. **Cypress Gardens** (US 52,
tel. 803/553–0515) was created as a freshwater reserve for Dean Hall,
a 160-acre rice plantation with moss-draped cypress trees. **Magnolia
Plantation and Gardens** (Ashley River Rd., tel. 803/571–1266) was acquired
in 1676 by the Draytons, whose tenth-generation descendants still occupy it.
The manor house depicts plantation life after the Civil War. The landscaped
gardens at **Middleton Place** (Ashley River Rd., tel. 803/556–6020) date to

1741, and the manor house has collections of family silver, furniture, paintings, and historic documents. In the plantation stableyards, Low Country rural life is depicted through displays of tools, artifacts, and crafts demonstrations.

Beaches
There are public beaches at Beachwalker Park on Kiawah Island, Folly Beach on Folly Island, Kiawah Island, and Sullivan's Island.

Restaurants
Charleston is known for its great restaurants. At **Carolina's** (10 Exchange St., tel. 803/724–3800), a local favorite, you might try the Carolina quail with goat cheese, sun-dried tomatoes, and chutney. **Restaurant Million** (2 Unity Alley, Charleston, tel. 803/571–1472), a Relais Gourmand (food only) affiliate of Relais & Chateaux, serves French food in an antique building (1788) with French antique furnishings. Or soak up the local atmosphere at the cozy **Moultrie Tavern** (18 Vendue Range, tel. 803/723–1862), in an 1833 brick warehouse where the menu has baked oysters and sausage pie with puff pastry. For more casual dining and great harbor views, try **California Dreaming** (1 Ashley Pointe Dr., tel. 803/766–1644) for the broiled seafood, barbecued chicken, or Texas-smoked ribs. **Gaulait and Maliclet French Café** (98 Broad St., tel. 803/577–9797) is a fast French eatery featuring soups, salads, and sandwiches. **Shem Creek Bar & Grill** (508 Mill St., tel. 803/884–8102), across the Cooper River in Mt. Pleasant, is a great place to sample oysters and fresh local seafoods in a laid-back setting.

Beaufort has several good restaurants, too. **The Anchorage** (1103 Bay St., tel. 803/524–9392), in a house built in 1770, features shrimp étouffé, seafood gumbo, and grilled tenderloin of pork with bourbon and apricot sauce. **Gatsby's** (822 Bay St., tel. 803/525–1800), overlooking the water, won a 1990 Silver Spoon Award for its steak and seafood dishes.

Tourist Information

Charleston Trident Convention and Visitors Bureau (Box 975, Charleston, SC 29402, tel. 803/577–2510). **Greater Beaufort Chamber of Commerce** (Box 910, Beaufort, SC 29901, tel. 803/524–3163). **South Carolina Department of Parks, Recreation, and Tourism** (1205 Pendleton St., Columbia, SC 29201, tel. 803/734–0122).

Reservation Service

Charleston Society B & B (84 Murray Blvd., Charleston, SC 29401, tel. 803/723–4948). **Historic Charleston B & B** (43 Legare St., Charleston, SC 29401, tel. 803/722–6606).

Kings Courtyard Inn

If you're a shop-till-you-drop person, you'll love staying at the Kings Courtyard. The inn is wedged between the city's best antiques shops and fashionable boutiques on King Street, one of Charleston's oldest shopping thoroughfares, one block from the Old City Market, with its souvenir shops, restaurants, and craft vendors. But you don't have to be a shopper to enjoy the Kings Courtyard Inn's universal appeal. The sophisticated traveler will quickly recognize the ambience, service, and respect for privacy that are characteristic here: The inn is much like a small European hotel.

Designed by architect Francie D. Lee and built in 1853, the two structures that compose the Greek Revival inn have the appearance of being only one because of their exterior stucco, which was added after the great earthquake of 1886. The buildings were restored in 1983 by Richard T. Widman, and converted into an inn, which had been their original use. Prior to the Civil War, plantation owners and shipping magnates stayed here when they came to do business in Charleston. The rooms are furnished with 18th-century reproductions, including canopied beds and French armoires, and decorated in elegant, traditional fabrics, with Oriental rugs, which look wonderful on the original heart-pine floors. There are guest rooms on all three stories; a few of them have fire-

places with gas-burning logs. Most of the rooms open onto the courtyard; the rest overlook King Street.

Guests are received in a small formal room off one of the two inner courtyards. When they are not in their rooms or out sightseeing, they can usually be found here, having cocktails or relaxing in the whirlpool—complimentary wine and sherry are always available here, as is brandy after dinner. Guests may have breakfast here, in their rooms, or in the breakfast room; a full meal is available upon order. Breakfast comes with a morning newspaper, and the nightly turndown service includes brandy and chocolates.

Address: *198 King St., Charleston, SC 29401, tel. 803/723-7000 or 800/845-6119, fax 803/720-2608.*
Accommodations: *44 double rooms with private baths, 2 suites.*
Amenities: *Air-conditioning; cable TV, phones, outdoor whirlpool, small meeting room; turndown service.*
Rates: *$110–$190; Continental breakfast. AE, MC, V.*
Restrictions: *No pets.*

Rhett House Inn

This 1820 Greek Revival mansion was the home of Thomas Rhett, a rich planter, who lived here with his wife, Caroline Barnwell, and their children. The house exemplifies the rich and lavish life-style of prosperous southern planters prior to the War Between the States, and nowhere in the South was wealth flaunted more than in Beaufort.

The three-story white building is square, with black shutters, and double-decker verandas on the second and third floors supported by 14 fluted Doric columns. It stands on the edge of Craven Street, with a huge live oak hung with Spanish moss directly in front and its gardens to the side and the rear.

The mansion was looking somewhat sad when Steve and Marianne Harrison, executives in New York's garment industry, first spied it on a vacation trip in 1988. But it was love at first sight. So Steve quit his job as president of Anne Klein, and Marianne gave up her knitwear company so they could move to Beaufort and become innkeepers.

The Harrisons completely renovated the mansion and filled it with their own antiques and art. Though elegant, the inn is warm and friendly with a country look; guests feel comfortable in sweaters and tennis shoes, and boaters on the Intracoastal Waterway (only a block away) often drop in. The most famous guests to date have been Barbra Streisand and Nick Nolte, when they were filming *Prince of Tides*.

Several works by Nancy Rhett, a local artist married to a descendant of Thomas Rhett, are exhibited throughout the inn, along with American primitives. The inn has some unusual amenities: each room has a full-length mirror, a double bathroom vanity, four pillows, a comforter, and satin-covered hangers. The lavish honeymoon suite has a whirlpool tub. The Harrisons serve a Low Country high tea every afternoon and provide complimentary bicycles for guests. Breakfast is served in the formal dining room or delivered to your room on a silver tray. Candlelight dinners are served by reservation.

Address: *1009 Craven St., Beaufort, SC 29902, tel. 803/524-9030, fax 803/524-1310.*
Accommodations: *9 double rooms with baths, 1 suite with a whirlpool.*
Amenities: *Air-conditioning, ceiling fans and phones in rooms, cable TV in 1 room and suite, pool table; bicycles, picnics on request.*
Rates: *$80–$115; Continental breakfast and tea. MC, V.*
Restrictions: *No smoking indoors, no pets.*

Two Meeting Street

You know this is a special place the minute you step through the iron gates onto a walk lined with flowers and shrubs. The landscaped gardens are manicured to perfection; the curved verandas, with their arched columns and balustrades, are freshly painted. The sparkle of the beveled glass and the polished brass on the heavy wooden door add to the welcome of the innkeeper's official greeting.

You enter the foyer, a large open room with richly carved oak paneling, stained glass windows, and a heavy stairway over which hangs a huge crystal chandelier. The reception rooms are also paneled, and the house has seven stained glass windows in all, two of them Tiffanys. The formal parlors, off the foyer, are furnished with overstuffed Victorian love seats and chairs, and the formal dining room has a dazzling crystal chandelier and silver that is polished like mirrors.

Each guest room has its own personality, and all are furnished with antique four-poster and canopied beds and Oriental carpets. The two honeymoon suites have working fireplaces and French doors that open to the outside, creating a feeling of privacy. The rooms on the first and second floors are the most sought after, but those on the third floor are just as appealing except that you must climb the stairs.

This Queen Anne Victorian built in 1892 is one of the most beautiful houses in the city's Historic District and is usually included in spring and fall house tours. Its location, overlooking the Battery and the harbor, makes it convenient to all of Charleston's pleasures. In 1946, it was turned into an inn, and it eventually passed to Jean and Pete Spell. Their daughter Karen, the official innkeeper, formerly worked on Capitol Hill for the Senate Budget Committee and for a Charleston congressman. The Spell family have made the house a showplace, one of the city's most popular lodgings, and raised innkeeping to an art. Karen says the profession is in her blood.

The staff members at Two Meeting Street go out of their way to please guests and make sure their stay in Charleston is one they'll remember for a long time. Guests are treated to afternoon sherry and given advice on what to see, where to go, and the best places to eat.

Address: *2 Meeting St., Charleston, SC 29401, tel. 803/723-7322.*
Accommodations: *9 double rooms with baths.*
Amenities: *Air-conditioning and TV in rooms.*
Rates: *$85–$150; Continental breakfast and afternoon sherry. No credit cards.*
Restrictions: *No smoking, no pets. Closed Christmas.*

Elliott House Inn

As you sip champagne in the courtyard of Elliott House Inn in the early evening, you can hear the chimes of St. Michael's Church. Occasionally, the clip-clop of a passing horse-drawn carriage will catch your ear, then fade away. Though you're secluded within the walls of the building behind the iron gate, you can walk to King Street, Battery Park, and the Old City Market. The inn provides bicycles and will furnish a picnic lunch upon request.

The courtyard is the inn's outdoor living room for most of the year. Tea and cookies are served here, and just before bed, you can slip into the Jacuzzi under the wisteria blossoms.

Guest rooms in the three-story pink stucco inn open onto the courtyard. Though they're a little small—the building is an 1861 Charleston single house—they're decorated with period furniture, including canopied four-poster beds, Oriental rugs, and fresh flowers.

Address: *78 Queen St., Charleston, SC 29401, tel. 803/723–1855 or 800/729–1855.*
Accommodations: *26 double rooms with baths.*
Amenities: *Air-conditioning, cable TV, and phones in rooms, elevator, turndown service; bicycles.*
Rates: *$100–$130; Continental breakfast. AE, D, MC, V.*

Guilds Inn

For most of its life, this 1888 Victorian building in Mt. Pleasant has been a grocery store, but more recently it has housed an inn and restaurant. A flower garden behind a picket fence is a pleasant introduction to the three-story cream-colored building, with its classic storefront, Charleston green shutters, and dormer windows with matching awnings. It was restored in 1985 by Guilds Hollowel, a retired tugboat owner, his wife, Joyce, and their five sons.

The Hollowels own a furniture store in the same neighborhood and have furnished the inn in handsome reproductions. The rooms have four-poster canopied queen or twin beds, secretaries, desks, and chests of drawers. All the bathrooms have whirlpool tubs (the bridal suite's is large enough for two), and some rooms have skylights.

Guests enjoy turndown service, and a newspaper with breakfast. Casual lunches are available in Captain Guilds Café (the original store) and dinner in Supper at Stack's, the formal dining room on the second floor, where chef Bill Stack offers a set menu and people usually dress.

Address: *101 Pitt St., Mt. Pleasant, SC 29464, tel. 803/881–0510.*
Accommodations: *6 double rooms with whirlpool baths, 1 suite.*
Amenities: *Restaurant, café, air-conditioning, ceiling fans, phones in rooms.*
Rates: *$70–$100; Continental breakfast. AE, MC, V.*

Maison DuPré

Around a quiet courtyard facing George Street in Charleston's Ansonborough district (a 15-minute walk to the Battery), is the walled enclave that is the Maison Dupré. Open since 1987, the inn is a complex of three restored houses and two carriage houses, some of them moved to the site of the original 1801 Federal house.

This Charleston inn is owned by Robert and Lucille Mulholland and their children and managed by son Mark. It is furnished in period antiques, including Charleston rice beds and four-poster canopied affairs. Each room is decorated around one of Lucille's paintings, with silk floral arrangements and fresh flowers contributed by daughter Teri.

The Mulhollands serve daily Low Country tea, with sandwiches, cakes, cookies, cheeses, wine, and coffee. They give complimentary tickets to the Nathaniel Russell house and do nightly turndowns with chocolates. They will even take care of dinner reservations and carriage rides.

Address: *317 E. Bay St., Charleston, SC 29401, tel. 803/723–8691 or 800/662–4667.*
Accommodations: *12 double rooms with baths, 3 suites.*
Amenities: *Air-conditioning, cable TV and phones in rooms; cribs and bassinets, tickets to house museum.*
Rates: *$82.50–$200; Continental breakfast and tea. AE, MC, V.*
Restrictions: *No smoking indoors, no pets.*

Two Sons Inn

This Neoclassical inn overlooking the Beaufort River was restored by Ron and Carroll Kay for the Fall Tour of Homes in 1990. The prairie-style sand-colored house, with wraparound verandas, was built in 1917, with every modern convenience: The Roman heat distribution system, steam radiators, skylight ventilation, and circular brass body shower all are operational again.

The Kays did the decorating with furniture they already had and Victorian pieces bought at antiques shops and flea markets. Carroll made the draperies and bedspreads and does handweaving on the loom in the parlor. Ron is a talented graphics artist.

The Kays put their hearts and souls into running the inn; they have a Tea and Toddy hour every afternoon, help with dinner reservations, give directions for walking tours, and serve a full breakfast every morning. They will even serve private champagne breakfasts and pack picnic baskets for an additional fee.

Address: *1705 Bay St., Beaufort, SC 29902, tel. 803/522–1122 or 800/552–4244, fax 803/522–1122.*
Accommodations: *5 double rooms with baths.*
Amenities: *Air-conditioning, ceiling fans, cable TV, phones in rooms; bicycles.*
Rates: *$90; full breakfast. MC, V.*
Restrictions: *No smoking indoors, no pets.*

Thoroughbred Country and the Old 96

The Sandhills region with its moderate climate first lured the wealthy to western South Carolina in the 1890s. They settled in and around Aiken, wintering in stately mansions, flinging lavish parties, and spending their time on hunting and racing. Many of their palatial vacation "cottages" (often surrounded by walls or hedges) are preserved in Aiken's three Winter Colony historic districts.

Among the top race horses that have been stabled and trained here are Kentucky Derby champion Pleasant Colony and Summer Squall, a Preakness winner. In late March and early April, people come to Aiken for the Triple Crown: three successive weekends of steeplechasing, Thoroughbred trials, and harness racing. Polo matches are held at Whitney Field, Sunday afternoons from September through November and February through July. On Saturday mornings, guided tours will take you to some of the local stables; at several you can ride and take lessons.

Golf is also popular; most of the year you can play any of 17 courses. In April, the tour of homes welcomes spring, and in May, the Strawberry Festival celebrates a luscious local product. Aiken's Makin' heralds autumn with arts and crafts demonstrations and displays, and then comes the Christmas Crafts Show.

History buffs interested in the Colonial and antebellum eras, the Revolution, or the Civil War should explore some nearby towns in the Old Ninety-six District 30 miles or so northwest of Aiken. At Abbeville, the Southern Cause was born and died. In 1860, the first organized secession meeting was held there, and scarcely less than five years later, Confederate President Jefferson Davis convened his last Council of War. In more recent times, Abbeville was the location for the filming of Sleeping with the Enemy, *and it has a number of antiques stores and boutiques. Your first stop here should be the Briefing Center at the Chamber of Commerce (104 Pickens Street) for an audiovisual presentation.*

In Greenwood, founded by Irish settlers in 1802, Andrew Johnson, the 17th president, ran a tailor shop at Courthouse Square before migrating to eastern Tennessee. In mid-July, the city hosts the South Carolina Festival of Flowers at the Park Seed Company, with home-and-garden tours, live entertainment, and a beauty pageant. Anglers, swimmers, and boaters head for nearby Lake Greenwood's 200-mile shoreline.

Along an Indian trade route near Greenwood is the little community of Ninety-six, located that number of miles from the Cherokee village of Keowee in the Blue Ridge Mountains. Two miles south, at the Ninety-six National Historic Site, South Carolina's first Revolutionary War battle was fought in 1775. Also commemorated is a more significant engagement in 1781, which pitted General Nathaniel Greene against a force of British Loyalists.

Places to Go, Sights to See

Abbeville County Museum (Poplar and Cherry Sts., tel. 803/459–2740). Historic memorabilia and a log cabin are housed in an old 1850s jail designed by Robert Mills, architect of the Washington Monument.

Abbeville Opera House (Town Sq., tel. 803/459–2157). Built in 1908, the structure has been restored to its original grandeur, and current productions range from contemporary comedies to Broadway musicals.

The **Aiken County Historical Museum** (433 Newberry St., SW, Aiken, tel. 803/642–2015), in a wing of **Banksia,** an 1860 estate, depicts the area's early history, with rooms furnished to reflect late 18th- and early 19th-century life-styles, a firearms collection, and Indian artifacts. On the grounds stand an 1890 one-room schoolhouse and an 1808 log cabin thought to be Aiken County's oldest building.

The **Burt-Stark House** (313 Greenville St. at N. Main, Abbeville, tel. 803/459–4600), site of Jefferson Davis's last Council of War, is open for tours Friday and Saturday or by appointment.

At the **George W. Park Seed Co.** (Rte. 254, 7 mi north of Greenwood, tel. 803/223–7333), the colorful experimental gardens and greenhouses put on vivid displays in summer. There are guided tours, and you may buy seeds and bulbs in the company's store.

The **Greenwood Museum** (106 Main St., tel. 803/229–7093) has more than 7,000 items in eclectic displays: Indian artifacts, natural history and geology exhibits, and a replica turn-of-the-century community.

At **Hickory Knob State Resort Park** (7 mi southwest of McCormick via U.S. 378, tel. 803/391–2450), you'll find a pool, nature trails, tennis courts, an equestrian center, and an 18-hole championship golf course. There's a lake where you can fish, rent sailboats and motorboats, and go waterskiing.

Hopelands Gardens/Thoroughbred Racing Hall of Fame (149 Dupree Pl., Aiken, tel. 803/648–5461). These gardens have seasonal plantings, summer concerts and plays, and a Touch and Scent Trail lined with plaques in Braille. The Thoroughbred Hall of Fame commemorates national champions from Aiken.

Montmorenci Vineyards (2989 Charleston Hwy., east of Aiken, tel. 803/649–4870) produces ten varieties of wine, including several award winners. Tours of the family-operated winery are available by appointment with two weeks' notice. Wine tastings are offered Monday and Wednesday through Saturday.

The **Ninety-six National Historic Site** (Rte. 248, 2 mi south of Ninety-six, tel. 803/543–4068) includes earthworks and old roadbeds, a reconstructed stockade fortification, a frontier settlement, and a trading post. National Park Service archaeological digs and historic restorations are still continuing. A visitor center displays relics and has descriptive exhibits.

Restaurants

The elegant **Pheasant Room of the Willcox Inn** (100 Colleton Ave., Aiken, tel. 803/649–1377) serves salmon steak and stuffed baked trout, and a lavish Sunday brunch. The **West Side Bowery** (151 Bee La., Aiken, tel. 803/648–2900), a popular casual spot, serves sandwiches, seafood, steaks, and poultry. On mild days, ask for a table on the sunny terrace. Across the street from the Bowery's rear entrance, **Up Your Alley** (222 In the Alley, Aiken, tel. 803/649–2603) offers steaks, seafood, and health-conscious alternatives in a cozy dining room. **No. 10 Downing St.** (241 Laurens St., Aiken, tel. 803/642–9062) offers upscale dining in a handsome suburban cottage. **Yoder's Dutch Kitchen** (US 72 E, Abbeville, tel. 803/459–5556) has a daily lunch buffet and evening smorgasbord and sells pies, Dutch bread, apple butter, and salad dressings to go.

Tourist Information

Greater Abbeville Chamber of Commerce (104 Pickens St., Abbeville 29620, tel. 803/459–4600). **Greenwood County Chamber of Commerce** (Box 980, Greenwood 29648, tel. 803/223–8431). **Ninety-six Chamber of Commerce** (Box 8, Ninety-six 29666, tel. 803/543–2900). **South Carolina Department of Parks, Recreation and Tourism** (1205 Pendleton St., Columbia 29201, tel. 803/734–0122). **Thoroughbred Country** (Box 850, Aiken, SC 29802, tel. 803/649–7981).

Annie's Inn

You won't be a stranger at this inn very long. Before you know it, you'll be sipping coffee by the wood cookstove, getting acquainted with the other guests (usually businesspeople during the week and couples on weekends). The experience is a lot like going to Grandma's because of the friendly, at-home atmosphere that pervades Scottie Peck's kitchen.

Scottie and her late husband bought the house several years ago, and after his death, she turned it into a bed-and-breakfast inn, the oldest B&B in town. The nearly 200-year-old farmhouse in the rural community of Montmorenci, just outside Aiken, stood at one time on a 2,000-acre cotton plantation. The crop is still grown nearby, but only 2 acres of the original tract remain with the house.

There were originally three floors, but the top floor was hit by a cannonball during the Civil War and subsequently removed. A doctor had his practice in the house for a time and used it as a hospital; the resident ghost is a child who cries.

The house's most distinguishing features are its big front porch and second-floor balcony. It has a central hallway, with formal rooms on either side, the kitchen to the back, and bedrooms upstairs. Scottie has furnished it in elegant French and English country style, with antiques, handmade quilts, area rugs, and lace. Small bathrooms with showers were carved out of existing space, so that each guest room has one. Guests who are staying for a long time usually choose one of the two completely equipped housekeeping cottages behind the house.

Scottie serves breakfast in the kitchen or in the dining room (when she has a full house). Because she is from Colorado, she doesn't serve grits but offers such entrées as waffles with fresh steamed apples on top, popovers served with locally produced honey, and eggs Benedict.

On nice days, guests gather at the swimming pool, play croquet, or pitch horseshoes, and Scottie always has plenty of books, magazines, and games on hand for rainy days.

Address: *Hwy. 78 E, Box 311, Montmorenci, SC 29839, tel. 803/649–6836.*
Accommodations: *5 double rooms with baths, 2 housekeeping cottages.*
Amenities: *Air-conditioning, ceiling fans, cable TV in rooms, cottages, and common rooms.*
Rates: *$55; full breakfast. No credit cards.*
Restrictions: *No smoking in bedrooms, no pets.*

The Belmont Inn

This three-story hotel, with its long, arched double veranda, planted on one corner of Abbeville Square, has played a prominent role in the history of the town. Built in 1903 and called The Eureka, it was the resort of famous statesmen, lawyers and judges during court sessions, drummers, and vaudeville actors in its heyday. The hotel went through hard times, eventually closed in 1974, and was reopened in 1984 after a complete restoration. It is currently managed by a Memphis-based group of investors, and once again, the verandas provide a ringside seat for the comings and goings on Court Square.

Since its rebirth, The Belmont has developed quite a following. Its guests like to combine a visit with a couple of nights at the Opera House, following the example of such as Jimmy Durante, Fanny Brice, Sarah Bernhardt, and Groucho Marx, who made overnight stops in Abbeville. The town calls itself the "birthplace and deathbed of the Confederacy," and there is a Confederate memorial in the town square that will move you to tears.

The guest rooms are furnished in period reproductions, with four-poster beds and armoires; the bathrooms are strictly functional. The heart-pine floors are original, but the fireplaces are now only decorative. The best lodging in the house, the John C. Calhoun Room, has two four-poster beds and opens onto the second-floor balcony. The public rooms of the hotel are also furnished in reproductions, with some period antiques. The lobby exudes a turn-of-the-century atmosphere, with its registration desk in the middle of the room and sitting areas and separate parlors off to the side.

The Heritage Room restaurant, serving French cuisine, offers all meals plus Sunday brunch, and light fare is served in the Curtain Call Lounge on the basement level. The meeting rooms, also on this level, were originally used by traveling salesmen to display their merchandise.

Address: *Court Sq., 106 E. Pickens St., Abbeville, SC 29620, tel. 803/459–9625, fax 803/459–9625, ext. 131.*
Accommodations: *24 double rooms with baths.*
Amenities: *Restaurant, lounge; air-conditioning, cable TV and phones in rooms; meeting rooms, parking.*
Rates: *$60–$85; Continental breakfast. AE, D, MC, V.*
Restrictions: *No pets.*

The Willcox Inn

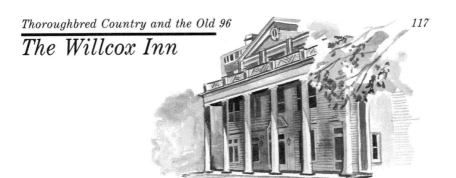

Were it not for the white-white paint on this three-story classic inn, you would hardly notice the building amid the trees and shrubbery in Aiken's historic district. But it's right there with the elaborate estates and horse farms belonging to the winter people, who come from everywhere year after year for the riding, racing, and hunting.

Frederick Sugden Willcox, an Englishman, came to Aiken around 1891 with his Swedish wife, Elise, and started the Willcox Inn. Response was so great that he had to enlarge it several times. Winston Churchill, Elizabeth Arden, Averill Harriman, and other luminaries slept here, and it's said that no room could be found for the Duke of Windsor during a Masters Golf Tournament (Augusta, Ga., is about 16 miles away). The Willcox family managed the inn until 1957, and after a succession of owners, Weldon Wyatt bought and restored it in 1987. Stig K. Jorgensen, a native of Denmark, is the general manager.

Second Empire and Colonial Revival in architectural style, the weatherboard inn has a front porch supported by six Doric columns, over which there is a balcony. The rosewood-paneled lobby has heart-pine floors, a stone fireplace at either end, and a smaller fireplace on the second landing, which was the original dining room. The back porch was recently enclosed to become the Pheasant Dining Room, where the inn's renowned meals are served, including the popular Sunday brunch. The Polo Lounge, with dark paneling and leather chairs, is a perfect setting for the horsey set during racing season. The light spacious guest rooms have traditional furniture with bright floral wallpapers and complementary fabrics. The Winston Churchill Suite, in shades of blue, is the most elaborate in the inn, with a separate sitting room, a private entrance, and a porch. Room 106, on the back side, is cool and quiet; its large bathroom has a claw-foot tub.

Though small compared with most hotels, the Willcox Inn has a friendly, service-oriented staff. You can get room service during the day, and the staff can arrange golf games, historic tours, and carriage rides. The inn offers golf and honeymoon packages as well as popular gourmet weekends, which begin with champagne and chocolates and revolve entirely around food.

Address: *100 Colleton Ave., Aiken, SC 29801, tel. 803/649–1377, fax 803/649–1377.*
Accommodations: *30 double rooms with baths.*
Amenities: *Restaurant, lounge, air-conditioning; cable TV and phones in rooms, meeting room, turndown service.*
Rates: *$93–$113. AE, MC, V.*
Restrictions: *No pets.*

The Briar Patch

You'll have a sense of what life is really like in Aiken when you stay at this unique bed-and-breakfast. From here you can walk down shady lanes and perhaps see over the walls of the surrounding farms where Kentucky Derby champions are raised. You can also walk to shops and restaurants.

Spending some time with innkeepers Martha Hair and her daughter Trisha will make you appreciate the contrasts of life in modern South Carolina. Martha has the aristocratic accent of plantation owners, and Trisha, a champion shagger, owns a dance hall.

The Hairs' two guest rooms—each with its own entrance and fireplace—are furnished in handsome antiques. One room is feminine, with French provincial furniture and a pink-and-blue color scheme; the masculine room has cable TV, pine furniture, and the original weathervane as a decoration over the mantel. Guests may have breakfast in their room, but most prefer to sit around the Hairs' big pine table in the breakfast room.

Address: *544 Magnolia La., SE, Aiken, SC 29801, tel. 803/649-2010.*
Accommodations: *2 double rooms with baths.*
Amenities: *Air-conditioning; tennis court.*
Rates: *$45; Continental breakfast. No credit cards.*
Restrictions: *No smoking indoors, no pets.*

The Constantine House

The Constantine House, opened in the fall of 1991, is Aiken's most elegant bed-and-breakfast. Completed in 1935, the white stucco Georgian mansion sits on 6½ acres on the highest point in Aiken. It is perfectly symmetrical, with elaborate friezes, four columns, and four chimneys (though only one fireplace). In back there's a terrace and a screened loggia on the second floor. The house was designed for entertaining, with formal rooms on each side of a central hallway and a spiral stairway in the middle.

Anne S. Smith, who also owns the Four Generations antiques shop in Aiken, has filled the house with treasures and fine accessories. One bedroom has burgundy walls, jewel-tone fabrics, and an Oriental rug; the peach-colored room has a four-poster bed and an 1830 chest; and the white room opens onto the loggia.

Anne serves breakfast to guests along with a morning newspaper in their room, on the loggia, or in the formal dining room.

Address: *3406 Richmond Ave., Aiken, SC 29801, tel. 803/642-8911 or 803/641-7477.*
Accommodations: *1 double room with bath, 2 doubles share a bath.*
Amenities: *Air-conditioning.*
Rates: *$69; Continental breakfast. AE, MC, V.*
Restrictions: *No pets.*

Hollie Berries Inn Bed & Breakfast

This century-old bright yellow two-story farmhouse offers simple bed-and-breakfast accommodations close to Aiken's race tracks. The house has a classic front porch, a narrow central hallway with rooms on either side, and a living room for guests. Most of the outbuildings, including a large barn, are still standing, and there is plenty of space for walking. There's a housekeeping cottage on the property that badly needs repair and redecoration.

Hollie Berries is owned by David and Wendy Mason, who also have a B&B in town. They plan to move to the farm when they retire, but Steve and Suzi Parrett are the resident innkeepers. Steve is an anchorman for a local television station, and Suzi runs the inn. You can have breakfast in bed or in the dining room; the large selection includes eggs, bacon, ham, grits, special casseroles, homemade muffins, waffles, French toast, and more.

Great ingenuity was used in creating private baths: the one in Room 1 has nine sides. Room 3, the smallest room, has the largest bed—a king-size one in brass. Antiques are used throughout the house, which has several nonworking fireplaces.

Address: *1560 Powderhouse Rd., Aiken, SC 29803, tel. 803/648-9952.* **Accommodations:** *4 double rooms with baths, 1 housekeeping cottage.* **Amenities:** *Air-conditioning, cable TV and phones in rooms.* **Rates:** *$40–$50; full breakfast. AE, DC, MC, V.*

The Inn on the Square

Greenwood's most elegant lodging, the Inn on the Square, was created out of an old warehouse and opened by Tom Fisher in 1986. The progression of the restoration project is highlighted in photographs displayed in the lobby. The new layout is spacious and modern, with all the components of a small luxury hotel, including a formal lobby, dining room, lounge, and meeting space. The building's central focus is the spacious lobby, with its reception and formal sitting areas. Continental breakfast is laid out here each morning, along with *USA Today* and the *Wall Street Journal.*

All the guest rooms are configured in typical hotel fashion, but the 18th-century reproduction furniture is a cut above the ordinary; there are four-poster beds, large writing desks, and armoires.

Guests receive a small bottle of wine and snacks in their rooms. Golf privileges can be arranged at Stoney Point Golf Club on Lake Greenwood.

Address: *104 Court St., Greenwood, SC 29648, tel. 803/223-4488, fax 803/223-7067.* **Accommodations:** *48 double rooms with baths.* **Amenities:** *Restaurant, air-conditioning; pool.* **Rates:** *$65–$71; Continental breakfast. AE, D, DC, MC, V.* **Restrictions:** *No pets.*

Georgia

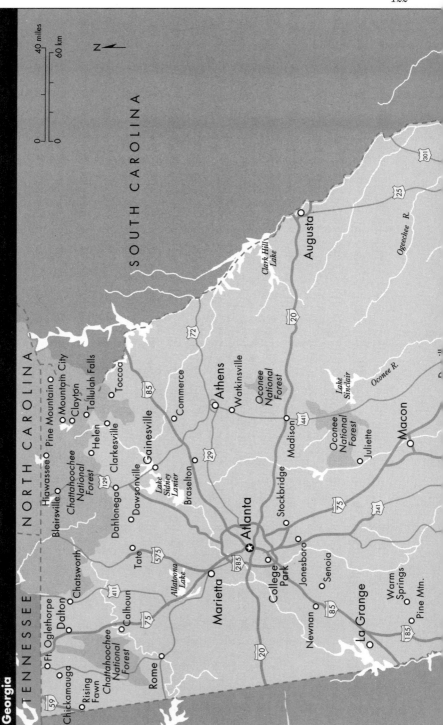

Georgia

40 miles
60 km

N

TENNESSEE   NORTH CAROLINA

SOUTH CAROLINA

Chickamauga
Rising Fawn
Ft. Oglethorpe
Dalton
Chatsworth
Chattahoochee National Forest
Calhoun
Rome
Tate
Allatoona Lake
Marietta
Atlanta
College Park
Jonesboro
Newnan
Senoia
La Grange
Warm Springs
Pine Mtn.
Blairsville
Hiawassee
Pine Mountain
Mountain City
Clayton
Tallulah Falls
Helen
Clarkesville
Dahlonega
Dawsonville
Gainesville
Lake Sidney Lanier
Braselton
Commerce
Athens
Watkinsville
Oconee National Forest
Madison
Lake Sinclair
Juliette
Macon
Oconee National Forest
Toccoa
Clark Hill Lake
Augusta
Oconee R.
Ogeechee R.
Stockbridge

Chattahoochee National Forest

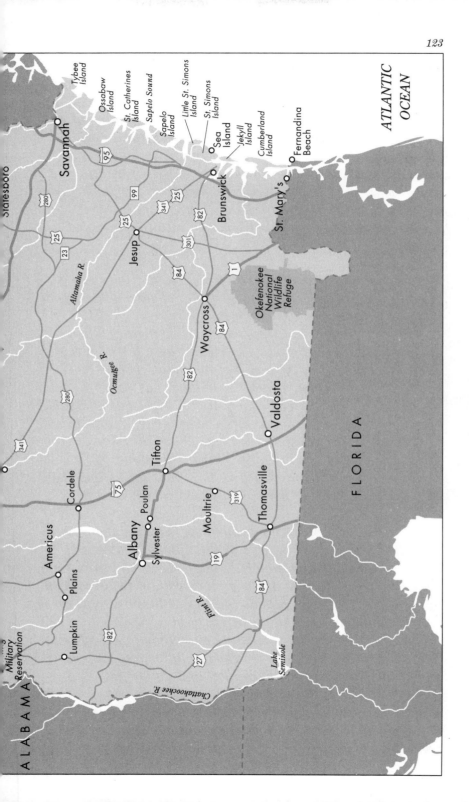

Atlanta to the Mountains

No other part of Georgia is as diverse in temperament and appearance as the area that encompasses Atlanta and stretches northward. There's the booming city and also quiet rural areas steeped in the lore of the Cherokees and dotted with Civil War battle sites. The region's rich heritage dates back to the 1700s, when adventurous pioneers moved from the crowded coastal settlements into the untamed upland territories.

Development has drastically altered Atlanta, the state capital, and its environs. Today steel-and-glass skyscrapers punctuate the city's downtown and perimeter profiles. A lingering presence of the area's earlier history is found only outside these populated centers, where the high-rise silhouettes fade into the distance and are replaced by lush valley pastures. Then, almost as suddenly as they appeared, the open green spaces lining highways and side roads give way to the smoky blue peaks of the mountains. The tone of these areas seems to change with the landscape—Atlanta's bustling metropolitan energy is transformed into tranquillity in the small towns and then into the casualness of lakeside and mountain resorts.

Atlanta has such big-city pleasures as the tony shops and restaurants lining the streets of the upscale Buckhead district. It also has a six-block underground mall and an unparalleled collection of Coke memorabilia in a recently opened pavilion. Just outside the city at Stone Mountain is a man-made marvel: the world's largest Civil War monument, carved into a granite cliff. Driving east from Atlanta brings visitors to the charming town of Athens, site of the state's botanical garden and its largest university. The rural appeal of the country north of Athens is epitomized by the year-round presence of roadside apple-cider, vegetable, and craft stands along the winding back roads and highways. In Dahlonega, in the uplands northeast of Atlanta, panning for gold is a favorite pastime, as are kayaking and river-rafting along the Chattooga River's white-water rapids. A serenity still blankets the popular resorts rimming the shores of pristine Lake Rabun and Lake Burton, though both lakes are reputed among weekend visitors and vacation-home residents to be the "in" spots for the pursuit of fishing, waterskiing, or dockside cocktails.

Annual crafts and cultural festivals, county agricultural fairs, and weekly markets are year-round attractions. The ideal time for a visit to Atlanta is spring, when the dogwood trees are in full bloom and temperatures are mild. The mountains draw visitors all year long, but especially in summer for their coolness and in autumn for their reds and golds.

Places to Go, Sights to See

Amicalola Falls State Park (16 mi northwest of Dawsonville via Rte. 183, tel. 404/265–8888) is where the state's highest waterfalls are found, and where the Georgia portion of the Appalachian Trail begins.

Athens. This small town is the northern gateway to the state's Antebellum Trail. It is also home of the nation's oldest state university, whose buildings date back to the early 1800s, and the *State Museum of Art* (North University Campus, tel. 404/542–3254). *The State Botanical Garden* (2450 S. Milledge Ave., tel. 404/542–1244) is a few miles from downtown.

Atlanta Botanical Garden (1345 Piedmont Ave., Atlanta, tel. 404/876–5859). On 60 acres of Atlanta's Piedmont Park are 5 acres of formal gardens, a 15-acre hardwood forest, a Japanese garden, and a conservatory for unusual and flamboyant tropical, desert, and Mediterranean plants.

Atlanta Cyclorama (800 Cherokee Ave., Atlanta, tel. 404/658–7625). A 105-year-old panoramic battle painting, 350 feet in circumference, is the focal point of this Civil War museum complex. A guided tour and short film are also provided.

Brasstown Bald. Often referred to as the "top of Georgia," this 4,784-foot peak is the state's highest point. Georgia, Tennessee, and the two Carolinas can be seen from here on a clear day.

Chateau Elan Winery (Braselton, tel. 404/658–9463). Vineyards surround the château-style visitors' center, casual and formal restaurants, an art gallery, and wine-tasting facilities. There's also a tournament-quality golf course.

Chattooga River. A first-class white-water river, the Chattooga annually draws over 100,000 visitors eager to ride its rapids. For information about river outfitters, contact the U.S. Forest Service's Tallulah Ranger District (tel. 404/782–3320).

Chickamauga National Military Park (Chickamauga, tel. 404/375–4728). The historic clash of Union and Confederate troops here in 1863 resulted in 34,000 casualties. Today, visitors can take an 11-mile self-guided tour following the battle's stages and see a display of weapons in the visitors' center.

Chief Vann House (Chatsworth, tel. 404/695–2598). This house was built by Cherokee Chief James Vann in 1804; it's now a showplace of Cherokee culture.

Cloudland Canyon (Rte. 2, Rising Fawn, tel. 404/657–4050). This scenic park, which straddles a deep gorge on the western side of Lookout Mountain, has waterfalls and dramatic land formations.

Dahlonega Gold Rush Museum (Public Sq., tel. 404/864–2257). The first American gold rush happened in Georgia, not California. Ore samples, early photographs, and mining tools are displayed in the former Lumpkin County Courthouse. Visitors can pan for gold in nearby mines.

Ft. Mountain Park (east of Chatsworth, tel. 404/695–2621). Ft. Mountain's origins are unknown, but this man-made prehistoric rock wall, extending 875 feet, is believed to have been a Native American religious site.

Helen. This small mountain town, a mecca of tourism, holds an annual Oktoberfest. Souvenir shops filled with European imports, Christmas ornaments, and local crafts line the main streets.

Kennesaw Mountain National Battlefield (U.S. 41 and Stilesboro Rd., tel. 404/427–4686). This 2,900-acre park outside Atlanta commemorates one of the Civil War's most decisive battles and offers 17 miles of hiking and biking trails.

Lake Burton. The largest of five state reservoir lakes has breathtaking scenery along its 62 miles of shoreline.

Lake Hartwell. This lake's thriving populations of largemouth bass, catfish, and crappie make it a fisherman's paradise.

Lookout Mountain (off Rte. 189, south of Rock City, tel. 404/398–3549). Hang gliders take off from this mountain's McCarty Bluff, but you can simply stop at the overlooks to get the view of the surrounding mountains and patchwork of farmlands and forest.

Marietta. Well-preserved homes, churches, a renovated business district, and a National Cemetery are some points of interest along this town's extensive walking and driving tour.

New Echota (Calhoun, tel. 404/629–8151). Indian mounds and restored buildings represent the history of the Independent Cherokee Nation, which resided here from 1825 until the Cherokees were removed to Oklahoma in 1838.

Stone Mountain Park (U.S. 78, Stone Mountain Freeway, tel. 404/498–5690) is a 3,200-acre recreation and amusement park centered on a massive Civil War relief sculpture. Also here are an antebellum plantation, a paddle-wheel riverboat, restaurants, and recreational sports.

Tallulah Gorge (Terrora Visitors Center, Tallulah Falls, tel. 404/754–3276), in the southern gateway to Rabun County, plunges to 1,100 feet. In *Terrora Park*, next to the gorge, the visitor center, run by the Georgia power company, has exhibits on the area's natural resources and pioneer past.

Traveler's Rest (Jarrett Manor, Toccoa, tel. 404/886–2256). This two-story frame house was a stagecoach inn and plantation home; it is furnished with locally crafted antiques.

Underground Atlanta (50 Alabama St., Atlanta, tel. 404/523–2311), a newly spruced up center encompassing six redeveloped city blocks, is filled with shops, restaurants, and entertainment.

World of Coca-Cola Pavilion (55 Martin Luther King Dr., Atlanta, tel. 404/676–5151). This new building's dazzling architecture is nearly as compelling as its spectacular collection of articles related to the Atlanta-based soft drink's history.

Restaurants

Deacon Burton's (tel. 404/525–3415) in Atlanta's Inman Park is a soul-flavored bastion of Southern breakfasts and lunches. The **Dillard House** (tel. 404/746–5348 or 800/541–0671), north of Clayton, offers family-style meals of country ham, chicken, and vegetables plus a panoramic view of the Nachoochee Valley. **Moon Valley** (tel. 404/746–2466), near Lake Rabun, serves the area's finest gourmet cuisine. **Taylor's Trolley** (tel. 404/754–5566), on the square in Clarkesville, is a throwback to soda fountain days and offers a modern American menu. **La Prade's Fishcamp** (tel. 404/947–3312), north of Clarkesville, is a family-style eatery, serving homegrown vegetables and fried chicken from April through November. **Cohutta Lodge** (tel. 404/695–9601) sits on top of Ft. Mountain and serves three meals daily to go along with the view. The **Smith House** (202 S. Chestatee St., tel. 404/864–3566) is a legendary all-you-can-eat institution in Dahlonega.

Nightlife

The **40 Watt Club** (tel. 404/549–7871), a popular fixture on the Athens music scene, is where homegrown bands like REM got their start. Dancing and dining are offered at **Petrus** (tel. 404/873–6700), a recent addition to Atlanta's club scene. Big-band sounds and danceable pop tunes are heard nightly at **Rupert's** (tel. 404/266–9834) in Atlanta's Buckhead district.

Tourist Information

Atlanta Convention and Visitors Bureau (233 Peachtree St., Atlanta, GA 30043, tel. 404/521–6628). **Blue Ridge Visitors Center** (Historic Depot, Blue Ridge, GA 30513, tel. 404/632–5680). **Calhoun Welcome Center** (300 S. Wall St., Calhoun, GA 30701, tel. 404/625–3200). **Dahlonega-Lumpkin County Chamber of Commerce** (Box 2037, Dahlonega, GA 30533, tel. 404/864–3711). **Gainesville Tourist & Convention Bureau** (Box 374, Gainesville, GA 30503, tel. 404/536–5209). **Greater Rome Convention & Visitors Center** (Box 5823, Rome, GA 30161, tel. 404/295–5576). **Marietta Welcome Center** (4 Depot St., Marietta, GA 30060, tel. 404/429–1115). **Rabun County Welcome Center** (Rte. 441, Clayton, GA 30525, tel. 404/782–5113).

Reservation Services

Atlanta Hospitality (2472 Lauderdale Dr. NE, Atlanta, GA 30345, tel. 404/493–1930). **Bed and Breakfast Atlanta** (1801 Piedmont Ave., Atlanta, GA 30324, tel. 404/875–0525 or 800/967–3224).

Ansley Inn

When you stay at the Ansley Inn, you're in the heart of seductive Midtown, a handsome landscape of park-lined streets that's one of Atlanta's oldest neighborhoods. The English Tudor yellow brick mansion trimmed with green shutters was built early in this century by a local philanthropist and then converted into a bed-and-breakfast in 1987. It is managed by a professional staff, who try, nevertheless, to give you personal attention.

Upon arrival, guests check in at the front desk, which is manned round-the-clock by a concierge. Before breakfast you'll find the morning papers stacked on a table in the main hallway. There's a formal dining room, where light buffet breakfasts are served, and a living room with a marble fireplace and comfortable seating, where afternoon appetizers and drink setups are laid out.

The well-equipped guest rooms range in size from spacious suites with four-poster beds to cozy double rooms. They are each individually decorated in a variety of paisleys and chintzes, flowers and stripes. The house is furnished throughout with dark mahogany reproductions: tables, bureaus, and armoires based on formal 18th-century designs. Two of the rooms have fireplaces and seating areas, and there's a new two-bedroom cottage with a fireplace and a kitchenette.

A conference area with a fireplace on the first floor can be reserved for business meetings. Health club privileges are offered at a nearby fitness club, but by the summer of 1992 the inn will have its own swimming pool. There is no restaurant, but the staff can order catered meals and serve them in your room. The house is within walking distance of the High Museum, Atlanta Botanical Gardens, Piedmont Park, and Woodruff Arts Center, where the city's symphony and theater company perform.

Address: *253 15th St., Atlanta, GA 30309, tel. 404/872–9000 or 800/446–5416, fax 404/892–2318.*
Accommodations: *11 double rooms with baths, 1 suite, 2-bedroom housekeeping cottage.*
Amenities: *Air-conditioning; wet bars, whirlpool baths, cable TV in rooms; laundry and dry cleaning service; small pets permitted; off-street parking.*
Rates: *$80–$275; Continental breakfast. AE, D, DC, MC, V.*

Glen-Ella Springs Hotel

len-Ella Springs Hotel, a rambling 100-year-old hideaway just outside Clarkesville, has been lovingly renovated, after years of neglect, by Barrie and Bobby Aycock. The small hotel, listed on the National Register of Historic Places, sits by a gravel road on 17 acres of meadows and woods laced with nature trails.

The Glen-Ella is packed with appeal all the way to its heart-of-pine ceilings, but along with its air of charming country freshness, it has the savvy of an uptown urban hotel. The front lobby, filled with chintz and antiques, serves as a parlor, and fires are lit here against the cool night air. From wide double porches you enter the guest rooms, where quilts, Oriental and hooked rugs, and primitive antiques warm the pine-paneled interiors, and the well-equipped bathrooms are brand-new.

The hotel's dining room, with a fireplace, is the realization of Barrie's original dream: to own her own restaurant. She approaches the business of food with a no-excuses attitude. Her kitchen is the source of the sweet baked goods—blueberry muffins and oat scones—served at breakfast; the salads, sandwiches, and chili enjoyed at lunch; and the American Creole cuisine served at dinner. The food here has so enhanced the inn's reputation that it has become a culinary hotspot for Atlantans, who will drive the two hours for the sumptuous meals.

Special weekend pursuits, such as herb-gardening conferences, are listed at the lobby desk, and there is a wide range of outdoor activities at hand. You can relax by the pool on the large sun deck surrounded by flower gardens or take a more active approach to your stay by hiking, sailing, golfing, horseback riding, boating, or rafting. In winter you can make day trips to nearby slopes.

Address: *Bear Gap Rd. (Rte. 3, Box 3304), Clarkesville, GA 30523, tel. 404/754-7295 or 800/552-3479.*
Accommodations: *14 double rooms with baths, 2 suites.*
Amenities: *Restaurant; air-conditioning and phones in rooms, whirlpool baths and fireplaces in suites; TV in lobby.*
Rates: *$70–$135; Continental breakfast. MC, V.*

The Tate House

This pink marble mansion, in woods that frame a picturesque view of the mountains, is a beacon of civility along a winding mountain road. The elegant interiors, luxurious accommodations, and formal gardens of the striking Tate House would surely have made Rhett and Scarlett feel at home.

Built in 1926 by Colonel Sam Tate, the marble baron who supplied the stone for the Lincoln Memorial in Washington, D.C., the house sat empty for more than 25 years until Ann and Joe Laird painstakingly restored it and opened it in 1985. They furnished the house in the ultimate of formal decor, with an impressive collection of antiques that includes a John Adams sideboard, a baby grand player piano, and a sparkling dining room chandelier that matches one hanging in Graceland, Elvis Presley's home in Tennessee.

Many of the decorative elements you might expect in a house on the National Register of Historic Places can be found just inside the front door: marble floors, a hand-painted mural, and a winding staircase. The bedrooms are furnished with heavy tapestry draperies, plush rugs, working fireplaces, antique bedsteads and furnishings, and chandeliers. One bedroom contains an antique game table for checkers, backgammon, and roulette.

During the week, Continental breakfast is served in the sun room overlooking the landscaped gardens; on weekends, guests receive a bottle of champagne and a traditional Southern breakfast. There's a solarium courtyard pub (beer, wine, and setups) with a 46-foot bar, antique beveled glass, and mahogany cabinets, which can be hired for large groups.

The property also offers country-style accommodations in nine cabins behind the main house; all have hot tubs, fireplaces, and wet bars. Guests have free run of the property's 27 acres, including the terrace dining areas, formal gardens, tennis courts, and heated swimming pool. There's also horseback riding on trails through 700 acres just opposite The Tate House, and tee times can be arranged at nearby courses.

Address: *Rte. 53 (Box 33, Tate), GA 30177, tel. 404/735-3122 or 800/342-7515 in GA, fax 404/735-4730.*
Accommodations: *4 suites; 9 cabins with sleeping lofts.*
Amenities: *Air-conditioning, cable TV in rooms; pool, riding, tennis courts, shuffleboard, gift shop.*
Rates: *$105 weekdays, $115 weekends. AE, D, MC, V.*

Captain's Quarters Bed & Breakfast Inn

The Captain's Quarters is one of 13 stately homes outlining Fort Oglethorpe's manicured grassy common. With lattice-trimmed twin porches and a quaint front sitting room, this captivating turn-of-the-century Greek Revival inn has all the charm of a chintz-decorated dollhouse. The airy, spacious rooms have an appealing Laura-Ashley-meets-Southern-country flair, with overstuffed armchairs, wicker settees, and floral borders.

After traveling through New England and staying in bed-and-breakfasts, sisters Pam Humphrey and Ann Gilbert bought the house in the late 1980s and renovated it. The downstairs bedroom has a private entrance and a porch. A small breakfast room at the end of the second-floor hall overlooks a grassy stretch of the Chickamauga National Battlefield. You can have breakfast here with the view, or on flowered china and lace tablecloths in the dining room downstairs.

Address: *13 Barnhardt Cir., Fort Oglethorpe, GA 30742, tel. 404/858–0624.*
Accommodations: *3 double rooms with baths, 1 suite.*
Amenities: *Air-conditioning; ceiling fans, cable TV, and ironing boards in rooms.*
Rates: *$50–$75; full breakfast. AE, MC, V.*
Restrictions: *No smoking indoors, no pets.*

The Gordon-Lee Mansion

The Gordon-Lee Mansion in Chickamauga was made a National Historic Site, and rightly so—the Greek Revival house survived the ravages of the war that raged near here more than a century ago. Visitors today who stay overnight or take a tour of the house can sometimes get a sense of the original inhabitants and the lifestyle they enjoyed.

Built in 1840–47 by James Gordon, an early Scottish settler, the house was used by the Union Army as a headquarters and hospital. A wide driveway lined with oaks and maples frames the grand Doric columns on the front veranda as you approach. A stroll across the shade-dappled lawn takes you to a brick slave cabin with two rooms and then into the heart of the small mountain town. The mansion's well-preserved rooms have 10- and 12-foot ceilings and are furnished with authentic period antiques. Frank Green, a retired dentist, and his wife, Maria, opened the house to the public in the late 1980s. They live on the grounds nearby, as does the manager, Richard Barclift.

Address: *217 Cove Rd., Chickamauga, GA 30707, tel. 404/375–4728.*
Accommodations: *2 double rooms with baths, 1 double and 1 housekeeping suite share 1 bath; 1 cabin sleeps four.*
Amenities: *Air-conditioning; TV in apartment, cabin, and parlor.*
Rates: *$63–$72; full breakfast, afternoon wine and cheese. MC, V.*
Restrictions: *No smoking indoors, no pets.*

The Pittman House

This 1890s-vintage Colonial-style house, in a small town outside Athens, is owned by Tom and Dot Tomberlin, longtime antiques dealers from Atlanta, who bought and restored the house in 1987 and opened it as an inn. Dot works full-time in a chemical plant, so Tom became the daytime manager. Typically found next door tending their antiques store or carving his wonderful wood figures, Tom runs the inn with an inviting warmth based on the old Southern saying, "If you ain't at home, you ought to be."

The house is just on the edge of the commercial district, but what it lacks in scenery it makes up for in homey comforts. In order to make guests "be at home," they are given the run of the downstairs parlor, the kitchen, and the dining room. The bedrooms are decorated with turn-of-the-century armoires and chests, reproduction Oriental rugs, and soft beds. In the afternoon, guests congregate in the rocking chairs on the front porch, in the sitting area on the landing, or on a screened back porch furnished with comfortable wicker.

Address: *103 Homer St., Commerce, GA 30529, tel. 404/335-3823.*
Accommodations: *2 double rooms with baths, 2 doubles share 1 bath.*
Amenities: *Air-conditioning, TV in common area.*
Rates: *$50–$55; full breakfast. MC, V.*
Restrictions: *No smoking indoors, no pets.*

Rivendell

Rivendell, a contemporary house with a Tudor-style exterior, is nestled in woodland along the Oconee River. Danny and Nancy Connell began their bed-and-breakfast after their children moved out, and the house is often the site of corporate working weekends.

Sunlight streams across the second-level deck into the spacious, beamed great room, with its comfortable seating arrangement and stone fireplace. On this level, there are plushly carpeted bedrooms and a suite with a canopy bed, antique furniture, and a whirlpool bath. A bedroom off the kitchen, done in English chintz, has white-painted Victorian furniture and its own bath, but less privacy than two others on a lower level, where there's a second living room.

Breakfast is served at the kitchen's counter, and in the den bowls of popcorn and movies are enjoyed in the evening. Armed with a raft or a float, you can escape to the cool, shallow waters of the river; golfers can play at the nearby Green Hills course; and arrangements can be made for riding.

Address: *3581 S. Barnett Shoals Rd., Watkinsville, GA 30677, tel. 404/769-4522.*
Accommodations: *2 double rooms with baths, 3 doubles and 1 single share 2 baths; 1 suite.*
Amenities: *Air-conditioning, common TV/VCR, phones in rooms.*
Rates: *$45–$60; full breakfast. AE.*
Restrictions: *Smoking on porches only, no pets.*

Stoneleigh Bed and Breakfast

A distinctive Southern sensibility permeates the homey Stoneleigh Bed and Breakfast. This wood-and-stone Craftsman bungalow is in a quiet, shady neighborhood off a main street. Owner Jim Lay, a former Peace Corps volunteer and educator, was born and raised here, and he runs the charming place with an unerring flair for hospitable traditions.

Jim opened his home as a B&B in 1989 as a side interest after retiring from teaching. It's furnished with family heirlooms, like the pre–Civil War cannonball bed and ancestral photographs, mixed with finds, like a Russian canopy bed, that Jim collected during his travels. A hunt-style breakfast with cereal, grits, eggs, and toast is set up in a very organized manner: You sign up the night before for your time and breakfast choices and are served the following morning.

The manicured backyard garden (site of family weddings and reunions) is a delightful place for evening cocktails in mild weather.

Address: *316 Fain St., Calhoun, GA 30701, tel. 404/629–2093.*
Accommodations: *2 double rooms share 1 bath, 1 suite with fireplace.*
Amenities: *Air-conditioning, phone in den, dinner available on request.*
Rates: *$60; full breakfast. No credit cards.*
Restrictions: *Smoking on porch only, no pets.*

The York House

T his old inn nestles at the base of a mountain with the serene air of days gone by. The original log cabin is today a two-story structure with double porches built in an L shape around a towering stand of trees. It is listed on the National Register of Historic Places. Now owned by Jim and Phyllis Smith and run by resident managers, it has been an inn since 1896 and remains much as it was when it opened.

The modestly furnished common parlor becomes a gathering place in cool weather, when fires are burning; there's another fireplace in the lobby. Guest rooms are simply furnished with assorted antiques and vintage pieces and have small sitting areas where breakfasts are served on a silver tray each morning. Each room has a small but efficient bathroom, and most have balcony entrances. Stacks of current magazines and newspapers cover the tops of bureaus and chests on stairway landings. Breezes blowing down the mountain cool the house, and rocking chairs line both porches.

Address: *York House Rd., Box 126, Mountain City, GA 30562, tel. 404/746–2068.*
Accommodations: *12 double rooms with baths, 1 suite.*
Amenities: *TV and ceiling fans in rooms, fireplace in suite, guest phone; shuffleboard.*
Rates: *$55–$75; Continental breakfast. MC, V.*
Restrictions: *No smoking indoors, no pets, 2-night minimum in Oct. and on holiday weekends.*

Coastal Georgia

Sandy white beaches and saltwater marshes rim the state's 100 miles of coast, from the mouth of the Savannah River at the South Carolina border south to the St. Marys River. The barrier islands (called the Golden Isles) and mainland towns that dot this coastline attracted Colonial settlers and later became the winter retreats of Carnegies, Rockefellers, and Vanderbilts. All were lured, as visitors are today, by the balmy winters, the promise of escape on sun-drenched beaches, and calm afternoons spent drifting along winding tidal creeks. Along with these timeless pleasures come exciting Independence Day celebrations, rowdy beach music, wonderful seafood, and jazz and art festivals. The area's diverse pursuits and sunny climate combine to make it a year-round vacation spot.

Historic Savannah boasts a Colonial setting with cobble-stone squares and parks draped with Spanish moss. The city's River Street waterfront gift shops and jazz bars bustle with visiting crowds, and the annual St. Patrick's Day parade is one of the country's largest. Travelers seeking a more informal setting can continue south toward St. Simons Island for swimming, fishing, golf, and tennis.

Little of urban America is evident in these rural, coastal areas, but glimpses of the lavish lifestyle of the 19th-century rich and famous remain on Jekyll Island in Millionaire's Village, where stately Victorian and shingled manses rim the waterway compound. Cumberland Island National Seashore's protected forests and 16 miles of pristine white-sand beaches and dunes offer isolated serenity. Inland near the Georgia-Florida state line lies the 700-square-mile Okefenokee Swamp, whose black waters are dotted with water lilies and inhabited by alligators.

During the off-season, before Memorial Day and after Labor Day, the crowds leave these seashore communities,

*and the already remote beaches become virtually private
playgrounds. If you visit at this time of year, you discover
what locals already know: that the humid temperatures
and the insects leave with the crowds.*

Places to Go, Sights to See

Cumberland Island. A National Seashore, this barrier island is distinguished
by an undisturbed landscape. Accessible only by boat, the island is
a sanctuary for wild horses, deer, and bobcats. It is popular for day trips and
overnight camping, and the park service (tel. 912/882–4335) operates a ferry
service on a limited, reservations-only schedule.

Darien. The British *Ft. King George* (tel. 912/437–4770), 19th century houses
and historic churches (including the smallest one in America) are some of
what you'll see in Darien, Georgia's second-oldest planned town.

Hofwyl-Broadfield Plantation (Rte. 2, Darien, tel. 912/264–9263), established
in the early 1800s, was one of the few that functioned around the turn of the
20th century. Visitors can tour the 1858 plantation house and walk along the
canals that were used to flood the rice fields lining the riverbanks.

Jekyll Island (tel. 912/635–3636). Named for Sir Joseph Jekyll, the largest
contributor to Georgia's colonization, the island is reached from Brunswick
by causeway. It offers 63 holes of golf, 10 miles of Atlantic Ocean
beachfront, and a historic district that was a turn-of-the-century private
winter playground for the Rockefellers, Cranes, Pulitzers, and Vanderbilts.
Many of their brick, shingle, and tabby manses stand today as architectural
landmarks of a bygone era.

Little St. Simons Island is a private getaway resort, accessible by small
plane or by boat from St. Simons Island. The 12,000-acre island is even more
secluded than Cumberland, and if you plan to stay over, reservations must be
made well in advance (Box 1078, St. Simons Island, GA 31522, tel. 912/638–
7472).

Okefenokee Swamp Park (U.S. 1, tel. 912/283–0583). This wildlife sanctuary
8 miles south of Waycross is one of the country's most acclaimed wilderness
areas. Guided boat tours highlight the swamp's flora and fauna, and
a network of bridged walkways allows visitors to penetrate the park on foot.

St. Simons Island. This seashore haven, connected to the mainland by
a causeway, is the most developed of the Golden Isles. Its southern tip is
rimmed by white sand beaches and dotted with souvenir shops, gift
boutiques, and restaurants; a network of bike paths extends across the
marshlands into the center of the island. Historic sites established by early
settlers include *Ft. Frederica* (tel. 912/638–3639) and *St. Simons Lighthouse*
(tel. 912/638–4666).

Sapelo. After the Creek Indians, Spanish missionaries, British soldiers, and rice planters came tobacco magnate R. J. Reynolds, who bought this barrier island in the 1930s for his own agricultural projects. Today the island is a state-owned protected area, accessible only by boat, which operates as an institute for the study of marine life and marshland. The Department of Natural Resources (tel. 912/437–4192) conducts tours three days each week.

Savannah. *The Green-Meldrim House* (1 West Macon St., tel. 912/232–1251), a Gothic Revival mansion with wraparound wrought-iron balconies, was built in 1850 for cotton merchant Charles Green. General Sherman stayed here during his occupation of Savannah; it was later occupied by a Judge Peter Meldrim, and is now the parish house of St. John's Episcopal Church. The house, in its original condition, is furnished with period antiques (some original to the house) and is open for tours. The *Owens-Thomas House* (124 Abercorn St., tel. 912/233–9743), built in 1817, was architect William Jay's first regency mansion in Savannah and is still the city's finest example of that style. In 1825 the Marquis de Lafayette bade Savannah goodbye from the house's wrought-iron balcony. Daily tours highlight its architectural details and priceless antique furnishings.

Tybee Island, east of Savannah on Victory Drive (U.S. 80), is a popular seashore escape for Savannah residents; seafood restaurants, shops, and summer cottages dot the island.

Restaurants

The Fourth of May (tel. 912/638–5444) on St. Simons Island and Savannah's **45 South** (tel. 912/354–0444) offer gourmet regional cuisine in cozy, contemporary settings. The **Crab Trap** (tel. 912/638–3552), a casual spot on St. Simons, serves fried and broiled seafood entrées caught locally. In Savannah's historic district, **Mrs. Wilkes Boarding House** (tel. 912/232–5997) serves Southern breakfasts and lunches in an appealing elbow-to-elbow family-style setting, while **Bobbie's** (tel. 912/238–2443), a vintage diner, offers burgers and fries. **Speeds Kitchen** (tel. 912/832–4643), amid the odd collection of house trailers and shingled buildings in Shellman's Bluff outside Darien, is considered by many locals to have the area's best fried seafood.

Tourist Information

Jekyll Island Convention and Visitors Bureau (901 Jekyll Island Causeway, Jekyll Island, GA 31520, tel. 912/635–3636). **St. Simons Chamber of Commerce** (Neptune Park, St. Simons Island, GA 31522, tel. 912/638–9014). **Savannah Visitors Center** (301 W. Broad St., Savannah, GA 31499, tel. 912/944–0455).

Reservation Services

Savannah Historic Inns (147 Bull St., Savannah, GA 31401, tel. 912/233–7660 or 800/262–4667).

The Gastonian

Two blocks from Forsyth Park in Savannah's historic district stands The Gastonian. The pineapple, symbol of hospitality, engraved on the brass sign outside hints at the congenial comforts within. Flame stitch-upholstered wing chairs on either side of the drawing room fireplace confirm them.

The inn comprises two adjacent Regency Italianate mansions beautifully restored by owners Hugh and Roberta Lineberger. After falling in love with Savannah on a first-time visit, they were inspired to sell their California home and head south, buying the buildings (then private homes) in 1985. The move seems to have been a good one, and The Gastonian is Savannah's only real owner-run inn.

Roberta Lineberger decorated the interiors with authentic 1800s Savannah colors and antiques. In the front parlor and formal dining rooms, fine 18th-century American and English furniture glows with the patina of much polishing. Both rooms are trimmed with wall coverings from Scalamandré's Savannah collection. Sideboards and tabletops are laden with heirloom crystal, silver, and fine china. The elegant, subdued, but unstuffy atmosphere of the reception rooms downstairs extends to the guest rooms. Each spacious bedroom has a 12-foot ceiling and contains a grouping of period furnishings, a working gas fireplace, and individ-

ually controlled heat and air-conditioning. The rooms are adjoined by well-lit private baths. The evening turndown service includes Savannah sweets and cordials placed by each bedside.

The Linebergers do all the cooking, and hot breakfasts are served at tables arranged intimately before the fireplace in a light-filled yellow room. If you like to move slowly in the morning, you can opt for a Continental breakfast served in your room with a complimentary newspaper of your choice. Guests gather for afternoon tea in the front parlor to talk about the day's sightseeing and to glean touring tips from the amiable desk clerk.

A wooden walkway across the back garden courtyard connects the inn to a carriage house suite with a private deck, kitchen, and bath done in Chinese red. An elevated sun deck has chaise longues, a vine-draped pergola, and a hot tub.

Address: *220 E. Gaston St., Savannah, GA 31401, tel. 912/232–2869, fax 912/234–0006.*
Accommodations: *10 double rooms with baths, 3 suites.*
Amenities: *Cable TV, gas fireplaces in bedrooms; off-street parking, sun deck with hot tub.*
Rates: *$98–$165, suites $150–$225; full breakfast, afternoon tea. AE, MC, V.*
Restrictions: *No smoking, no pets.*

Greyfield Inn

The only hotel on Cumberland Island, accessible only by ferry, boat, or private plane, Greyfield Inn is a symbol of civility in the wilds. The turn-of-the-century house stands by itself in the primitive landscape, its wide colonnade porches inviting all to step in and stay.

Built in 1901 by tycoon Thomas Carnegie for his daughter, the two-story Victorian house retains much of its original glory. The inn is operated by Mitty Ferguson, great-great-grandson of Thomas Carnegie, and his wife, Mary Jo, who carefully preserve the structure's ties to the past. They furnished the inn as if it were still a private residence; it is filled with an inviting mix of dark, heavy heirloom furniture, family photographs, tabletop collections of seashore memorabilia, and antique rugs. The formal dining room is typically decorated with freshly cut greenery—vines and berries collected on the island.

The inn's enthusiastic staff is dedicated to making guests feel comfortable. The nine bedrooms are spacious, the linens crisp, and the hardwood floors burnished to a glossy shine. The spit-and-polished shared bathrooms have three tubs, and there's an enclosed backyard shower house that is another full bath.

The best times to visit are in spring and early autumn, when the insect population and level of humidity remain low. In the winter, guests can go on beach excursions and guided jeep tours of the island's historic ruins.

All meals are included in the rates. Breakfasts are informal affairs of baked apples, ginger flapjacks, sausages or bacon, and coffee. Hors d'oeuvres are served at the cocktail hour, and afternoon tea is a winter ritual. The ring of a bell announces the evening meal, which often includes tasty soups, pasta and shrimp dishes, and always wonderful desserts. The staff's tradition of dressing for dinner transforms the nightly ritual into a festive occasion.

Greyfield's atmosphere is relaxed. Lunches are packed and left in the old-fashioned kitchen. The Fergusons are happy to let you follow your own agenda or they'll help plan a day's activities.

Address: *Cumberland Island, GA (Drawer B, Fernandina Beach, FL 32034, tel. 904/261-6408).*
Accommodations: *1 double room with bath, 7 doubles and 1 suite share 3 baths; outdoor shower house.*
Amenities: *Air-conditioning in dining room; shuttle to ferry, bike rentals, guided tours.*
Rates: *$190–$210; American Plan. MC, V.*
Restrictions: *No smoking indoors, no pets.*

Open Gates

A brick-and-white-picket fence outlines the perimeter of Open Gates bed-and-breakfast, the home of Carolyn and Philip Hodges. The white frame house with blue shutters, built in 1876, is tucked beneath a canopy of Spanish moss cascading from live oaks on the corner of Vernon Square, a National Historic District. It is three blocks from the river, historic Darien's major thoroughfare.

Founded in 1736, the town was a shipping center for cotton and a busy lumber port. It is now a jumping-off point for boat tours to Sapelo (a nearby barrier island), a shrimping port, and a center of domestic caviar production. It was recently profiled in the nonfiction bestseller *Praying for Sheetrock*, by Melissa Fay Green.

Carolyn Hodges, an avid preservationist and nature lover, eagerly shares her knowledge with interested visitors. She pulls a vintage fishing boat behind her vintage car for the bird-watching expeditions she conducts. Philip is a professional philatelist.

In a sunny den, a game table is set for chess or backgammon, and shelves are filled with books on coastal history, including the diary of the English actress Fanny Kemble, who recorded her controversial stand against slavery while living in the area briefly. One guest bedroom, in robin's-egg blue, has a sleigh bed and a display of old doll clothes and children's books; another, done in peach and blue, has twin beds; and an upstairs room painted dark green has wood floors and framed botanical illustrations. A room above the garage with a private entrance has natural wood walls adorned with antique quilts.

A canoe standing on the back porch, the aquarium gurgling away in the den, and the baby grand, family portraits, and photographs in the deep-orange front parlor remind you that this is a family's home.

Address: *Vernon Sq. (Box 1526), Darien, GA 31305, tel. 912/437–6985.*
Accommodations: *2 double rooms with baths, 2 double rooms share 1 bath.*
Amenities: *Air-conditioning, TV in common area; pool.*
Rates: *$40–$53; full breakfast. No credit cards.*
Restrictions: *No smoking indoors.*

Ballastone Inn

This handsome stucco inn was originally built for a well-to-do Savannah shipping magnate, later became the residence of a bank president, and today is run by innkeeper Timothy Hargus. Its central location along Savannah's Oglethorpe Avenue in the historic district puts you on the main bus line, a quick walk from the Civic Center and other points of interest. It also makes the first-floor guest rooms a bit noisy.

The Ballastone has Old World flair. It's similar to The Gastonian but not as lavish; the linens are not as fine and the guest rooms are smaller. Though many of the rooms have tall canopy beds, the bathrooms have linoleum floors and plastic shower curtains.

Tea is served in the genteelly elegant public rooms, which are done with authentic Savannah color schemes and period antiques. Evening nightcaps are mixed at a full-service bar along the back wall in the double parlor, where breakfast is set out each morning.

Address: *14 E. Oglethorpe Ave., Savannah, GA 31401, tel. 912/236–1484 or 800/822-4553.*
Accommodations: *17 double rooms with baths, 3 suites.*
Amenities: *Air-conditioning, cable TV/VCRs in rooms, fireplaces in 9 rooms and suites, elevator; off-street parking.*
Rates: *$95–$145, suites $175; Continental breakfast, afternoon tea. AE, MC, V.*
Restrictions: *No pets.*

Brunswick Manor

The ticktock of an antique clock resounds through the handsomely renovated interior of Brunswick Manor, a stately Victorian in the historic district. Claudia and Harry Tzucanow, whose enthusiasm for sailing brought them to the Georgia coast, opened the inn in 1989.

In a setting of oak trees, with generous porches and antique-filled interiors, the house lets visitors sample an aristocratic lifestyle. The furnishings complement the ornate oak staircase, high ceilings, and beveled glass mirrors of the 1886 house. Deluxe frills are the trademark of this bed-and-breakfast: plush bathrobes and fresh flowers in each room, and at extra cost, a chauffeured Jaguar limousine and sailing aboard a 51-foot ketch.

The sleeping quarters are typically Southern, with ornate antique bedsteads, bureaus, and decorations, and the suite has a small kitchen. A simply decorated efficiency housekeeping cottage that sleeps four is ideal for groups traveling together.

Address: *825 Egmont St., Brunswick, GA 31520, tel. 912/265–6889.*
Accommodations: *3 double rooms with baths, 1 housekeeping suite, 1 cottage.*
Amenities: *Air-conditioning, phone in common area; airport transportation available, bicycles.*
Rates: *$80–$85; cottage $70; full breakfast. No credit cards.*
Restrictions: *No smoking indoors, no pets in main house.*

Magnolia Place Inn

After passing through the front yard gate, you climb steep steps softly carpeted with fern to reach Magnolia Place. Striking two-story verandas wrap around the front of this 1878 Savannah house, where poet Conrad Aiken was born. There's a sophisticated elegance to the well-proportioned house, but inside you find that the front parlor has been sacrificed for bedrooms, giving the inn a claustrophobic feeling. The rose-toned back parlor, furnished in Colonial style (except for the glow of a clock radio), is the only reception room.

Though the guest rooms aren't as well decorated as in the other historic houses, there's a mixture of old and new, with canopy beds, Oriental rugs, and in 11 rooms fireplaces and in six, whirlpool baths. Breakfast is served Southern style on fine china either in the parlor, in the garden, or on the veranda.

What the Magnolia lacks in ambience it makes up for in its unbeatable location, overlooking the lush landscaping of Forsyth Park.

Address: *503 Whitaker St., Savannah, GA 31401, tel. 912/236-7674 or 800/238-7674.*
Accommodations: *13 double rooms with baths.*
Amenities: *Air-conditioning, phones, cable TV/VCR in rooms; off-street parking, garden hot tub.*
Rates: *$85–$185; Continental breakfast. AE, MC, V.*
Restrictions: *No pets; closed mid-Jan.–mid-Feb.*

Olde Harbour Inn

The Olde Harbour Inn, in a converted three-story warehouse, has been open since 1987 under the direction of innkeeper Pamela Barnes. It offers prime access to the many gift shops, restaurants, and bars lining the city's popular River Street district.

The inn's white-on-white interiors may lack the flavor of the historic mansions, but they do have a clean, crisp appeal and contemporary conveniences: Each bedroom is carpeted and has a fully equipped kitchen.

You can reserve a studio unit, a two-room suite, or a deluxe suite on the fourth floor, with a sleeping loft overlooking two entertaining rooms. Some units have a spacious riverfront balcony. Light breakfasts are served in the downstairs sitting rooms, where wine, cordials, and cheese are set out in the late afternoon.

Address: *508 E. Factors Walk, Savannah, GA 31401, tel. 912/234-4100 or 800/553-6533, fax 912/233-5979.*
Accommodations: *24 units with baths.*
Amenities: *Cable TV, concierge service; off-street parking.*
Rates: *$79–$135; Continental breakfast, afternoon wine and cheese. AE, D, DC, MC, V.*
Restrictions: *Smoking in guest rooms only, no pets.*

Pulaski Square Inn

Designed in 1853 by the Colonial architect William Jay, the Pulaski Square Inn retains the grandeur of the city's early days. The stucco building four blocks from Savannah's Civic Center stands as one of the city's finest examples of town-house architecture. Johnny B. and Hilda Smith, the current proprietors of the inn, are, according to available records, only the third owners of the house, which they opened as a bed-and-breakfast in 1984.

The entire inn is beautifully restored and finished with the finest touches, from the polished heart-of-pine floors and period antiques to the Oriental rugs on the bathroom floors and the gold-plated fixtures. Chandeliers hang from 11-foot ceilings illuminating the inn's bedrooms. Each floor has a separate living room, and the main-floor parlor can be rented with an adjacent bedroom as a suite. Beyond the garden courtyard is a carriage house that's a two-bedroom suite with a Japanese-style tiled bath.

Address: *203 W. Charlton St., Savannah, GA 31401, tel. 912/232–8055 or 800/227–0650.*
Accommodations: *5 double rooms with baths, 2 doubles share 1 bath; 1 suite; carriage house.*
Amenities: *Air-conditioning, phones, cable TV in rooms, elevator; off-street parking.*
Rates: *$48–$88, suites $75–$196; Continental breakfast. AE, MC, V.*
Restrictions: *Smoking in guest rooms only.*

Rose Manor Guest House

Hanover Square in Old Town Brunswick is an appropriate setting for the old-fashioned charm of Rose Manor. A steeply pitched tin roof shades the white-columned porch of this pale pink 'bungalow, where Rachel Rose converted the entire downstairs of her family's circa-1885 home into guest quarters. She and her family reside on the second floor.

Rachel's love of old textiles and floral prints shines through in Rose Manor's comfort and its nostalgic decor. Pastel-toned, small, but comfortable guest rooms are equipped with designer sheets, layered with heirloom linens, and furnished with cushy upholstered sofas and antique bedsteads. The bathrooms have claw-foot tubs and tiled showers.

Afternoon tea is served in the parlor or garden, and later, sherry, fresh fruit, and tea are set out on the porch so you can watch the sun set across the marsh.

Address: *Hanover Sq., 1108 Richmond St., Brunswick, GA 31520, tel. 912/267–6369.*
Accommodations: *4 double rooms share 3 baths.*
Amenities: *TV and phones in rooms; croquet, badminton.*
Rates: *$45–$85; full breakfast, afternoon tea, sherry. No credit cards.*
Restrictions: *Smoking only on porches and in sun room, no pets.*

Middle Georgia

*When Margaret Mitchell modeled Tara and its
surroundings in* Gone with the Wind *on the Jonesboro part
of Clayton County, she immortalized this area of Georgia.
The landscape here has remained relatively undisturbed
since the days when cotton was king; you can still drive for
hours through flat fields planted in rows as far as the eye
can see. Except for the occasional man-made shape of
a town, barn, or house, you see nothing but soybeans,
tobacco, tomatoes, corn, peanuts, cotton, and the famous
Vidalia onions stretching across the horizon. The daily
rhythm of the area's rural life has also surfaced in other
works by native writers: the colorful Uncle Remus tales, by
Joel Chandler Harris, and* The Color Purple *and other
books by Alice Walker.*

*The restored antebellum estates, Federal-era plantation
houses, and Victorian bungalows that dot the urban and
rural landscapes are reminders of the area's early settlers
and their history. Well-marked driving trails bearing
names like Peach Blossom and Antebellum take you
through thriving historic towns filled with homes of
architectural distinction and then past lushly landscaped
gardens. In Macon (once the Queen City of the South),
crowds gather annually for the cherry blossom festival and
to visit Jarrell Plantation, a working farm outside town.
The beauty of Madison, a "cultural and aristocratic town,"
is said to have protected it from destruction by General
Sherman on his march to the sea. Augusta, the state's
second-oldest city, is called the Garden City of the South.
A remote trading outpost during frontier times, it is now
the center of much activity. In addition to the thriving new
Riverwalk complex, there are six historic districts in which
attractions abound. Of particular interest are Oldetown,
one of the largest neighborhoods of Victorian homes in the
state, and Summerville, known as "the Hill," a summer
retreat built by John D. Rockefeller.*

Places to Go, Sights to See

Ashley Oaks (144 College St., Jonesboro, tel. 404/478–8986). Built between 1879 and 1880, this Jonesboro mansion remains the town's most elegant residence. It is renovated, furnished with period pieces, and open for tours by appointment.

Augusta. A new five-block complex on the Savannah River, with shops, restaurants, entertainment, and *The Shoppes of Port Royal* shopping center, is part of the city's newly revitalized center. Antiques stores line *Broad Street* in the walkable historic district. Augusta has the state's second-oldest opera, a symphony, and a ballet company, all of which perform in the gilded Romanesque-style *Sacred Heart Cultural Center* (tel. 404/826–4700).

Callaway Plantation (U.S. 78, 5 mi west of Washington, tel. 404/678–7060). This 56-acre working farm outside Washington has been under the control of the same family since the late 18th century and today is an example of the way the area's early settlers lived. Tour a ca.-1869 Greek Revival house, a log cabin, and a two-story Plain-style house, open daily March–December.

Hawkinsville Historic Opera House (100 N. Lumpkin St., tel. 912/783–1717). The original turn-of-the-century glamour of this elaborately decorated performance hall has been restored, and cultural events, concerts, and plays are presented here once more.

Macon, incorporated in 1823, has three National Historic Districts, with large garden squares and wide streets lined with Greek Revival mansions and Victorian bungalows. *Pleasant Hills Historic District,* one of the first black neighborhoods on the National Register of Historic Places, and the *Harriet Tubman Museum* (340 Walnut St., tel. 912/743–8544) are dedicated to the preservation of black history. The *Ocmulgee National Monument* (1207 Emery Hwy., tel. 912/752–8257) commemorates 12,000 years of Southeast Indian culture with a museum, a film, and exhibits from the excavated Indian mounds. *Hay House* (934 Georgia Ave., tel. 912/742–8155), a spectacular 24-room Italian Renaissance Revival mansion (1855–1860), was built with an elevator, a secret room, and an early ventilating system. Today it is filled with the art and antiques collections of the Georgia Trust for Historic Preservation. *Woodruff House* (988 Bond St., tel. 912/744–4187) is a Greek Revival mansion built in 1863, owned and operated by Mercer University. It was the scene of a ball for Winnie Davis, daughter of Confederate President Jefferson Davis. The *Jarrell Plantation* (Rte. 1, Juliette, tel. 912/986–5172) outside Macon consists of 20 historic buildings dating between 1847 and 1940, including a three-story barn, a bee-keeping house, a gristmill, a cane mill, smokehouses, and an extensive collection of domestic artifacts of the period.

Madison is often called "the town Sherman refused to burn" on his march to the sea. Stringent restoration codes have preserved its architectural heritage, and the Federal and Victorian mansions, churches, and public buildings make it the state's antebellum showcase.

Massee Lane Gardens (tel. 912/967–2358), outside Fort Valley, is the home of the American Camellia Society. The 9 acres of gardens are in full bloom from November to March; azaleas, banksia roses, daylilies, and other bulbs take their turn in season.

At the **Monastery of the Holy Spirit** (2625 Rte. 212, 8 mi southwest of Conyers, tel. 404/483–8705), the grounds offer a pastoral spot for picnics and contain a greenhouse where bonsai trees are sold and a gift shop that sells baked goods.

Museum of Aviation at Robins Air Force Base (7 mi from I–75, at Exit 58, tel. 912/923–6600). This collection on 43 acres outside Perry contains more than 70 historic airplanes, an original Norden bombsight, and an SR–71 Blackbird spy plane.

Panola Mountain State Conservation Park (2600 Rte. 155SW, Stockridge, tel. 404/389–7801), in Henry County, has hiking trails, picnic areas, covered shelters, and playgrounds.

Robert Toombs House (216 E. Robert Toombs Ave., Washington, tel. 404/678–2226). This completely restored house in downtown Washington was built in 1794. Once the home of Confederate General Robert Toombs, secretary of the Confederacy, it is now a state park, whose exhibits tell the story of the fiery planter and lawyer.

Washington Historical Museum (308 E. Robert Toombs Ave., Washington, tel. 404/678–2105). Elegant antebellum furnishings, Civil War mementos, and an Indian collection are on display in this historic house.

Restaurants

Another Thyme (tel. 404/678–1672), in Washington's historic Fitzpatrick Hotel, serves Continental breakfasts, lunch, and dinner. **Beall's 1860** (tel. 912/745–3663), a columned mansion in a historic district in Macon, serves prime rib and daily specials at lunch and dinner. Hawkinsville's **Black Swan Restaurant,** in the Black Swan Inn (tel. 912/783–4466), serves entrées like veal marsala, grilled swordfish, and peach-glazed chicken. **Ed's Steakhouse** (tel. 912/892–3383), in Hawkinsville, is open for lunch and dinner, with beef, chicken, and seafood entrées. **Fincher's Barbecue,** with two Macon locations (tel. 912/743–5866 and 912/742–2220), has been serving pit-cooked pork, ribs, chicken, and Brunswick stew for 50 years. **Len Berg's** (tel. 912/742–9255), in Macon, serves fresh vegetables, fried oysters, macaroon pie, and other Southern delights. **The Raines Room** (tel. 912/489–8628), in the Statesboro Inn, serves Continental cuisine Tuesday through Saturday nights.

Tourist Information

Clayton County Convention & Visitors Bureau (8712 Tara Blvd., Jonesboro, GA 30237, tel. 404/478–4800). **Macon-Bibb County Convention and Visitors Bureau** (Terminal Station, 300 Cherry St., Macon, GA 31201, tel. 912/743–3401). **Madison-Morgan County Chamber of Commerce** (Box 826, Madison, GA 30650, tel. 404/342–4454). **Monroe County Chamber of Commerce** (Box 811, Forsyth, GA 31029, tel. 912/994–9239). **Peach County Chamber of Commerce** (Box 1238, Fort Valley, GA 31030, tel. 912/825–3733). **Perry Area Convention & Visitors Bureau** (Box 1619, Perry, GA 31069, tel. 912/988–8000). **Washington-Wilkes Chamber of Commerce** (104 E. Liberty St., Box 661, Washington, GA 30673, tel. 404/678–2013).

The 1842 Inn

This imposing Greek Revival mansion stands in the heart of Macon's historic neighborhood, a few blocks from Mercer University, a five-minute drive from downtown, and practically next door to the acclaimed Beall's 1860 restaurant.

The medium-size inn, named for the year its oldest portion was built, was enlarged around the turn of the century, has been professionally restored, and has earned many preservation awards. It was bought in late 1991 by Philip Jenkins, a Georgia native and fund-raising consultant, and his silent partner Richard Meils, a Michigan physician. Philip or one of the friendly staff members will show you to a spacious, well-appointed guest room in the main house or in the Victorian cottage, which was saved from demolition by being cut in half, moved to the property, and installed in back, past the brick courtyard.

The white-pillared front porch opens to the traditional center hall found in many Southern houses. Cream-colored bedrooms with overhead ceiling-fan lamps have brass or four-poster beds made up with eyelet-trimmed linens, and small dining areas where breakfast is served along with the morning paper. There are fresh flowers in the rooms, evening turndown service with chocolates, overnight shoe shining, and cocktails at any hour in the library.

Six of the rooms have working fireplaces, and four have whirlpool baths.

High tea is served on the grand porch each Saturday and Sunday afternoon when weather permits, and the end of each week is celebrated at a cocktail hour with live jazz on Thursday and Friday.

Address: *353 College St., Macon, GA 31201, tel. and fax 912/741–1842 or 800/336–1842.*
Accommodations: *12 double rooms with baths in house, 9 cottage rooms with baths.*
Amenities: *Air-conditioning, phones, cable TV, ceiling fans in rooms.*
Rates: *$65–$95; Continental breakfast and hors d'oeuvres. AE, MC, V.*
Restrictions: *No pets.*

The Black Swan Inn

This Greek Revival house in Hawkinsville, outside Macon, was named for the steamboat that used to take produce and cotton downriver to Savannah. The town is the state's harness-racing capital, and during the season, the inn is filled by the horse-racing crowd.

Built in the early 1900s, the house was a private residence until 1990, when corporate investors converted it into a fine inn. You will be surprised by its deluxe accommodations. Under manager William Pace, the inn stays beautifully maintained, with everything inside—from the hardwood floors to the four-poster beds—polished and shining. The decor is simple and pretty in an authentic, old-fashioned Victorian style that makes many other inns in the area seem contrived. The bedrooms are the epitome of comfort, with high ceilings, period furnishings, ceiling fans, and access to wide porches set with hanging swings. One of the rooms has a whirlpool bath. The large dining room doubles as a restaurant except Sunday.

Address: *411 Progress Ave., Hawkinsville, GA 31036, tel. 912/783-4466.*
Accommodations: *6 double rooms with baths.*
Amenities: *Restaurant, air-conditioning, cable TV and phones in rooms.*
Rates: *$55–$70; Continental breakfast. AE, DC, MC, V.*
Restrictions: *No pets.*

The Brady Inn

The Brady Inn sits on a velvet lawn in the heart of Madison's historic district, near antebellum mansions and historic churches.

The clapboard Victorian inn with its deep rocking-chair porches consists of two connected turn-of-the-century bungalows. The owners, Chris and Lynn Rasch, left New England in the late 1970s, bought the two houses, and built a walkway to connect them. All the guest rooms have adjoining baths, and some rooms boast hand-stenciled ceiling borders.

The Rasches' background as restaurant owners contributes to their success as resident innkeepers. They skillfully prepare individual breakfasts according to orders placed the night before. Despite a busy schedule catering weddings and luncheons, they serve guests and the public lunch or dinner with advance notice.

In the cozy family atmosphere, you'll see the Rasches' cat and dog around the house, and congregate with others by the parlor television.

Address: *250 N. 2nd St., Madison, GA 30650, tel. 404/342-4400.*
Accommodations: *5 double rooms with baths, 1 double suite with 2 baths.*
Amenities: *Restaurant, air-conditioning, refrigerator and TV in suite, telephone and TV in common room.*
Rates: *$45–$70, suite $100; full breakfast. MC, V.*
Restrictions: *No pets, closed late Dec.*

Statesboro Inn

This large cream-colored Neoclassical frame house with shaded verandas was built in 1903. In 1981 after a year's renovation, it was turned into a bed-and-breakfast equipped with luxuries as modern as whirlpool baths and as old-fashioned as front-porch rockers. New owners John and Valerie Tulip and their daughter Claudine took over in 1991 and have enlarged the place.

The guest rooms have sophisticated country charm, with brass beds and love seats; some rooms have private porches or working fireplaces. In a restored cabin behind the house Blind Willie McTell wrote the Greg Allman hit "Statesboro Blues."

Chef Tom Williams takes command in the kitchen, turning out elaborate breakfasts, as well as the dinners served in their restaurant, the Raines Room. Claudine presides in the kitchen at lunch.

Address: *106 S. Main St., Statesboro, GA 30458, tel. 912/489–8628.*
Accommodations: *14 double rooms with baths, 2 suites.*
Amenities: *Restaurant; airconditioning, cable TV, phones in rooms; large banquet hall, 5 meeting rooms, off-street parking.*
Rates: *$49–$72, suites $80–$90; full breakfast. AE, DC, MC, V.*
Restrictions: *No pets.*

Victorian Village

This complex of four restored Victorian houses, though convenient to Macon's downtown, faces a borderline inner-city neighborhood and fast-food restaurants just off an I–75 exit. Despite these drawbacks, you will be surprised by the decor and friendly staff.

Turrets, gazebos, and wraparound porches give each house a Victorian fantasy appearance that is repeated inside with decorative accents like floral balloon shades, tasseled lamps, dark paneling, and heavy moldings. Bedrooms furnished with antiques also offer whirlpool baths. The third-floor Hardeman Suite boasts a stained-glass window and cupola windowseat overlooking a garden. Covered breezeways between the houses connect brick patios.

Breakfast is served in the main building, Hardeman House, and the first floor of another house is a public restaurant.

Address: *1841 Hardeman Ave., Macon, GA 31201, tel. 912/743–3333 or 800/832–0641.*
Accommodations: *22 double rooms with baths, 3 double suites, Hardeman Suite.*
Amenities: *Restaurant, airconditioning, whirlpool baths, cable TV, and phones in rooms; complimentary newspapers.*
Rates: *$85, Hardeman Suite $125; Continental breakfast, sherry or wine on arrival. AE, MC, V.*
Restrictions: *No smoking in Hardeman House, no pets.*

The Southwest Corner

*Though it's steeped in Civil War history, landscaped with
lush gardens, and rich in plantation lore, this corner of
Georgia is frequently overlooked. A hundred years ago,
however, the southwest's low-key charm developed
a following among the celebrated and wealthy, and the area
is associated with two American presidents. Franklin D.
Roosevelt's Little White House in Warm Springs, the only
home he ever owned, is now a museum, preserved as it was
on the day he died there. And when a peanut farmer from
Plains named Jimmy Carter was elected president, the
small town west of Americus became instantly famous.*

*Columbus, on the Chattahoochee River, the region's largest
city, is surrounded by the huge Fort Benning Military
Reservation. It was the home of John Pemberton, the
inventor of Coca-Cola, and is the site of the PGA Southern
Open Golf Tournament. North of Columbus, in the
Appalachian foothills, are Franklin D. Roosevelt State
Park and Callaway Gardens, a resort development on
14,000 acres comprising woodlands, lakes, gardens, and
wildlife that's the center of the spring Azalea Festival and
an annual November steeplechase.*

*Near the Florida border lies Thomasville, a town of
architectural grandeur, where the turn-of-the-century elite
built hunting lodges and plantations and spent the winters
entertaining. Many of the sporting retreats are still
occupied, and a few are open to the public.*

*In addition to touring landmark houses in town after
town, you can visit outlet shops; go camping, hunting, and
whitewater rafting; and try some of Georgia's famous
Alberta peaches. At the Andersonville National Historic
Site, Civil War buffs can delve into the past.*

Places to Go, Sights to See

Andersonville National Historic Site (Rte. 49, 10 mi north of Americus, tel. 912/924–0343). In 14 months between 1864 and 1865, 13,000 Union prisoners died in the Confederate prison on this site. The reconstructed portion of the stockade is open for tours and the museum chronicles prisoners of war in all the American conflicts from the Revolution to Vietnam. A nearby village comprises a log church, prison officials' quarters, a pioneer farm, and crafts and antiques stores.

Bellevue (204 Ben Hill St., LaGrange, tel. 404/884–1832). This Greek Revival house, famous for its Ionic columns, portico, and upstairs balcony, was built in the early 1850s.

Callaway Gardens (U.S. 27, Pine Mountain, tel. 404/663–2281 or 800/282–8181). Spread across 14,000 acres of woodlands, lakes, and gardens near LaGrange, this family resort has four golf courses, soft and hard tennis courts, swimming, sailing, quail hunting, and the Cecil B. Day Butterfly Center (tel. 404/663–5102).

The **Chattahoochee Valley Art Association** (112 Hines St., tel. 404/882–3267), in a restored Victorian house in LaGrange, displays a permanent collection of regional and local artists' works Tuesday through Sunday and puts on special monthly exhibits.

Columbus may have more museums than any other Georgia town. It also boasts a downtown historic district with well-preserved residential and commercial buildings that you can see on a walking tour. At the *Columbus Museum* (1251 Wynton Rd., tel. 404/322–0400), a multimillion-dollar expansion completed in 1989 houses an outstanding regional history section, a fine arts area, and a hands-on exhibit for children. The museum also has an excellent folk art collection. The *Confederate Naval Museum*, on the riverfront (202 4th St., Columbus, tel. 404/327–9798), contains the remains of two Confederate warships, the *Muscogee* and the *Chattahoochee*.

Cordele. This small town established in 1888 by the Americus Investment Company grew from the junction of two railroads and was the state capital during the final stage of the Civil War. The Chamber of Commerce runs walking tours of the turn-of-the-century downtown, which is on the National Register.

The **Fort Benning National Infantry Museum** (Baltzell Ave., Fort Benning Reservation, tel. 404/545–2958) traces the evolution of the infantry from the French and Indian War to the present.

Jimmy Carter National Historic Site (Main St., Plains, tel. 912/824–3413). The 39th president's first campaign headquarters, in his hometown, houses a museum, informative collections of pictures, and memorabilia from his boyhood.

Little White House (Rte. 85W and U.S. 27A, Warm Springs, tel. 404/655–3511). Franklin D. Roosevelt, afflicted with infantile paralysis, built this small house in Warm Springs as a vacation retreat during the early 1900s, so he could be near the beneficial waters. Open daily for tours.

Male Academy Museum (30 Temple Ave., tel. 404/251–0207). A restored 1883 schoolhouse in Newnan interprets Coweta County's history through education, industry, architecture, and costume, from Indian days through the late 19th century. Civil War and *Gone With the Wind* collections are displayed with rotating exhibits.

Providence Canyon (30 mi south of Columbus, tel. 912/838–6202), a natural wonder of spectacular color and shape, was formed entirely by rainwater erosion. There's an interpretive center, picnic areas, and hiking trails.

Senoia. You can pick up a pamphlet at city hall or the town library that outlines a driving tour around the National Historic District to see 24 houses that date from antebellum days through the late 19th century.

Thomasville. This storybook town in a scenic setting was a booming winter resort during the late 19th and early 20th centuries. The rich and famous invested in its development by buying acreage and building mansions. Today, 71 plantations still stand (on 300,000 acres), many still owned by original-family descendants. One of them, the *Lapham-Patterson House* (626 N. Dawson St., tel. 912/225–4004), a landmarked Queen Anne 20-room cottage, is an architectural tour de force without a single right angle. It is open for tours, as is *Pebble Hill Plantation* (U.S. 319S, tel. 912/226–2344), a former hunting retreat. Memorabilia from the 1800s is displayed in the *Thomas County Museum* (725 N. Dawson St., tel. 912/226–7664).

Trebor Plantation (Macon Rd., Andersonville, tel. 912/924–6887). In the 1840s, one of Sumter County's earliest settlers built this white frame house with double galleries, home to the same family for five generations. It is nicely restored, has furnishings of the period, with a few original pieces, and is open for tours.

Westville (S. Mulberry St., tel. 912/838–6310). This living history museum south of Lumpkin town square depicts 19th-century Georgia life with its authentically restored buildings and daily crafts demonstrations.

Restaurants

Blue Willow Café (tel. 404/655–2195) in Warm Springs serves home-style southern entrées. **Daphne Lodge** (tel. 912/273–2596), nestled in a pine grove setting near Lake Blackshear outside Cordele, is renowned for catfish, seafood, steaks, and melt-in-your-mouth biscuits. The cafeteria-style **Deutsche House** (tel. 912/472–2024) outside Montezuma is famous for its authentic Mennonite cuisine and the adjacent bakery. A rambling Victorian building furnished with period antiques in LaGrange houses **In Clover** (tel. 404/882–0883), a Continental restaurant. Dine American style at **J. Henry's** (tel.

404/228–1762) outside Griffin in a turn-of-the-century mill. **Old Courthouse Square Restaurant** (tel. 912/924–2481) in Americus offers old-fashioned Southern hospitality and live entertainment each evening. **Robin's** (tel. 912/924–4258) in Americus serves home-cooked vegetables, sandwiches, and salads. Barbecued pork is the specialty at **Sheppard House** (tel. 912/924–8756) in Americus.

Tourist Information

Albany Local Welcome Center (225 W. Broad St., Albany, GA 31701, tel. 912/434–8700). **Americus–Sumter County Chamber of Commerce** (Box 724, Americus, GA 31709, tel. 912/924–2646). **Andersonville Local Welcome Center** (Old Railroad Depot, Andersonville, GA 31711, tel. 912/924–2558). **Columbus Convention & Visitors Bureau** (Box 2768, Columbus, GA 31902, tel. 404/322–1613). **Newnan-Coweta Chamber of Commerce** (Box 1103, 23 Bullsboro Dr., Newnan, GA 30264, tel. 404/253–2270). **Plains Visitors Information Center** (U.S. 280, Plains, GA 31780, tel. 912/824–7477). **Thomasville–Thomas County Local Welcome Center** (401 S. Broad St., Thomasville, GA 31792, tel. 912/226–9600).

Reservation Service

Quail Country Bed and Breakfast, Ltd. (1104 Old Monticello Rd., Thomasville, GA 31792, tel. 912/226–7218).

The Veranda

wo oak trees canopy the walk leading up to The Veranda's wide front porch, and rows of green rockers and shutters are outlined against the white paint. The two-story Neoclassic house, on the National Register of Historic Places, is in Senoia, near both Callaway Gardens and the Little White House in Warm Springs, 20 miles south of Atlanta.

The quality of this inn's hospitality, cuisine, and charm has earned it several "inn of the year" awards. Jan Boal, a college mathematics professor, and his wife, Bobby, an extraordinarily good cook, run the place as if every guest is a cherished friend: you are greeted in the foyer by a sign printed with your name, and you are regaled with home-cooked breakfasts into which Bobby has put her heart and soul—fruit cups topped with sorbets, freshly baked cinnamon rolls, and three-cheese omelets. On weekends it's Belgian waffles cooked to order, fresh fruit, and a hot buffet.

You'll go off to bed with an armload of children's books, because, having written one, Jan believes they're just right for bedtime reading. In your room you'll find miniature homemade fruitcakes or other goodies cushioned on each pillow. Guest rooms have themes, like birdwatching, or the Civil War, or butterflies, and are equipped accordingly, with binoculars, an army drum—

even a group of walking sticks. The hallways are also full of curiosities: antique tools and an old portable record player.

Downstairs in a room with a player piano and an organ is a gift shop, with the Boals' huge collection of kaleidoscopes for sale. The house is furnished throughout with antiques, such as southern walnut pieces and much family memorabilia, and as a crowning touch that's not to be missed, there's the culinary indulgence of Bobby's home-cooked dinners, with French onion soup, sourdough brown bread, broccoli and chicken casserole, shrimp mousse, and raspberry layer cake.

Address: *252 Seavy St., Senoia, GA 30276, tel. 404/599–3905.*
Accommodations: *9 double rooms with baths.*
Amenities: *Air-conditioning, TV in common area, whirlpool bath in 1 room.*
Rates: *$70–$90; full breakfast. AE, MC, V.*
Restrictions: *No smoking indoors, no pets.*

Evans House Bed & Breakfast

This tailored yellow and white Victorian is across the street from the 27 acres of Paradise Park, in the heart of Thomasville's historic district.

Leverne Puskar, whose husband, John, is a hotel executive, runs the house with a polished professionalism that stems from a wealth of experience and insight accumulated over the years. She seems to anticipate every need, providing such luxuries as crisply pressed linens, fresh flowers, plates of homemade cookies at bedtime, and made-to-order breakfasts served on china and linen.

The bedrooms are isolated from each other and from the Puskars' quarters. All have 11-foot ceilings, well-cared-for antiques and reproductions, and the convenience of modern baths.

Address: *725 South Hansell St., Thomasville, GA 31792, tel. 912/226–1343, fax 912/226–0653.*
Accommodations: *4 double rooms with baths.*
Amenities: *Air-conditioning, cable TV/VCR and movie library in living room. Guest kitchen; bicycles.*
Rates: *$45–$85; full breakfast, snacks, drinks, and evening sherry. No credit cards.*
Restrictions: *No smoking indoors.*

Merriwood Country Inn

Clustered around a fishing pond and ringed by woods, nearly a mile from the nearest neighbor, a log cabin, a carriage house, and a low-country cypress farmhouse make up this inn complex outside Americus.

In 1985, Tony and JoAnn Davis opened one room in their farmhouse to visitors after Tony retired from corporate life, and one year later they added the two smaller houses. Tony recently opened the Merriwood Café in the carriage house, where he skillfully prepares dinner six nights a week and lavish breakfasts tailored to each guest.

At the Merriwood, you can sleep in a burl walnut sleigh bed, an old-fashioned country iron bed, or an English spindle bed; many pieces are English oak, with quilts and collectibles and antique decorations. The downstairs room in the log cabin, occupied by honeymooners, has a tub for two and a romantic look.

Address: *Mask Rd., Americus, GA 31709, tel. 912/924–4992.*
Accommodations: *4 double rooms with baths.*
Amenities: *Café; air-conditioning, TV, phones, ceiling fans, coffeemakers, and refrigerators in rooms.*
Rates: *$45–$65; full breakfast and bedtime snacks. MC, V.*
Restrictions: *No pets.*

Morris Manor

The family home of Betsy and Troy Morris, a stately brick Georgian Colonial house, stands on a 4-acre lawn rimmed by age-old pecan, apple, and peach orchards. Since 1989, the Morrises have been treating guests like family, and you'll find yourself eating breakfast at their kitchen table and swapping stories in their downstairs den.

There's privacy even in this informal atmosphere: the bedrooms are totally separate from the Morrises' quarters, and the efficiency apartment has a semiprivate entrance. Carpeted bedrooms with modern baths open onto a sitting area, where Betsy serves pots of morning coffee.

Year-round, the outdoors is appealing; you can fish in the pond or just mess around in a small rowboat, and in late summer and early fall, in the orchard, you can pick fruits and nuts and distinctively pungent muscadine grapes.

Address: *425 Timberlane Dr., Americus, GA 31709, tel. 912/924-4884.*
Accommodations: *4 double rooms share 2 baths; efficiency apartment.*
Amenities: *Air-conditioning, TV in apartment and sitting room, phone in common area.*
Rates: *$45-$55; full breakfast. MC, V.*
Restrictions: *No smoking, no pets.*

A Place Away

In Andersonville, you can spend the night in the shadow of southern history in a red brick building built as a schoolhouse and later used as a bird-dog kennel, or in a trim white cottage across the street that was the principal's residence. Now the well-worn floors of the schoolhouse are warmed with scatter rugs, and the spacious rooms are furnished with a mix of reproductions, easy chairs, dining sets, and armoires. The Cottage has a front porch with rockers and a back deck with a grill and picnic tables. Two large bedrooms open onto a kitchen and breakfast nook, where made-to-order breakfasts are served. The furnishings are in a comfortable country style.

Fred and Peggy Sheppard are the knowledgeable owners. Peggy, Andersonville's director of tourism, organizes the October fair, which brings 30,000 people to town to see the costumed battle reenactments and memorabilia dealers. Peggy and Fred run A Place Away with smooth efficiency.

Address: *110 Oglethorpe St., Andersonville, GA 31711, tel. 912/924-1044 or 912/924-2558.*
Accommodations: *5 double rooms share 4 baths; cottage has 2 rooms with baths.*
Amenities: *Cable TV, coffeemakers, ceiling fans, and refrigerators in rooms.*
Rates: *$30-$65; full breakfast. No credit cards.*
Restrictions: *No pets.*

Susina Plantation Inn

Time stops as you enter the 115 acres of lawn and woodlands to Susina Plantation Inn. Magnificent magnolias and centuries-old live oaks drip with Spanish moss.

The Greek Revival house, built in 1841, is owned by Anne-Marie Walker, who came from Sweden, via California, determined to have the area's most upscale inn. She seems to have succeeded, and among her guests have been Paul Newman and Joanne Woodward, who stay at Susina when visiting Georgia relatives.

Guests have the run of the house, which has an Old World feeling: large, antique-filled public rooms, high-ceilinged bedrooms furnished with heavy Empire mahogany, opening onto verandas.

Instead of television, there is a well-stocked bookcase. Lavish breakfasts and optional five-course dinners are served beneath the glow of a crystal chandelier.

If the tennis court, stocked fish pond, walking trails, and swimming pool don't keep you busy, you can go antiquing or take a plantation tour in nearby Thomasville.

Address: *Route 3 (Box 1010), Thomasville, GA 31792, tel. 912/377-9644.*
Accommodations: *8 double rooms with baths.*
Amenities: *Restaurant, air-conditioning, phone in common area.*
Rates: *$100; full breakfast. No credit cards.*

Alabama

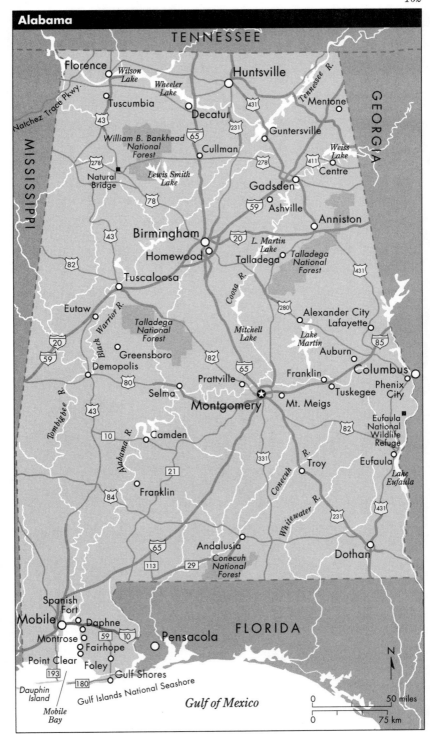

The Highlands

*From a tourist's point of view Alabama, like all Gaul, can
be divided into three parts: the upland country from
Birmingham north, the belt of black earth where the
plantations grew, and the Gulf coast. The rocky and
mountainous land in the northern section, called the
Highlands, has none of the expected flavor of antebellum
life. The region is made up of unproductive small farms,
which sell their produce in charmless towns that look like
the poor relations of other communities that are moving
ahead.*

*The largest of the latter is Huntsville, home of the Redstone
Arsenal (forerunner of NASA), the world's largest space
museum, and in its Twickenham section, more pre–Civil
War houses than anywhere in the state, many dating from
1814. The most sophisticated city in Alabama, Huntsville
has many foreigners, the space and rocket scientists who
have added considerable panache to the community and
who have even made it possible to find restaurants that do
not serve collard greens.*

*There are nine covered bridges left in this part of the state,
as well as a number of state and national parks that offer
recreation and interesting sights. The longest natural
bridge east of the Rockies is near Haleyville; in DeSoto
State Park there's the 110-foot DeSoto Falls in the
beautiful Little River Canyon. Russell Cave National Park
has the remains of Indian tribes dating back 8,000 years.*

*Farther south, set in a valley amid rolling hills, is
Birmingham, the state's largest city and in the '20s and
'30s the South's major industrial area. Atop Red Mountain
on the city's south side is a park surrounding a huge
statue of Vulcan, symbol of the iron and steel industry on
which the city's wealth was founded. Though the steel mills
are now closed, one is still used as an outdoor theater for*

summer concerts, its enormous furnaces rising against the skyline. The city now dedicates itself to medicine instead of the steel industry and is one of the country's leading centers of medical care and study. An impressive fine arts museum that specializes in Oriental and French art hosts traveling exhibitions from national galleries and contains a scholarly library.

Places to Go, Sights to See

In the 67 acres of the **Birmingham Botanical Gardens** (2612 Lane Park Rd., tel. 205/879-1227), a Japanese garden, a rose garden, and fern and rock gardens are intermingled with fountains and plantings of azaleas, camellias, and dogwood.

Birmingham Museum of Fine Arts (2000 8th Ave. N, tel. 205/254-2565 or 205/254-2566) has the S.H. Kress collection of Oriental porcelains and bronzes, paintings, and silver and the newly acquired Hitt collection of 18th-century art and decorations.

Depot Museum (320 Church St., Huntsville, tel. 205/539-1860; closed Mon.), in one of the country's oldest surviving railway stations, built in 1860, covers the history of the region's transportation.

Ivy Green (300 W. North Commons, Tuscumbia, tel. 205/381-7074) is the birthplace of Helen Keller, the house where her teacher, Annie Sullivan, taught her to communicate despite her deafness and blindness. It is complete with Keller's furniture, schoolroom, and clothes.

Museum of Art in Huntsville (700 Monroe St., tel. 205/535-4350; closed Mon.) has changing exhibits and permanent collections of American paintings, sculpture, and Japanese netsuke.

Schloss Furnaces National Historic Landmark (between 1st Ave. and University Blvd., Birmingham, tel. 205/324-1911; closed Mon.). In this open-air concert hall, converted from a steel mill, rock, symphonic, and popular music performances are held—also festivals and picnics.

Space and Rocket Center (1 Tranquility Base, Huntsville, tel. 205/837-3400 or 800/637-7223). The largest space museum in the world shows the development of space exploration, displaying the 354-foot *Saturn V* moon rocket and 60 exhibits where you can experience the effects of weightlessness and see a piece of moon rock.

Vulcan State Park (20th St. at Valley Ave., Birmingham, tel. 205/328-6198) surrounds a huge statue of Vulcan, the god of metalworking, which sits atop

Red Mountain overlooking the city. A small booth at the foot of the statue has information on the museums of Birmingham.

Restaurants

In Birmingham, at the moderately priced **Highland Bar & Grill** (2011 11th Ave. S, tel. 205/939–1400), a chef with Cordon Bleu training serves extraordinary French food. **Botega** (2240 Highland Ave., tel. 205/939–1000) offers fine Northern Italian food, good wine, and luscious bread. **Dexter's Restaurant** (354 Hollywood Blvd., tel. 205/870–5297) serves mesquite-grilled fresh seafood and hickory-grilled steak of high quality.

Muffins Café (U.S. 411 just outside Centre, tel. 205/927–2233) is the place for home cooking, with three meats and 23 vegetables at every meal. **Shelley's Irongate Restaurant** (402 Johnston St. SE, Decatur, tel. 205/350–6795) is a homey restaurant in a restored Victorian house, where everything served is made from scratch, including unusual desserts.

The Right Track Restaurant (1001 Shop Pike Rd., Florence, tel. 205/381–8295), in a restored railroad depot, serves Southern cooking, with fried chicken, hot biscuits, and notable baked goods.

The **Victoria Inn** (1604 Quintard Ave., Anniston, tel. 205/236–0503) serves seafood, steaks, and chicken, as well as domestic and imported wines at very reasonable prices.

Tourist Information

Birmingham Convention and Visitors Bureau (2200 9th Ave. N, Birmingham, AL 35203-1100, tel. 205/252–9825).

Reservation Service

Country Shine Bed-and-Breakfast (Rte. 2, Box 275, Leeds, AL 35094, tel. 205/699–9841).

Mentone Inn

L ookout Mountain in northeastern Alabama forms the background for the Mentone Inn, a building perfectly suited to its setting. Stone steps, dark wood, flagstone paths, flowers, and evergreens show you the way to the entrance. A stone foundation supports screened or glassed-in porches, set with rocking chairs and small tables where breakfast can be served. Striped awnings over most of the bedroom windows confirm the impression that this is a house from the early days of the century. And the rolling hills and valleys providing dark-green views on all sides are ablaze in fall with foliage too dramatic to seem real.

Amelia Kirk has owned the inn since 1976. She keeps it open from April through November, but says it's impractical to try to heat a building constructed in 1927. Many of Kirk's guests flock to these parts for the festivals and craft shows that take place during the summer and autumn.

The living room is paneled in natural-colored old pine. There is comfortable beige furniture, a grandfather clock, a plate rack circling the room, and a stone fireplace. In this room, guests play dominoes or bridge; then for a change they sit on the porch and spin tall tales as they rejoice in not being back home in the heat. In the glassed-in dining area, more plate racks and more paneling surround one long table and six or seven smaller ones, all with views of the mountains. Everything feels the way a relaxed country inn should.

A handsome staircase made of pale wood leads upstairs. All the walls in the house are wood paneled, some painted, some left the natural color. The bedrooms are full of furniture from the 1920s. One has a bookcase with glass doors, a tall oval mirror on a stand, walls painted a pale blue, and a blue and white flowered bedspread. In the corner is a flowered washbowl with matching towels and soap. All rooms have queen-size beds with multicolored matching spreads and curtains, and most have Art Deco night tables.

Several yards behind the house, backed by a grove of trees, is a wooden deck, weathered a soft gray, holding lounge chairs, small tables, and a hot tub.

Address: *Box 284, Mentone, AL 35984, tel. 205/634–4836.*
Accommodations: *12 double rooms with baths.*
Amenities: *Air-conditioning; dinners from nearby restaurant available by prior arrangement.*
Rates: *$55; full breakfast. No credit cards.*
Restrictions: *Smoking only on porches, no pets, BYOB. Closed Dec.–Mar.*

Noble House

In 1886 Samuel Noble, from England, arrived in Alabama, built an impressive house, and thereby founded the city of Anniston. Today that house, restored and refurbished with tender loving care, is the most stunning bed-and-breakfast in Alabama. Built of brick painted a dark Victorian red, it has spanking-white trim, a leaded-glass entrance door, a cupola in one corner of the encircling porch, a freestanding balcony, and old brick paths around a copper fountain and herb garden. The towering magnolias and laurel trees, whose fragrance in spring wafts about the property, shade lawns and flower beds, planted to re-create 19th-century designs.

The owners, Prudence and Robert Johnson, sold their engineering business and bought Noble House. Then Robert and his crew spent over a year restoring it. Prudence knits and crochets, has an herb garden, and produces for breakfast piping hot rolls or breads and coffee cake.

Over the entrance door is a double fanlight, one light above the other; a sweeping staircase leads to the bedrooms. The stately public areas—hallways, parlor, and dining room—have 11-foot ceilings, and each room measures 20 by 20. Victorian furniture often looks as though it were designed for mastodons, but here the pieces are original French ones, whose proportions are suited to humans. Marble-top tables, cabinets

with elegantly turned legs, a 9-foot gilt mirror on one wall, and Victorian lamps with deep fringe all take you back to an earlier time.

Throughout the house, wallpapers reproduce old English papers, and curtains and bedspreads are copies of original materials. In some rooms the floors are painted with designs, carrying out a favorite Victorian decorating technique. All the furniture is of the period, including an elegantly carved mahogany bed from the Noble family's earliest days.

The bedrooms are worthy of the rest of the house. Blue, green, and red swag curtains swoop across wide windows, and the rooms have fireplaces with the original mantels. Fans of brass and wood turn softly above rare bureaus, perfectly placed. It all makes you think of the days when you could pull a velvet cord and someone would come to do your bidding. Though the whole house is quintessentially Victorian, it is neither overdone nor cutesy.

Address: *1025 Fairmont Ave., Anniston, AL 36201, tel. 205/236–1791, fax 205/237–5997.*
Accommodations: *6 double rooms with baths.*
Amenities: *Air-conditioning, cable TV in lounge.*
Rates: *$95–$115; morning coffee, full breakfast. AE, DC, MC, V.*
Restrictions: *No smoking indoors, no pets.*

Wood Avenue Inn

This three-story Queen Anne house lifts square and octagonal towers high above its garden on a busy street in Florence. Built in 1889, it is pure, concentrated Victorian, with 14-foot ceilings, multipane leaded windows, and an assortment of nooks, crannies, and bay windows—the deepest, in one of the drawing rooms, holding a large piano.

The owners are Alvern and Gene Greeley. They have both worked in various fields, he as a clergyman turned auto-parts salesman, she as a dean of Bible studies and then as a real estate agent. With her radiant smile and enveloping warmth, Alvern makes innkeeping an art form. Since she likes to pamper people, she is doing what comes naturally in running a bed-and-breakfast, and she delights in making home-cooked delicacies for her guests. The zucchini bread served at breakfast is unsurpassed in the world of cookery.

The house has an inviting porch with white wicker furniture and petunias growing in flower boxes. Two formal parlors open off the wide central hall, which bisects the two lower floors. One drawing room has dark-green walls with gleaming white woodwork, a red velvet sofa 150 years old, a cabinet in a corner whose rosewood shelves have held someone's china for over a century. But it's the bric-a-brac that sets the tone. Arranged among and around the furniture are enough figurines, artificial flowers, bows, wreaths, footstools, and ruffled cushions to stock a theatrical warehouse. Five minutes in that room and you know exactly how the well-to-do characters in a Dickens novel used to live.

Fireplaces are in every room, even the bathrooms, two of which have narrow tubs resting on claw feet. Beside the tub a table holds a bottle of sparkling cider and two silver-wrapped chocolates. After a good soak, you climb into a huge bed, its salmon-colored satin spread topped by matching pillows against the 19th-century-look wallpaper.

Outside the back door, wisteria climbs over an arbor, and a black carriage handmade by the Amish stands under a protective roof. Not far away a winding path leads to the bridal cottage and to other accommodations kept readied for guests who want to reserve for longer stays.

Address: *658 Northwood Ave., Florence, AL 35630, tel. 205/766-8441.*
Accommodations: *6 double rooms and 2 singles with baths, 2 suites.*
Amenities: *Air-conditioning in bedrooms, TV, special catering on request; ping-pong, badminton, horseshoes.*
Rates: *$60–$80; full breakfast. No credit cards.*
Restrictions: *No smoking, no pets, BYOB.*

Roses and Lace

Roses and Lace sits beside a rose garden on 11 acres of farmland in the historic town of Ashville, where in front of the county courthouse stands a statue of a Confederate soldier, trying to look fierce in spite of his teenage softness.

On the wraparound porch, large clay pots hold ferns, spreading their greenness among the wicker furniture. The pinkish mauve Queen Anne Victorian house retains its stained-glass windows, fireplaces, wide-board floors, and crystal chandeliers hanging from 12-foot ceilings. Innkeeper Shirley Sparks makes quilts, and her husband, Mark, is a cabinetmaker, so they decided to restore the house themselves, spending two years on the downstairs alone. Though lace curtains hang at the windows and lace cloths cover tables, the rooms don't look cluttered in the classic Victorian way. One bedroom holds a headboard 8 feet high, a fireplace, a carved walnut wardrobe, and a china pitcher and basin for rinsing upwardly mobile mustaches.

Address: *Box 852, Ashville, AL 35953, tel. 205/594–4366.*
Accommodations: *2 double rooms with baths, 2 doubles share 1 bath.*
Amenities: *Air-conditioning, ceiling fans, cable TV in common room.*
Rates: *$55–$75; full breakfast. MC, V.*
Restrictions: *No smoking.*

Plantation Country

*The Plantation Country, called the Black Belt because of
its rich black soil, runs through the center of Alabama
from the Mississippi line to the area around Montgomery.
This is the land that produced King Cotton and that until
the Civil War supported the immensely rich plantations.
It's a flat, gentle land, wooded with oak, hickory, sweet
gum, and beech trees, magnolias, sycamores, and
semitropical bay trees and palmettos. Most of the large
holdings have now become cattle farms.*

*On the eastern edge of Plantation Country lies Tuskegee,
an extraordinary community, where in 1881 Booker T.
Washington founded a university for blacks. Here, in
a largely black town, the university provides an
intellectual and educational haven and carries on the
research begun by George Washington Carver, whose work
with peanuts and sweet potatoes helped to change the life of
southern farmers.*

*The Black Belt now provides a background for little old
towns like Selma, Franklin, Demopolis, and Greensboro,
full of antebellum houses and cemeteries—the one in
Selma holds the grave of Abraham Lincoln's sister-in-law.
Many of these homes are in a fine state of preservation and
look as though Scarlett O'Hara should come strolling
through the white columns on their encircling porches.
Some of them are open to the public during spring
festivals and pilgrimages, for a few weeks allowing visitors
to relive the dear dead days when great-great-
grandmother's silver teapot was used regularly and had no
need to be hidden from the Yankee soldiers.*

*Montgomery, the state capital and center of both Civil War
recollections and the civil rights movement, is, with its
historic Old Town district, a quintessential Southern city,
where people who moved here 30 years ago are still*

considered outsiders. Martin Luther King Jr. preached here regularly from the pulpit of the Baptist church on Dexter Avenue. The church is almost cheek by jowl with the state capitol, where the Confederate flag is kept flying and the bronze star where Jefferson Davis stood to be sworn in as president of the Confederacy is still kept brightly polished. The Montgomery bus boycott began here, and the Selma march ended here, not far from the First White House of the Confederacy.

Places to Go, Sights to See

Alabama Shakespeare Festival (1 Festival Dr., Montgomery, tel. 205/277–2273) comprises two theaters, with a professional repertory company that presents classical and modern plays from December to August.

Alabama State Capitol (Bainbridge St. at Dexter Ave., Montgomery). The double curving staircase without supports is one of only a few left in the United States. Closed for renovation, the capitol is scheduled to reopen in late 1992.

Civil Rights Memorial (400 Washington Ave., Montgomery, tel. 205/264–0286). Designed by Maya Lin, who did the Vietnam Memorial in Washington, the Alabama one of black granite and flowing water honors those people killed in the struggle for black equality.

Dexter Avenue King Memorial Baptist Church (454 Dexter Ave., Montgomery, tel. 205/263–3970) has a large Civil Rights mural in the basement. It is open to the public weekdays. To visit on holidays and weekends, call two weeks in advance.

Tuskegee Institute, a national historic site on the campus of Tuskegee University, is managed by the National Park Service. The *Carver Museum* (Tuskegee campus, tel. 205/727–3200) has artifacts, photo displays, and films on the institute and on George Washington Carver's research with peanuts and sweet potatoes. Park rangers conduct guided tours of *The Oaks*, home of Booker T. Washington (1212 Old Montgomery Rd., tel. 205/727–3200). This house, built in 1899, is a fine example of Queen Anne Victorian architecture and was designed and built by blacks. Its furnishings are suitable to the period and include a few Washington family pieces.

Victoryland Greyhound Park (in Shorter, off I–85 east of Montgomery, tel. 205/727–0540) is open year-round, with races held in the afternoon and evening. Minimum age: 19.

Restaurants

In Montgomery, try **Le Bistro** (1059 Woodley Rd., tel. 205/269–1600) for imaginative French cooking, an adequate wine list, and faultless service. Reservations are necessary, and a coat and tie will make you feel more comfortable. At the moderately priced **Vintage Year** (405 Cloverdale Rd., tel. 205/264–8463), you'll get luscious Northern Italian food, crunchy bread, and a large wine list. The even less expensive **Young House Restaurant** (231 N. Hull St., tel. 205/262–0409), in an 1850 house in Old Town, specializes in local cuisine.

In Demopolis, at **The Red Barn** (905 U.S. 80, tel. 205/289–0595), you'll find reasonably priced Southern cooking: steaks, catfish, hush puppies, and chicken. The elegant **GainesRidge Supper Club,** 2 miles east of Camden (Rte. 10, tel. 205/682–9707) in a 19th-century house, serves 13 entrées, gumbo, and homemade hot rolls at very reasonable prices from Wednesday to Saturday. At the **Cotton Patch** in Eutaw (tel. 205/372–4235) there's homespun Southern cooking, with fried chicken, barbecue, and hot biscuits.

Tourist Information

Alabama Bureau of Tourism & Travel (532 S. Perry St., Montgomery, AL 36102, tel. 205/242–4169).

Reservation Service

Anne B. Waldo (Box 1026, Montgomery, AL 36101, tel. 205/264–0056).

The Colonel's Rest

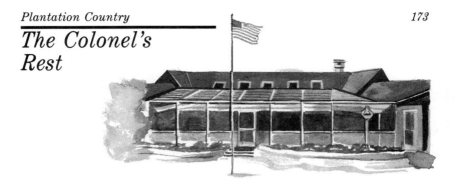

On the northeastern outskirts of Montgomery is The Colonel's Rest, an 80-acre property that's one of the most unusual bed-and-breakfasts in Alabama. The brick and cedar central building is long and low, wrapping in a wide U shape around a screened patio with a pool. There's a duplex cabin, an A-frame with one bedroom, and the Carriage House—a large hall for dinners, receptions, and wedding rehearsals. Discreetly hidden in the bushes and among groves of trees sloping away from the main house are spaces for 50 recreational vehicles—on that much land the RVs can be kept out of sight.

The four rooms in the main house face the patio, where azaleas and camellias are spaced on paths around the pool and a fountain's music soothes guests at breakfast. A stone fireplace warms the paneled living room, lit by a huge, sparkling chandelier and full of chairs so soft you think you'll sink down to China.

Each bedroom is decorated in a different style. The Oriental Room has grass-paper wall covering, pagoda paintings, and black lacquer furniture with black and white accessories. The nautical room is white and blue, with a striped bedspread, paintings of sea gulls, white rattan furniture, and a ship's wheel over one door. In the Early American room, a cannonball bed is set against dark wainscoting and an oak chest's mirror has Victorian gingerbread.

The property was developed by Jim and Jane Watson, he a retired colonel in the Air Force, she a gifted musician. Though the Watsons can produce a seated meal for 100 in the Carriage House (which has a professional kitchen and a barbecue large enough to roast an ox), the property's wide-open spaces ensure silence and solitude.

The Colonel's Rest looks out on fields and heavily forested areas. Stargazing, bird-watching, and walks in the woods are especially enchanting during Alabama's early spring. The Watsons encourage extended stays on a weekly or monthly basis. Several repeaters have been snowbirds from Canada, who find wearing only a sweater in the middle of January little short of miraculous. And then of course there's that red-eye gravy and grits, considered by most Southerners to be one of civilization's highest achievements.

Address: *Box 133, Mt. Meigs, AL 36057, tel. 205/279–0380.*
Accommodations: *7 double housekeeping rooms with baths.*
Amenities: *Restaurant, air-conditioning, TV/VCR in public area; fax machine, copier, laundry; pool and 2-acre pond.*
Rates: *$48 ($130/week, $350/month); full breakfast. No credit cards.*

Grace Hall

Among the stately homes of Selma is Grace Hall, built in 1857 and now restored. In its shifting past the wealthy mansion became run-down apartments and then a grungy boardinghouse, but today, resplendent again, with many of its original antiques brought home, it shines as brilliantly as ever.

The owners are Coy and Joey Dillon, he a former executive of a steel company, she a designer. Since the age of 16, when Joey bought her first antique (an oval mirror for $10), she has been interested in old buildings. She jumped at the chance to buy and restore Grace Hall. The Dillons drifted into bed-and-breakfast management by the back door when the mayor of Selma asked them to put up a visiting dignitary. The occasion has led to considerable corporate business.

The house is a certified restoration of a Victorian home. It is stunningly beautiful, with double parlors, a pressed-tin ceiling in the study, heart-of-pine floors throughout, and windows 10 feet tall. The dining room has its original mahogany pedestal table, seating 12, and there's a smaller breakfast room behind, where guests may help themselves to a three-course breakfast. Solid brass chandeliers light the house; on the south porch overlooking the manicured garden, the original wicker furniture invites you to relax.

All the bedrooms in the main house have marble fireplaces, where fires are lit as soon as guests arrive. These large rooms are furnished with carved rosewood beds, Oriental rugs, and hand-painted enameled clocks. The wallpapers are copies of 19th-century paper; in one bedroom, the Brighton pattern fits perfectly with a four-poster bed flanked by brother-and-sister walnut chests. TV sets in the bedrooms are carefully concealed in cabinets.

Leading off the back is a latticed, galleried wing, whose porches, facing the garden, provide open-air sitting space for three more bedrooms, smaller than those in the main house but charmingly decorated in the same 19th-century style. So that you cannot possibly forget your Southern surroundings, in each room an overhead fan turns lazily above a large bowl holding branches full of cotton bolls.

Address: *506 Lauderdale St., Selma, AL 36701, tel. 205/875-5744, fax 205/875-9967.*
Accommodations: *6 double rooms with baths.*
Amenities: *Air-conditioning, TV, phones, and fans in rooms.*
Rates: *$65–$95; full breakfast. AE, MC, V.*
Restrictions: *No smoking indoors, no pets.*

Oakwood

Oakwood, which is on the National Register of Historic Places, was commissioned in 1847 by the first mayor of Talladega. Painted white, with green shutters, tall columns, chimneys, and a freestanding balcony over the front porch, Oakwood resembles the quintessential Southern mansion of antebellum days. It is even set in the right kind of garden—full of azaleas and dogwoods—and faces a pretty street lined with carefully tended houses and yards.

Naomi and Al Kline, the owners, have agreed to a perfect division of labor: The house is in her name, but Al does all the work. He's chef, gardener, and singing waiter, for he is a professional musician. When he is not sweeping off the front porch, he teaches voice, piano, and organ, and he conducts the Talladega Community Chorus. Naomi commutes to Birmingham, where she is a registered nurse at St. Vincent's Hospital. A unique feature of the house is the well-equipped recording studio, where guests may play the organ or piano, even lifting up their voices in deathless song, and preserve for posterity their performances.

Like so many houses built for the wealthy in the mid-19th century, Oakwood is done on a large scale: The rooms are 20 feet by 20, the ceilings are 11 feet, and the windows almost as tall. The original heart-pine floors have been redone, adding a special gleam. In the wide entrance hall, a broad staircase invites you upstairs and contributes an air of welcome and elegance. Throughout the house, the wallpapers have been copied from original designs. They make a fitting background for the original furniture, most of it English Victorian, with some delicate French pieces. One nice touch is a table from an English pub; its brass hinges allow it to unfold to seat eight hungry or thirsty people.

One bedroom has a spool bed, the others four-posters. In two you will find English armoires, washstands, 1895 dressers, and (in one) a strange hand-carved curio cabinet. One room is decorated as if for a young girl, with light, floaty curtains, old white wicker chairs and sofas, and an antique doll propped against cushions. Everywhere else, the long sweeps of draperies at the windows are copies of fabrics of the period. The house is all of a piece, everything blending to give a glimpse of how the gentry of yesteryear managed to enjoy life.

Address: *715 E. North St., Talladega, AL 35160, tel. 205/362–0662.*
Accommodations: *4 double rooms share 2½ baths.*
Amenities: *Air-conditioning, TV in common area; horseshoes, croquet.*
Rates: *$55–$65; full breakfast. No credit cards.*
Restrictions: *No smoking, no pets.*

The Plantation House

Ten miles northwest of Montgomery is Prattville, once the home of Daniel Pratt, who, according to Alabama lore—Eli Whitney supporters to the contrary notwithstanding—invented the cotton gin. The Plantation House sits amid magnolias, azaleas, and dogwoods, sheltering under other trees 150 years old on a property originally granted by President Andrew Jackson. The 2½-story white clapboard house, its columns rising past a freestanding balcony, is an example of Greek Revival at its best.

John and Bernice Hughes had another life before they bought and rebuilt The Plantation House after a fire. She worked for the state of Alabama, and he was a Montgomery businessman; the idea of a bed-and-breakfast was suggested by her son. They are talkative, knowledgeable, walking examples of Southern hospitality.

You enter the spacious hall under a spreading fanlight, which shows up the gleam of the wide, heart-pine floorboards. The house, built in 1832, is supported on joists a foot and a half thick, which contain enough lumber to build a small bungalow. Walls throughout are painted off-white. There are nine fireplaces in the house, eight of them original. A portrait of Jenny Lind in a formal pose, surrounded by the furs worn when she once sang in Prattville, hangs on one wall of the living room. In the formal parlor with its 11-foot ceiling, a crystal chandelier hangs from an enormous plaster medallion. The furniture is a mixture of easy, comfortable modern blended with many pieces from John Hughes's mother. There's a lady's love seat wide enough for hoop-skirts, a chair whose back is carved in delicate swirls, and a heavy oak poker table from a Mississippi riverboat.

The wainscoted upstairs hall leads to bedrooms lit by tall windows. There are four-poster beds, white chenille spreads, and pale ruffled curtains. At the end of the hall is a small sitting room with green rattan furniture, where guests are served breakfast if they prefer not to go downstairs to the formal dining room. Every bedroom has a fireplace; in front of one of them sits a tiny antique child's rocking chair. Each room also boasts an oak washstand, and one of the beds is so tall you must climb up via a set of narrow steps.

Address: *752 Loder St., Prattville, AL 36067, tel. 205/361–0442.*
Accommodations: *2 double rooms with baths, 1 with Jacuzzi.*
Amenities: *Air-conditioning, cable TV, phones in rooms; pool, nature trail.*
Rates: *$65; Continental breakfast. MC, V.*
Restrictions: *No smoking, no pets.*

Blue Shadows

Isolated on 320 acres of fields and woods, this white frame house backs up on a 2-mile nature trail to a bird sanctuary, a wildflower preserve, and a pond. Its undistinguished 1930s exterior is belied by the colorful interior, where everything glows, from the apricot walls and carpet of the living room to the burnished grass-cloth walls in the foyer.

Thaddeus May, a retired pilot, has lived in this house all his life. His wife, Janet, an artist and decorator, opened the B&B as an antidote to boredom. The inviting bedrooms have antique beds with ruffled pillows, chandeliers, French provincial mirrors, and prints and drawings by Janet. The bathroom has bright-blue figured wallpaper and matching towels that look almost a foot thick. The small guest sitting room, with its private entrance, 10-foot windows, and soft, pale rug, is a quiet haven. In the comfortable but blandly furnished garage apartment, guests can stuff themselves on goodies from the fridge, then luxuriate in the large bedroom and bath.

Address: *Rte. 2, Box 432, Greensboro, AL 36744, tel. 205/624–3637.*
Accommodations: *2 double rooms share 1 bath, 1 apartment.*
Amenities: *Air-conditioning, TV in lounge.*
Rates: *$55; Continental breakfast, afternoon tea. No credit cards.*
Restrictions: *No smoking indoors, no pets.*

Hill-Ware-Dowdell House

Althea and Nicolas Mendeloff, from Pennsylvania, had always wanted to move south. They answered an ad, and in 11 days had sold their home and bought the Ware House.

The massive white columns are the first thing you notice about this Greek Revival house built in 1840. The impressive public rooms have 11-foot ceilings, but their dark red and green paint makes them somewhat somber. Refinished heart-pine floors gleam between flowered carpets, and the elegant staircase is dramatic.

The bedrooms have fireplaces with original hand-carved mantels and wallpaper copied from old patterns; they are furnished mostly with reproductions of 19th-century pieces. The 20-by-20 master bedroom has a king-size bed, a small white iron bed with curlicues and ruffled pillows, and an early spinning wheel.

Address: *203 2nd Ave. SW, Lafayette, AL 36826, tel. 205/864–7861.*
Accommodations: *4 double rooms with baths.*
Amenities: *Air-conditioning, cable TV; souvenir shop; pool, dinner served with advance notice.*
Rates: *$79–$125; full breakfast. MC, V.*
Restrictions: *No smoking indoors, no pets. BYOB.*

Red Bluff Cottage

Red Bluff Cottage, built to accommodate guests, sits high above the Alabama River, a raised cottage with public rooms on the second floor and the bedrooms below.

Mark Waldo, a retired Episcopal rector, is straight out of central casting—tall, slim, and intellectually gray. His wife, Anne, is gardener and chef, and also an accomplished musician.

The public rooms have Oriental rugs, a fireplace, and the kind of soft lamplight that makes you want to sit down and tell someone the story of your life. Guests may play an ancient harpsichord in the music room. Breakfast is served on a mahogany table, with family china and silver; on the porch amid hanging baskets of pansies; or in a white lattice gazebo in the garden.

The bedrooms are full of light, with large windows and starched white curtains. Old carved cherry pieces are arranged among framed photos of ancestors taken against sepia backgrounds.

Address: *551 Clay St., Montgomery, AL 36104, tel. 205/263-1727.*
Accommodations: *4 double rooms with baths.*
Amenities: *Air-conditioning, cable TV, laundry.*
Rates: *$50; full breakfast and pre-breakfast coffee. No credit cards.*
Restrictions: *No smoking, no pets.*

Gulf Coast Delta

The southwestern part of Alabama, the Gulf Coast Delta, is dominated by water: by the rivers and streams of the delta, draining into Mobile Bay, and by the Gulf of Mexico, whose beaches have sand so gleaming white it looks as though it has been scooped up from the streets of paradise. The flat and uninteresting area approaching the coast, however, has no distinctive features but heat, insects, and high humidity. Throughout much of the region large trees support gray-green curtains of Spanish moss that festoon their branches, hanging down 10 or 15 feet in irregular clusters and adding an air of mystery to the silent, motionless landscape.

Mobile, with its active shipping industry, is Alabama's only important port. The French settled it in 1711, and many of the older parts of the city hold fast to bits and pieces of their French ancestry. Live oaks, 100 years old and riotous, and exploding stretches of azaleas turn the town into fairyland in early spring.

Strung along the eastern shore of Mobile Bay is a scattering of small towns with evocative names: Point Clear, Fairhope, Daphne, Montrose, and Spanish Fort. Point Clear has one of the South's most famous hostelries, the 140-year old Grand Hotel, whose half-moon dining rooms overlook the bay and whose sweeping lawn is so manicured guests are almost afraid to walk on it.

Places to Go, Sights to See

Fairhope, the most interesting village on Mobile Bay, was settled about 1900 by a group of high-minded midwesterners; all land was owned collectively by the religious community. Now a growing art colony with 20 antiques shops and several potteries, it is also a center for fishing, boating, and marine services.

At **Dauphin Island,** a gateway to Mobile Bay, regattas and fishing tournaments take place, notably the Deep-sea Fishing Rodeo, which has been held every July for 50 years.

Mobile. The *Cathedral of the Immaculate Conception* (Dauphin at Claiborne St., tel. 205/432–6684) is a Greek Revival masterpiece built in 1835, with German art-glass windows. Three museums featuring city life in the 19th century—the *Carlen House,* the *Phoenix Fire Museum,* and the *City Museum*—are in the center of town, all within walking distance of each other. The Museum Office (tel. 205/438–7569) provides information about all three. Moored offshore in Mobile Bay is the USS *Alabama* (Battleship Pkwy., tel. 205/433–2703), which was called "the hero of the Pacific." The ship is a popular tourist attraction, but during the summer months it's likely to be full of crowds dripping ice cream and perspiration.

Bellingrath Gardens (Theodore, tel. 205/973–2217), on 800 acres 20 miles south of Mobile, are famous for their imaginative landscaping with traditional southern flowers, shrubs, and trees. The house contains a collection of Boehm porcelains.

Restaurants

At **The Gift Horse,** in Foley (209 W. Laurel Ave., tel. 205/943–3663), reasonably priced Southern cooking (but no wine) is served buffet-style in an elegant old house built in 1912. In the dining room of Point Clear's **Marriott Grand Hotel** (U.S. 98, tel. 205/928–9201), the French cuisine tries to be light and nonfattening, but the desserts are sinfully tasty. **Maggie's Bistro** (800 N. Section St., Fairhope, tel. 205/928–8323) serves Continental cuisine and a nice selection of wines. Just south of Mobile, right on the water, is **Nan Seas** (4170 Bayfront Rd., tel. 205/479–9132); one could write paeans to the seafood fresh from Mobile Bay.

Tourist Information

Mobile Chamber of Commerce (Box 2187, Mobile, AL 36652, tel. 205/433–6951). **Fort Condé Welcome Center** (150 S. Royal St., Mobile, AL 36602, tel. 205/434–7304).

Rutherford Johnson House

Much of Monroe County seems to have slid through the 20th century untouched by change of any kind. Guests at the Rutherford Johnson House in Franklin will sleep in a grey-timbered Federal-style house (built by a riverboat captain in 1840), whose later Victorian facade has white porch railings and intricate gingerbread.

Co-owner Mary Johnson is an editor, a published writer on quilting and crafts, and a historic preservationist. John Huff, her husband, was a businessman from Mobile, but now is turning the Rutherford Johnson House into a working example of an antebellum plantation. He produces pecans, eggs, dairy products, and fruits, and will soon have repainted and refurbished the potato house, the molasses house, the cotton house, and the separate kitchen, those "dependencies" so necessary to an authentic farm setting.

Through the original Empire doorway guests enter a long hall, brightened by a collection of kilims. In the drawing room and office-library, on either side, the furniture is heavy and formal, almost all original Empire. The dining room has an Empire chest and an elegant mahogany table, where breakfast for guests is served, and in the cozy, intimate sitting room, a carved mahogany mantel clock ticks away, flanked by two old-fashioned bronzes from New Orleans. An old pine dresser serves as

a bar, and the flowered draperies are held in place by antique mercury-glass tiebacks.

The bedrooms have light-grained rock maple floors, tongue-and-groove paneled walls and 14-foot ceilings. One contains a rare suite of carved oak furniture, with an unusual fainting couch—the daybed where Victorian ladies reclined when life became simply too much. All the beds are covered by handmade quilts, which blend nicely with the bed hangings and the curtains at the tall windows. There are rocking chairs and ladder back chairs, carved and mirrored dressers, and footstools with colorful needlework; in the upstairs bathroom little handcarved hippopotami follow each other across the mantelpiece.

The welcoming warmth of the house is helped by prints, paintings, quilted wall hangings, old family photographs, and a seemingly limitless collection of books and magazines; even out on the porch there are folk art and primitive carvings.

Address: *Box 202, Franklin, AL 36444, tel. 205/282-4423.*
Accommodations: *1 double room with bath, 3 doubles share 1½ baths.*
Amenities: *Air-conditioning, TV, phone in common area; badminton, croquet, pets permitted.*
Rates: *$75; full breakfast. No credit cards.*
Restrictions: *No smoking indoors.*

The Guest House

The Guest House in Fairhope is a low, turn-of-the-century structure that's been added to and subtracted from several times. It's saved from blandness by fresh pink paint and a church door of antique leaded glass with glass side panels. Its busy location is noisy, but that's compensated for by its nearness to the center of the village of Fairhope, with pleasant places to walk.

The owner, Betty Bostrom, was formerly in real estate and now operates not only her bed-and-breakfast enterprise but also a completely separate conference and reception center. A staff of 13 keeps her two establishments running smoothly.

One of the B&B's public rooms has attractive traditional decor, including a Chinese rug, potted plants, and big chairs that invite guests to sit and snooze. But the nearby lounge looks somewhat bare and cramped. Bedrooms are decorated in pink and gray candy stripes with wicker furniture, or yellow floral prints on curtains and bed. Breakfast is often served in the New Orleans–style brick courtyard, as are afternoon tea and wine and cheese.

Address: *63 S. Court St., Fairhope, AL 36532, tel. 205/928–6226.*
Accommodations: *1 double room with bath, 2 doubles share 1 bath.*
Amenities: *TV in lounge.*
Rates: *$65; full breakfast, afternoon tea, wine and cheese. No credit cards.*
Restrictions: *No smoking, no pets.*

Merschon Court

Merschon Court is a small Victorian town house built at the turn of the century. The entrance is dominated by a rolltop desk and a heart-pine staircase. A high-ceilinged, bright living/dining room is done in grays and aquamarine, with one wall filled with books and another with white-shuttered windows. Though the house is small, the effective use of color and light prevents the visitor from feeling cramped.

The owner, Susan Glickman, is pert and efficient, shooting off almost visible rays of energy. Her businesslike exterior can't quite hide her concern for the comfort of her guests, as she is everywhere at once, taking care of all details.

Two of the bedrooms have French doors that open onto an upstairs deck sitting area, with a treetop feeling and nice views of the surrounding gardens. Weathered decks and porches, a gazebo, a Victorian veranda, and huge live oaks overhanging a shadowed pool are welcome retreats in this warm climate.

Address: *203 Fairhope Ave., Fairhope, AL 36532, tel. 205/928–7398.*
Accommodations: *2 double rooms with baths, 2 doubles share 1 bath.*
Amenities: *Air-conditioning, TV in lounge, ceiling fans in rooms.*
Rates: *$55–$69; Continental breakfast. MC, V.*
Restrictions: *No smoking, no pets.*

Mississippi

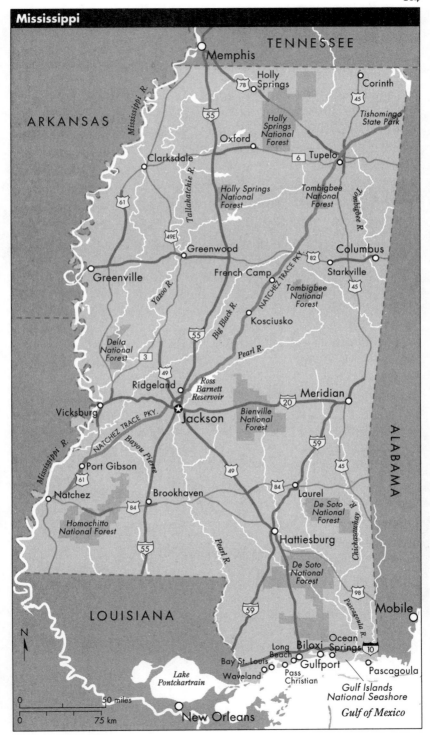

Mississippi

TENNESSEE

Memphis

78 Holly Springs

Corinth

45

Tishomingo State Park

55

Oxford

Holly Springs National Forest

6 Tupelo

ARKANSAS

Clarksdale

Holly Springs National Forest

Tombigbee National Forest

Mississippi R.

61

Tallahatchie R.

Tombigbee R.

49E

Greenwood

French Camp

NATCHEZ TRACE PKY.

82 Columbus

Starkville

45

Greenville

Yazoo R.

Tombigbee National Forest

Kosciusko

Big Black R.

55

Pearl R.

Delta National Forest

3

49

Ridgeland

Ross Barnett Reservoir

20 Meridian

Bienville National Forest

Vicksburg

★ Jackson

NATCHEZ TRACE PKY.

Bayou Pierre

59

45

Mississippi R.

Port Gibson

61

49

84

Laurel

Natchez

Brookhaven

De Soto National Forest

Homochitto National Forest

84

Chickasawhay R.

55

Pearl R.

Hattiesburg

De Soto National Forest

98

Pascagoula R.

Mobile

59

LOUISIANA

N

ALABAMA

Long Beach

Biloxi

Ocean Springs

10

Bay St. Louis

Gulfport

Waveland

Pass Christian

Pascagoula

Lake Pontchartrain

Gulf Islands National Seashore

Gulf of Mexico

New Orleans

0 50 miles

0 75 km

Oxford, Holly Springs, and the North Mississippi Hills

Though Holly Springs and Oxford are within an hour or so of Memphis, Tennessee, they are very much a part of the rural Deep South. This "big woods" region was introduced to the world by Oxford native William Faulkner, who won the 1949 Nobel Prize in Literature for his depictions of small-town life. Faulkner fans may recognize his mythical Yoknapatawpha County when they visit Lafayette County, of which Oxford is the seat.

Even before Faulkner made Holly Springs famous, it appears that the Union soldiers who were bivouacked there during the Civil War were quite enamored of the town. Rumor has it that because of certain blandishments of local women determined to save their homes, the Yankees chose not to burn the town. Today, those private houses are open for the Pilgrimage tour in late April, and some by appointment. The entire Courthouse Square, with its neat box of shops and offices, is on the National Register of Historic Places.

In Oxford, there's little need to plan activities, for the town itself is an attraction. The neat and pretty square is dominated by the courthouse. Faulkner wrote in Requiem for a Nun, *"But above all, the Courthouse: the center, the focus, the hub; sitting looming in the center of the county's circumference like a single cloud in its ring of horizon. . . ." The University of Mississippi (Ole Miss) has excellent museums, one with an extensive collection of Greco-Roman antiquities. The University Museums also maintain Faulkner's home, Rowan Oak.*

Side trips within a couple of hours of Oxford include the pretty and historically significant towns of Corinth and Columbus both steeped in yet more Civil War history—and herstory. The women of Columbus, for example, in 1866

*helped to heal the nation by placing flowers on the graves
of both Confederate and Union soldiers at Friendship
Cemetery. "Decoration Day," initiated by those genteel
ladies, evolved into the nation's Memorial Day. In 1884, the
first state-supported college for women was founded here.
Corinth, a town of tree-canopied streets and quiet, historic
neighborhoods, was of strategic importance during the
Civil War because the railroads met and crossed here. It
changed hands more than once, and the Battle of Corinth
cost thousands of lives. The major Battle of Shiloh occurred
just across the state line in Tennessee.*

*Nearby there are several serene and pretty state parks and
lakes. In bustling Tupelo you'll find plenty of shopping
and fine restaurants (see Along the Natchez Trace).
Starkville, west of Columbus, is the home of many
museums and Mississippi State University, where SEC
(Southeastern Conference) sports offer year-round
activities.*

Places to Go, Sights to See

The **Kate Freeman Clark Art Gallery** (292 E. College Ave., Holly Springs)
exhibits more than 1,000 paintings by the Holly Springs native who left her
home in the 1890s to study with William Merritt Chase at the Art Students
League in New York. By choice, she never sold a painting.

Marshall County Historical Museum (220 E. College Ave., Holly Springs,
tel. 601/252-3669) is full of interesting artifacts and artful conversation.

Blues Archives (Farley Hall, University of Mississippi, Oxford, tel. 601/232-
7753). See how singin' the blues evolved from Mississippi Delta roots. B. B.
King's collection of memorabilia and recordings is exhibited, as are the
works of other blues musicians.

The **Center for the Study of Southern Culture** (tel. 601/232-5993), housed in
the antebellum Barnard Observatory on the University of Mississippi campus
in Oxford, examines the region's music, folklore, literature, and other things.

Rowan Oak (Old Taylor Rd., Oxford, tel. 601/234-3284) is writer William
Faulkner's antebellum home. His outline of the prizewinning story, *A Fable*,
is still written on the wall of his study.

Corinth National Cemetery (tel. 601/286–5782), once a major battlefield, is now the gravesite of 6,000 Civil War soldiers.

The **Northeast Mississippi Museum** (204 4th St., Corinth, tel. 601/286–3120) contains Indian relics and artifacts and Civil War maps and battle plans.

Antebellum Home Tours (Columbus, tel. 601/329–3533 or 800/327–2686). The town opens at least three of its mansions—all of them antebellum, with period antiques—for tours every day, year-round.

Waverley Plantation (between Columbus and West Point, tel. 601/494–1399) is one of the South's favorite historic houses, a spectacular mid-1800s showplace built around an octagonal rotunda.

Agricultural Laboratory Tours (Food and Enology Lab, Mississippi State University, Starkville, tel. 601/325–3200). Those who appreciate wine and wine making will enjoy the excellent tour of the lab.

The **Cobb Institute of Archaeology** (Mississippi State University, Starkville, tel. 601/325–3826) has North American Indian artifacts and much more.

Restaurants

Harvey's, in Tupelo, Columbus, and Starkville, specializes in mesquite-grilled fish, steak, and chicken, and dressed-up hamburgers and salads. All locations are relaxed and casual, and the service is unusually good. In Tupelo, **Jefferson Place** (tel. 601/844–8696) serves the finest cuts of beef and lighter fare of sandwiches, salads, and burgers. **The Front Porch** (tel. 601/842–1591) is known for the best Mississippi catfish, with hush puppies and cole slaw. And yes, it actually boasts a front porch with rocking chairs.

Tourist Information

Columbus Convention & Visitors Bureau (Box 789, Columbus, MS 39703, tel. 601/329–1191 or 800/327–2686). **Corinth Chamber of Commerce** (Box 1049, Corinth, MS 38834, tel. 601/287–5269). **Holly Springs Chamber of Commerce** (Box 12, Holly Springs, MS 38635, tel. 601/252–2943). **Oxford Tourism Council** (Box 965, Oxford, MS 38655, tel. 601/234–4651). **Starkville Visitors & Convention Council** (Box 2720, Starkville, MS 39759, tel. 601/323–3322).

Reservation Services

Columbus Historic Foundation (Box 46, Columbus, MS 39703, tel. 601/329–3533) can make reservations at four houses in Columbus. **Lincoln, Ltd. Bed & Breakfast Mississippi Reservation Service** (Box 3479, Meridian, MS 39303, tel. 601/482–5483 or 800/633–6477).

Hamilton Place

Throughout the South, cotton money built lavish houses, and Holly Springs, in the northwest corner of Mississippi, is a case in point. The impressive Hamilton Place was built in 1838 as a grand three-story Greek Revival mansion with massive columns. The house plays a prominent role in Holly Springs's Civil War history; in fact, its then mistress, Mrs. Carrington Mason, is said to have saved the town from destruction. According to legend, it was discovered quite by accident that Maria Mason and Union Gen. B. H. Grierson had both studied piano under a renowned professor in New York. Each day during the Union occupation, the general and Mrs. Mason gave "concerts" (performing in compatible styles). Finally, he told her that though his mission had been to destroy Holly Springs, he had, instead, reported to superiors that he'd found intelligent, cultivated people, some of whom were nursing wounded Federals in their homes. "You and your piano can take credit for saving Holly Springs," he said to Maria Mason. Thus, Hamilton Place survived the war.

But the house was not so lucky with the elements. During a fierce storm in 1923 it was struck by lightning and incurred damage so severe that the third story and the columns had to be removed. The facade was converted to the style of a Louisiana raised cottage, though the proportions remain grand and the high ceilings, ornate moldings, and original interior design elements are still in place.

The house, now the residence of Jackson and Linda Stubbs, is the only bed-and-breakfast in town. He is with the Social Security Administration, she is a registered dietitian, and both serve as innkeepers. Among their treasures are a Mallard tester bed and exquisite blue-and-gold antique French twin beds. They've combined inherited pieces with collected items to complete the elegant decoration.

Three of the guest rooms are in the main house; one is in the carriage house, where there is also an antiques shop. Guests are encouraged to enjoy the hot tub and the pool or take a bike ride through Holly Springs. Breakfast is served in the formal dining room, on the veranda, or in the gazebo.

Address: *105 E. Mason Ave., Holly Springs, MS 38635, tel. 601/252-4368.*
Accommodations: *4 double rooms with baths.*
Amenities: *Air-conditioning, TV in sitting room; bicycles, hot tub, pool.*
Rates: *$65; Continental breakfast. MC, V.*
Restrictions: *No pets.*

The Isom Place

Travelers who stay in bed-and-breakfast inns to meet interesting people should all head for The Isom Place in Oxford. Opal Worthy, a lady of more than 80 who says that her varied interests and cherished memories have preserved her vitality, is certainly interesting and indeed somewhat phenomenal. Mrs. Worthy is a retired professor from the University of Mississippi and other colleges, who has taught English and French. After traveling the world, she came home to Mississippi and now owns one of Oxford's few remaining antebellum houses.

The Isom Place, listed on the National Register of Historic Places, was originally a three-room log house built in 1838 by Dr. T. D. Isom for an office. As the physician's practice grew, so did the building, becoming his office/home and over the years evolving into a rambling two-story house that exemplifies planter-style architecture. It was built entirely of native timber, hand-planed by local workmen. According to legend, Dr. Isom treated wounded Federal soldiers in his clinic during the Civil War, and in 1862, General U. S. Grant placed officers in The Isom Place to protect the house and residents.

Mrs. Worthy and her late husband, Dr. H. D. Worthy, bought The Isom Place in 1958 and began a two-year renovation. She says house guests asked her to set a fee so they wouldn't feel they were imposing, and that is how she got into the B&B business. "Guests provide a touch of the outside world; I give them a touch of the Old South," she says.

The house contains Victorian furniture and a mixture of other antiques accumulated by the Worthys, including a pre-Revolutionary table. The "parlor bedroom" features a Thomas McIntyre bed dating from 1810 and a rare Tiffany lamp. The Isom Place is almost a house museum, for in the attic, accessible from an upstairs bedroom, fashions dating back 150 years are exhibited on mannequins and in armoires. Of particular interest is an 1851 French wedding gown.

Throughout the house, Mrs. Worthy displays her special treasures—antique dolls, old trunks, christening gowns, and other relics of a gentler time. She says that every room has been decorated with precious things to remind guests that the house is quite old. Mrs. Worthy prefers a relaxed atmosphere; breakfast is "an informal occasion" served most anytime.

Address: *1003 Jefferson St., Oxford, MS 38655, tel. 601/234-3310.*
Accommodations: *3 double rooms with baths.*
Amenities: *Air-conditioning.*
Rates: *$55–$70; Continental breakfast. No credit cards.*
Restrictions: *No smoking, no pets.*

The Amzi Love House

In the town of Columbus where women have made a mark, one of the many antebellum homes was built for a woman, and her descendant, Sid Caradine, now runs it as a bed-and-breakfast. Built in 1848 for the bride of Amzi Love, the Italian-style villa in the historic district is much the way it was originally, because seven generations have intentionally preserved its unique character. In fact, Sid tells his guests that it's like a journey back in time, complete with original Empire and Victorian furnishings and such accessories as the crocheted bedspreads and needlepoint done by Amzi Love's five daughters.

Sid returned to his birthplace in 1989, after deciding that writing poetry was preferable to working in the stock market. He has made the house more appealing to guests by providing extra amenities like bicycles and lush terry-cloth robes for use after bathing. He offers beverages upon arrival and serves lunch and dinner on request.

Address: *305 7th St. S, Columbus, MS 39701, tel. 601/328–5413 or 601/329–3533.*
Accommodations: *3 double rooms with baths, 1 suite.*
Amenities: *Air-conditioning, phones in rooms, bicycles.*
Rates: *$75–$100; full breakfast, refreshments. MC, V.*
Restrictions: *No smoking in bedrooms, no pets.*

The General's Quarters B&B

The town of Corinth goes about its daily business, greeting the historians and tourists who come to see the battlefields. Other than pursuing the connection with Civil War history there's not a lot to do in town, but a walking tour of the neat, tree-canopied streets is a plus. This quietly charming house is in a serene, old residential neighborhood in the historic district.

Built around 1870, the Victorian house features a nice mixture of antiques of varying styles. Canopy beds, brass beds, armoires, and marble-top dressers create a pleasing decor for an old house.

Owners J. L. and Rosemary Aldridge, who work in insurance and real estate, try to make The General's Quarters a home away from home. They also have a gift shop in the house, where Corinth art and local items are sold. The staff says that guests love the big Southern breakfasts. Dinner is served at the restaurant every night but Sunday, and bed-and-breakfast guests often join the locals for fish, filet mignon, or one of the other house specialties.

Address: *924 Fillmore St., Corinth, MS 38834, tel. 601/286–3325.*
Accommodations: *5 double rooms with baths.*
Amenities: *Restaurant; air-conditioning, coffee makers, phones, and TV in rooms.*
Rates: *$70; full breakfast. AE, MC, V.*
Restrictions: *No pets.*

Ivy Guest House

The Ivy Guest House is a wonderfully restored hotel in downtown Starkville, about 30 minutes east of the Natchez Trace. Built in 1925 as the Hotel Chester, the hotel was expertly renovated and renamed in 1985. It is small and elegant, with amenities one seldom finds in an old hotel in a college town.

The lobby, with its marble floors, grand piano, period furnishings, and crystal chandelier transport's you back in time, perhaps abroad. The Ivy has a definite European feel, and the ambience was there even before general manager Gerald Hemery, from France, arrived on the scene.

The spacious, comfortable guest rooms feature four-poster beds, coverlets, dust ruffles, beveled-glass mirrors, and period reproductions; the executive suites have wet bars and sitting areas. Colors are muted roses, peaches, greens, and blues.

The Ivy serves good Southern food in its restaurant, The Waverly; The Library's mahogany paneling, marble-top bar, and Empire furniture make a nightcap very appealing.

Address: *Main and Jackson Sts., Starkville, MS 39759, tel. 601/323-2000.*
Accommodations: *40 double rooms with baths.*
Amenities: *Restaurant, bar; air-conditioning, phone and TV in rooms.*
Rates: *$45–$75; full breakfast. AE, MC, V.*

Oliver-Britt House

The Oliver-Britt House in Oxford is named for sisters Mary Ann Britt and Glynn Oliver, two young women who understand Southern hospitality and enjoy people. The fact that they just happen to be great cooks is a plus for their bed-and-breakfast guests and for those who use the sisters' catering facility for special festivities. It seems, in fact, that catering has top priority at the Oliver-Britt House.

Oliver and Britt have turned a former two-story physician's clinic, built in Victorian style around 1905, into an inn. Catering kitchens and dining room are downstairs; guest rooms are upstairs. Nice oak-strip flooring complements old iron and four-poster beds. One particularly pleasant room has a canopy bed, lots of flowered chintz and prints, and an antique slipper sofa at the foot of the bed. All rooms have some antiques interspersed with older contemporary furniture. French windows open onto the upstairs gallery and overlook the street below.

The Oliver-Britt House & Tea Room's welcoming hospitality and the homey smell of hot bread baking may be as welcome to some travelers as historic houses and antiques.

Address: *512 Van Buren Ave., Oxford, MS 38655, tel. 601/234-8043.*
Accommodations: *5 double rooms with baths.*
Amenities: *Air-conditioning.*
Rates: *$40–$50; full breakfast. MC, V.*

Along the Natchez Trace

The two-lane paved road crossing Mississippi from southwest to northeast, connecting Natchez to Nashville, Tennessee, has had a long and colorful past. It began about 8,000 years ago, when a path was "traced out" by buffalo and Indians. By 1800, the well-worn Old Trace was the route used by post riders, settlers, outlaws, peddlers, and "Kaintucks," or boatmen, from all points north. They came down the Mississippi River to New Orleans, sold their goods and boats, then headed home via the Trace, hoping not to encounter hostile Indians, bandits, or wild animals on the way. Those who could spare a few pennies slept inside— often on the floor—at inns (called "stands") scattered along the Trace, sharing "mush and milk" with other wayfarers pleased to have the simple luxury of hot food and a roof over their head.

After the late 1820s, when steamboats began to offer better accommodations and shorter trips, the wilderness path to the new frontier fell into disuse. The Old Trace had been taken over by weeds when, about 1909, the Mississippi chapter of the Daughters of the American Revolution waged a campaign to mark it. Their exemplary efforts resulted in the 450-mile, limited-access Natchez Trace Parkway, a long, thin park running from Natchez to Nashville.

Travelers today who seek historic places and a slower pace choose this road. The Trace is safe, scenic, and impeccably maintained by the National Park Service and has been landscaped to open up peaceful vistas in the dense woodland. Uniformed rangers patrol it, enforcing the 50 mph speed limit, and commercial vehicles and outdoor advertising are prohibited. You can drive the Trace from Natchez to Tupelo in seven hours, but to appreciate fully its beauty and history requires a more leisurely approach—perhaps a week-long odyssey.

Expect to see abundant tall timber, historic markers, wild game, and nature trails, but plan to leave the Trace for restaurants, shopping, and city sights. They're available in Natchez, Jackson, and Tupelo right on your way, and in Vicksburg, on the Mississippi River, 15 miles west.

In Natchez, one of the South's favorite destinations, many antebellum houses are open for daily tours throughout the year, and travelers today catch a glimpse of the way things were in the Old South.

Near Jackson, swaying pines and moss-draped oaks are replaced by sailboats and the glistening waters of the Ross Barnett Reservoir. Jackson is the best choice for restaurants, museums, and entertainment.

Tupelo offers museums, Southern fare, mall shopping, fine restaurants, and Elvis Presley's birthplace, the city's stellar attraction. Five miles north of Tupelo, on the Trace, is the Natchez Trace Parkway Visitor Center, which is open every day but Christmas. It has exhibits, a 12-minute film, a hands-on area for children, a bookstore, and the Official Map and Guide, which opens to a four-foot length, laying out the Trace mile by mile and giving detailed information.

Places to Go, Sights to See

Natchez's grand mansions attest to the former wealth of this old and colorful river town, recalling a time when lavish entertaining was de rigueur for the landed gentry. About 30 of the more than 500 mansions are on parade during the spring and fall "pilgrimages." A carriage ride through the historic district is a memorable way to see the houses and hear their history. The riverboats *Delta Queen* and *Mississippi Queen*—calliopes playing, flags flying, passengers cheering—make regular stops at Natchez Under-the-Hill, the riverbank area that was the former hangout of rowdy boatmen and gamblers.

Mount Locust Inn, at milepost 15.5, is the only remaining example of a frontier "stand," or inn. Built around 1780, it is furnished accordingly and is closed during January and February.

Port Gibson features quaint churches, historic houses of varying architectural styles, and the towering columns at the "Windsor Ruins," remnants of another time. In contrast, you can take a tour of the *Grand Gulf nuclear plant*, a futuristic facility.

Vicksburg, on the Mississippi, approximately 25 miles west of the Trace, is a lively and appealing river town known for its Civil War significance. Its historic antebellum houses are open for tours year-round. The *Vicksburg National Military Park* (3201 Clay St., tel. 601/636–0583) encompasses more than 1,800 acres of hills, fortifications, monuments, and the USS *Cairo*, a Union gunboat.

Jackson, Mississippi's capital, is the place to stop for cultural events and tours of historic sites and old government buildings. You can see the *Governor's Mansion* (300 E. Capitol St., tel. 601/359–3175) on 30-minute tours Tuesday through Friday. The *Old Capitol* and *State Historical Museum* (100 S. State St., tel. 601/359–6920) are open daily for self-guided tours. The *Jackson Zoological Park* (2918 W. Capitol St., tel. 601/352–2580) is open year-round, and the *Russell C. Davis Planetarium* (201 E. Pascagoula St., tel. 601/960–1550) gives multiscreen space and nature shows Tuesday through Sunday. The *Mississippi Museum of Art* (201 E. Pascagoula St., Jackson, tel. 601/960–1515) contains continuing and changing exhibits, often international in scope, and a gallery for children with interactive high-tech exhibits. At the *Mississippi Agricultural and Forestry Museum* (1150 Lakeland Dr., Jackson, tel. 601/354–6113), which has farm buildings and exhibits on the state's agrarian roots, you can see an orientation film and a re-created small town, ca. 1920, complete with farm animals and living-history enactments. Juried works and native crafts are sold here at the *Chimneyville Crafts Gallery* (tel. 601/981–2499 or 601/981–0019).

Mississippi Crafts Center (just north of Jackson, at Ridgeland, tel. 601/856–7546), a quaint log cabin with front porch rockers, sells local crafts, including quilts, baskets, and jewelry.

French Camp Log Cabin (milepost 180.8, tel. 601/547–6657) is a "dog trot" cabin (whose center hall, open on both ends, separates the two sides) built in the early 1800s, containing Indian and French artifacts, and with an operating sorghum mill.

Tupelo Visitors Center/Natchez Trace Parkway Headquarters (Tupelo, tel. 601/842–1572). The Visitors Center houses a museum pertaining to the Trace and offers an audiovisual program. Antique toys are displayed.

Tupelo City Museum (Ballard Park, tel. 601/841–6438) runs the gamut of the past, present, and future with permanent and traveling exhibits ranging from the arts (paintings and sculpture) to astronauts, plus Elvis Presley memorabilia.

Elvis Presley Birthplace (306 Elvis Presley Dr., Tupelo, tel. 601/841-1245). Take an interesting look at the humble beginnings of Elvis Presley, perhaps the world's best-known entertainer. There are ongoing tours daily.

At **Tishomingo State Park** (milepost 302.8, tel. 601/438-6914), in northeast Mississippi, the Appalachian Mountains begin. The park has nature trails, canoe trips, and beautiful rustic settings.

Restaurants

In Natchez-Under-the-Hill, try the casual **Cock of the Walk** (15 Silver St., tel. 601/446-8920), in an old cypress house, for catfish, shrimp, and gumbo; or **Natchez Landing** (11 Silver St., tel. 601/442-6639) for catfish and barbecue. **Café La Salle** (110 N. Pearl St., tel. 601/445-6000), in the restored Eola Hotel, serves Continental food in an elegant setting; the food at **Brothers** (209 Franklin St., tel. 601/442-1777) has an unmistakable New Orleans flavor; and **The Pompous Palate** (409 Franklin St., tel. 601/445-4946), in a historic bank building, has critics raving about the quality and presentation of Mississippi's best food.

Among Vicksburg's popular restaurants are the rather formal **Delta Point** (4155 Washington St., tel. 601/636-5317), overlooking the Mississippi River and serving a variety of good food, from Cajun to Continental; **Tuminello's** (500 Speed St., tel. 601/634-0507), a tradition since 1899 for seafood, steaks, and veal, which is also near the river; and the **Old Southern Tea Room** (801 Clay St., tel. 601/636-4005), for "plantation cooking" downtown, in the Vicksburg Hotel.

In Jackson, **400 East Capitol** (tel. 601/355-9671), in the downtown Emporium Building, offers live jazz nightly and "classic American" poultry, beef, and game. The casual **Amerigo** (6592 Old Canton Rd., tel. 601/977-0563) serves grilled seafood, steaks, veal, and pasta. A local favorite, **Hal & Mal's** (200 S. Commerce St., tel. 601/948-0888), in a 1920s warehouse, serves such good Mississippi cooking it's sure to be packed. The prime ribs and Gulf seafood at **Primo's** (4330 N. State St., tel. 601/982-2064) are a Jackson tradition.

Tourist Information

Jackson Convention & Visitors Bureau (Box 1450, Jackson, MS 39215, tel. 601/960-1891 or 800/354-7695). **Mississippi Department of Economic Development**, Division of Tourism Development (Box 22825, Jackson, MS 39205, tel. 601/359-3297 or 800/647-2290). **Natchez Convention & Visitor Bureau** (311 Liberty Rd., Natchez, MS 39120, tel. 601/446-6345 or 800/647-6724). **Natchez Pilgrimage Tours** (Box 347, Natchez, MS 39121, tel. 601/446-6631 or 800/647-6742). **Natchez Trace Parkway Visitor Center** (milepost 266, Rte. 1, NT-143, Tupelo, MS 38801, tel 601/680-4025). **Port Gibson Chamber of Commerce** (Box 491, Port Gibson, MS 39150, tel. 601/437-4351). **Tupelo Convention & Visitors Bureau** (Box 1485, Tupelo, MS 38802, tel.

601/841–6521). **Vicksburg Convention & Visitors Bureau** (Box 110, Vicksburg, MS 39180, tel. 601/636–9421 or 800/221–3536).

Reservation Services

Lincoln, Ltd. Bed & Breakfast Mississippi Reservation Service (Box 3479, Meridian, MS 39303, tel. 601/482–5483 or 800/633–6477). **Natchez Pilgrimage Tours Bed & Breakfast Reservations** (Box 347, Natchez, MS 39121, tel. 601/446–6631 or 800/647–6742).

The Briars

One of Mississippi's prettiest and most serene B&Bs, The Briars is quietly tucked away on a bluff high above the Mississippi River. The Federal-style house, built around 1818, with its 80-foot veranda, dormer windows, and fanlight doorways, is one of the finest examples of Southern plantation-style architecture extant and one of the state's most historically significant houses. In the mid-1800s it was the home of the Howell family, whose beautiful Varina was called "the Rose of Mississippi." In the parlor of The Briars in 1845, Varina Howell married a dashing young graduate of West Point, Jefferson Davis, who was to become a Mexican War hero, a member of the Senate, Secretary of War under U.S. President Pierce, and, in 1861, President of the Confederate States of America. The Briars is listed on the National Register of Historic Places.

Interior designers Robert E. Canon and Newton Wilds purchased the house in 1975, and since that time, their talents have produced a retreat as grand as it is gracious. Each bedroom has a different color scheme and fabric, and as one would expect of a house done by designers, it is a showplace, although not so design perfect as to be uncomfortable. On the contrary, it's a warm and congenial place with lots of special features. It contains an enclosed gallery supported by arches and fluted columns, unusual fan-shaped windows, and walk-in closets in some rooms. In the pretty and spacious guest rooms, antiques and reproductions are amicably mixed and there's a choice of king-size, queen-size, or extra-long twin beds. Many guests enjoy early morning coffee on the veranda or in their rooms.

From an observation point on the grounds, you can see the flatlands of Louisiana and many miles of the busy Mississippi River, where there's always something going on, from tugboats pushing barges to festive riverboats up from New Orleans. The flowering plants and foliage offer almost as nice a view as the river. The pavilion dining room, where guests are served breakfast, is another choice spot for outstanding views. The Briars is, understandably, one of eight Mississippi properties given a Four-Diamond rating by the American Automobile Association.

Address: *31 Irving La., Box 1245, Natchez, MS 39120, tel. 601/446–9654 or 800/634–1818.*
Accommodations: *13 double rooms with baths.*
Amenities: *Air-conditioning, cable TV in rooms; pool.*
Rates: *$120–$135; full breakfast. AE, MC, V.*
Restrictions: *Smoking only in foyer and on porches, no pets.*

The Burn

The name of this impressive Greek Revival house dates to 1836 and the occupation of Natchez Mayor John Walworth, who chose the Scottish word for "small brook" to commemorate the one that once meandered through the property. Though it's only a punny coincidence, Loveta Byrne and her children own the place now, and the Byrnes are in residence at The Burn.

The house was built in 1832 as a pure Greek Revival cottage, and from the street, it does not appear to be the three-story mansion that you find upon closer inspection. Doric columns support the portico; as you enter through the transomed and sidelighted Grecian doorway, the first thing you see is the unique spiral staircase with its delicate spindle banisters. Dramatic red and green Natchez Collection wall covering and fabric by Schumacher are used in the music room, and in the formal dining room Schumacher wallpaper and draperies draw attention even when the Empire table is set with the 1820 Old Paris china. Outstanding woodwork and plaster moldings enhance the quality you note at The Burn.

Guest rooms in the main house are downstairs in the original house-servants' quarters, where quiet and comfort prevail. Bedrooms boast Mallard furniture, pastel walls, and exquisite Belgian fabrics on windows and beds. The Pink Room is elegantly furnished in Rococo Revival style, which was a Natchez favorite in the mid-1800s; in fact, The Burn is a treasure trove of 19th-century European antiques and accessories throughout. The house retains its Old South charm while offering modern conveniences. Guest-room TVs in the main house are discreetly hidden in antique armoires. There are additional guest rooms across the courtyard in the dependency, a building formerly used as servants' quarters.

Loveta encourages guests to enjoy the house and to explore the lush and lovely grounds. Though it is located in the city, The Burn has a country feel about it. The property is on a rise, surrounded by tall trees and flowering shrubbery, except for the clearing of the pool and courtyard areas. Loveta and a partner also own and operate Natchez's first-rate gourmet restaurant, the Pompous Palate.

Address: *712 N. Union St., Natchez, MS 39120, tel. 601/442-1344 or 800/654-8859.*
Accommodations: *2 double rooms with baths in main house, 4 doubles with baths in dependency.*
Amenities: *Air-conditioning; pool.*
Rates: *$75–$125; full breakfast. AE, MC, V.*
Restrictions: *No smoking in house, no pets.*

Cedar Grove

Vicksburg's Cedar Grove is a house of rather eclectic Greek Revival style that's a National Historic Landmark. The "grand antebellum mansion" has also been described as "a Southern experience relived," although the two-story house, with its round columns and wings, in all its stucco glory, is on a much grander scale than most Southerners, or otherners, have ever lived.

Imagine 25 ornately designed, spacious rooms filled with rare and important antiques that about 30,000 people come to see each year on daily tours. B&B guests, however, are isolated from the tourists, so that their privacy is ensured, whether their room is in the main house or in the former carriage house.

Guests are invited to a complimentary tea in the garden room with mint juleps and piano music. Dinner is provided on request, with advance notice. Owners Ted and Estelle Mackey mix and mingle with guests if they're in town. He's a native Mississippian who left a law practice in Los Angeles to return to the South. They both love antiques and old houses, so they bought Cedar Grove a few years back and have spent the time since on various restoration projects on the property (about 4 acres). The Mackeys strongly impress upon the staff the importance of making guests feel most welcome and very comfortable, and the result has earned Cedar Grove AAA's Four-Diamond award.

The house was built in 1840 and still has a Union cannonball from the Battle of Vicksburg lodged in a parlor wall. Amazingly, the original heavy furnishings made for the house remain in the master bedroom and the children's rooms. Many of Prudent Mallard's dark, massive pieces are in evidence, including a specially made king-size bed. All rooms are opulent and colorful, and they feature elaborate moldings, woodwork, wallpaper borders, gaslit chandeliers, gold-leaf pier mirrors, Italian marble mantels, and rich draperies reminiscent of those that Scarlett O'Hara made into a dress in *Gone with the Wind*. The house also boasts a grand ballroom and many choice spots from which to view the Mississippi.

Address: *2300 Washington St., Vicksburg, MS 39180, tel. 601/636–2800, 800/862–1300, or 800/448–2820 in MS.*
Accommodations: *10 double rooms with baths, 9 suites.*
Amenities: *Air-conditioning, phones, TV in rooms; pool, hot tub.*
Rates: *$85–$115, suites $110–145; full breakfast. AE, MC, V.*
Restrictions: *Smoking permitted in garden room and Rooms 3 and 8 only, no pets.*

Dunleith

Dunleith is one of the South's most beautiful houses, from the colonnaded galleries that encircle it to the superior antiques within and the 40 acres of landscaped grounds, wooded bayous, and green pastures without. It is constantly photographed, often written about, and occasionally appears in films. Dunleith is also a National Historic Landmark on the National Register of Historic Places and is one of the AAA's Four-Diamond inns.

The palatial mansion (ca. 1856) is owned by William Heins III of Natchez. A resident manager and staff run the business of daily tours and lodging, and it is, quite noticeably, a business. Fortunately, the magnificence of Dunleith's architecture and interiors neutralizes the regimented recitations of the staff and their curt responses to questions. The grandeur of the place prevails.

Among the elegant furnishings are the dining room's French Zuber wallpaper from 1855 woodblocks that was hidden in a cave in France during World War I. The V'Soske carpet in the front parlor determined the color scheme for the room's walls, draperies, and upholstery; the greenish-gold walls and draperies perfectly complement the peachy pinks and gold tones in the carpet. A Louis XV ormolu-mounted mahogany Linke

table is in a prominent place in the front parlor.

Three of the guest rooms at Dunleith are in the main house, and eight are in the former servants' wing. The rooms are quiet and private and are well decorated in mid-19th-century style, with a mixture of reproductions and antiques. All of them have working fireplaces.

Another nice feature is that the grounds are subtly lighted at night, so that guests can stroll in the "moonlight" or enjoy the romantic views from wicker rockers on the galleries.

Old brick and warm woods set the stage for the big plantation breakfast served in the restored poultry house. Exposed beams, lots of windows, and wood floors add a homey touch that guests may have missed in the elaborate, museumlike main house.

Address: *84 Homochitto St., Natchez, MS 39120, tel. 601/446-8500 or 800/433-2445.*
Accommodations: *11 double rooms with baths.*
Amenities: *Air-conditioning, TV in rooms, phones in common area.*
Rates: *$85–$130; full breakfast. AE, D, MC, V.*
Restrictions: *No pets.*

Millsaps Buie House

Though its location in Mississippi's busiest city keeps it from being just another moss-and-magnolia bed-and-breakfast inn, the Millsaps Buie House in Jackson is grand and historic and filled with antiques. It's actually an elegant Victorian mansion, built in 1888 in the heart of downtown. Everything about the house says "quality," from exterior construction to interior details like the hand-molded plaster frieze work, bay windows, and other elements of the Queen Anne influence.

Once the home of Major Reuben Webster Millsaps of the Confederate Army, banker, financier, and founder in 1892 of the distinguished Millsaps College, the house has been in the same family for five generations. It has been a B&B inn since 1987 and is described as "a 19th-century urban retreat for the 20th-century traveler." One might add "business traveler," for although it contains priceless heirlooms, each room has a telephone with computer dataport and a small, unobtrusive bedside radio, and TVs are concealed in old armoires.

Guests are encouraged to relax in the drawing room, parlor, or library before retiring to their room for the evening. Pier mirrors in the parlor reflect the grand piano and a French "courting bench," as the house as a whole reflects the style and taste of the distinguished interior designer who also refurbished the Governor's Mansion, the New State Capitol, and Florewood Plantation in Greenwood.

Bedrooms are furnished in a pleasing mixture of period antiques and reproductions, including tester or canopy beds, rosewood chairs, and marble-top tables. Original mantelpieces add detail and interest, while old family portraits add authenticity. The rich, pleated draperies in one of the rooms are made of solid fabric in a shade matching the dominant color in the flowered wallpaper; carpet color matches the draperies.

A resident manager and full staff keep the Millsaps Buie House in mint condition and see that guests' needs are met. The staff members here are truly gracious, unlike those efficient but impersonal people at some other inns. The Millsaps Buie House won AAA's Four-Diamond Award.

Address: *628 N. State St., Jackson, MS 39202, tel. 601/352–0221, fax 601/352–0221.*
Accommodations: *11 double rooms with baths.*
Amenities: *Air-conditioning, cable TV, and phones in rooms.*
Rates: *$87–$142; full breakfast. MC, V.*
Restrictions: *Smoking on porches only, no pets.*

Monmouth

The massive Monmouth (ca. 1818) may lack the delicate lacelike ornamentation of some other Natchez homes, but it is no less interesting in monumental architecture and Victorian furnishings. Its sturdy appeal inspired a daughter of the house to write this in her diary in 1868: "Dear old Monmouth, within whose substantial weather-beaten walls it used to seem to my childish imagination that care and trouble could never come."

Staying at Monmouth still evokes such feelings of security and well-being, and touring the house is a treat. Perhaps the children of owners Ron and Lani Riches will someday write such tributes, though the Riches actually live in Los Angeles, where he is a land developer. A resident manager and full staff keep the inn ready for guests.

The Riches bought Monmouth in 1978, then spent two years restoring it, recapturing the grandeur it knew in earlier days. The interior mood is formal, with the blue-silk-covered Rococo Revival furniture in the double parlor made even prettier by the glow of a Waterford crystal chandelier. The windows are done with fanciful swags, valances, fringes, and lace. The "courting chair" in the parlor, a major conversation piece, is a three-cornered contraption just suited for a couple and a chaperone.

The bedrooms in the main house are a decorator's dream. The peach bedroom, a favorite, features peach walls and fabrics, including magnificent draperies on the windows and the canopy bed. Lacy accessories add to the beauty of this bedroom. Other rooms are less feminine but equally grand, and 10 have working fireplaces.

Monmouth's Greek Revival portico was added in 1853, at which time the original brick was covered with eggshell stucco and scored. The grounds, all 26 acres, are immaculate, and there's always something in bloom. Though the interior of the main house is designer perfect, the four garden cottages, the carriage house, and the servants' quarters are great to stay in too. They are cozy and intimate and far removed from the hustle and bustle of the house, with its tours and gift shop.

Address: *36 John A. Quitman Pkwy., Natchez, MS 39120, tel. 601/442–5852 or 800/828–4531.*
Accommodations: *6 double rooms and 1 suite in main house; 11 doubles and 1 suite in garden cottages and outbuildings; all with baths.*
Amenities: *Air-conditioning, TVs, phones in rooms, free house tour.*
Rates: *$90–$160; full breakfast. AE, D, MC, V.*
Restrictions: *No smoking indoors, no pets.*

Mount Repose

While Natchez is often busy entertaining guests, the surrounding countryside is so quiet you can almost hear the Spanish moss gently swaying in the breeze. Though only 7 miles from downtown, the aptly named Mount Repose seems to be a world away. This roomy, rambling plantation house listed on the National Register of Historic Places is a perfect spot in which to rest and regroup. Mount Repose has high ceilings, lots of doors, tall windows, and fireplaces in every room; it is not delicately ornate but "country comfortable," the way planters' homes were meant to be.

The house was built in 1824 in the Federal style, with a central 2½-story facade. When the Greek Revival style became popular in Natchez in the 1830s, one-story wings were added to each side, resulting in a carefully planned and pleasingly eclectic building. Square columns across the front support double-tiered galleries; matching doors with oval fanlights and sidelights open onto both galleries, where porch swings wait to be used. In front you'll see magnolias and dogwood trees, rows of centuries-old live oaks draped with Spanish moss, a circle of azaleas, and perhaps a fat bullfrog resting on the rim of the brick lily pond. The back porch, shaded by a big ginkgo tree, offers views of rolling hills, woods, and a lake, as well as glimpses of

a plethora of birds, squirrels, maybe even a wild turkey or two. Mount Repose is indeed a country place.

William Bisland built the house, and it has been occupied since by Bisland descendants. The walls are filled with portraits of ancestors, and many of Mount Repose's original furnishings are still in place, among them tester beds by Mallard, the New Orleans cabinetmaker; armoires; and dressers. Various Bisland descendants have added such items as an Italian palace chair and rare porcelains from Paris.

Off the front bedroom, which has Mallard furniture, an Oriental carpet, and rose-flowered wallpaper, is the children's room and nursery, where old christening gowns, porcelain dolls, and first-edition children's books are displayed. Mount Repose is a place where guests come for one night and stay for several. They particularly enjoy relaxing on the shaded galleries and strolling the well-kept grounds.

Address: *Pine Ridge Rd., Natchez, MS 39120, tel. 601/446–6631 or 800/647–6742.*
Accommodations: *3 double rooms with baths.*
Amenities: *Air-conditioning, phones in rooms.*
Rates: *$90–$105; full breakfast. AE, MC, V.*
Restrictions: *No smoking indoors, no pets.*

Natchez Eola Hotel

This wonderfully restored 1927 hotel, a Natchez treasure, has earned recent accolades and awards and is now basking in renewed glory. The historic hotel began a decline in the 1960s and closed its doors in 1974. In 1978, renewed interest in preservation and rehabilitation induced investors to buy the property, and by 1980 work had begun on the $6.5 million job.

The hotel's main entrance was changed to face an open brick courtyard filled with foliage, flowers, and a fountain. The old coffee shop was updated and upscaled to become the formal dining room, Café LaSalle; a glass-enclosed casual restaurant called Juleps and the relatively new Juleps Bar & Lounge also overlook the courtyard and fountain. In the lobby, a raised dais called Le Pavillion is the site for afternoon tea. The seventh floor was made into suites and a meeting room, which have choice views of the meandering Mississippi River and rich delta land far beyond. (The smaller rooms have balconies overlooking the courtyard.)

Today, under the direction of owners Larry L. "Butch" Brown of Natchez and Baxter H. Turnage of Memphis, the genteel Eola once again exhibits Southern charm and myriad amenities. The guest rooms, which have Georgian reproduction furniture, recently received extensive refurbishment, with new draperies and upholstery.

The lobby, with pastel colors, elaborate chandeliers, marble trim, massive yet stately columns, arched doorways and windows, and outstanding millwork, was decorated by Henredon Furniture, Schumacher, and eight other licensees with the new Natchez Collection of furnishings and fabrics. It is the center of activity for functions ranging from annual Opera Festival recitals and the new Natchez Literary Celebration to afternoon tea. Since 1932 the Eola has been host to events surrounding the busy Pilgrimage weeks in April and October.

The Eola—one of the South's grand old landmarks—is the only hotel in Mississippi among the 60 or so Historic Hotels of America. The National Trust for Historic Preservation selects hotels for their historic character, architectural quality, and the preservation efforts of the owners. The Natchez Eola is also listed on the National Register of Historic Places.

Address: *110 N. Pearl St., Natchez, MS 39120, tel. 601/445–6000 or 800/888–9140, fax 601/446–5310.*
Accommodations: *118 double rooms with baths and 7 suites.*
Amenities: *Air-conditioning, TVs, phones, and ceiling fans in rooms, room service, gift shop, 2 restaurants, bar, 4 small meeting rooms.*
Rates: *$60–$150; breakfast extra. AE, DC, MC, V.*

Pleasant Hill

leasant Hill, with its perfect name, is one of the most pleasant and cheerful bed-and-breakfasts in all the South and is listed on the National Register of Historic Places. Called a "raised cottage," it is a large house elevated from a fully raised basement, three-storied and elegant. It is known in architectural circles for its well-planned space and the high quality of its Greek Revival trim.

The house was initially built on the site now occupied by the larger mansion, Magnolia Hall. In 1858, the owner developed more grandiose plans for a new home, so he had Pleasant Hill pulled on log rollers by a team of oxen to its new address one block south, for his sister's family. Rumor has it that the mistress of the manor gave birth in the middle of Pearl Street while the house was en route.

When you walk up about 12 steps to the entrance, you see the wide central hall that separates the formal parlor and dining room on the right from the library and a bedroom on the left. At the end of the hall rises a gracefully winding stairway. Across the back of the house is an enclosed porch with rooms at each end. The woodwork in the house is magnificent, and so are the furnishings, mostly Empire, Federal, and Victorian antiques.

You expect to see fine antiques in the home of dealers, and owners (since 1991) Brad and Eliza Simonton, proprietors of Simonton Antiques in Natchez, do not disappoint you. Guests immediately notice a Boston recamier from 1815 and a New York breakfast table from about the same year, possibly a Duncan Phyfe. In fact, the entire house reeks of quality, from the exquisite furniture to the custom-made Stark carpet and the Italian marble mantels.

The colors are warm and glowing: shades of peach and terra-cotta, bordered by rich cream. There are lots of cinnamons and creams, too, in the ground-level bedrooms. Guests congregate on the glass-enclosed porch or in the spacious sitting room around which the bedrooms are situated. All the rooms are quiet, private, and appealing, and each one has a different name and unique furnishings: The Canterbury Room sports a "field bed," one supposedly used by generals encamped with troops in the field.

Address: *310 S. Pearl St., Natchez, MS 39120, tel. 601/442-7674.*
Accommodations: *4 double rooms with baths.*
Amenities: *Air-conditioning, phones and TV in rooms.*
Rates: *$90–$115; full breakfast. MC, V.*
Restrictions: *Smoking on porches only, no pets.*

Stanton Hall

Stanton Hall is perhaps the grandest of the grandes dames of Natchez's antebellum houses. From the massive Corinthian columns and lacy iron railings on the front gallery, through the 72-foot central hallway, and on to the magnificent ornamentation found in every room, Stanton Hall is a treasure. The front parlor features elaborately carved wood moldings, which tower over the matched Victorian parlor set and Rococo Revival side chairs.

Like the palatial Dunleith, however, Stanton Hall is very much a business. Proceeds from the mansion's bed-and-breakfast, daily tours, functions, the gift shop, and the Carriage House Restaurant fund projects of the Pilgrimage Garden Club.

Since the club bought it in 1938, Stanton Hall has been its headquarters and major revenue producer. The imposing mansion and grounds command an entire city block in the downtown historic district, four blocks east of the river. The house was built in 1858 by cotton broker Frederick Stanton, who lived there only a month before he died. Stanton Hall became Stanton College for Young Ladies, after which hard times forced several sales of the property. When it came into the hands of the garden club, the members vowed to furnish the house in the "most fashionable style or manner." Indeed they did. The members

commenced to gather furnishings from their own collections and borrowed and bought pieces from other Natchez mansions. Their influence was far-reaching, for in 1940, the Scalamandré Company of New York City donated fabric for the parlor draperies. The elaborate architectural details—arches, plaster moldings, and cornices—are so overpowering, however, it's difficult to pay close attention to fabric or furniture, even the outstanding carved mahogany Belter window seat.

Mantels of white Carrara marble, carved with fruit and flowers, adorn many rooms. The upstairs hall and bedrooms repeat the layout and scale of the first floor, though the design features are not as ornate. Bedrooms have full- or half-tester beds, armoires, dressers, and appropriate chairs and accent pieces.

Ruth Havard, Stanton Hall's resident manager, greets guests and presents them with complimentary wine and Natchez chocolates.

Address: *401 High St., Natchez, MS 39121, tel. 601/442–6282 or 800/647–6742.*
Accommodations: *4 double rooms with baths.*
Amenities: *Air-conditioning, guest phone and TV in common area after 5 PM; off-street parking.*
Rates: *$120–$125; full breakfast. AE, MC, V.*
Restrictions: *No smoking, no pets.*

Anchuca

Time seems to have stood still at Anchuca. It may be the most authentic—in style, decor, and attitude—of Vicksburg's antebellum bed-and-breakfasts. The owner, May Burns, is about as Southern a belle as you'll find, for she hails from the Mississippi Delta, upriver from Vicksburg. Anchuca (ca. 1830) was the first Vicksburg B&B, and in the 10 years since it began, guests have experienced the South the way it must have been in the pre-1860 days. It has consistently earned the AAA Four-Diamond rating.

You step into the music parlor, where the Knabe grand piano shares billing with a pair of exquisite watermelon-colored recamiers, on which many a belle probably swooned over men and music. Though the master suite with its pink tufted furniture can be reserved, most guests are put up in an original dependency formerly used by house servants or in a turn-of-the-century guest cottage. Antiques and period reproductions are used throughout the guest rooms.

Address: *1010 1st East St., Vicksburg, MS 39180, tel. 601/636–4931 or 800/262–4822.*
Accommodations: *9 double rooms with baths, 1 suite.*
Amenities: *Air-conditioning, TV and phones in rooms.*
Rates: *$75–$115; full breakfast. AE, D, MC, V.*
Restrictions: *No smoking in main house, no pets.*

Balfour House

In this land of stunning architecture, the mere fact that the columned 1835 Balfour house is one of the finest examples of the Greek Revival in the state or that it has a graceful, elliptical spiral staircase rising three stories may not impress you. But the really interesting thing here is that while watching from a window in her home in 1863, Emma Balfour wrote an evocative account of the 47-day siege of Vicksburg. She saw mortar shells passing over the house and heard the conversations of friends who fought on opposite sides. Emma Balfour's important diary is now in the Mississippi archives.

The square, redbrick Balfour House was restored to the meticulous specifications of the U.S. Deptartment of the Interior, and owner Terry Weinberger says the workmen uncovered such items as a cannonball in the walls. Original features include parquet floors, outstanding millwork, and *faux marbre*. The original pastel wall colors and period antiques are used throughout.

Address: *1002 Crawford St., Vicksburg, MS 39181, tel. 601/638–3690 or 800/844–2500.*
Accommodations: *2 double rooms with baths.*
Amenities: *Air-conditioning, phones in rooms, TV in master bedroom.*
Rates: *$85–$95; Continental breakfast. MC, V.*
Restrictions: *No smoking, no pets.*

The Corners

The Corners has had a happier history than many other Vicksburg dwellings. No cannonballs are lodged in the walls, and there are no stories of the siege, just interesting anecdotes about the house and its times. The Corners sits almost in the shadows of Cedar Grove, because John Klein, Cedar Grove's builder, presented the smaller and more intimate one-story frame house to his daughter as a wedding gift.

The late Greek Revival/early Victorian house was built in 1873 and bought by Texans Bettye and Cliff Whitney in 1986. It was not a planned purchase but a fortuitous happening: On a trip, the Whitneys saw the delightful house and bought it the same day. Today you can enjoy the river sights and sounds from the 65-foot front gallery. All the guest rooms are furnished with antiques, each with a different color combination. The master bedroom is "on the mauve side," with a half-tester bed and a river view. The Corners is a AAA Four-Diamond Award winner and is on the National Register of Historic Places.

Address: *601 Klein St., Vicksburg, MS 39180, tel. 601/636-7421 or 800/444-7421.*
Accommodations: *6 double rooms with baths, 1 suite, 2-bedroom housekeeping cottage.*
Amenities: *Air-conditioning, TV in rooms.*
Rates: *$75-$95; full breakfast. AE, MC, V.*
Restrictions: *No pets.*

Duff Green House

Times were good when Duff Green built a house for his bride, Mary, back in 1856—a grand Palladian-style house, with elaborate cast-iron grillwork on the second- and third-floor galleries. A few years later, however, Confederate Vicksburg was under siege by Union forces. The Green family joined other local citizens and moved to the safety of nearby caves, where Mary gave birth to a son she named Siege. The house survived and later served as a hospital with Confederate wounded downstairs, it is said, and Union wounded upstairs.

The Duff Green House stands tall and proud, a little heavier with cannonballs, but as elegant and graceful as ever. The interior proportions are grand, with outstanding millwork and plaster ornamentation, solid cypress doors, and exquisite Waterford chandeliers. Fifteen fireplaces still keep the house warm and cozy. Owners Alicia and Harry Sharp, who also own the Gentlemen's Haberdashery in Vicksburg, bought the house in 1985 and restored it. The original wall and trim colors were duplicated; the furnishings are of the period, but none are original to the house.

Address: *1114 1st East St., Vicksburg, MS 39180, tel. 601/636-6968, 601/636-6662, or 800/992-0037.*
Accommodations: *4 double rooms with baths, 3 suites.*
Amenities: *Air-conditioning, phones in rooms; pool.*
Rates: *$75-$150; full breakfast. AE, MC, V.*

French Camp Academy Bed and Breakfast

The settlement on the Natchez Trace called French Camp got its name when Louis le Fleur built an inn on the Trace back in 1812. Le Fleur, a French Canadian, married a Choctaw woman; their son changed his name to Greenwood Leflore and became a Choctaw chief, a state senator, and a colorful figure in Mississippi history. Today, Leflore's ornate carriage is on display at French Camp Academy, a small secondary school begun in 1885.

Sallie and Ed Williford, both associated with the school (she teaches algebra and tutors math; he is director of development), manage the academy's nearby bed-and-breakfast. The inn on the Natchez Trace (ca. 1850) is intentionally rustic; it is made from two log cabins now joined together, each more than 100 years old. Rich, warm wood, chinked log walls, antiques, iron beds, and handmade quilts give the B&B the right touch of Old World charm mixed with its 20th-century conveniences. Big windows with forest views plus Sallie's bread and jams are a bonus.

Address: *French Camp, MS 39745, tel. 601/547–6835.*
Accommodations: *2 double rooms with baths.*
Amenities: *Air-conditioning.*
Rates: *$53; full breakfast. No credit cards.*
Restrictions: *No smoking indoors.*

Governor Holmes House

Walk through the historic door at the "Governor's House" and hear marvelous Mozart extending a melodious welcome. Built in 1794, the Federal brick town house was the residence of David Holmes, the last governor of the Mississippi Territory and the first governor of the state of Mississippi. The house is also rumored to have once been owned by Jefferson Davis, president of the Confederacy.

Perhaps these high-powered former occupants inspired the present owners when they set about making the remarkably well preserved house reflect its history and happenstance; it is now a National Historic Landmark. In the Governor's Suite, beamed ceilings and ecru walls provide a perfect background for the colorful Oriental carpet and canopies that cover the two double beds. The fabric is by Scalamandré. Leather wing chairs positioned beside the fireplace are inviting. Co-owners Rivet Hedderel (an interior designer who owns an antiques shop in New Orleans) and Hermann Stenz have put their time, talents, and expertise to good use in the Governor Holmes House.

Address: *207 S. Wall St., Natchez, MS 39120, tel. 601/442–2366.*
Accommodations: *3 double rooms with baths, 1 suite.*
Amenities: *Air-conditioning and TV in rooms.*
Rates: *$85–$115; full breakfast. MC, V.*
Restrictions: *No pets.*

Hope Farm

All the bed-and-breakfasts in Natchez are old, but Hope Farm is surely the oldest. The original portion, now the B&B wing, was built of heavy cypress around 1775. Don Carlos de Grand Pré, the Spanish commandant of the Natchez District, bought the house in 1789, built the main house, and commenced to entertain distinguished guests. Perhaps he set the precedent for the lavish entertaining that is still part of the Natchez lifestyle.

Hope Farm is now owned by Ethel Banta, a Natchez native who moved to New York after graduating from Sweet Briar College. She "came home" in 1986; bought the house, 15 acres of land, and the furnishings as well; and became the fifth owner of Hope Farm. One of the many treasures is a Duncan Phyfe dining room table, which is often set with Old Paris china and exquisite Gorham silver. The cream-colored parlor is dressed with early American Empire furniture; the guest rooms are furnished with some plantation-made pieces, a chair designed by Thomas Jefferson, and other important antiques.

Address: *147 Homochitto St., Natchez, MS 39120, tel. 601/445-4848 or 800/647-6742.*
Accommodations: *4 double rooms with baths.*
Amenities: *Air-conditioning; tour of house.*
Rates: *$80–$90; early coffee on the porch, full breakfast, refreshments upon arrival.*
Restrictions: *No smoking, no pets.*

Lansdowne

The entrance to Lansdowne leads one on a tunnellike trail through thick woods and foliage, across a narrow bridge over a deep ravine. It is civilized isolation in its purest form and a marvelous country retreat for city dwellers. Lansdowne was built in 1853 by George Marshall. His descendants are still in residence, and so are many of the original furnishings. The style is Greek Revival, with fine accent work, pale pink brick, and dark-green shutters, reminiscent of Italianate style. All is contained on one floor and two dependencies, which used to be the governess's room and schoolrooms.

Lansdowne's guest rooms are quiet and comfortable, furnished with antiques and reproductions, but plain in comparison with the main house and its treasures. High ceilings emphasize the plaster medallions and chandeliers, though it is the outstanding Rococo Revival parlor furniture that catches the eye. The exquisite old family silver in the formal dining room is a treat for guests to see at breakfast, and so are the old wood-graining and marbleizing, which have been preserved.

Address: *M. L. King Rd., Natchez, MS 39121, tel. 601/446-9401 or 800/647-6742.*
Accommodations: *2 double rooms with baths.*
Amenities: *Air-conditioning, TV in rooms.*
Rates: *$90; full breakfast. AE, MC, V.*
Restrictions: *No pets.*

Linden

Linden's ornately carved Federal-style doorway may be familiar to movie fans, because it was copied for the doorway to Scarlett O'Hara's Tara in *Gone with the Wind*. The house was built around 1800 and was sold in 1818 to the first U.S. senator from Mississippi. Linden is a sprawling, two-story house with wings on each side, known for its 98-foot front gallery and for the Federal furniture found inside. Hepplewhite, Sheraton, and Chippendale are well represented at Linden; other treasures include three original paintings by Audubon and a portrait of Jenny Lind.

The guest rooms are furnished in antiques and some heirlooms, for one family's descendants have been in residence here since 1849. The east-wing bedrooms open onto a back gallery, which overlooks the garden and courtyard. The owner, Jeanette Feltus, a former teacher, conducts free tours of the house and joins guests for breakfast. The house is listed on the National Register of Historic Places and is also a AAA Three-Diamond property.

Address: *1 Linden Pl., Natchez, MS 39120, tel. 601/445–5472 or 800/647–6742.*
Accommodations: *7 double rooms with baths.*
Amenities: *Air-conditioning.*
Rates: *$90; full breakfast. AE, MC, V.*
Restrictions: *No pets.*

Oak Square

Port Gibson's massive white-frame Greek Revival–style Oak Square (ca. 1850), whose white columns support a second-story porch, was built as the town home of a cotton planter who apparently wanted his family to enjoy culture as well as comfort. The house features a foyer/ballroom with a wide stairway leading to a "minstrel gallery." The gentility of the old house (a AAA Four-Diamond Award winner) has been retained by owners Martha and William Lum, former retail merchants in Port Gibson. Both the Lums inherited massive antiques from old family plantations, and their treasures are now on display at Oak Square.

Elaborate crown moldings and ornate plasterwork adorn the ceilings, and Empire and Rococo Revival furniture fills all 30 rooms in the mansion. Guest rooms are in the main house or in the guest house, originally two buildings. One, an 1848 Vicksburg town house with galleries, was dismantled and moved to Port Gibson; the other was servants' quarters. The guest house is also furnished with heirlooms and antiques.

Address: *1207 Church St., Port Gibson, MS 39150, tel. 601/437–4350 or 800/729–0240.*
Accommodations: *10 double rooms with baths.*
Amenities: *Air-conditioning, TV and phones in rooms.*
Rates: *$75–$95; full breakfast. AE, MC, D, V.*
Restrictions: *No smoking indoors, no pets.*

Ravenna

Visitors will remember Ravenna for its remarkable elliptical stairway, which gracefully spirals from the first to the third floor. A magnificent hallway arch sets the stage for the stairway and the other architectural elements of the interior. The Greek Revival house was built in 1835 for a prominent cotton broker who spared no expense, and people still look in awe at the staircase.

Ravenna, the home of Catherine Morgan and her family, is furnished mostly in period antiques and family heirlooms; it has a nice "lived-in" appeal. The guest rooms, with old armoires and tester beds, are restful and gracious, and their decor matches the age and style of the house, with no unnecessary adornment.

Catherine is known for her culinary talent, and each morning she serves up Southern delicacies with all the trimmings.

The gardens are lush and lovely at any time of year, with foliage so thick the house appears to peek from behind the leaves and Spanish moss. In springtime, azaleas and dogwood provide a haven of color.

Address: *S. Union at Ravenna La., Natchez, MS 39121, tel. 601/446–9973 or 800/647–6742.*
Accommodations: *2 double rooms with baths; housekeeping cottage with fireplace.*
Amenities: *Air-conditioning.*
Rates: *$85–$100; full breakfast. AE, MC, V.*
Restrictions: *No pets.*

Redbudd Inn

The Redbudd Inn is as pretty as the name sounds, and the 1885 Victorian house has other attractions, too. A popular restaurant on the first floor that serves lunch to the public will prepare private candlelit dinners for bed-and-breakfast guests, if requested in advance. The inn is also an antiques shop where English and Victorian antiques may be admired or purchased.

Owners Rosemary Burge, an interior designer; Maggie Garrett, a teacher; and Kevin Lawrence, a floral designer, have done wonderful things with the Redbudd Inn in the years they've owned it. Each room is decorated with period antiques and individual colors and appointments. The peach room, for example, features a big

Victorian bed so tall it has antique steps beside it. Flowers and accessories complement the decor.

This B&B, right in the heart of Kosciusko, is a fine example of Queen Anne architecture and is listed on the National Register of Historic Places. It is within walking distance of the town square and other charming Victorian houses.

Address: *121 N. Wells St., Kosciusko, MS 39090, tel. 601/289–5086.*
Accommodations: *4 double rooms with baths.*
Amenities: *Restaurant; air-conditioning, TV, phones in rooms.*
Rates: *$75; full breakfast. MC, V.*
Restrictions: *Smoking in restaurant and on porches only, no pets.*

Mississippi Gulf Coast

Despite its late-17th-century beginnings as the region's first permanent European settlement, the Mississippi Gulf Coast has few vestiges of the French and Spanish period. Today, the international influence in this seaside resort area comes from workers in the seafood business, which, along with tourism, ranks as the leading industry.

A drive along scenic U.S. 90 reveals palatial beach "cottages" and a 26-mile strip of man-made beach, said to be the world's longest. It's hard to tell one coastal town from the next, but whether you're in Biloxi, Gulfport, Long Beach, Pass Christian, or Bay St. Louis, a stop at any one of many restaurants will turn up the coast's specialty: fresh seafood.

Biloxi's Old Lighthouse is a landmark for tourists today as it has been for sailors since 1848. Other points of interest here are the Seafood Industry Museum, the Mardi Gras Museum, and Beauvoir, the last home of Jefferson Davis, president of the Confederacy.

Daily excursions can be made to the barrier islands, where water is blue and beaches are white; there are scheduled departures on daily cruise ships, and West Ship Island can be reached by passenger ferry. Charter boats go out deep-sea fishing, and 14 golf courses attract the sports-minded year-round.

Inland from the Gulf but considered somewhat coastal in attitude and climate are Hattiesburg and Laurel. Hattiesburg is a shopping hub for south Mississippi, and the site of the University of Southern Mississippi. There's a plethora of university-related activities: theater, art galleries, and SEC sports, and Hattiesburg hosts the popular Deposit Guaranty Golf Classic, a PGA tour, each April. Outdoor recreational areas and water parks abound

*along the nearby Pat Harrison Waterway. Laurel has one
of the country's best small museums, the Lauren Rogers
Museum of Art. The privately endowed museum, set in
a neo-Georgian building and known for the quality of its
exhibits and permanent collections, is a surprise and
a delight.*

*Still farther inland lies Meridian, whose Highland Park
has a museum for country-music legend Jimmy Rodgers
and a one-of-a-kind antique carousel. Meridian's downtown
area has not been altered in the name of progress. It's still
much as it was in the 1940s and appears to be thriving.*

Places to Go, Sights to See

On the Coast

Beauvoir (224 Beach Blvd., Biloxi, tel. 601/388–1313). This beachfront
dwelling was the last home of Jefferson Davis, president of the Confederate
States of America. The 1854 house museum contains Civil War artifacts and
Confederate memorabilia.

Biloxi Lighthouse (Hwy. 90, tel. 601/435–6294). This 65-foot cast-iron
structure, built in 1848, is the area's major landmark. The base holds
a permanent exhibit of the lighthouse's history.

Fort Massachusetts (West Ship Island, tel. 601/875–9057) was built in 1858,
captured by Union forces, and used as a prison for Confederate soldiers and
civilians. The ferry trip takes 1 hour and 15 minutes and costs $11 for adults,
$5 for children.

Gulf Islands National Seashore (3500 Park Rd., Ocean Springs, tel.
601/875–9057). The National Park Service runs this 400-acre park on the
mainland (with a visitor center, campground, and nature trail), which offers
fishing and, in summer, free bayou excursions and ferry trips to West Ship
Island, 12 miles out in the Gulf, where there are unspoiled beaches and blue
water, bathhouses, umbrellas, and food stands.

J. L. Scott Marine Education Center & Aquarium (115 Beach Blvd., Biloxi,
tel. 601/374–5550). The 26 aquariums and other exhibits serve as an
introduction to the sea life of the region.

John C. Stennis Space Center (Hwy. 70, Bay St. Louis, tel. 601/688–3390).
The facility offers a guided tour and a look at space shuttle testing. See
films on space and more.

Magnolia Hotel/Mardi Gras Museum (119 Rue Magnolia, Biloxi, tel. 601/432–8806). Mardi Gras is a big celebration on the Gulf Coast, complete with parades and festive costumes. It warrants its own museum, which is located in the only remaining pre–Civil War hotel on the Gulf.

Old Spanish Fort & Museum (4602 Fort Dr., Pascagoula, tel. 601/769–1505). Built by Frenchmen in 1718, the oldest building in the Mississippi Valley has thick walls made of oyster shell, mud, and moss. The museum has a varied collection of 18th-century items and a children's hands-on exhibit.

Seafood Industry Museum (Point Cadet Plaza, Biloxi, tel. 601/435–6320). A tribute to the industry that helps to keep the coast afloat, the museum features tools of the trade and even an architectural exhibit called "The houses that seafood built."

Inland

De Grummond Children's Literature Research Collection (University of Southern Mississippi campus, Hattiesburg, tel. 601/266–4345). More than 1,100 authors and illustrators are included in this extensive collection of original children's works.

Cruises and Charters. *Biloxi Schooner* (tel. 601/435–6320) sails on daily cruises and special charters. *Fiesta Charters* (tel. 601/875–9462) runs fishing charters, and the cruise ship *Southern Elegance* (tel. 800/441–7447) offers day and evening cruises complete with a casino.

Dentzel Carousel (Highland Park, Meridian, tel. 601/485–1801). Painted ponies and other hand-carved animals on this antique carousel, one of three in the United States, have thrilled children and adults since 1892.

Grand Opera House (2208 5th St., Meridian, tel. 601/693–5239). The state's grand lady of opera has been restored. See the stage where Lillian Gish, the Barrymores, Sarah Bernhardt, and others performed after 1890.

Jimmy Rodgers Museum (Highland Park, Meridian, tel. 601/485–1808). Rodgers, called the "father of country music," was the first inductee into the Country Music Hall of Fame.

Lauren Rogers Museum of Art (5th Ave. at 7th St., Laurel, tel. 601/649–6374). Recognized as one of the country's best small museums, the Lauren Rogers shows works by John Singer Sargent, Jean-François Millet, Winslow Homer, "Grandma" Moses, and others. It houses 19th- and 20th-century American landscapes, European salon paintings, an outstanding Georgian silver collection, and more than 600 baskets of Native American and other cultures.

Restaurants

For an authentic coast atmosphere and great gumbo, try **McElroy's Harbor House Seafood Restaurant** (tel. 601/435–5001), overlooking the Gulf, at the

Biloxi Small Craft Harbor. **Baricev's Seafood Restaurant** (899 Beach Blvd., Biloxi, tel. 601/435–3626) has been around since 1948, a proven favorite. **Trilby's** (Hwy. 90, Ocean Springs, tel. 601/875–4426) is another coast tradition, with steaks and seafood much in demand. The famous **Mary Mahoney's Old French House** restaurant (138 Rue Magnolia, Biloxi, tel. 601/374–0163) is in one of the oldest houses in America, built in 1737, and has served two U.S. presidents with seafood and steaks. **Layne's,** a roadhouse in Waveland (U.S. 90, tel. 601/467–2072), has a splendid all-you-can-eat buffet for $3.99. **Weidmann's** in Meridian (210 22nd Ave., tel. 601/693–1751) has served fresh vegetables and Gulf seafood since 1870, to the delight of Mississippians and travelers, too.

Tourist Information

Harrison County Tourism Commission (Box 6128, Gulfport, MS 39506, tel. 601/896–6699 or 800/237–9493). **Meridian-Lauderdale County Tourism Commission** (Box 5866, Meridian, MS 39302, tel. 601/483–0083).

Reservation Service

Lincoln, Ltd. Bed & Breakfast Service (Box 3479, Meridian, MS 39303, tel. 601/482–5483 or 800/633–6477).

Hamilton Hall

After General William T. Sherman burned Meridian's lifeline, the railroad, during the Civil War, he supposedly proclaimed, "Meridian no longer exists." Little did he know that the industrious Meridianites not only would rebuild very quickly but would preserve what they'd built. The bustling, thriving city still boasts turn-of-the-century architecture in the downtown business district. And Victorian architecture is what guests can expect at Meridian's stellar bed-and-breakfast, Hamilton Hall, a raspberry-colored (actually, deep mauve) grand Victorian house built downtown in 1890. It was completely dismantled, stored for a year, then about 16 years ago moved to its present site—10 wooded acres just within the city limits, with an ambience that can be classified only as country quiet.

The colorful exterior is a jigsaw of nooks and crannies and doors and porches, and the massive wood and beveled-glass door opens on an interior full of Victorian treasures. Rosewood furniture and fine antique pieces that caught the eye of the owner (though not necessarily "of the period") are appropriately and pleasingly mixed. Raspberry is the dominant color inside, too, though the extensive and ornately carved woodwork seems to overpower everything else. Guest bedrooms are upstairs, where 13-foot ceilings and Victorian-print wallpaper comple-

ment the canopy beds, marble-top dressers, washstands, and Victorian accessories.

Hamilton Hall could (and should) appear in the pages of a magazine of Victorian design, yet it is comfortable and cheerful, and usually something wonderful is baking in the kitchen. The lady of the house, Nashville native Edna Holland, is a well-known gourmet cook and professional caterer. Years ago, she was a recording engineer before moving to Meridian with her husband, Bob Holland, general manager of Meridian's WTOK-TV.

The Hollands collect fine china. A dozen sets of old Limoges are displayed in the formal dining room, where sumptuous breakfasts (including such dishes as eggs Benedict) are served to bed-and-breakfast guests. Edna also serves other excellent, reasonably priced meals with advance reservations.

Address: *4432 State Blvd., Meridian, MS 39307, tel. 601/483–8469 or 601/482–4611.*
Accommodations: *1 double room with bath, 1 double shares bath with a family member.*
Amenities: *Air-conditioning; phone and TV in den.*
Rates: *$65; full breakfast. No credit cards.*
Restrictions: *No smoking indoors, no pets.*

The Hamill House

he comfortable, contemporary home of Rowena Hamill of Meridian is a prime example of how a nonhistoric house can become a successful bed-and-breakfast inn. The Hamill House is a good-looking brick, frame, and glass dwelling surrounded by tall trees and shrubbery, situated in one of Meridian's prettiest neighborhoods. Inside, American antiques are interspersed with good-quality conventional furniture. The guest rooms are furnished with such heirloom pieces as a high-back bed of heavy oak, an oak sleigh bed, and antique dressers, washstands, and rocking chairs. The rooms are colorful and crisp, with floral chintz spreads and curtains; one room contains a parlor set that came from Rowena's childhood home.

Rowena Hamill is a busy, energetic lady who owns an antiques shop. She's never too busy, however, to see that her guests have all the comforts of home. Some of them stay a week or longer, and many write to say how much they appreciate her attentiveness and wonderful breakfasts.

Address: *3111 29th Ave., Meridian, MS 39303, tel. 601/483–5565 or 800/633–6477.*
Accommodations: *2 double rooms share 1 bath.*
Amenities: *Air-conditioning; phone and TV in den.*
Rates: *$55–$70; full breakfast. MC, V.*
Restrictions: *No smoking indoors, no pets.*

Lincoln, Ltd.

or those who want complete privacy in a bed-and-breakfast suite with no owners around, Lincoln, Ltd. is just the place. The house is a 1905 cottage in Meridian's historic district that serves a dual purpose. The front portion is the office of Lincoln, Ltd. Bed & Breakfast Reservation Service, where B&B pro Barbara Hall and her staff work. They have all the answers to questions concerning B&Bs and inns in Mississippi, plus a few listings in adjoining states. Their office closes about 5 PM; from then until 9 AM or so, guests have the charming house to themselves.

The back suite has a private entrance, use of the kitchen, a carport, and other comforts of home. The suite's living room is cheerful, with pretty plaid sofas, nice woodwork and accessories, and, in the connecting bedroom, walls of a restful, light sea green with rich cream-colored trim and cream curtains. A fireplace, a rocking chair, and flowered chintz cushions and spread enhance the antique walnut bed and chest. The adjoining bathroom has a footed tub and plenty of storage space.

Address: *2303 23rd Ave. (Box 3479), Meridian, MS 39303, tel. 601/482–5483 or 800/633–6477.*
Accommodations: *1 suite.*
Amenities: *Air-conditioning, phone, TV.*
Rates: *$55–$65; kitchen privileges but no food. AE, MC, V.*
Restrictions: *No pets.*

Red Creek Colonial Inn

When guests are asked their favorite things to do at the Red Creek Colonial Inn, just 5 miles from the Gulf of Mexico, they invariably say, "Swinging on the front porch and walking on the beach," according to innkeeper Betty Gray. She adds that guests who come for one night always either end up staying longer or wish they could.

Built around 1899, the three-story brick and frame raised cottage boasts a 64-foot front porch, six fireplaces, and interesting antiques like an electric pump organ and working Victrola. Better still, the inn sits on 11 lush acres, with 300-year-old trees that are registered with the Live Oak Society.

The inn is the brainchild of owner Karl Mertz, from Atlanta, who grew up on the Mississippi Gulf Coast. He and Claudia, his wife, have spent the past few years collecting and restoring antiques and decorations for the inn, and their efforts have paid off in a homey atmosphere that pleases most everyone. Rooms are clean, cozy, and comfortable rather than lavishly done in heavy antiques.

Address: *7416 Red Creek Rd., Long Beach, MS 39560, tel. 601/452–3080 or 800/729–9670.*
Accommodations: *3 double rooms with baths.*
Amenities: *Air-conditioning, TV in den, portable phone for guest use.*
Rates: *$44–$64; Continental breakfast. No credit cards.*
Restrictions: *No smoking, no pets.*

Tally House

Hattiesburg is a town that officially got its start in the late 1800s; thus it is only fitting that the only bed-and-breakfast inn in town should be a Victorian-style, red-roofed white frame building. In fact, the Tally House is pure turn of the century, complete with dormers and a double-tiered porch wrapping around three sides, from which to admire the flower borders, well-manicured lawn, and brick walkway.

The Tally House was built in 1907, and since that time has welcomed three Mississippi governors as overnight guests. The 13,000-square-foot two-story house boasts 11 fireplaces and a nice collection of well-displayed antiques and artifacts. The house is listed on the National Register of Historic Places.

Overnight guests of the Tally House are greeted by the owners, Mr. and Mrs. C. E. Bailey, and are offered a mint julep made with mint grown in the Baileys' herb garden. The bedrooms are done with Victorian furniture and accessories and decorated with fresh flowers. In the morning, breakfast is served with homemade jellies and jams.

Address: *402 Rebecca Ave., Hattiesburg, MS 39401, tel. 601/582–3467.*
Accommodations: *4 double rooms share 2 baths.*
Amenities: *Air-conditioning.*
Rates: *$50–$75; Continental breakfast. MC, V.*
Restrictions: *No smoking, no pets.*

Louisiana

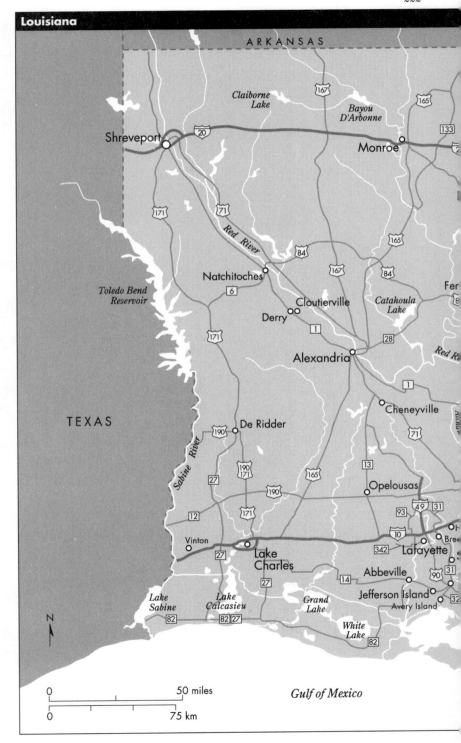

Louisiana

ARKANSAS

Claiborne Lake

167

165

Bayou D'Arbonne

133

Shreveport

20

Monroe

171

71

Red River

84

167

84

165

Natchitoches

6

Cloutierville

Catahoula Lake

Fer

Derry

1

Alexandria

Toledo Bend Reservoir

28

Red R

1

TEXAS

Cheneyville

71

Sabine River

190

De Ridder

13

190 171

27

165

Opelousas

12

171

190

93 49 31

10

342

Lafayette

Lake Sabine

Vinton

27

Lake Charles

27

14

Abbeville

90 31

Lake Calcasieu

Grand Lake

Jefferson Island

Avery Island

32

82 27

White Lake

82

N

0   50 miles

0   75 km

Gulf of Mexico

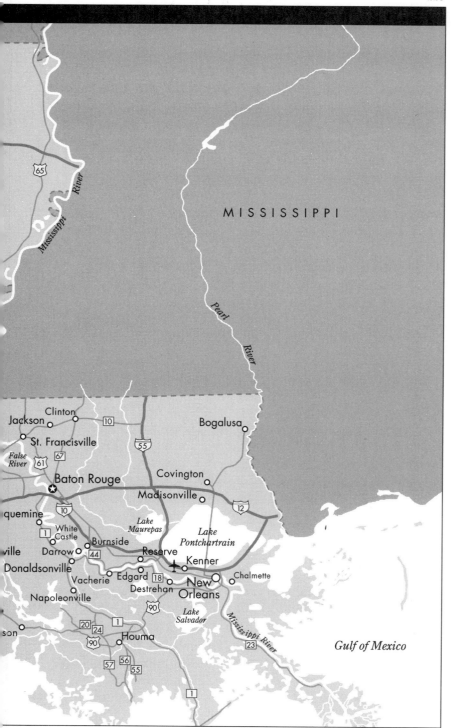

MISSISSIPPI

Mississippi River

Pearl River

65

Jackson

Clinton

10

Bogalusa

St. Francisville

55

False River

67

61

Covington

Baton Rouge

Madisonville

12

quemine

10

White Castle

Lake Maurepas

Lake Pontchartrain

1

Burnside

Reserve

Kenner

ville

Darrow

44

Donaldsonville

Vacherie

Edgard

18

Destrehan

New Orleans

Chalmette

Napoleonville

90

Lake Salvador

Mississippi River

son

20

24

1

Houma

23

57

56

55

1

Gulf of Mexico

Greater New Orleans

*Internationally known for its fine French Creole cuisine
and great jazz, New Orleans basks in the sun smack on the
Mississippi River about 110 miles inland from the Gulf of
Mexico. The city is something of a paradox: It's a major
convention city and one of the world's largest ports; some 6
million visitors come to call annually; and Mardi Gras is
but the best known of dozens of annual festivals (New
Orleanians do love to party)—all of which means there is
a great deal of activity here. And yet, this is a very laid-
back, Caribbeanesque city that much prefers to operate on
"island time." Not for naught is it called The Big Easy. The
Crescent City (another sobriquet) is unlike any other
American city; certainly it is different from other
Southern cities. It has been promoted as "America's
European Masterpiece"—yet there is nothing quite like it
in Europe, either. It is, in a word, unique.*

*Within the city proper, the French Quarter is the prime
tourist target. Comprising about a square mile, the
Quarter is an easily walkable, perfect grid. Its narrow
streets are lined with picturesque, pastel-painted buildings
garnished with fanciful ironwork or dollops of gingerbread.
It is both a carefully restored living museum whose
structures date from the 18th and 19th centuries and
a residential district with about 7,000 somewhat smug
inhabitants. Most of the famed French Creole restaurants
are in the Quarter, and Bourbon Street is lined with music
clubs of every description. This is a 24-hour town, which
means there is no legal closing time. At almost any hour of
the day or night, you can stroll down Bourbon and hear
the syncopated rhythms of Cajun, rhythm and blues,
gutbucket (that's low-down, mean blues), Dixieland, rinky-
dink piano, ragtime, and even Irish music. The heartbeat of
the Quarter is Jackson Square, a pedestrian mall where
stately St. Louis Cathedral soars like a hymn over
a riotous scene of Dixieland bands, red-nosed clowns,*

sidewalk artists, costumed kooks, tap dancers and break dancers, fire-eaters, bongo players, unicyclists, nonchalant New Orleanians, and curious tourists.

Almost as much activity, frivolous as well as serious, takes place in the Central Business District (CBD), adjacent to the Quarter. The Foot of Canal Street, as it's known to locals, boasts several splashy attractions. From the downtown area, the St. Charles Streetcar, a National Historic Landmark, makes a jolly rumble upriver via St. Charles Avenue. It chugs through the Garden District, a residential area in which posh, palatial mansions are surrounded by luxuriant gardens, and on past pretty Audubon Park with its magnificent live oaks dressed in Spanish moss and its wonderful zoo. Lake Pontchartrain drapes for 40 miles over the northern border of the city, and the lakefront area is a favorite summertime playground for locals. There are several marinas, sailboats to be rented, and a plethora of funky restaurants frequented by hard-core, no-nonsense seafood eaters. The metropolitan area extends across the lake to the piney woods of St. Tammany Parish, where fishing and boating are popular.

Six miles east of the city lies Chalmette National Historical Park, on whose rolling green fields Andy Jackson whipped the Brits in the 1815 Battle of New Orleans. And to the west of town, the Great River Road, which follows the meandering Mississippi from New Orleans to Baton Rouge, is decorated with handsome, restored antebellum plantation homes. Many are open to the public, and several companies offer tours to plantation country. If you fly into New Orleans, you'll note that dry land seems to sort of fizzle out the closer you get to the city. These flat marshlands are laced with waterways, and swamp tours, which sneak into erstwhile pirates' lairs and give you a tempting taste of Cajun Country to the west, are extremely popular outings.

Places to Go, Sights to See

Carriage Rides. Decatur Street at Jackson Square is lined with fringed carriages drawn by mules in silly hats. The lively raconteurs at the reins dispense a wealth of misinformation but give a pleasant half-hour overview of the Quarter.

Cemeteries. Reminiscent of Père Lachaise in Paris, New Orleans's aboveground cemeteries are usually high on visitors' must-see lists. The oldest, *St. Louis No. 1,* lies on the fringes of the Quarter; the largest, and most photographed, is *Metairie Cemetery.* Many of these Cities of the Dead are in high-crime areas; visitors should not venture into them alone. For a group tour on Sunday, contact Save Our Cemeteries (tel. 504/588–9357).

City Park. Home of the *New Orleans Museum of Art* (Lelong Ave., tel. 504/488–2631), this is one of the nation's largest city parks. Within its 1,500 acres are golf courses, tennis courts, baseball and softball diamonds, lagoons and boat rentals, botanical gardens, and, for the little ones, Storyland and an amusement park with a delightful antique carousel.

Foot of Canal Street. If you keep on going toward the river on Canal Street, you'll drive right off dry land and onto the commuter ferry (free outgoing, $1 returning) that sidles across the Mississippi to the neighborhood of Algiers on the West Bank. Smack at the river and the CBD, there are several diversions. A good place to get your bearings is *Viewpoint* (2 Canal St., tel. 504/581–4888), a glass-enclosed observation deck on the 31st floor of the World Trade Center. The *Aquarium of the Americas* (Canal St. and the river, tel. 504/861–2537), which boasts four major exhibits and a plethora of sea creatures, sits in the handsomely landscaped Woldenberg Riverfront Park. *Riverwalk,* sprawling upriver from the ferry landing, comprises Spanish Plaza—a broad, open expanse with mosaic pavement and a huge fountain—and a festival marketplace with some 200 specialty shops and restaurants. Several of the sightseeing boats dock at Riverwalk. On Lundi Gras (the Monday night before Fat Tuesday), the city tosses a huge, free-to-the-public masked ball on Spanish Plaza, replete with live music, fireworks, and much merriment.

House Museums. Several restored homes (almost all in the Quarter) provide a glimpse of old New Orleans. *Pitot House* (1440 Moss St., tel. 504/482–0312) is a West Indies–style house typical of those built by early planters. *Gallier House* (1118–32 Royal St., tel. 504/523–6722) was designed and built by noted 19th-century architect James Gallier Jr. as his family home. The *Hermann-Grima House* (820 St. Louis St., tel. 504/525–5661) is an 1831 mansion in whose outbuildings Creole cooking demonstrations (and tastings) are held on Thursday, October–May. *Beauregard-Keyes House* (1113 Chartres St., tel. 504/523–7257), a Greek Revival raised cottage, was home to Confederate General P. G. T. Beauregard and, much later, to novelist Frances Parkinson Keyes. *Longue Vue House & Gardens* (7 Bamboo Rd., tel. 504/488–5488), set on 8 acres of manicured gardens in Mid-City, resembles an English country estate and is filled with priceless French, American, and Oriental antiques.

Nightlife. *Tipitina's* (501 Napoleon Ave., tel. 504/895–8477) is arguably the city's most popular club. Laid back, with a loyal following, Tip's is the place where Dennis Quaid romanced Ellen Barkin in *The Big Easy.* Live reggae, rock, rhythm and blues, and Cajun music entertain a dressed-down crowd. *Michaul's* (701 Magazine St., tel. 504/522–5517) offers live Cajun music, Cajun food, and free Cajun dance lessons on Monday and Tuesday night. The *Maple Leaf Bar* (8316 Oak St., tel. 504/866–9359) features live music seven nights a week. The dance floor is the proverbial postage-stamp size, and the dancing often overflows out onto the street. For great traditional jazz sans dancing (and creature comforts), *Preservation Hall* (726 St. Peter St., tel. 504/522–2238 or 504/523–8939) is the place to hear the city's jazz legends. Next door, *Pat O'Brien's* (718 St. Peter St., tel. 504/525–4823)—perhaps the world's most famous bar and birthplace of the now ubiquitous Hurricane— features a raucous sing-along piano bar that roars long after the fat lady sings. *Pete Fountain's Club* (Hilton Hotel, 2 Poydras St., tel. 504/523–4374) is home base for the world-famous New Orleans clarinetist, and *Lulu White's Mahogany Hall* (309 Bourbon St., tel. 504/525–5595) is stomping ground for the Dukes of Dixieland. Many of the city's best jazz and rhythm and blues musicians perform regularly at the *Palm Court Jazz Café* (1204 Decatur St., tel. 504/525–0200). The popular *Napoleon House* (500 Chartres St., tel. 504/524–9752) and *Lafitte's Blacksmith Shop* (941 Bourbon St., tel. 504/523–0066) are marvelous, musty old bars in buildings that date from the 1700s. Napoleon House features taped classical music, and Lafitte's showcases pianist-vocalist Lily Hood.

Riverboats. Frilly riverboats kicking up froth on the mighty Mississippi offer a variety of excursions. Among the most popular are the *Steamboat Natchez* (tel. 504/586–8777) and the *Creole Queen* (tel. 504/524–0814), both of which operate evening dinner/jazz cruises as well as daytime outings.

Restaurants

The city's most famous restaurant, **Antoine's** (713 St. Louis St., tel. 504/581–4422), established in 1840, serves fine French Creole cuisine in several grand, Old World dining rooms. **Arnaud's** (813 Bienville St., tel. 504/523–5433) and **Galatoire's** (209 Bourbon St., tel. 504/525–2021) are two other venerable and fashionable French Creole restaurants. **Commander's Palace** (1403 Washington Ave., tel. 504/899–8221), in a splendid Victorian mansion in the Garden District, is a great favorite for its innovative French-American menu and weekend jazz brunches. The estimable Brennan family, of Commander's Palace fame, also operates the **Palace Café** (605 Canal St., tel. 504/523–1661), which serves creative versions of Parisian bistro fare. For Cajun cooking, try **K-Paul's Louisiana Kitchen** (416 Chartres St., tel. 504/942–7500), bastion of celebrity chef Paul Prudhomme.

Tourist Information

Greater New Orleans Tourist & Convention Commission (1520 Sugar Bowl Dr., New Orleans, LA 70112, tel. 504/566–5011).

Reservation Services

Bed & Breakfast, Inc. (1021 Moss St., Box 52257, New Orleans, LA 70152–2257, tel. 504/488–4640 or 800/749–4640, dial tone 184). **New Orleans Bed & Breakfast** (Box 8128, New Orleans, LA 70182, tel. 504/822–5038 or 504/822–5046). **Bed, Bath & Breakfast** (Box 52466, New Orleans, LA 70152, tel. 504/897-3867).

Note: The rates quoted below do not apply during special events. Prices skyrocket for Mardi Gras, Sugar Bowl, Jazz Fest, and Super Bowl; also, in addition to three- to five-day minimums, hotels sometimes request full payment in advance.

Hotel Maison de Ville and Audubon Cottages

The Maison de Ville is tucked behind an etched-glass door, a half block off the French Quarter's bawdy Bourbon Street. It's easy to stroll right by it; only a discreet coat-of-arms sign heralds the three-story European-style hotel, which dates from the late 1700s.

To the rear of the small lobby is a sedate parlor, with a fireplace and marble mantel. The parlor opens onto one of the city's prettiest courtyards, with a tiered fountain, banana trees, and flowers. Two-story, balconied former slave quarters extend from the rear of the main house and border the courtyard.

Rooms in the main house are small, but all are done in 18th- and 19th-century French and American antiques, with four-posters, marble fireplaces, swagged draperies, and matching quilted spreads. The small marble baths have brass fittings. The slave-quarter rooms are more rustic, with beamed ceilings and small fireplaces. (Tennessee Williams once lived in No. 9.) It's necessary to draw the draperies for privacy, which darkens the rooms. The hotel can be noisy. Light sleepers should avoid the front rooms overlooking Toulouse Street.

More luxurious (and pricier) are the one- and two-bedroom Audubon Cottages, two blocks from the main building. They are so named because John James Audubon lived in Cottage No. 1 in 1821. Set behind a high stucco wall, the quiet, secluded cottages have kitchens and walled private patios. They're clustered around a landscaped patio, with statuary and a pool (which is available to all hotel guests). The spacious rooms have slate or brick floors, antique furnishings, and a French country flavor.

Breakfast, served on a silver tray and accompanied by the morning paper and a rose, can be taken in your room or in the courtyard.

Despite its corporate ownership and noisy location, the hotel maintains the ambience of a small country inn.

Address: *727 Toulouse St., New Orleans, LA 70130, tel. 504/561–5858 or 800/634–1600.*
Accommodations: *14 double rooms with baths, 2 suites, 7 housekeeping cottages.*
Amenities: *Air-conditioning, cable TV, phones, and minibars in rooms, turndown and overnight shoe-shine services, restaurant, concierge; pool.*
Rates: *$125–$385; Continental breakfast; afternoon port, sherry, and tea. AE, DC, MC, V.*
Restrictions: *No pets, 3-night minimum during Mardi Gras and Jazz Fest.*

Lamothe House

Esplanade Avenue, a broad, tree-shaded boulevard that constitutes the lower border of the French Quarter, stretches from the river to City Park. In 1829, Miss Marie Virginie Lamothe bought property here, which she subsequently sold to her brother, Jean. It was he who, in 1839, built the handsome three-story double town house. Later, 19th-century owners added the four white Corinthian columns and converted the carriageway to a central hallway with twin winding stairways leading to the second-floor reception room. The flagstones in the spacious courtyard originally came to New Orleans as ship's ballast.

The inn's public rooms are decorated with Victorian furnishings upholstered with rich fabrics, framed oil paintings, and magnificent gilt-and-etched-glass chandeliers. The reception area gives onto a formal dining room. Original fireplaces with ornately carved mantelpieces can be seen (though not used) throughout the property.

Guest rooms and suites are in the main house, the attached slave quarters, and a carriage house. Though they differ in size and design, the rooms feature an array of Victorian antiques—four-poster beds, velvet and brocade chairs and settees, chaise longues, carved armoires, and marble-top tables. The two suites in the main house—large bedroom/

sitting rooms—are marvels of Victoriana, but baths in each are quite small, with pedestal lavatories. Conversely, the slave-quarter rooms are smaller and somewhat cramped but have bigger, more modern baths. In the carriage house, suite No. 117 is a spacious affair whose sitting room and bedroom are separated by a brick fireplace; there is a second, very small bedroom, and a big modern bath. Apart from those in the carriage house, many rooms are dark.

Address: *621 Esplanade Ave., New Orleans, LA 70116, tel. 504/947–1161 or 800/367–5858, fax 504/943–6536.*
Accommodations: *11 double rooms with baths, 9 suites.*
Amenities: *Air-conditioning, cable TV and phones in rooms, 2 small meeting rooms.*
Rates: *$85–$95, suites $125–$195; Continental breakfast. AE, MC, V.*
Restrictions: *No pets, 5-night minimum during Mardi Gras, 4-night minimum for Jazz Fest and Sugar Bowl.*

Melrose Mansion

This splendid Victorian Gothic on the fringe of New Orleans's French Quarter was built in 1884. It has a turret, dormers, stained-glass windows, a steeply pitched roof, Corinthian columns, and a guest list that includes Lady Bird Johnson. The former first lady attended the grand opening of the bed-and-breakfast in 1990 and was the first person to sign the register.

Each of the large, high-ceilinged rooms is furnished differently, but all feature handsome 19th-century Louisiana antiques, including canopy beds and four-posters. The usual amenities include down pillows, fine-milled soaps, monogrammed robes and towels, coffee makers, and small refrigerators stocked with mineral water, soft drinks, and a split of complimentary champagne. Fresh flowers and a decanter of Courvoisier are placed in each suite, where there are also wet bars, private balconies, and whirlpools.

The star is the Donecio Suite, in the turret, with its 18-foot ceiling, chandelier of brass and etched glass, and ecru-and-ivory lace touches. All the mansion's baths are sumptuous affairs, but in this suite the whirlpool bubbles in the turret, a huge window overlooks the French Quarter, and a frosted silver ice bucket containing a bottle of champagne is within easy reach.

Melrose's owners, Melvin Jones and Sidney Torres, bought the building in 1976 from New Orleans entertainer Chris Owens. It was an apartment house then and remained so for more than 10 years. Melvin, a general contractor, spent more than two years in extensive renovations, and his wife, Rosemary, did the interior decoration.

Guests can take breakfast in their room, at the pool, or in the formal dining room. An astonishing array of hors d'oeuvres is served with afternoon cocktails.

The Melrose is not in an entirely safe neighborhood; guests should avoid walking around the area at night.

Address: *937 Esplanade Ave., New Orleans, LA 70116, tel. 504/944–2255.*
Accommodations: *4 double rooms with baths, 4 suites.*
Amenities: *Air-conditioning, library, 1 meeting room, turndown service; complimentary airport limousine, heated pool.*
Rates: *$195–$395; full breakfast, cocktails and hors d'oeuvres. AE, MC, V.*
Restrictions: *No pets, 4-night minimum during Mardi Gras, Jazz Fest, and Sugar Bowl.*

Soniat House

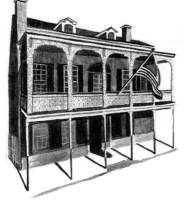

The two 1830s town houses that comprise the Soniat House were among the first Greek Revival houses in New Orleans. The green shutters across the front are kept closed for privacy and security, which gives the building a somewhat austere look despite its lacy ironwork galleries. But behind the shutters a graceful flagstone carriageway leads from the street to a small landscaped courtyard with a lily pond, a softly gurgling fountain, and a profusion of gardenias, night-blooming jasmine, and banana plants. The courtyard is particularly romantic at night, when it's lit by candles. The tiny office and the elegant First Empire parlor that adjoins it are just off the courtyard.

Rodney and Frances Smith have furnished their French Quarter guest house with English, French, and Louisiana antiques gathered during 25 years of world travel. Rooms are uncluttered and have a starkly elegant look. Each is decorated differently, right down to the colors of the paint and custom-made fabrics. Four-poster and canopy beds are complemented by framed contemporary paintings, some of them on loan from the New Orleans Museum of Art. The polished hardwood floors are covered with thick Oriental rugs. All the rooms have fireplaces except one. Beds are made with luxurious 200-count cotton percale bed linens and goose-down pillows (extra ones for reading in bed). The baths are large and well appointed, all with bathside phones and most with whirlpools.

A private elevator takes guests to the secluded third-floor rooms, which offer even more peace and privacy, but the second-floor rooms require a long haul up a graceful but steep spiral staircase. Small and intimate though it is, the Soniat House has a sophisticated business center with' fax and photocopying machines and a modem for personal computers.

A breakfast of plump, hot biscuits, homemade strawberry jam, freshly squeezed orange juice, and chicory coffee on a silver service can be taken in your room or on white-clothed tables in the courtyard.

Address: *1133 Chartres St., New Orleans, LA 70116, tel. 504/522-0570 or 800/544-8808, fax 504/522-7208.*
Accommodations: *14 double rooms with baths, 3 singles with baths, 5 suites.*
Amenities: *Air-conditioning, concierge, room service, honor-system bar, phones and TV in room, VCRs in suites, 1 meeting room, business center.*
Rates: *$115–$195, suites $275–$425; Continental breakfast extra. AE, MC, V.*
Restrictions: *No pets, 3-night minimum on weekends, 5-night minimum during Mardi Gras, Jazz Fest, and Sugar Bowl.*

Terrell House

From the outside, the Terrell House—with its tall French doors, shutters, and frilly iron galleries—looks much like any other Greek Revival house in the lower Garden District. But it contains one of the city's most extensive and impressive collections of antiques.

Built in 1858 by a cotton merchant, the house is currently owned by Fred Nicaud, whose collections of gaslight fixtures and lamps, European and Louisiana antique furniture, Oriental rugs, and antique carnival memorabilia are displayed everywhere. The furnishings are true to the style and period of the house, and many are Nicaud family heirlooms. Some of the ornate beds and armoires were hand carved in the studio of Prudent Mallard, a well-known 19th-century New Orleans craftsman. On display in one of the twin parlors is a full set of 1850 doll furniture in the Mallard style. A Waterford crystal chandelier sparkles in the formal dining room, where breakfast is served.

Guest rooms in the main mansion are original bedrooms of the house and have balconies overlooking a landscaped courtyard with a fountain and an ancient crape myrtle tree. Rooms 1 and 3 contain Mallard armoires, washstands, and marble-top tables and dressers. (No. 3 is a two-bedroom suite with half-tester beds and a sitting room.) There are two attic rooms with sloping ceilings and brass beds. Room 10, in the servants' quarters, has twin white iron beds with half testers and crocheted coverlets. The four rooms in the carriage house have balconies or patios opening onto the courtyard.

Harry Lucas, the affable manager, operates Terrell House in laid-back style. He began at the guest house as a gardener and still loves landscape gardening. Harry's wife, Alma, occasionally comes in to cook special dinners for guests; she gets raves for her crawfish étouffée, bread pudding, and other regional dishes.

The lower Garden District is in the midst of a project called Operation Comeback, which aims to restore the neighborhood to its former grandeur and create safer streets.

Address: *1441 Magazine St., New Orleans, LA 70130, tel. 504/524–9859 or 800/878–9859.*
Accommodations: *8 double rooms with baths, 1 2-bedroom suite.*
Amenities: *Air-conditioning, cable TV and phones in rooms, room service.*
Rates: *$80–$100; Continental breakfast, cocktails. AE, MC, V.*
Restrictions: *3-night minimum during Mardi Gras, Jazz Fest, and Sugar Bowl.*

Cornstalk Hotel

Set well behind an elaborate cast-iron "cornstalk" fence two blocks from Jackson Square, this hotel is in a gleaming white historic Victorian house with Corinthian columns, a crenellated tower, and a bull's-eye window. White iron furniture decorates the lawn, the front porch, and the upstairs balcony.

A leaded-glass door gives onto a long narrow entrance hall, where a crystal chandelier hangs from a carved medallion. The crown moldings are trimmed with gold leaf, as are the ornate mirrors. You register at a 19th-century desk tucked into an alcove at the end of the hall, where Debi Spencer is usually presiding. She and her husband, David, have owned the hotel since 1980.

Some of the guest rooms have vaulted ceilings, crystal chandeliers, Oriental rugs, and fireplaces; all are individually decorated with 19th-century American antiques, including marble-top tables and intricately carved tester and canopy beds.

Address: *915 Royal St., New Orleans, LA 70116, tel. 504/523–1515 or 504/523–1516.*
Accommodations: *14 double rooms with baths.*
Amenities: *Air-conditioning, newspaper, TV and phones in rooms.*
Rates: *$75–$105; Continental breakfast. AE, MC, V.*
Restrictions: *No pets, 2-night minimum on weekends, 5 nights during Mardi Gras, 3-4 nights for Jazz Fest and Sugar Bowl.*

Hotel Villa Convento

The three-story Villa Convento, on a quiet residential street in the French Quarter a block from the French Market, was built for a French family in 1848. It is not an elegant hotel; in fact, the carpets and reproduction furniture are somewhat worn. But the warmth of the Campo family—Lela, Warren, and son Larry—draws repeat guests year after year. The hotel is popular with European budget travelers.

The building boasts six ornate iron balconies with tables and chairs, where guests can sit and take in the passing street scene. Off the narrow entrance hall there's a tiny elevator lined with tapestries. Most rooms are average size, but No. 305 is a large bedroom/sitting room from which steep stairs lead to a Spartan, twin-bedded loft. The other suite, No. 400, has an Oriental silk screen, a four-poster bed with quilted spread, and a pink chaise lounge among its traditional furnishings. In the morning, guests gather on a tree-shaded patio for breakfast.

Address: *616 Ursulines St., New Orleans, LA 70116, tel. 504/522–1793, fax 504/525–6652.*
Accommodations: *22 double rooms with baths, 2 suites.*
Amenities: *Air-conditioning, TV and phones in rooms, concierge.*
Rates: *$59–$95; Continental breakfast. AE, DC, MC, V.*
Restrictions: *No pets, 5-night minimum during Mardi Gras and Jazz Fest.*

Josephine Guest House

A block from St. Charles Avenue is the home of Jude Daniel Fuselier and his wife, Mary Ann Weilbaecher. The large Italianate mansion dates from 1870, and Mary Ann calls the furnishings "Creole baroque"; indeed, cherubs and angels decorate virtually everything. The most elaborate piece is a massive ebony bed inlaid with ivory and bone. Dutch marquetry daybeds are a focal point of the downstairs guest room. The couple's passion for antique-collecting is everywhere apparent; French Empire and English Gothic are among the periods represented. There is a Gothic refectory table in the cluttered country-style kitchen and an 18th-century mahogany banquet table in the formal dining room.

Dan and Mary Ann are eager to acquaint their guests with the "real New Orleans." Mary Ann, a former home economics teacher, makes the fresh breads that accompany morning café au lait and juice. Breakfast is served on Wedgwood china.

Address: *1450 Josephine St., New Orleans, LA 70130, tel. 504/524–6361.*
Accommodations: *6 double rooms with baths.*
Amenities: *Air-conditioning, cable TV in some rooms.*
Rates: *$75–$135; Continental breakfast. AE, MC, V.*
Restrictions: *Smoking only in courtyard, 3- to 4-night minimum during Mardi Gras and Jazz Fest.*

Lafitte Guest House

S mack in the middle of the French Quarter, the Lafitte Guest House is a restored French manor house that dates from 1849. The red and gold Victorian parlor is resplendent with velvet chairs, matching swag curtains, fringed lampshades, and an Oriental rug. Public areas are adorned with art from the private collection of owner Dr. Robert Guyton.

For the most part, guest rooms are large and bright, and some have private balconies. Most are done in early 19th-century Louisiana antiques—four-poster, canopy, and tester beds; crystal chandeliers; carved wood armoires. The room on the fourth floor has beamed ceilings and wicker furnishings, and the suite has a splendid view of the Quarter from

its balcony across the front. Tucked away behind the courtyard is the former carriage house, with a parlor, a bedroom, and a bath that was cleverly converted from a coal bin.

Address: *1003 Bourbon St., New Orleans, LA 70116, tel. 504/581-2678 or 800/331-7971.*
Accommodations: *13 double rooms with baths, 1 suite.*
Amenities: *Air-conditioning, color TV and phones in rooms, 1 small meeting room.*
Rates: *$59–$165; Continental breakfast, afternoon wine and hors d'oeuvres. AE, MC, V.*
Restrictions: *No pets, 4-night minimum during Mardi Gras, 3 night minimum during Jazz Fest and Sugar Bowl.*

Plantation Bell

Lila Rapier's late-Victorian house is painted dark maroon with cream-colored trim. Named for the antiques shop Lila once owned, it's on a quiet residential street in Covington, about 35 miles from New Orleans. Shrubs nestle against the wraparound porch, where Domino, Lila's black and white cat, is often curled up in a rocking chair. A small plantation bell hangs by the steps.

During extensive renovations on the house, Lila herself painted the 13-foot-high ceilings and hung the bold Schumacher wallpaper. Her eye for details is apparent: Bath towels exactly match the color of a tiny flower in the wallpaper. The house is furnished primarily with 18th- and 19th-century American antiques.

The front guest room is large and airy, but it's necessary to go through the hall and kitchen to reach the private bath. The smaller guest room has an adjoining shower bath. A two-bedroom attic apartment with sloping ceilings and a private entrance is sometimes available.

Address: *204 W. 24th Ave., Covington, LA 70433, tel. 504/893-7693.*
Accommodations: *2 double rooms with baths, 1 housekeeping suite.*
Amenities: *Air-conditioning; free use of bikes and canoe.*
Rates: *$30–$40; full breakfast. No credit cards.*
Restrictions: *No smoking in bedrooms or baths.*

River Run Plantation

The large double-galleried home of Liz and Richard Kempe is on one of the main streets of Madisonville, a boating and fishing community about 35 miles from New Orleans. Built in 1888, it has broad central hallways upstairs and down. There are rocking chairs and swings on the porches; in the backyard a galvanized cattle trough serves as a children's pool.

The house is simply furnished with 19th-century American and European antiques collected on the Kempes' world travels (they met while serving in the Peace Corps). The walls are adorned with tapestries and Haitian art. A downstairs guest room, which shares a bath with the Kempe family, is across the hall from the rustic breakfast room. The other three

rooms and bath are off the upstairs hall.

The healthy breakfasts Liz prepares include homemade multigrain breads, fresh juices, fruit, and even fruit crepes.

Address: *703 Main St., Madisonville, LA 70447, tel. and fax 504/845-4222.*
Accommodations: *4 double rooms share 2 baths.*
Amenities: *Air-conditioning; bike.*
Rates: *$50; Continental breakfast. AE, MC, V.*
Restrictions: *Smoking only on porches, no pets, 3-night minimum during Mardi Gras, Jazz Fest, Christmas, and New Year's.*

St. Charles Guest House

Joanne and Dennis Hilton describe their guest house as "simple, cozy, and affordable." It comprises four 19th-century buildings in the lower Garden District, a block from the St. Charles streetcar line.

Rooms vary; some are large enough for a family of four, and some are small "backpacker" rooms with no air-conditioning and shared baths. (All the rooms with private baths are air-conditioned.) None of the rooms are grand; they are all functionally furnished, clean, and well maintained. A breakfast room with a large picture window overlooks the pool and sun deck. In the morning, guests help themselves to rolls and doughnuts, juice, and paper cups of coffee.

The Hiltons provide guests with a "survival manual," containing safety hints and suggestions for inexpensive dining. And they sometimes treat their guests to a crawfish boil or special meals of other regional specialties.

Address: *1748 Prytania St., New Orleans, LA 70130, tel. 504/523–6556.*
Accommodations: *22 rooms with baths, 4 rooms share 1 bath.*
Amenities: *Air-conditioning in 18 rooms, pay phones; pool.*
Rates: *$25–$60; Continental breakfast. AE, MC, V.*
Restrictions: *No smoking indoors, no pets, 5-night minimum during Mardi Gras, Jazz Fest, and Sugar Bowl.*

Sully Mansion

Most of the Garden District's fine mansions are private houses, not open to the public. But one of them—a huge Queen Anne with wraparound veranda, dormers, turrets, and frilly trim—is a bed-and-breakfast. New Orleans architect Thomas Sully built it, it's now Maralee Prigmore's home.

In the spacious foyer, sunlight filters through original stained-glass windows and falls on a grand piano. An ornate carved staircase spirals up to the second floor. The house has 12-foot coved ceilings, 10-foot cypress doors, and heart-of-pine floors covered with Oriental rugs. Swagged, floor-length draperies hang from tall windows. Porcelain figurines are displayed on the fireplace mantels.

Guest rooms are eclectically furnished. One is 1950s French provincial, while the "downstairs peach" (which has a sitting area and huge modern bath) features a four-poster bed with a diaphanous canopy. In the downstairs "gathering room," guests can watch television or play Scrabble and backgammon.

Address: *2631 Prytania St., New Orleans, LA 70130, tel. 504/891–0457.*
Accommodations: *5 double rooms with baths.*
Amenities: *Air-conditioning, phones in rooms.*
Rates: *$65–$100; Continental breakfast. MC, V.*
Restrictions: *2-night minimum on Jazz Fest weekends.*

North-Central Louisiana

*Many people predicted that Interstate 49, to join North
Louisiana and South Louisiana, would never be completed.
Well, the highway has been finished, and the two "states"
are now connected. By car, at least, if not in spirit.
Louisiana has always been a divided state. Natives
invariably refer to North Louisiana and South Louisiana,
and even in conversation you can detect a capitalized
distinction. North Louisiana is Southern, and South
Louisiana is not. (New Orleans, which is way down south,
has neither a Northern nor a Southern flavor but is in
a class by itself.)*

*Alexandria, in the middle of the state, is Louisiana's own
unofficial but acknowledged Mason-Dixon Line. North of
Alex (or "Elleck," as it's pronounced around here), the
terrain, accents, customs, and cuisine change. Flat
marshlands, moss-draped cypress trees, and gray earth give
way to rolling green hills, pine forests, and rich red clay—
stained, as they say in these parts, by the blood of the
Confederacy. The area around Alexandria has several
notable Civil War sites, including a cemetery and
antebellum houses.*

*Natchitoches (pronounced "nack-i-tish"), about two hours
northwest of Alexandria, is the oldest permanent
settlement in the entire Louisiana Purchase—four years
older than the more highly publicized French Quarter of
New Orleans. The town's restored historic district is
a 33-block area containing fine old homes. Front Street,
paved with old brick, stretches along the pretty Cane River
Lake. Created when the Red River changed its course, Cane
River Lake not only decorates Natchitoches but meanders
on down through the region's plantation country.*

*Natchitoches gained fame as the town of Chinquapin in the
film* Steel Magnolias. *The film, which was shot here in 1988,*

has virtually transformed this sleepy little town. You can't walk 2 feet in any direction without encountering someone who wants to tell about the "part"—on camera or off—he or she played in the film.

In these parts, Natchitoches has long been known for its Christmas Festival of Lights, now more than 65 years old. The monthlong festival, which begins the first Saturday of December, draws about 150,000 people to town. The historic district, on which the festival centers, is a riot of twinkling lights, and the first weekend is a continuous festival of food and fun.

Another celebrated, though slightly smaller, event is the two-day Natchitoches Pilgrimage, held in October, which includes walking tours of the historic district, admission to some of the landmark homes and plantations, and candlelight tours.

Although I–49 makes the drive easy, you should get off onto the state and parish roads to explore the backcountry of Louisiana and visit the house museums and plantations. State Route 1 slips diagonally from the northwest corner all the way to the Gulf of Mexico. Although the road is substandard along some stretches, the scenery is prettier, and you'll pick up more flavor than on the interstate. Routes 494 and 493 are also picturesque, drifting alongside Cane River Lake between Natchitoches and Melrose. And the drive through the Kisatchie National Forest is spectacular.

Places to Go, Sights to See

Kisatchie National Forest. South of Natchitoches, a 100,000-acre division of this national forest contains the 17-mile Longleaf Trail Scenic Byway, which crosses a beautiful bayou; an 8,700-acre wilderness with hiking and riding trails; and several strategically placed viewpoints. For further information, write to the District Ranger, Kisatchie Ranger District, Box 2128, Natchitoches, LA 71457.

Bayou Folk Museum (Cloutierville, tel. 318/352–8072). In the late 1800s, Kate Chopin, who wrote the book on which the recent film *The Awakening* was based, lived for a time in this region. Her home was what is now the museum, which contains costumes, furnishings, and various memorabilia pertaining to Chopin's life and times.

Beau Fort Plantation (Rte. 494 south of Natchitoches, tel. 318/352–9580) is a 265-acre working cotton plantation. A long alley of live oaks leads to the mansion, which has an 84-foot gallery and the ambience of the Old South.

Magnolia Plantation (Rte. 119, 1 mi north of Derry, tel. 318/379–2221), one of the largest homes in the area, is a 2½-story structure with 27 rooms. The only cotton press in the country still in its original location is housed in a barn behind the house.

At **Melrose Plantation** (at Melrose, Exit 119 off I–49, tel. 318/379–0055), tours take in the main mansion, the blacksmith shop, the doctor's office, and the African House, the most famous structure, the second floor of which boasts murals by primitive artist Clementine Hunter. The "black Grandma Moses" lived and painted here till her death in 1988, just short of her 102nd birthday.

Kent House (3601 Bayou Rapides Rd., Alexandria, tel. 318/487–5998), built around 1800, is the oldest known structure still on its feet in central Louisiana. Its outbuildings—milk house, carriage house, and kitchen—have been preserved, and a variety of activities, including cooking and quilting demonstrations, take place here on a regular basis.

Trolley Tours (tel. 318/352–7093 or 318/352–2577) has an open tram that rattles around Natchitoches on a Steel Magnolia Tour, with a narrator who does a colorful commentary on who lived where and what happened here during the filming of the movie. If you're curious about where the stars— Dolly Parton, Shirley MacLaine, Sally Field, Olympia Dukakis, Julia Roberts, and Tom Skerritt—lived, this is the way to find out.

Cane River Cruises (tel. 318/352–7093 or 318/352–2577) runs an easygoing narrated cruise on scenic Cane River Lake—a pleasant way to while away an hour. Boats leave from Roque House on Natchitoches's downtown riverfront.

Restaurants

Finding good food is not a problem anywhere in Louisiana. In the Natchitoches/Alexandria area, there are two standouts. People who travel frequently between North and South Louisiana plan things so that at feeding time they'll be near **Lea's Lunchroom** (Rte. 71, Lecompte, tel. 318/776–5178), a big, noisy down-home café that dishes out zillions of plate lunches, sandwiches, and mouth-watering homemade pies. Natchitoches is known for meat pies, and the best place to get them is **Lasyone's Meat Pie Kitchen & Restaurant** (622 2nd St., tel. 318/352–3353).

Tourist Information

Natchitoches Parish Tourist Commission (Box 411, Natchitoches, LA 71458, tel. 318/352–8072). **Rapides Parish Convention & Visitors Bureau** (Box 8110, Alexandria, LA 71306, tel. 318/443–7049).

Reservation Service

Southern Comfort Reservation Service (2856 Hundred Oaks Ave., Baton Rouge, LA 70808, tel. 504/346–1928 or 800/749–1928).

Cloutier Townhouse

Adorned with filigreed cast-iron galleries that were assembled in France, the Cloutier (pronounced "cloo-chee") Townhouse sits smack in Natchitoches's historic district. Conna Cloutier's elegant home is the only bed-and-breakfast that offers an unobstructed view of Front Street and Cane River Lake. This is the center of the town's famed Christmas Festival of Lights, when the trees, buildings, and bridges are ablaze. Conna opens her home for group tours (by appointment) during the month of December.

The town house occupies the top two floors of a three-story building that dates from the 1830s. In the European style, the first floor is a commercial establishment—in this case, an antiques shop. A carriageway leads from Front Street to a courtyard paved with old brick. From there, behind an iron gate, steps lead to the broad rear porches, where there are tables and rocking chairs. At both the front and back, French doors open onto the galleries.

In the large open area that contains the foyer, living room, and dining room, polished hardwood floors are covered with Oriental rugs, and paneled walls reach to a 30-foot ceiling. A winding central staircase leads to the part of the third floor where Conna lives. Most of the furnishings are of the American Empire period. An Empire sideboard and a gold-leaf mirror supported by rosewood piano legs on a marble base were made for an early nearby plantation. Bookcases are filled with books, and oil paintings hang on the walls, one of them a portrait of the wife of a 19th-century owner of the property.

The front guest room, which has a four-poster bed and other Louisiana antiques, opens onto the gallery and is somewhat noisy; the master bedroom, which opens onto the foyer and the rear gallery, is both larger and quieter. Its focal points are a full-tester bed with an embroidered spread, old-brick walls, and a fireplace with gas logs. Wing chairs and an upholstered settee (with good reading lamps) are tempting places to curl up and read the many books that lie about. Twin dressing areas, each with a spacious marble vanity and ample wall mirrors, are outside a large carpeted bath which has a platformed whirlpool and a wood-paneled lighted shower stall.

Address: *8 Ducournau Sq., Natchitoches, LA 71457, tel. 318/352-5242.*
Accommodations: *2 double rooms with baths.*
Amenities: *Air-conditioning, cable TV in master bedroom, 2 fireplaces in public rooms.*
Rates: *$65 and $85; Continental breakfast with home-baked breads. MC, V.*

Loyd's Hall

oyd's Hall is a 640-acre working plantation that grows cotton, corn, and soybeans. Frank Fitzgerald's father bought the land in 1949, unaware that a deteriorated 19th-century mansion was buried beneath a tangle of trees and bushes. Frank and his wife, Anne, now live in the restored house. Frank is a veterinarian, and in addition to chickens, cattle, horses, and other farm critters, a small army of cats and dogs calls Loyd's Hall home. Two Catahoula hog dogs—each with the one blue eye and one brown eye that distinguish the breed—make it a point to befriend guests who stay in the farmhouse cottage.

The little cottage, which sits near the mansion, appears to be a restored 19th-century plantation outbuilding, with a sloping shingled roof and a front porch. But it was built in 1971 to look old. Frank's mother had an antiques shop, and the cottage is furnished with some of her 19th-century Louisianiana.

The front room, with a low, beamed ceiling, is a combination living room and kitchen. At one end, before a wood-burning fireplace and brick hearth, brass lamps hang over an upholstered sofa, an old wooden chest that serves as a coffee table, a reclining chair, and an inviting leather chair. Healthy-looking green plants dangle from the ceiling. In addition to plenty of books and magazines, there are games, including backgammon and Chinese checkers. The front-porch rocking chairs are fine for listening to the crickets.

Separated from a small dining area by an island, the fully equipped kitchen has modern appliances, including a dishwasher, toaster, and electric coffee maker. It's stocked with a chilled decanter of wine, homemade muffins, milk, juice, and all the ingredients for a bacon-and-eggs breakfast, which guests prepare at their leisure.

Each bedroom has a big four-poster bed covered with a plump comforter, but the larger one has a rocking chair, a cheval mirror, and ample closet space. There is a claw-foot tub in the bath and plenty of vanity space.

Because of its small size, the cottage is rented only to a family or to people who know each other well.

Address: *292 Loyd Bridge Rd., Cheneyville, LA 71325, tel. 318/776–5641 or 800/749–1928, fax 318/279–2335.*
Accommodations: *2 double rooms share 1 bath in housekeeping cottage.*
Amenities: *Air-conditioning, TV; pool, bicycles, fishing rods.*
Rates: *$75; full breakfast. AE, MC, V.*
Restrictions: *Smoking only on porch.*

Fleur-de-Lis

The Fleur-de-Lis, opened in 1983, is the granddaddy of Natchitoches bed-and-breakfasts. Bert Froeba's home, built in 1902, is a two-story frame house painted beige with brown trim. A front porch, with a swing and rocking chairs, is shaded by a roof that juts out beneath a second-story bay window topped by a gable. Behind leaded-glass doors are a large foyer and stairway. Adjoining the foyer, a cozy family room has a sofa and chairs grouped around the TV. Bert whips up breakfast and serves it family-style at a long table in the dining room. Knickknacks and framed family pictures are displayed throughout.

Guest rooms feature four-poster, white iron, or brass beds and patchwork quilts; some have white wicker furnishings and headboards. The quietest room is the Blue Room, which has a country French flavor. All the baths are tiny but have modern fixtures.

Address: *336 2nd St., Natchitoches, LA 71457, tel. 318/352-6621.*
Accommodations: *5 double rooms with baths.*
Amenities: *Air-conditioning, cable TV in living room; wheelchair ramp.*
Rates: *$55; full breakfast. AE, MC, V.*
Restrictions: *No pets, 2-night minimum during Christmas Festival.*

Jefferson House

The back veranda of Gay and L. J. Melder's contemporary white frame home affords a mesmerizing view of Cane River Lake. Although the house sits on a busy extension of Front Street, within walking distance of the historic district, the weeping willows, herb garden, rocking chairs on the veranda, and pier sneaking onto the lake create a bucolic ambience.

The house is a split-level whose lower floor is hidden from the street. The Melders live on the lower floor; guests occupy the entire street-level floor. Gay, who has an upmarket gift shop, has decorated the house with a blend of exquisite Oriental objets d'art and traditional furnishings. The large, stately parlor has a high, beamed ceiling, a brick fireplace, and doors opening to the veranda. Bedrooms are done with quilted spreads and matching draperies. The larger room has an adjoining tile bath that's big enough for a fair-size cocktail party!

Address: *229 Jefferson St., Natchitoches, LA 71457, tel. 318/352-3957 or 318/352-5756.*
Accommodations: *2 double rooms with baths.*
Amenities: *Air-conditioning, large-screen cable TV in living room.*
Rates: *$45-$55 ($85 if rented as suite); full breakfast, afternoon cocktails. MC, V.*
Restrictions: *Smoking only on porch, no pets.*

William and Mary Ackel House

Named for her two children, Margaret Ackel's home is on a peaceful tree-lined street near Natchitoches's historic district. Built in 1820 of cypress and brick, it is the oldest two-story house in town. Mrs. Ackel, a retired home economist, began restoring it with her late husband in 1967. She now lives upstairs with her mother.

A private entrance from the garden leads into the sunny, spacious guest room, which is furnished with a Victorian Eastlake carved walnut bed and a matching pier mirror and marble-top dressing table. The embroidered pillowcases, quilts, and rugs are all handmade. Gas logs burn in the fireplace, and above the mantel hangs a large oil portrait of the Ackel children; other framed family pictures are placed here and there, and antique high-button shoes sit on the hearth. The tiny bath is modern, with a small vanity.

Address: *146 Jefferson St., Natchitoches, LA 71457, tel. 318/352–3748.*
Accommodations: *1 double room with bath.*
Amenities: *Air-conditioning.*
Rates: *$75; full breakfast. No credit cards.*
Restrictions: *Smoking only on porch, no pets.*

Plantation Country

From north to south, the state of Louisiana is graced with fine old plantation homes, but the area officially designated Plantation Country begins with a reservoir of grand houses north of Baton Rouge and stretches all the way down the Mississippi River to New Orleans.

As the crow flies (or Interstate 10 runs), the distance is about 80 miles (wherever you stay in Plantation Country you'll not be far from the bright lights of a big city), but as the river flows—and twists and curves—the going is much slower. The romantic-sounding Great River Road (Rte. 61) follows its serpentine meanderings between Baton Rouge and New Orleans, but unfortunately, it is less scenic than the interstate—huge industrial and chemical plants line the road and the river. The stretch of Route 1 between Baton Rouge and Donaldsonville on the west bank is a scenic alternative.

This is the proverbial moonlight-and-magnolias country; there are more mint juleps sipped on sweeping verandas than you can shake a swizzle stick at. Homes with sky-high ceilings and rows of white columns are filled with such 19th-century necessities as petticoat mirrors, hoopskirt chairs, courtship settees, and fire screens. The hostesses and docents tell tales of Union gunboats, Yankee soldiers, the valorous men and women of the Confederacy, and the tons of silver that were buried to keep the Bluebellies from stealing it. Ghosts are also favorite topics; it seems that almost every mansion is haunted—by a tiny child, an entire massacred family, or a wild-eyed murderer dragging around chains.

Less than a half hour north of Baton Rouge lies St. Francisville, a town that's been described as "two miles long and two yards wide." Much of the long, skinny little city is listed on the National Register of Historic Places. In

*the early 19th century, West Feliciana Parish, in which it
lies, was the seat of government for the short-lived Republic
of West Florida. Antique-seeking is popular here; the
Feliciana towns (including St. Francisville, Clinton, and
Jackson) are loaded with wonderful old poke-around places.*

*The terrain above Baton Rouge—rolling hills, high bluffs,
deep valleys, and piney woods—is much more akin to
North Louisiana than to South Louisiana. But as the
Mississippi nears New Orleans, the land flattens out and
becomes marshy. Stark cypress trees poke up through the
swamplands, and pirogues bob lazily on sluggish bayous.
You can almost hear Cajun fiddles tuning up to the west
and Dixieland bands stomping off to the east but much of
the charm of Plantation Country is in . . . well, sipping
mint juleps on the veranda and listening to tales of
carpetbaggers, scalawags, and Yankees.*

Places to Go, Sights to See

False River is one of several oxbow lakes left behind when the Mississippi
River changed its course. Route 1 sashays south from New Roads right
along the "river," which, unlike the muddy Mississippi, has pretty, deep-blue
water and is a fine place for fishing and boating, as evidenced by all the
fishing camps that line the banks.

In the wooded, 100-acre **Audubon State Commemorative Area** (Rte. 956 near
St. Francisville, tel. 504/635–3739) you can tour *Oakley Plantation*, where
John James Audubon created many of the paintings for his *Birds of
America* series.

The **Port Hudson State Commemorative Area** (756 W. Plains–Port Hudson
Rd., south of St. Francisville, tel. 504/654–3775) encompasses part of the
Port Hudson battlefield, a Civil War site that saw the longest siege in
American military history. There are an interpretive center and a picnic area,
as well as 6 miles of hiking trails on the 650 acres.

Plaquemine Lock (downtown Plaquemine at the Mississippi River, tel.
504/687–0641), built in 1909 and no longer in use, has the original lock house
and an interpretive center with displays and exhibits that examine the history
of the river and its boat traffic.

Plantations

Rosedown Plantation House and Gardens (U.S. 61 at Rte. 10, tel. 504/635–3332), a restored 1835 mansion with original furnishings, on 28 acres of landscaped gardens, is one of the state's most impressive houses.

Catalpa Plantation (3½ mi north of St. Francisville, tel. 504/635–3372), reached by an elliptical oak alley, has been in the same family since the 18th century and contains fine antiques, silver, and family heirlooms.

San Francisco Plantation (Rte. 44 at Reserve, tel. 504/535–2341) is a steamboat Gothic structure noted for its ornate frescoes and millwork.

Houmas House (Rte. 942, Burnside, tel. 504/473–7841), a large white Greek Revival house, was the setting for the Gothic thriller *Hush, Hush, Sweet Charlotte,* starring Bette Davis and Olivia DeHaviland.

Ashland/Belle Helene (Rte. 75 between Darrow and Geismar, tel. 504/473–1207), a Greek Revival mansion surrounded by 28 columns, is a magnificent if somewhat ghostly unrestored house that has been used as a set for more films than any other plantation in the area.

Restaurants

Lafitte's Landing (Sunshine Bridge Access Rd., Donaldsonville, tel. 504/473–1232) features South Louisiana specialties in a quaint raised Acadian plantation house. **The Cabin** (intersection of Rtes. 22 and 44, Burnside, tel. 504/473–3007), in a rustic, 150-year-old former slave cabin, is an informal place for sandwiches as well as hearty Cajun and Creole fare. Decorated with wonderful stuffed bears, **Bear Corners** (Bank St. at Rte. 10, Jackson, tel. 504/634–5349) is a friendly fried chicken-y sort of place.

Tourist Information

Baton Rouge Area Convention & Visitors Bureau (Drawer 4149, Baton Rouge, LA 70821, tel. 504/383–1825 or 800/527–6843). **Greater New Orleans Tourist & Convention Commission** (1520 Sugar Bowl Dr., New Orleans, LA 70112, tel. 504/566–5011). **West Feliciana Tourist Commission** (Box 1548, St. Francisville, LA 70775, tel. 504/635–6330).

Reservation Service

Southern Comfort Bed & Breakfast Reservation Service (2856 Hundred Oaks Ave., Baton Rouge, LA 70808, tel. 504/346–1928 or 800/749–1928).

Cottage Plantation

The country road to Cottage Plantation ambles across a wooden bridge and through a splendid wooded area thick with moss-covered live oaks, as well as dogwood, mimosa, and crape myrtle trees. The plantation nestles in 400 such idyllic acres, far from traffic noises and other 20th-century distractions.

Built between 1795 and 1850, Cottage is one of only a handful of antebellum plantations that still have their original outbuildings. The office and one-room schoolhouse, kitchen, tiny milk house, barns, slave quarters, and other dependencies that comprised a working plantation are intact, though weathered with time. One outbuilding is now a rustic restaurant called Mattie's House (open for dinner only); another is an antiques shop.

The well-maintained main building is a long, low yellow frame structure with green shutters outlining the gallery and dormer windows. The sloping roof is punctuated with chimneys and dormers from which window air-conditioning units jut anachronistically. A variety of dogs and cats nap or amble around the grounds.

Angling off from the main house is a similar structure—also original to the plantation—which houses the guest rooms. Downstairs rooms open onto the porch and get more light than those upstairs. All have four-posters and baths with modern plumbing and fixtures.

A tap on the door in the morning signals the arrival of a demitasse of coffee, accompanied by a flower. A serious breakfast is later served in the formal dining room, which, like the rest of the house (including guest rooms), is furnished with antebellum Louisiana pieces that might have been in the house when General Andrew Jackson called on the original owners after the 1815 Battle of New Orleans.

The plantation has been in the Brown family since 1951; Harvey and Mary Brown, the present owners, moved to St. Francisville from Miami to take charge in 1984. One of Mary's hobbies is apparent in the flower gardens that decorate the grounds near the main building.

Address: *U.S. 61 at Cottage La., HC 68, Box 425, St. Francisville, LA 70777, tel. 504/635-3674.*
Accommodations: *5 double rooms with baths.*
Amenities: *Air-conditioning, TV in rooms, restaurant, antiques shop; pool.*
Rates: *$85; full breakfast. MC, V.*
Restrictions: *Smoking only on porch, no pets, closed Christmas Eve.*

Madewood Plantation

I n a lush country setting about midway between New Orleans and Baton Rouge, this handsome 21-room Greek Revival mansion offers a nostalgic glimpse of 19th-century life.

Built in 1846 for Col. Thomas Pugh, the house had fallen into a terrible state of repair when, in 1964, it was bought and restored by the Harold K. Marshall family of New Orleans. It is now owned by the Marshalls' son Keith and his wife, Millie, who will tell you, laughing, that the mansion became a bed-and-breakfast as the result of an exorbitant electric bill. Keith had just seen the bill when the phone rang and a caller asked if Madewood accepted paying guests. He replied, "Yes!" The Marshalls sometimes spend weekends at Madewood, but the resident managers are Janet Ledet and Dave D'Aunoy, who preside at the informal wine-and-cheese gatherings and candlelit Southern dinners served to guests in the main mansion. There's additional lodging in Charlet House and the cabin, two restored outbuildings on the property.

Madewood has spacious rooms with high ceilings, hardwood floors, handsome carved moldings, Oriental rugs, and sparkling crystal chandeliers. In addition to 18th- and 19th-century Louisiana antiques in the mansion and in Charlet House, there are English antiques collected by Keith when he was a Rhodes Scholar. The house has served as a set for films, among them *A Woman Called Moses*, starring Cicely Tyson.

Address: *4250 Rte. 308, Napoleonville, LA 70390, tel. 504/369–7151, 800/749–7151, or 800/375–7151 in LA.*
Accommodations: *5 rooms with baths in the main mansion, 3 suites in Charlet House, 1 double housekeeping suite in the cabin.*
Amenities: *Air-conditioning, turndown service, free tour of house and grounds.*
Rates: *$159 in the main mansion, including dinner and full breakfast; $90 in the cabin or Charlet House, including Continental breakfast. AE, MC, V.*
Restrictions: *Smoking only on porches, no pets. Guest rooms must be vacated for tours from 10 AM till 5 PM in the main mansion and from noon till 3 PM in the outbuildings. Closed Christmas Eve and Day, Thanksgiving Eve and Day, New Year's Eve and Day.*

Milbank

On special occasions, such as the Jackson Assembly Antique Show and Sale, Milbank co-owner Leroy Harvey dons a frock coat and acts as tour guide of his historic house. He loves talking about the history of the quiet town and his plans for a winery, a tourist railroad, and other entrepreneurial attractions. Leroy was instrumental, as it were, in obtaining the Wurlitzer theater pipe organ that now graces the Republic of West Florida Historic Association Museum, which he and others founded.

Milbank is an impressive two-story pink house on a downtown street, surrounded by a dozen 30-foot Doric columns. One of Jackson's oldest commercial buildings, it dates from 1836. Its name commemorates a former owner named Miller and a former occupant—the Clinton Port Hudson Railroad Banking House.

Leroy and his wife, Lynette, bought Milbank in 1982 in partnership with Leroy's sister Rosemary and her husband, Thomas Jackson. None of the owners—nor anyone else, for that matter—lives in the house. Overnight guests stay here as if they owned the place, a situation ideal for a family or for couples traveling together. (There is only one "guaranteed private bath"; it adjoins the downstairs bedroom and was once a bank vault.) There is a full kitchen upstairs and another one down, and lunch and dinner are available in the homey Bear Corner Restaurant.

The house has an opulent display of 18th- and 19th-century American and European antiques, including ornate hand-carved tester and half-tester beds and a pair of sterling silver candelabra commissioned by Napoleon III and bearing his crest. Also prominently displayed is Leroy's collection of unique and antique clocks. The staff likes to challenge overnight guests to see how many hidden drawers and little secret compartments they can find in the desks, dressers, and other antique furnishings. It's amazing what the touching of an inkwell will reveal.

Address: *102 Bank St., Jackson, LA 70748, tel. 504/634-5901.*
Accommodations: *1 double room with bath, 3 doubles share 1 bath.*
Amenities: *Restaurant (closed Mon.), air-conditioning, free house tour; gift shop.*
Rates: *$65-$75; full breakfast. MC, V.*
Restrictions: *No smoking indoors, no pets, closed major holidays. Rooms available 4 PM-10 AM.*

Barrow House

Barrow House was built in 1809 as a two-story saltbox; iron-work double galleries and a one-story Greek Revival wing were added in the 1850s. Located on pretty, tree-lined Royal Street, the house is owned by Shirley and Lyle Dittloff, who opened it as a bed-and-breakfast in 1985. The Dittloffs live in separate quarters, giving guests their own entrance and much privacy.

All the guest rooms are large and light, with lace-curtained French doors opening onto the gallery. The furnishings, dating from the 1840s to the 1870s, include etched-glass chandeliers, carved armoires, and a Mallard bed whose mattress is stuffed with Spanish moss. Baths are modern; the share-a-bath double suite is rented only to people traveling together.

Address: *524 Royal St., St. Francisville, LA 70775, tel. 504/635-4791.*
Accommodations: *3 double rooms with baths, 1 double suite.*
Amenities: *Air-conditioning, cassette walking tour.*
Rates: *$75–$85; Continental breakfast, wine (full breakfast and candlelit dinner available). No credit cards.*
Restrictions: *No pets, closed Dec. 22–25.*

Nottoway

This three-story Italianate/Greek Revival mansion built in 1859 is a knockout. The interior, which was restored in 1980, has undergone extensive recent refurbishment, and at press time the exterior was getting a badly needed coat of paint. Sitting in a lush country setting, across a quiet road from the Mississippi River levee, it has 22 white columns, 200 windows, and 53,000 square feet of living space.

Guest rooms are in the main mansion (the best are those facing the river) and the overseer's cottage, which overlooks sculpted gardens and a duck pond. Four-posters, testers, brass beds, and armoires are among the 19th-century furnishings; the master bedroom's Rococo Revival furniture, made in New Orleans by McCrackin, is original to the house.

Address: *Hwy. 1 (Box 160), White Castle, LA 70788, tel. 504/545-2730 or 504/346-8263 in Baton Rouge.*
Accommodations: *10 double rooms with baths, 3 suites.*
Amenities: *Restaurant, air-conditioning, phones in 11 rooms, free house tour; pool.*
Rates: *$125–$250; wake-up Continental breakfast in rooms, full breakfast, sherry. AE, D, MC, V.*
Restrictions: *Smoking only on verandas, no pets, closed Dec. 24–25. Randolph Suite and Master Bedroom must be vacated for tours 9 AM–5 PM.*

Ormond Plantation

Typical of the houses of early Louisiana planters, Ormond (built sometime prior to 1790) is a two-story West Indies–style home with double galleries, a sloping roof, and attached garçonnières (young men's quarters). It is currently owned by Ken and Dede Elliott, who completed extensive restoration before opening as a bed-and-breakfast in 1989.

Large, sunny rooms have high ceilings, hardwood floors, and lace-curtained French doors opening onto the galleries. In addition to furnishings representative of Louisiana in the 18th and 19th centuries, the house contains a roomful of adorable antique dolls and carriages, a display of antique guns, and a collection of antique one-armed bandits. From the rocking chairs on the upstairs gallery, you can watch the parade of boats on the Mississippi. Bowls of potpourri and miniature picture hats add warmth. The baths have modern tub/showers, but they lack vanity space for toiletries.

Address: *8407 River Rd., Destrehan, LA 70047, tel. and fax 504/764–8544.*
Accommodations: *3 double rooms with baths.*
Amenities: *Air-conditioning, free house tour, meeting room.*
Rates: *$125; full breakfast. AE, MC, V.*
Restrictions: *Smoking only on veranda, no pets. Rooms must be vacated for tours 9 AM–5 PM.*

Cajun Country

*The Cajun craze of recent years has had the whole world
two-stepping and tasting such hot-peppery dishes as Cajun
chef Paul Prudhomme's blackened redfish. For the
residents of South Louisiana, "Cajun" denotes not
a passing fad but a way of life that spans almost 400 years.
This way of life involves hard work, a strong Catholic faith,
devotion to family and friends, plenty of good food, and an
exuberant joie de vivre. In these parts, the Cajun motto is*
Laissez les bons temps rouler *(Let the good times roll). And
roll they do; though for the rest of the world fads may come
and fads may go, there is still plenty big fun down on the
bayous.*

*The Cajuns are descendants of the French who settled in
what is now Nova Scotia and New Brunswick, Canada; they
called their colony l'Acadie. The Acadians ("Cajun" is
a corruption of the word) were expelled by the British in
the mid-18th century, and a few thousand of them came to
South Louisiana. Henry Wadsworth Longfellow's epic poem*
Evangeline *is based on the true story of Emmeline Labiche
and Louis Arceneaux (Evangeline and Gabriel in the
poem), the real-life lovers who were separated during the
arduous exile—called by the Cajuns Le Grand
Dérangement.*

*Cajuns speak an antique 17th-century form of French,
though they can understand and speak standard French
(as well as English). Radio stations sometimes broadcast in
French, and French-speaking disc jockeys spin Cajun
music. Billboards touting a local fried chicken chain
proclaim, "J'aime cette poule!" (Love that chicken!), and at
Evangeline Downs, races begin, "Ils sont partis!" (They're
off!). Most shops have a sign in their window announcing,
"Ici on parle français." Needless to say, this is a great place
to brush up on your French.*

Not surprisingly, given the Cajun exuberance, festivals pop up almost every 10 minutes in this neck of the bois. *Events celebrate alligators, crawfish, strawberries, cotton, shrimp, tomatoes, and potatoes—and in between festivals, the Cajuns simply celebrate themselves.*

The interstates that race through the region are the quickest routes from there to there, but the best way to savor the scenery is by taking the state and parish roads that follow twisting bottle-green bayous or amble by canebrakes, rice paddies, exotic old plantations, and immense live oak trees whose gnarled boughs are draped with gray shawls of Spanish moss. South Louisiana is sprinkled with salt domes, called "islands," which have nudged up from under the flatlands over a few thousand millennia and look a bit like dry-land islands. There are several picturesque state parks that are ideal for hiking, picnicking, boating, or building castles in the air.

Places to Go, Sights to See

Lafayette, a city of some 150,000, which proudly calls itself the capital of French Louisiana, lies less than two hours west of New Orleans. Lafayette's museums and music halls are good places in which to get acquainted with Acadian lore and life. The city is also a hub for exploring the smaller towns and villages in the area. *Cajun Mardi Gras* in Lafayette and environs is second only to its sister celebration in New Orleans. Picture a few hundred masked and costumed horsemen thundering around the countryside during the annual Courir de Mardi Gras (Mardi Gras Run). Lafayette is also home to the *Festival International de Louisiane,* which brings musicians, actors, dancers, jugglers, and all sorts of other performers and aficionados from all over the world. *The Lafayette Natural History Museum and Planetarium* (637 Girard Park Dr., tel. 318/268–5544) has an adjunct *Acadiana Park Nature Trail and Station* (E. Alexander St., tel. 318/235–6181), with an interpretive center. It organizes bird-watching walks, hikes, and other field trips.

Acadian Village (south of Lafayette off Rte. 342, tel. 318/981–2364), a rural folk-life museum, is a re-creation of a bayou village, with a cluster of authentic 19th-century houses, a church, a blacksmith shop, and a general store.

Vermilionville, the Cajun answer to Colonial Williamsburg, is another re-created village (1600 Surrey St., Lafayette, tel. 318/233–4077 or

800/992–2968), where costumed docents provide entertainment and lots of food, perform chores, and create early Acadian crafts.

Breaux Bridge, whose chief claim to fame is Mulate's (*see* Restaurants, *below*), draws some 100,000 visitors at its Crawfish Festival, held every other year. East of the village is the huge *Atchafalaya Basin* (800,000 watery acres), an eerily beautiful place where stark cypress trees dripping with Spanish moss rise from the murky waters. Just east of Breaux Bridge, at *Henderson,* where the levee is lined with tour and fishing boats, a host of operators will take you gliding out beneath canopies of trees to find alligators, herons, egrets, beavers, and all manner of critters. Try *McGee's Landing* (tel. 318/228–2384) for pontoon-boat tours or *Angelle's Atchafalaya Swamp Tours* (Whiskey River Landing, tel. 318/667–6135).

St. Martinville, a little town nearby, was a major debarkation point for the Acadians. There, on the banks of Bayou Teche, stands the *Evangeline Oak,* a giant tree that was the legendary last meeting place of the two lovers. It is one of the region's most photographed sights. In the late-18th century, St. Martinville was a haven for French aristocrats who fled from France during the revolution. The town was known then as Petit Paris because of the elaborate balls and operas staged there. St. Martinville is also home to St. Martin de Tours, the mother church of the Acadians. In the church square, the *Petit Paris Museum* (103 S. Main St., tel. 318/394–7334) has carnival costumes and historical displays pertaining to Cajun country. And behind the church, where Emmeline Labiche is buried, there is a statue of Evangeline. In 1929, *The Romance of Evangeline,* starring Delores del Rio, was filmed in the town; Ms. del Rio posed for the statue, and it was given to St. Martinville. Just north of town is the *Longfellow-Evangeline State Commemorative Area* (1200 N. Main St., St. Martinville, tel. 318/394–3754), a 157-acre park with an interpretive center, an early 19th-century Creole home, an Acadian craft shop housed in a Cajun cottage, picnic grounds, and a boat launch.

New Iberia, proclaiming itself the Queen City of the Teche, is a picturesque town that was settled by Spaniards from the Iberian coast. One of the South's best-known antebellum homes—*Shadows on the Teche* (317 E. Main St., tel. 318/369–6446)—is a perfect example of what went with the wind. The *Konriko Rice Mill and Company Store* (tel. 800/551–3245 or 800/737–5667 in LA) is the country's oldest rice mill, and *Trappey's* (tel. 318/365–8281) turns out red-hot spices. Both are open for tours.

Avery Island (south of New Iberia on Rte. 329, tel. 318/369–6243) boasts both a 300-acre *Jungle Garden* (tel. 318/369–6243), thick with subtropical trees, plants, and flowers, and an aviary fluttering with egrets. Here you can also tour the *Tabasco Sauce factory* (tel. 318/365–8173), where the McIlhenny family still makes the red-hot condiment created by Edmund McIlhenny in the 1800s.

At **Jefferson Island,** you can visit *Live Oak Gardens* (284 Rip Van Winkle Rd., tel. 318/367–3485), once the winter home of 19th-century actor Joseph

Jefferson, which features landscaped grounds, a boat ride on the lake, and tours of Jefferson's lavish three-story house.

Franklin, sitting smugly on the Teche to the south, is a lush little Main Street USA town that boasts a half-dozen antebellum mansions open for tours. Oddly, for this part of Louisiana, Franklin was settled by the English. Nearby live some 300 Chitimacha Indians on a 280-acre reservation (Rte. 326, Charenton, tel. 318/923–4830) under the auspices of the Jean Lafitte National Historical Park. Besides the tribal center, the reservation has a museum, a trading post, a craft shop, a park, and picnic areas. The Chitimacha were known for basket weaving, and their colorful crafts can be purchased on the reservation.

Restaurants

You'd be hard-pressed to find any bad food in this part of the country. Standout Cajun restaurants include **Enola Prudhomme's Cajun Café** (4676 N.E. Evangeline Thruway, Carencro, tel. 318/896–7964) and **Prejean's** (3480 Hwy. 167, Lafayette, tel. 318/896–3247), both housed in cypress Cajun cottages; **Mulate's** (325 Mills Ave., Breaux Bridge, tel. 800/422–2586 or 800/634–9880 in LA), a wildly popular dance hall–cum–café with live Cajun music; and **Café Vermilionville** (1304 Pinhook Rd., Lafayette, tel. 318/237–0100), which serves Creole cuisine in a lovely restored 1799 inn. **Lagniappe Too** (204 E. Main St., New Iberia, tel. 318/365–9419) is a good lunch spot for salads, quiches, and sandwiches. **Dwyer's Cafe** (323 Jefferson St., Lafayette, tel. 318/235–9364), a down-home place, opens for breakfast at 4 AM.

Tourist Information

Atchafalaya Delta Tourist Commission (Box 2332, Morgan City, LA 70381, tel. 504/395–4905). **Iberia Parish Tourist Commission** (2690 Center St., New Iberia, LA 70560, tel. 318/365–1540). **Lafayette Convention & Visitors Commission** (1400 N.W. Evangeline Thruway, Box 52006, Lafayette, LA 70505, tel. 318/232–3737, 800/346–1958 in the United States, or 800/543–5340 in Canada).

Reservation Service

Southern Comfort Reservation Service (2856 Hundred Oaks Ave., Baton Rouge, LA 70808, tel. 504/346–1928 or 800/749–1928).

A la Bonne Veillée

Off a country road between Lafayette and Abbeville stands A la Bonne Veillée, a two-story Acadian cottage. Moss-draped live oaks shade it, and ducks waddle about a nearby pond. Their quacking and the songs of birds are about the only sounds that can be heard.

Made of hand-cut cypress timbers, the house has a steeply pitched wood-shingled roof through which pokes a chimney made of old brick. Wood for the two fireplaces is stacked neatly on the front porch, where there are rocking chairs. American Empire antiques and plenty of books grace the parlor; adjacent is a master bedroom with a huge tiger maple Sheraton canopy bed and scatter rugs on the cypress floors. The other downstairs rooms are a full kitchen and the only bath (it's almost as big as the bedroom). Steep, unfriendly stairs lead to an attic room with a brass bed, patchwork quilts, a trundle bed, and other pieces "from grandmother's attic," says owner Carolyn Doerle.

Carolyn and her husband, Ron Ray, who live in the historic LeBlanc House a stone's throw away, saved the cottage from demolition and had it moved to their 30-acre farm. (Ron, a psychotherapist, also raises Gertrudis cattle. Carolyn is CEO of Doerle Food Services, her family's wholesale food concern.) The two love restoring old houses, and the

cottage was special. More than 100 years ago it was a *maison dimanche* (Sunday house)—it was customary for prosperous rural plantation owners to keep a town house to use on weekends.

The cottage is rented only to a family or to two couples traveling together. Breakfast is brought in, and there is an intercom to the main house, which guests may tour; apart from that, they have absolute peace and privacy. (Those who want to pick up the pace can drive to the Cajun dance halls in Lafayette, about 15 minutes away.)

The unusual name of the guest house derives from a Cajun phrase, "Let's go *veiller*." It means to make long evening visits after supper, chatting, gossiping, and telling stories.

Address: *Rte. TI 21 off Rte. 339; LeBlanc House, Rte. 2, Box 2270, Abbeville, LA 70510, tel. 318/937–5495.*
Accommodations: *2 double rooms share 1 bath in housekeeping cottage.*
Amenities: *Air-conditioning and TV in rooms, guest phone.*
Rates: *$100 ($140 for 2 couples); Continental breakfast. No credit cards.*
Restrictions: *No smoking indoors, no pets.*

Chrétien Point Plantation

In the early 1930s, a local photographer took pictures of this house and sent them to Hollywood. As a result, the stairway and the window above it were used as a model for those in Scarlett O'Hara's Tara. Then, too, there's the tale of the long-ago lady of Chrétien Point who shot a man on the steps, as Scarlett shot the Union soldier. Owners Jeanne and Louis Cornay will point out the very step on which the man was standing when he was killed.

Of solid brick construction, with six round white columns and double galleries across the front, the two-story house was built in 1831 for Hypolite Chrétien II and his wife, Félicité. During the War Between the States, the house figured in a major battle. There is still a bullet hole in one of the front doors. The last Chrétiens lost the house a few years after the war, and it began to fall into a sorry state.

Louis found the deteriorated mansion while looking for a barn in which to keep his son's horse. Hay was stored in it; chickens, cows, and pigs roamed through it. The Cornays bought the house and restored it to its former grandeur.

The colors used in the house are those of nature's sunsets. Silk wall coverings are in vivid scarlets and pinks; one of the ceilings is painted a cool blue. There are six working fireplaces with imported French Empire marble mantels. The 19th-century Louisiana antiques include a carved armoire and four-poster by Mallard. Two rooms have full-tester beds, one with a pale gold sunburst canopy and crocheted spread, the other with canopy and spread in rich fabrics and bold colors. A downstairs room, formerly the wine cellar, has redbrick floors, pink velvet chairs, a marble-top dresser, and a hand-carved bed. The bins that once held wine are now filled with books.

The only guest room with an adjoining bath is the master bedroom upstairs. Most other rooms have private hall baths.

There is no restaurant, but Louis says that in bad weather they'll rustle up something for hungry guests.

Address: *Rte. 1, Sunset (1108 Johnston St., Lafayette, LA 70501), tel. 318/233-7050 or 318/662-5876.*
Accommodations: *3 double rooms with baths, 2 doubles share 1 bath.*
Amenities: *Air-conditioning, tour of mansion, 1 meeting room; pool, tennis court.*
Rates: *$95–$200; full breakfast. MC, V.*
Restrictions: *Smoking only on galleries, no pets, rooms must be vacated 10 AM–5 PM for tours.*

Mouton Manor Inn

A wide green lawn shaded by pecan trees stretches between a quiet city street and Mouton Manor Inn, a small, two-story Acadian cottage made of cypress. A trim white picket fence surrounds the house, which has a high-pitched shingled roof. On the double porches, there are clay pots of geraniums and ferns, a redwood swing, and rocking chairs where cats curl up for a snooze. Squirrels scurry across the lawn, birds can be heard singing, and a friendly Labrador named Kilo waits for a playmate in the fenced-in backyard.

Owners Rita and Frank Preston occupy a renovated barn in back. The cottage is for the exclusive use of their guests, who number no more than four at a time.

The downstairs living room has whitewashed walls, a fireplace with an old-brick hearth, beamed ceilings, and a big, round hooked rug on the cypress floor. A wooden bowl of fruit sits on the table, eyed by the stuffed dolls and teddy bears perched here and there. Furnishings are reproductions of simple early Acadian pieces.

All the rooms open onto the upstairs or downstairs porch. The downstairs guest room, adjacent to the living room, is larger than the one upstairs and has a big bathroom with a cypress vanity. In addition to the bed, there is an upholstered love seat and a dresser with a small TV set. Steep stairs curve from the living room to a spacious den with an upholstered sofa and wing chairs, a TV set, and a coffee table stacked with magazines like *Southern Living* and *Archaeology*, as well as books of Acadiana. There are also good reading lamps. A narrow hallway, with pad and pencil placed thoughtfully by the phone, connects the den to the upstairs guest room and bath. Though the bath has a modern tub and shower, it's small, and the only place to put toiletries is the floor.

Rita Preston instinctively knows how to make guests feel at home and when to leave them alone. And those who don't like to be herded at an early hour will be happy to know she prepares breakfast at whatever time a guest requests it. Her breakfasts, which may be mouth-watering cream-filled crepes, are well worth getting out of bed for.

Address: *310 Sidney Martin Rd., Lafayette, LA 70507, tel. 318/237–6996.*
Accommodations: *2 double rooms with baths.*
Amenities: *Air-conditioning, cable TV in 1 room, cable TV/VCR in den, guest phone.*
Rates: *$65. Full breakfast. MC, V.*
Restrictions: *Smoking only on porches.*

Bois des Chênes

Beneath the branches of huge live oaks, peacocks preen in a thatch-roofed aviary, while a Labrador and a miniature poodle greet visitors. The setting is so serenely bucolic that it seems to be deep in the woods rather than just off a busy thoroughfare.

This historic plantation is home to Marjorie and Coerte Voorhies, who have restored the mansion and carriage house. All the guest rooms are in the carriage house and have private entrances. Spacious, airy rooms have hardwood floors and Oriental rugs; one of the rooms has cypress beams. Marjorie, a former antiques dealer, furnished the rooms with 18th- and 19th-century American and Louisiana French pieces. Four-posters have patchwork quilts and a crocheted canopy or a filmy mosquito net. Baths are especially well done: large and modern, with brass fittings.

Address: *338 N. Sterling St., Lafayette, LA 70501, tel. 318/233-7816.*
Accommodations: *3 suites.*
Amenities: *Air-conditioning, cable TV, small refrigerators; fenced yard and kennel for small pets.*
Rates: *$75–$105; full breakfast, wine. AE, MC, V.*
Restrictions: *Smoking only on porch, closed Christmas Eve and Christmas Day.*

Old Castillo Hotel/Place d'Evangeline

Hard by Bayou Teche, beneath the branches of the Evangeline Oak (which suggests the rooms with the best view), this three-story brick building looks like a "little red schoolhouse." In fact, in its more than 150-year history it has *been* a school, as well as a 19th-century inn (the Castillo Hotel) and a hall for operas and balls.

The Place d'Evangeline restaurant opened in 1987; two years later owners Peggy and Gerald Hulin began restoring the upstairs rooms for overnighters. Restoration continues, and there is a rather unfinished look. Windows have only venetian blinds, but Peggy plans to add curtains and fresh flowers, both of which will improve things. The rooms are enormous (ceilings are sky-high) and at present somewhat sparsely furnished with 19th-century Louisiana French antiques. Room 5 is of awesome size, with a four-poster and a book-filled breakfront. Its bath is also large, with double marble vanities. All baths are adjoining and have modern fixtures and vanities complemented by old-fashioned touches like porcelain washbowls and pitchers.

Address: *220 Evangeline Blvd., St. Martinville, LA 70582, tel. 318/394-4010 or 800/621-3017.*
Accommodations: *5 double rooms with baths.*
Amenities: *Air-conditioning, restaurant.*
Rates: *$75; full breakfast. AE, MC, V.*
Restrictions: *No pets.*

Ti' Frère's House

A trim white gazebo stands on the spacious lawn of Ti' Frère's House, which sits well back from a busy thoroughfare. "Little Brother's House," a gabled Acadian cottage, was built about 1880 of cypress and brick.

A leaded-glass door opens to a central hallway with a crystal chandelier and ornate gold-leaf mirror. Two guest rooms are to the right of the hall; a formal parlor and dining room are opposite. There are two side porches—one glassed in and the other enclosed in latticework.

The big front room has an 1840s full-tester bed, floor-length draperies with lace valances, a working fireplace, and a whirlpool bath (accessible from the hall). This room is a bit noisy, but better suited for a couple than the smaller room, which has a tiny bath with a footed tub and spray shower. Up the steep stairs is another room, with twin beds and an old-fashioned bath.

Address: *1905 Verot School Rd., La-fayette, LA 70508, tel. 318/984-9347.*
Accommodations: *3 double rooms with baths.*
Amenities: *Air-conditioning and TV in rooms; fireplaces in 1 bedroom, parlor, and kitchen, terry-cloth robes.*
Rates: *$60–$65; full breakfast. MC, V.*
Restrictions: *Smoking only on porches or in gazebo, closed Thanksgiving week and Christmas week.*

Tennessee

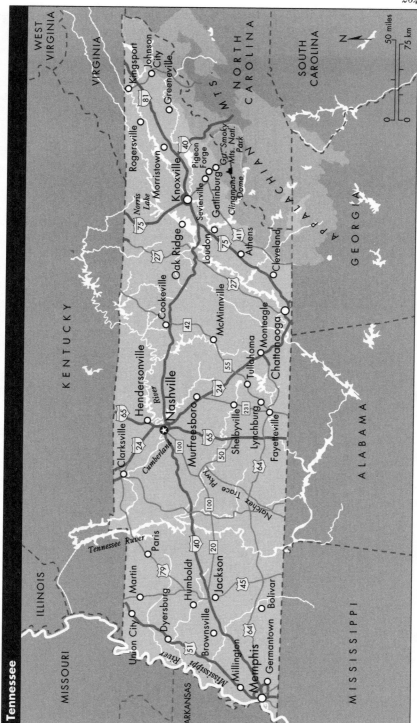

Tennessee

East Tennessee

High above a patchwork of rolling farmland and forests, the peaks of the Great Smoky Mountains dominate the landscape of East Tennessee. Covered with a dense carpet of wildflowers in spring and ablaze with foliage in autumn, the Smokies—named for the mantle of blue haze that so often blankets them—are a joy to hike, meander, or drive through.

The highest and most rugged elevations are in the Great Smoky Mountains National Park, a cool and scenic retreat from the heat of summer. The gateway city to the park is Gatlinburg, not too long ago a remote little place with a few hotels and some mountain crafts shops. Now hordes of visitors are attracted here for outdoor recreation. Neighboring Pigeon Forge—site of Dolly Parton's theme park, Dollywood, and numerous other tourist attractions— has become a favorite with family vacationers.

Less commercialized is the Great Smoky Mountains Arts and Crafts Community just outside Gatlinburg. Pretty byways into the national park take travelers far from the crowds to stunning vistas and roadside trailheads that mark the start of tranquil walks. Mountain folkways often persist in smaller communities, preserved by artisans who practice age-old crafts and traditional cooks who conjure up hearty meals from surrounding streams, fields, and woodlands. Most bed-and-breakfast inns are serenely located off the beaten path, but within a few miles of the major attractions. City lovers will find urban bustle and diversity at Knoxville and Chattanooga.

Places to Go, Sights to See

Andrew Johnson National Historic Site (College and Depot Sts., Greeneville, tel. 615/638–3551). The 17th president's home, grave, and simple tailor shop are preserved here in the smallest national park in the country.

Chattanooga Choo-Choo and Terminal Station (1400 Market St., Chattanooga, tel. 615/266-5000). This renovated facility commemorating the heyday of railroads has several good restaurants, shops, and train exhibits.

The **Dixie Stampede** (3849 Parkway, Pigeon Forge, tel. 615/453-4400). This live dinner-show features barbecue and a musical Wild West rodeo.

Dollywood (700 Dollywood La., Gatlinburg, tel. 615/428-9400). Dolly Parton's popular theme park offers the food, music, and fun of the region in a re-created 1880s mountain village with modern rides and professional entertainment throughout the day.

The **Gatlinburg Skylift** (tel. 615/436-4307) offers a bird's-eye view of the town, as does the **Ober Gatlinburg Tramway** (tel. 615/436-5423), which goes to a ski area and mountaintop amusement park.

Great Smoky Mountains Arts and Crafts Community (take U.S. 321 east of Gatlinburg and turn left on Glades Rd., tel. 615/436-9214 or 615/436-7671) is an enclave of 70 shops and galleries scattered along the back roads outside Gatlinburg.

At the **Great Smoky Mountains National Park** (tel. 615/436-1200), shared by North Carolina and Tennessee, the Southern Appalachians reach their ultimate grandeur as 16 peaks soar more than 6,000 feet. Highlights of the park include *Clingmans Dome,* which, at 6,643 feet, is the highest point in Tennessee; you can take a spiral pathway to the top of an observation tower here for panoramic views of the Smokies. *Cades Cove* (tel. 615/448-6967) is an isolated mountain valley within the park where farmhouses, barns, churches, and an old gristmill still in operation can be seen and visited via a scenic loop road.

Knoxville Zoological Gardens (Chilhowee Park on Rutledge Pike S, Exit 392, tel. 615/637-5331). Home to more than 1,000 animals, this zoo is famous for breeding big African cats and elephants.

Museum of Appalachia (on TN 61, 1 mi east of I-75, Exit 122, tel. 615/494-7680). Three dozen log buildings are preserved in a compound in Norris. The historical displays and exhibitions are sometimes punctuated by musical hoedowns.

Restaurants

The **Apple Tree Restaurant** (Parkway and Frances Rd., Pigeon Forge, tel. 615/453-4961) offers a traditional and inexpensive menu of mountain cuisine, including fried chicken and barbecue. The **Green Valley Restaurant** (804 S. Parkway, tel. 615/453-3500) just up the road has similar fare, offering such dishes as biscuits and gravy with ham as well as seafood in a rough-hewn room with a fireplace.

In Gatlinburg, the **Burning Bush Restaurant** (1151 Parkway, tel. 615/436–4669), decked out with Colonial-era antiques, is a favorite for its sumptuous breakfasts and Continental menu, and the **Smoky Mountain Trout House** (410 N. Parkway, tel. 615/436–5416), aptly named, serves eight separate trout dishes in a cozy restaurant also known for its country fried chicken and prime rib.

The **Copper Cellar/Cumberland Grill** in Knoxville (1807 Cumberland Ave., tel. 615/522–4300), serving sandwiches and drinks, is a fun place to grab lunch or Sunday brunch.

Tourist Information

Chattanooga Area Convention and Visitors Bureau (1001 Market St., Chattanooga, TN 37402, tel. 615/756–8687, 800/338–3999, or 800/322–3344 in TN). **Knoxville Convention and Visitors Bureau** (500 Henley St., Box 15012, Knoxville, TN 37901, tel. 615/523–7263). **Northeast Tennessee Tourism Council** (Box 375, Jonesborough, TN 37659, tel. 615/753–5961). **Smoky Mountain Visitors Bureau** (309 S. Washington St., Maryville, TN 37801, tel. 615/984–6200).

Reservation Services

Bed & Breakfast Host Homes of Tennessee (Box 110227, Nashville, TN 37222, tel. 615/331–5244 or 800/458–2421). **Tennessee Bed & Breakfast Innkeepers Association** (3313 South Circle, Knoxville, TN 37920, tel. 615/579–4508).

Big Spring Inn

On a shady street near Greeneville's historic district sits Big Spring Inn, a short walk from the burial site of the old town's most famous former citizen, Andrew Johnson.

The turn-of-the-century inn has Victorian touches inside and out and is owned and operated by a mother-daughter team whose interests range from cooking, quilting, and gardening to aviation. Jeanne Dries taught elementary school before taking on the inn; her daughter, Cheryl Van Dyck, is a former air-cargo pilot. Together, they impart a breezy sort of efficiency to the restored inn with its beveled, leaded-glass windows and original chandeliers and dining room wallpaper.

Built in 1905 as a wedding present, the house does show its age in places; the big front porch, for example, sags a bit. Bedrooms are generously furnished with antiques: One has a king-size brass bed, one has a pair of doubles reproduced from a 1920s design, and country oak furniture fills another. There is also a room with a good view of the lush backyard and one that used to be the maid's chamber, with a back entrance and a step-up level to the bathroom, whose tin shower dates from 1935. Much of the attraction of the Big Spring Inn is in its dinner and luncheon menus and the personal touch that comes with the meals, served at the 1790 Hepplewhite dining table or in guests' rooms on request. Jeanne and Cheryl are attentive and outgoing, but they respect their guests' privacy, puttering about the place in a low-key fashion. A downstairs common room with a fireplace is stocked with games, books, and a wide-ranging music collection, from Vivaldi to bluegrass. There is another common area upstairs.

Attractions within a short drive of the inn include hiking trails through the Great Smoky Mountains, whitewater rafting, and covered bridges and waterfalls. Greeneville remains distant enough from the mountains, however, to avoid being overrun by tourists. The town retains a New England ambience, with Colonial brick buildings and white church steeples. Antiques shops abound downtown.

Address: *315 N. Main St., Greeneville, TN 37743, tel. 615/638-2917.*
Accommodations: *6 double rooms with baths.*
Amenities: *Air-conditioning, cable TV, 24-hour room service, restaurant; pool.*
Rates: *$60–$78; full breakfast. MC, V.*

Blue Mountain Mist Country Inn

The Blue Mountain Mist Country Inn sits high on a hill amid a 60-acre farm at the foot of the Smoky Mountains, and the owners of this Victorian-style inn, Sarah and Norman Ball, have played their vantage point to the hilt. A wraparound porch is well equipped with leather deck chairs and wicker rockers, and a trail encircles the farm. In spring, flowers blossom in the yard; by summer, the pond, a short distance from the porch, is abloom with water lilies.

The Balls have deep family roots in the area: Their parents grew up in the rugged terrain that is now Great Smoky Mountains National Park (one set lives on another farm across the road), so they know the history and geography of the area—Sarah is a former elementary school teacher, and Norm is principal at a vocational center.

Built in 1987, the inn has little history but is modeled after local farmhouses in a bright and airy fashion, and is furnished with family heirlooms. Old photographs and paintings of the area hang on the walls, and two rooms are equipped with claw-foot tubs. The Bridal Room has a whirlpool bath in the inn's turret. It shares a balcony and the mountain view with The Rainbow Falls Room, which has its own hot tub, tucked behind a stained-glass parti-

tion, and with The LeConte Suite, the most spacious of the rooms.

Common areas upstairs and down have fireplaces, and the inn has shiny hardwood floors throughout. The Balls say the resident hound, Smoky the Husky, has a following all his own and that guests come back just to visit the dog. The inn is on a country road that serves as a back door into both the park and the Great Smoky Mountains Arts and Crafts Community, circumventing much of the local traffic. Pigeon Forge is just 4 miles away.

At press time the Balls were busy building five new cottages in the woods behind the house. They will have fireplaces and whirlpool baths, and are due to be completed by the Spring of 1992.

Address: *1811 Pullen Rd., Sevierville, TN 37862, tel. 615/428-2335.*
Accommodations: *12 double rooms with baths, 5 cottages.*
Amenities: *Cable TV, meal service for groups; outdoor hot tub.*
Rates: *$75–$125; full breakfast and evening refreshments. MC, V.*
Restrictions: *No smoking, no pets, 2-night minimum on summer holiday weekends and in Oct.*

Buckhorn Inn

T he lobby of the Buckhorn Inn, which is on a wooded hillside at the very edge of Great Smoky Mountains National Park, commands one of the best views of the local peaks, and several of the rooms have good views as well. Designed to blend in with its surroundings, the inn has a rustic flavor much as it must have had when it was built in 1938. The Buckhorn is in the middle of a 35-acre compound surrounded by pine trees; comfortable fireside chairs in the sitting and dining rooms invite guests to relax with a glass of wine and look out on Mt. Le Conte. A Steinway grand piano rests in one niche of the lobby, and a library dubbed the "hikers' corner" is in another spot.

Rooms are small—almost to the point of being cramped—but all are carpeted and furnished with simple but understated grace. On all but the warmest days of the year, the scent of wood smoke lingers in the air. In the dining room, meals are served on small tables with green tablecloths.

Four cottages and two relatively spacious guest houses are on the grounds, but the cottages are a cut or two below the inn rooms. Each is equipped with a fireplace and a screened-in porch with a good view, but the carpets are worn, the beds are on the soft side, and the buildings themselves are made of cinder blocks, with concrete decks.

The guest houses have much more room but are not much more comfortable than the cottages. The most interesting bedroom is in the inn's original water tower, where bath facilities are on one level and the bedroom is above.

The Buckhorn Inn is 1 mile from the entrance to the national park and about 5 miles from Gatlinburg and its myriad activities. It is in the midst of some 70 shops, galleries, and eateries of the secluded Great Smoky Mountains Arts and Crafts Community.

Address: *2140 Tudor Mtn. Rd., Gatlinburg, TN 37738, tel. 615/436–4668.*
Accommodations: *14 double rooms with baths (6 inn rooms, 4 cottages, 2 2-bedroom guest houses).*
Amenities: *Air-conditioning, cable TV, restaurant (dinner and breakfast).*
Rates: *$75–$95, cottages $115–$125, guest house $130, guest house/conference center $230; full breakfast. No credit cards.*
Restrictions: *No smoking in main building, no pets, 2-night minimum on holiday weekends and in Oct.*

Milk and Honey Country Hideaway

Fern Miller taps her Amish background to create the homey charm at Milk and Honey Country Hideaway, in the valley between Chilhowee Mountain and Great Smoky Mountains National Park. The two-story cedar inn sits on a slope covered by pine trees, where the scent is unmistakable. The neighborhood is tranquilly rural, to say the least; about the loudest noise to be heard is the occasional creak of the front screen door, and the only traffic is that lined up in late spring and summer at the hummingbird feeders on the wide porch.

Fern, a matronly woman, is a registered nurse who has retained the homemaker skills she learned while growing up in a family of 12 children. Her hobbies run to handicrafts and cooking, and she bakes cookies, cakes, or pies daily for guests.

The inn is Victorian on the inside, rustic country on the outside. The shaded porch is a good place to sip coffee in the morning while listening to the neighbor's roosters crow. A railroad-tie staircase leads down the steep slope to a road lined with wildflowers in spring and summer. Fern opened the inn in 1989, adding a range of distinct touches to the rooms. One is decked out with such Victorian furnishings as an ornate, high white-iron bed covered with a hand-crocheted bedspread made by Fern's mother. Another room has a Shaker-style bed; another has twin beds with splendid handmade quilts. The most personal of the rooms is the Amish one, which includes items from Fern's childhood, like the paddle her parents used on the children, an old-time kitchen sink, the washboard her mother toiled over, and a cast-iron buggy seat. The room's authenticity is unquestionable, except for the floral wallpaper, which seems a bit bold for Amish tastes.

The inn is small but has been made to feel cozy rather than cramped. Guests enter through a common room with a low tongue-and-groove ceiling and a fireplace kept crackling when it's cold outside. The two rooms without private baths are equipped with sinks in wooden vanities. This inn is in the same neighborhood as the Blue Mountain Mist Country Inn, and it enjoys the same back-door entrance to local attractions.

Address: *2803 Old Country Way, Sevierville, TN 37862, tel. 615/428–4858.*
Accommodations: *4 double rooms with baths, 2 doubles share 1 bath.*
Amenities: *Air-conditioning.*
Rates: *$60–$90; full breakfast. MC, V.*
Restrictions: *No smoking, no alcohol, no pets.*

River Road Inn

The River Road Inn sits on a farm-country back road beside the Tennessee River just south of Knoxville. Pamela Foster, a former education counselor for the Air National Guard, is the down-to-earth proprietress who runs the place with her husband, Kent, a contract manager for a Tennessee environmental group. The inn has a lived-in feel thanks in large part to the presence of the couple's three young children. Though the mountains are out of sight beyond the surrounding pastureland, Great Smoky Mountains National Park is 35 minutes away.

The Fosters bought the Greek Revival antebellum home from absentee landlords in 1988 and immediately made improvements. Their renovations continue, though the 134-year-old plantation home still has some rough edges. There is a certain historic charm, however, to features like the original brick floor downstairs and the former slave quarters that are now a pair of guest houses with a shared veranda overlooking the river. Each has a fireplace. Neither is plush, but one has a kitchen and a whirlpool, the other a nursery crib. The original kitchen doubles as a simple guest room equipped with a sofa bed; the house has two other guest rooms and a suite.

One of the Fosters' musical neighbors makes frequent weekend appearances to play the 1880 rosewood grand piano for guests. The inn is decorated in Victorian style throughout, with such Southern touches as the burgundy swag curtains on the windows that look out onto the farm from the breakfast room.

The house was built by the architect who laid out the city of Chattanooga; it has the original winding staircase between three of the four floors, as well as four fireplaces, 12-foot ceilings, and some of the original cabbage-rose wallpaper. Outside, box elders dating from the mid-1800s tower in the yard where General Sherman bivouacked with Union troops. The Fosters are Civil War buffs and can recite local details about the conflict. They say bullets and other artifacts from the war still can be found on the land. Various farm animals lend an agricultural feeling to the place, and visitors are welcome to dip a fishing line into the river.

Address: *River Rd., Box 372, Loudon, TN 37774, tel. 615/458-4861.*
Accommodations: *6 double rooms with baths, 1 suite.*
Amenities: *Air-conditioning; pool.*
Rates: *$65–$95; full breakfast. MC, V.*
Restrictions: *No smoking, no pets.*

Von-Bryan Inn

The Von-Bryan Inn commands what may well be the best mountaintop bed-and-breakfast view in the Smokies. A crooked dirt road climbs to the inn, situated on a knoll with a 360-degree vista of the surrounding mountains. Morning mist typically blankets the patchwork farmlands in the valleys below and the wooded dales beyond.

Jo Ann and D.J. Vaughn bought the house from the original owner, who built it in 1986 as a private retreat, and they now run the place with their college-age sons, David and Patrick. Jo Ann, who operated a telephone-answering service in Knoxville, and D.J., a retired corporate accountant, opened the Von-Bryan after traveling extensively in surrounding states to research country inns. They are quiet but amicable people who offer plentiful advice on the area. D.J., a woodworker by hobby, made many of the pendulum clocks in the house and some of the furniture.

The inn's builder emphasized wood surfaces and soaring, cathedral-like ceilings. Bright skylights filter in the sunshine, and big windows frame the view.

Every room in the inn has a view, in fact, and all are furnished in a blend of traditional and country antiques. The honeymoon suite—one of two with a whirlpool—is appropriately decorated in passionate red hues.

A plush canopy bed graces another room, two brass beds from the Middle East are in another, and a queen spool bed anchors yet another room. Soft jazz is usually on the stereo in the common area upstairs, and a fireplace blazes beside the television in the downstairs living room. In summer, the pool is a good place to bask in the sun; the deck out back is open year-round—it's just off the garden room, which has its own hot tub. The inn is aptly equipped with a telescope for a closer look at distant sights.

The chalet, designed for families, has a full kitchen and a television room as well as a living room with a fireplace, three bedrooms (one with a balcony), and two bathrooms. It has a wraparound deck, too, and a whirlpool bath. Gatlinburg, Pigeon Forge, and the entrance to the national park are within 30 minutes of the inn.

Address: *2402 Hatcher Rd., Sevierville, TN 37862, tel. 615/453–9832.*
Accommodations: *5 double rooms with baths, chalet with 2 baths sleeps up to 6.*
Amenities: *Air-conditioning, TV in living room, dinner service; pool.*
Rates: *$80–$125, chalet $150; full breakfast. AE, MC, V.*
Restrictions: *Smoking in garden room only, no pets.*

Hale Springs Inn

Overnighters at the Hale Springs Inn stay in the same high-ceilinged rooms that hosted presidents James Polk, Andrew Jackson, and Andrew Johnson. Once an important stop in the westward expansion of America, Rogersville is now off the beaten path, a Colonial-style burg known mostly for its tranquillity. The town is away from the hubbub adjacent to the Great Smoky Mountains but close enough to enjoy the national park, about an hour away.

Built in 1824–25 of bricks made from a formula that slaves imported from Virginia, the inn was restored in 1981–82. Ed Pace, a retired Tennessee Valley Authority administrator, is the garrulous manager who supervises the small staff. The inn's lobby has a friendly, small-town quality about it, and the rooms are decorated in the austere fashion of its frontier heyday. Twelve-foot ceilings remain, and each bedroom has a working fireplace. Central heating helps take the drafty chill off the spacious rooms, and the slight mustiness is overshadowed by the air of authenticity. There is a porch off the hallway on each of three levels; a small garden with a gazebo is next door.

Address: *110 W. Main St., Rogersville, TN 37857, tel. 615/272-5171.*
Accommodations: *9 double rooms with baths.*
Amenities: *Air-conditioning, cable TV, restaurant.*
Rates: *$35–$50; Continental breakfast. MC, V*

Seaton Springs Inn

This 1880 farmhouse is off a back road to Gatlinburg, in a narrow valley near Pigeon Forge. Bob and Barbara Kacin turned it into an inn after retiring from the restaurant business in Florida. The farm is named for springs near the house; the supposedly medicinal waters drew summer visitors years ago. An old footbridge crosses a stream just behind the house, where the farm peacocks promenade daily. Out back is a well-preserved cantilevered barn harboring dark nooks and crannies for exploring. The old peach and apple trees still bear fruit, as do the wild blackberry bushes.

The farmhouse ceilings were lowered from their original 12-foot height in the late 1970s, but the place still retains its historic feel. The bedrooms have fireplaces, and parts of the house still have the original tiger oak floors. One room's bed was imported from Scotland in the 1870s, and in most of the windows the original glass shows its age in wavy distortions.

Address: *2345 Seaton Springs Rd., Sevierville, TN 37862, tel. 615/453-1583.*
Accommodations: *1 double room with bath, 2 doubles share 1 bath.*
Amenities: *Air-conditioning, dinner by reservation.*
Rates: *$65–$75; full breakfast. MC, V.*
Restrictions: *No pets.*

Central Tennessee

The sprawling city of Nashville (population about 1 million) extends over eight counties in the middle Tennessee heartland, a pocket of rolling Cumberland Mountains foothills and bluegrass meadows that's one of the state's richest farming areas. Its impressive skyline, dotted with high-rise office towers, is a vivid reminder that it has been a long time indeed since Christmas Day 1779, when James Robertson and a small, shivering party of pioneers began to build a fortress and palisades on the Cumberland River's west bank.

Heralded as the world's Country Music Capital and birthplace of the "Nashville Sound," it also proudly calls itself the Athens of the South. Far from developing a case of civic schizophrenia at such contrasting roles, Nashville has made both labels fit, becoming one of the middle South's liveliest and most vibrant cities in the process. Its role as a cultural leader is enhanced by an impressive performing arts center and the many colleges, universities, and technical schools located here, most notably Vanderbilt University.

A rich Southern heritage is evident in the surrounding countryside, where highways meander through farmland punctuated by small towns. Lynchburg, home of the Jack Daniels Distillery, is among the most famous of the outlying communities. Franklin, not quite as well-known, has much to offer in the way of Civil War history, and Columbia, site of the family home of President James K. Polk, is famous for its antebellum architecture. West of Nashville, Clarksville boasts its very own vineyards and winery as well as several sites memorializing the colorful past of the Old South, from its frontier heyday to its Civil War pain.

Places to Go, Sights to See

Belle Meade Mansion (110 Leake Ave., Nashville, near Centennial Park off West End Ave., tel. 615/356–0501). One of the grand old houses of Nashville, this Greek Revival home set on a 5,300-acre estate is known for its thoroughbred horse stables and a Victorian carriage museum.

Cheekwood (1220 Forest Park Dr., Nashville, tel. 615/356–8000). This verdant estate and Georgian-style mansion is now a fine arts center. It's surrounded by the 55-acre *Tennessee Botanical Gardens*, a showcase picnic ground graced by roses, herbs, and Southern wildflowers.

Country Music Hall of Fame (4 Music Sq. E, Nashville, tel. 615/256–1639). The definitive collection of country music memorabilia is housed here—from Elvis Presley's "solid gold" Cadillac to Kris Kristofferson's songwriting scribbles and Marty Robbins's six-string guitar. The museum ticket is also good for admission to nearby *Studio B*, where Dolly Parton, Elvis, and Roy Acuff—among many others—recorded classic hits.

The Hermitage (4580 Rachel's La., 12 mi east of Nashville, tel. 615/889–2941), built by Andrew Jackson for his wife in a bucolic setting just beyond the urban sprawl of Nashville, is the perfect place for a stroll beneath huge live oaks.

Jack Daniels Distillery (¼ mi northeast of Lynchburg on TN 55, tel. 615/759–4221). Demonstrations on the art of making Tennessee sourmash whiskey are given on daily tours.

Opryland USA (2802 Opryland Dr., Nashville, tel. 615/889–3060). The only musical show park in the country offers performances of 12 different musicals and an array of rides, restaurants, and shops. Opryland is also home to the Grand Ole Opry House.

The Parthenon (in southeast-central Nashville off West End Ave., Centennial Park, Nashville, tel. 615/259–6358). This exact replica of the Grecian original was recently renovated to include a gigantic statue of the goddess Athena and a basement museum.

Nashville's historic **Second Avenue Business District.** Two blocks off the Cumberland River in the Church Street vicinity is one of the country's best-preserved rows of 19th-century commercial buildings.

Restaurants

In Nashville, **Arthur's** (1001 Broadway, tel. 615/255–1494) offers fine Continental fare and seafood specialties in an upscale atmosphere. The **Elliston Place Soda Shop** (24th Ave. and Elliston Pl., tel. 615/327–1090), an out-of-the-way Nashville café not generally known to tourists, serves wonderful diner-style lunches and malts big enough for two. The **Loveless**

Café (3001 West End Ave., tel. 615/320–7778, reservations advised) continues to draw lovers of Southern food to its almost rural Nashville setting for a menu rich in local cuisine. **Maude's Courtyard** (1911 Broadway, tel. 615/320–0543), another venerable Nashville institution, specializes in seafood and some of the world's best Louisiana seafood gumbo. At **Miss Mary Bobo's Boarding House** (Main St., tel. 615/759–7394), an 1867 white frame home in Lynchburg, chatty hostesses serve a midday all-you-can-eat dinner of country fare every day but Sunday to a usually talkative crowd.

Tourist Information

Nashville Area Chamber of Commerce (161 4th Ave. N., Nashville, TN 37219, tel. 615/259–4700). **Nashville Tourist Information Center** (I–65 and James Robertson Pkwy., Exit 85, tel. 615/259–4747). **Tennessee Department of Tourist Development** (Box 23170, Nashville, TN 37202, tel. 615/741–2158) is good for information on outlying areas.

Reservation Services

Bed & Breakfast Host Homes of Tennessee (Box 110227, Nashville, TN 37222, tel. 615/331–5244 or 800/458–2421). **Tennessee Bed & Breakfast Innkeepers Association** (3313 South Circle, Knoxville, TN 37920, tel. 615/579–4508).

Edgeworth Inn

The Edgeworth Inn is located atop the Cumberland Plateau inside a Victorian community nicknamed "the Chautauqua of the South." It is a Southern hotel in the grand, old-fashioned sense, with a broad wraparound porch, screen doors, and—to preserve the timeless spirit of the place—no airconditioning. Every summer, the Monteagle Assembly, the community surrounding the inn, hosts an eight-week program of events that range from literary seminars to classical music concerts. Most of the assembly is vacant during the rest of the year, and guests at the inn are free to wander the enclave of whitewashed houses and scenic paths. Originally a boarding house, the inn was built in 1896 but was renovated and reopened in 1977; none of its authenticity seems to have been lost in the remodeling. The entire compound is listed on the National Register of Historic Places.

David and Wendy Adams, the owner-proprietors, recently retired from prominent jobs in Atlanta. Wendy was director of fund-raising for the city's opera and ballet, and David headed the research department at a brokerage firm. They are an outgoing, articulate couple who know the area well. The Edgeworth library boasts some 2,000 volumes, and its art collection ranges from old-master paintings to contemporary art and items of antiquity picked up during the Adamses' extensive travels.

A gentle quiet pervades the Edgeworth, where guests read, talk, or play board games. The rooms are comfortable and border on the luxurious, with a mix of Victorian antiques and modern furniture. Some rooms have four-poster beds; others have twin brass beds. In warm weather, the porch is the perfect place to spend an evening in a rocking chair; in the afternoon, the hammocks are irresistible. Breakfast is served in a cozy dining room, where guests cannot avoid socializing with other visitors.

Nearby attractions include the University of the South at Sewanee, a small, well-respected school, and the South Cumberland State Recreation Area, which has some trails. The nearby Monteagle Winery produces a nice selection of sweet German wines. A memorable dining spot is up the road at the Four Seasons, a noisy, ramshackle restaurant where wonderful country cuisine is served buffet style.

Address: *Monteagle Assembly, Box 372, Monteagle, TN 37356, tel. 615/924-2669.*
Accommodations: *10 double rooms with baths, 1 suite.*
Amenities: *Pool.*
Rates: *$65, suite $100; full breakfast. MC, V.*
Restrictions: *No pets, 2-night minimum during summer assemblies at Monteagle.*

Hachland Hill Dining Inn

Hachland Hill Dining Inn is a treat for the traveler in search of a rustic evening beside a fireplace. Forty-five minutes north of Nashville in a rural part of Clarksville, it is surrounded by an 80-acre park full of raccoon, deer, and other wildlife. Trails from the inn wander into the woods, and guests wake up to the sound of bird song.

Phila Hach is an extraordinary hostess, a worldly and well-traveled woman who was an airline stewardess before settling down with her late husband, Adolph Hach, and founding the inn 35 years ago. She appears on local television shows that feature the cooking for which she is regionally famous. Part of the attraction of staying at Hachland Hill is having dinner from a menu laden with Southern specialties (pricey but worth the splurge) or indulging in the decadent, full Southern breakfast.

Phila designed the inn after Federal-style Cape Cod homes, and on winter nights, soup bubbles in a pot dangling on a fireplace crane. The bedrooms are neat and comfortable, with historic touches: One has a spool bed with a wedding-ring quilt, and many of the furnishings throughout are Early American. Some have Germanic touches, heirlooms from the time when Phila's family emigrated from their North Sea environs. The mantel keystone over the main fireplace is from the long-since-demolished local tobacco exchange (Adolph was a tobacconist). An 1870 cigar store Indian is on the premises, and a 150-year-old, 2,000-piece "postage-stamp" quilt hangs from a wall. The Hachs are widely traveled, and bits and pieces from their sojourns are in evidence: a Japanese print here, a Swiss vase there.

One wing of the inn branches off into a little cedar wedding chapel and a small guest house. Out back sit a pair of cabins, perfect for either romantic solitude or family lodging. Each cabin has two levels and modern bathrooms and comes with a guarantee of tranquillity; though the cabins are equipped with phones on which guests can dial out, the phones do not ring. The cabins are on a wide, shady terrace, where warm-weather cookouts are held, looking down on a wooded ravine near a pen where a pair of goats live.

Address: *1601 Madison St., Clarksville, TN 37043, tel. 615/647-4084.*
Accommodations: *4 double rooms in main inn, 3 guest houses sleeping up to 4, 6, and 9.*
Amenities: *Air-conditioning, restaurant, fax and other office facilities.*
Rates: *$78; Continental breakfast. AE, V.*

McEwen Farm Log Cabin Bed & Breakfast

The McEwen Farm Log Cabin Bed & Breakfast features a trio of buildings for rent on a farm 2 miles from the Natchez Trace, hidden away on a back road. No signs point the way, but it's easy enough to find: just north of the crossroads community of Duck River, named for the local stream known for smallmouth bass and summertime canoeing. Bill and Helen McEwen run the place from their house on a hilltop pasture several hundred yards from the well-spaced lodgings, evidently situated with privacy in mind. The farm is a popular stopover for bicyclists traveling the Natchez Trace Parkway, and it attracts visiting joggers and walkers as well to its big, quiet fields.

Helen is a homemaker, and Bill, a former community college administrator, raises hunting dogs; the hounds are kept in pens near the barn, their howls occasionally piercing the otherwise quiet night. The McEwens began hosting guests in 1987, after restoring a log cabin that dates back to the 1820s. They designed the cabin on the back of a paper sack with the intention of turning it into a guest house for family and friends, but passersby were drawn to it immediately. The original structure belies its age; its floors and walls are rugged but clean, and a ceiling fan twirls above the main room, which has a fireplace and leads into a modern kitchen. Outside there is a porch swing; up-stairs are three beds. Cabin No. 2— next to a railroad sign that says, "McEwen Crossing, elevation 607"— is much like No. 1.

Downhill in an adjacent dale is No. 3, which is not a cabin at all but a restored 1879 Victorian passenger train depot from nearby Centerville, where it served the North Carolina and St. Louis Railways. The most secluded of the lodgings, it is completely wrapped by a wooden deck generously furnished with rocking chairs that face a tiny stream. It has two bedrooms, two baths, and a kitchen beneath its original 14-foot ceilings; the ticket window has been turned into a reading nook.

Guests at McEwen Farm are welcome to meet the hunting dogs or wander the grounds at will. Nashville is 45 minutes away, and—this being Tennessee walking horse country—stables abound.

Address: *Bratton La., Box 97, Duck River, TN 38454, tel. 615/583-2378.*
Accommodations: *3 cabins with baths.*
Amenities: *Air-conditioning; canoe rental; pets allowed.*
Rates: *$85; Continental breakfast. MC, V.*

Monthaven
Bed & Breakfast

To meet the host of Monthaven Bed & Breakfast is to encounter something of Nashville's fabled country-music world. Musician Hugh Waddell maintains a record library of 10,000 albums he shows to his guests, and he happily talks about the industry he has come to know through his role as Johnny Cash's publicist. Hugh, an intelligent and witty man whose business cards say "Johnny Cash Sent Me," seems too young to be in charge of a Greek Revival mansion, but he operates the inn with panache. The place has been in his family for years; Hugh inherited it from his mother, who opened Monthaven in the early 1980s as a casual lodge for family and friends but gradually accepted other visitors.

Monthaven, decorated with Victorian elements inside and out, was built as a plantation home around 1840 on the site of a former Indian campground and today remains separated by considerable acreage from its closest neighbors. It sits well above a busy highway, maintaining a tranquil air, though it's within 30 minutes of every Nashville attraction. No sign marks the driveway, noted only by an old-fashioned mailbox and a simple stone gate. Old trees ring the mansion, and cows amble in fields beyond a white barn. The place is rich in history, including a Civil War association that saw it used as a military hospital for both Union and Confederate soldiers.

A guest cabin nearby was reconstructed in 1938 from logs that went into a similar structure almost 200 years ago. Finished inside with white oak and cedar, it is a roomy but romantic building with a big fireplaced living room. The cabin also has a full kitchen and sports some oddities, such as a ping-pong table and a museum-style glass case that holds local memorabilia running the gamut from old pharmaceuticals to Civil War bullets.

The house itself has two guest rooms—one upstairs and one down—that are far less rustic than the cabin, furnished with antiques and four-poster beds beneath high ceilings. The small library just off the main hall features some striking French provincial parlor furniture, and a hallway chandelier adds to the inn's feel. Animal lovers will appreciate the Monthaven fauna, which includes cats as well as a dog named Elvis.

Address: *1154 W. Main St., Hendersonville, TN 37075, tel. 615/824–6319.*
Accommodations: *2 double rooms with baths, 1 cabin.*
Amenities: *Air-conditioning, cable TV; pool.*
Rates: *$75–$85; Continental breakfast. AE, D, DC, MC, V.*

Old Cowan Plantation

The Old Cowan Plantation captures some of the genteel charm of the Old South in an 1886 Colonial home beside a country road. Hostess Betty Johnson's ambition was to open an antiques shop in the house, but after deciding there was a glut of such businesses in nearby Fayetteville, she turned the house into an inn and gift shop, filling a void in local lodging. Though it was modernized in 1985, the place clings tenaciously to its farmhouse ambience.

Betty's demeanor reflects her profession: She works as a personal-growth consultant and communications-skills therapist. Her hobbies show up around the house in various handicrafts, quilts, and cross-stitch items, many of them priced for sale in the downstairs room that doubles as the gift shop when it isn't occupied. The room has a gas-log fireplace and a pedestal tub in its shared bath.

One upstairs room has a brass bed and a spacious bath and shower; the other is equipped with a pair of twin beds and shares the downstairs bath. The home's original staircase leads to a narrow landing with an antique pie safe that now serves as a linen closet. Breakfast is served at a lace-covered table with a view of the neighboring pasture.

The inn's setting is one of its biggest draws. In spring, the yard is full of flowers; when snow is on the ground, trees frame the house in a striking winter scene. Guests usually gravitate to the front-porch rocking chairs, particularly in the early evening, when deer graze across the road and sometimes even come into the yard.

The Old Cowan Plantation is 15 miles from the Jack Daniels Distillery at Lynchburg. It is also 30 miles from the Space and Rocket Center in Huntsville, Alabama, where visitors can tour NASA labs and space shuttle test sites and wander through a park full of rockets, tour the center's hands-on museum, or view an Omnimax space film. Fifteen minutes away is Tims Ford Lake, with waterskiing in summer and fishing year-round. The inn is just north of U.S. 64, which has been designated an official scenic highway east to Chattanooga and as far west as Shiloh National Military Park, site of a bloody Civil War battle.

Address: *Rte. 9, Old Boonehill Rd., Box 17, Fayetteville, TN 37334, tel. 615/433-0225.*
Accommodations: *1 double room with bath, 2 doubles share 1 bath.*
Amenities: *Air-conditioning, cable TV.*
Rates: *$40; Continental breakfast. No credit cards.*
Restrictions: *No smoking.*

Lynchburg Bed & Breakfast

The Lynchburg Bed & Breakfast serves as a cozy, centrally located inn near the famous Jack Daniels Distillery in Lynchburg, a speck of a town in the farmland of south-central Tennessee. The proprietors, Virginia and Mike Tipps, opened the inn seven years ago. Lifelong residents of the area—Virginia is a former mail clerk and Mike is a manager at the distillery—they know what to see and do around Lynchburg.

The 1877 farmhouse (built for the county's first sheriff) is on a residential back street and is decorated with simple antiques. Both of its slightly cramped bedrooms are up a narrow staircase, and the second-floor common area leads to a balcony that's a good place to sip coffee in the morning. The distillery has tours daily, and visitors won't want to miss late lunch or dinner at nearby Miss Mary Bobo's Boarding House. The town square is a short walk away and has a handful of arts and crafts shops centered around a monument to Confederate soldiers.

Address: *Mechanic St., Box 34, Lynchburg, TN 37352, tel. 615/759–7158.*
Accommodations: *2 double rooms with baths, 1 suite.*
Amenities: *Air-conditioning, cable TV.*
Rates: *$42–$45, suite $85; Continental breakfast. MC, V.*
Restrictions: *No pets.*

West Tennessee

*The mighty Mississippi River defines the western boundary
of this section of Tennessee, rolling through the fertile
plain of the Delta and past the "cradle of the blues" on its
way to the sea. Stretching east and north from Memphis,
the western plains where cotton was king are interspersed
with hardwood forests, wildlife refuges, and state parks.
Outdoor people flock to the region's lakes and rivers, and
to Kentucky Lake, on the Kentucky border, the second-
largest man-made lake in the world.*

*You'll hear of folk heroes Davy Crockett and Casey Jones,
explore the Civil War battlefield at Shiloh National
Military Park, and visit Alex Haley's hometown of
Henning, where the story of his roots began.*

*The culture of the Mississippi Delta converges in Memphis,
a city with a uniquely American music heritage that is
well preserved today behind the gates of Graceland, on
stage at the Beale Street nightclubs, and in the old stories
told at Sun Studio. Memphis also retains a small-town feel,
its past still alive in 28 separate historic districts.*

*The city has used its riverside well, placing an entertain-
ment park on an island and the brand-new Great
American Pyramid complex beside the Hernando DeSoto
Bridge. The Memphis in May International Festival,
scheduled before the arrival of summer's heat and
humidity, pays tribute to the city's music and features the
open-air World Championship Barbecue Cooking Contest.
In November, there's Blues Music Week. Memphis honors
the civil rights movement and Martin Luther King at the
new National Civil Rights Center in the former Lorraine
Motel.*

Places to Go, Sights to See

Alex Haley State Historic Site Museum (Haley St., Henning, 50 mi north of Memphis via U.S. 51, tel. 901/738–2240). The boyhood home of the Pulitzer Prize–winning author of *Roots* is in this charming little river town.

Beale Street Historic District. A restored row of nightclubs and shops pays homage to the Memphis blues. Highlights include the *W. C. Handy Memphis Home and Museum* (352 Beale St., call ahead, tel. 901/527–2583); the *Old Daisy Theatre* (329 Beale St., tel. 901/525–1631), which shows continuously running silent short films; and any of 10 nightclubs, whose acts are advertised in the *Memphis Commercial Appeal* and other local papers. The *Rum Boogie Café* (182 Beale St., tel. 901/528–1050) has one of the best house bands in the city, and *B. B. King's Memphis Blues Club* (139–147 Beale St., tel. 901/527–5464) features appearances by its famous eponym.

The **Casey Jones Home and Railroad Museum** (U.S. 45 Bypass and I–40, Jackson, tel. 901/668–1223), adjacent to an old-fashioned ice-cream shop, houses an excellent collection of train memorabilia.

Dixon Gallery and Gardens (4339 Park Ave., Memphis, tel. 901/761–5250) blends art with nature, displaying Impressionist paintings and 18th-century Germanic porcelain in a museum surrounded by 17 acres of flowers.

Graceland (3717 Elvis Presley Blvd., tel. 901/332–3322 or 800/238–2000), Memphis' most popular attraction, offers a glitzy and sometimes poignant look at Elvis Presley, who lived and is buried here and whose memory generates a sizable souvenir industry from a row of shops across the street.

The **Great American Pyramid** (on the Mississippi River at I–40, Memphis, tel. 901/576–7241) finally opened in the fall of 1991. The 32-story stainless-steel structure pays tribute to Memphis's Egyptian namesake with a 20,000-seat sports arena. It will also house the American Music Awards Hall of Fame, the College Football Hall of Fame, and a Hard Rock Café, among other restaurants and shops.

Mud Island. The 53-acre Memphis park is accessible by walkway, boat, or monorail (boat terminal, 125 Front St., tel. 901/576–7241). Attractions include the 18-gallery *Mississippi River Museum* and the exceptional *River Walk*, a scale model of the great river 5 blocks long, tracing every bend of the Mississippi on its journey from Minnesota to the Gulf of Mexico.

National Civil Rights Center (450 Mulberry St., Memphis, tel. 901/521–9699). The civil rights struggle of the 1950s and '60s is documented in the former motel where the Rev. Martin Luther King Jr. was assassinated in 1968.

National Ornamental Metal Museum (374 W. California St., Memphis, tel. 901/774–6380). This one-of-a-kind place is devoted to preserving the art of metalworking from gold to iron; exhibits include a working blacksmith shop.

Peabody Hotel (149 Union Ave., Memphis, tel. 901/529–4000 or 800/732–2639). This Memphis treasure was restored and reopened in 1981 after two decades of neglect. It's worth a trip just to see the resplendent lobby, where the hotel's famous ducks spend the day.

Shiloh National Military Park (100 mi east of Memphis, off U.S. 64 on TN 22, tel. 901/689–5275). A beautiful country setting is a grim reminder of the horrific Civil War battle and of the 4,000 soldiers buried here.

Sun Studio (706 Union Ave., Memphis, tel. 901/521–0664), a recording venue by night, offers daytime tours on the hour through the famous studio where Elvis Presley, Carl Perkins, Johnny Cash, and Jerry Lee Lewis made their first records. The adjacent *Sun Studio Café* sells burgers and chili.

Restaurants

In Memphis, **Captain Bilbo's Restaurant** (263 Wagner Pl., tel. 901/526–1966) isn't much to look at, but it draws a loyal following for its seafood. For something fancier, **Chez Philippe** in the Peabody Hotel (149 Union Ave., tel. 901/529–4188) is worth the splurge. For sandwiches and pastries made daily, try **Café Espresso** (tel. 901/529–4165), also in the Peabody. **Charlie Vergos' Rendezvous** (General Washburn Alley, tel. 901/523–2746), famous for its pork barbecue, is a real Memphis institution. **Hemmings** (7615 W. Farmington Rd., Saddle Creek shopping center, Germantown, tel. 901/757–8323) is a departure from traditional Delta dining, serving excellent Southwest and California cuisine. **John Wills' Bar and Grill** (5101 Sanderlin Rd., tel. 901/761–5101) serves good barbecue, baked beans, and mustard-spiced coleslaw in an upscale atmosphere, while **Corky's Bar-B-Q** (5259 Poplar Ave., tel. 901/685–9744) is the place to do some down and dirty barbecue eating. The elegant **La Tourelle** (Overton Sq., 2146 Monroe Ave., tel. 901/726–5771) is one of the best French restaurants in the area.

Tourist Information

Memphis Convention and Visitors Bureau (Morgan-Keegan Tower, 50 N. Front St., Suite 450, Memphis, TN 38103, tel. 901/576–8181). **Memphis Visitors Information Center** (207 Beale St., Memphis, TN 38103, tel. 901/526–4880). **Tennessee Department of Tourist Development** (Box 23170, Nashville, TN 37204, tel. 615/741–2158).

Reservation Services

Bed & Breakfast Host Homes of Tennessee (Box 110227, Nashville, TN 37222, tel. 615/331–5244 or 800/458–2421). **Bed & Breakfast Memphis Reservation Service** (Box 41621, Memphis, TN 38174, tel. 901/726–5920). **Tennessee Bed & Breakfast Innkeepers Association** (3313 South Circle, Knoxville, TN 37920, tel. 615/579–4508).

Magnolia Manor

Well off the beaten path in southwest Tennessee, Magnolia Manor creates an imposing presence along Main Street in tiny Bolivar, a historic burg that boasts the oldest courthouse in West Tennessee. It is one of two dozen or so antebellum homes in the neighborhood that were spared from Union torches during the Civil War; tours of the area can be arranged.

The two-story house is built in the Colonial Georgian style, its 1849 construction date noted on a bronze eagle mounted onto one corner. The walls, made of sun-dried, slave-laid red brick, are 13 inches thick. It was constructed as a symmetrical rectangle, with center halls upstairs and down running the depth of the house and separating the spacious rooms.

Elaine and Jim Cox, a reserved but polite couple, were inspired to open the inn in 1984 by the bed-and-breakfasts they'd stayed in on a long trip through Europe. Elaine is a former cosmetology instructor; Jim is a retired hospital administrator. Beyond travel, the Coxes' hobbies are interior decorating and cooking, both of which are evident at the manor; the house is ornately restored, and guests can order a home-cooked dinner by reservation. Downstairs, the inn's 14-foot ceilings allow space to relieve the heavy furnishings and a lingering, musty scent reminiscent of old houses in distant childhood memories. The downstairs

suite, a double parlor, is furnished opulently with early Victorian pieces: a big rosewood headboard, a rosewood gentleman's chair, and others with hand-carved flowers. Upstairs are two double rooms and a spacious suite, all sharing a common bath. One bed is graced with a massive walnut canopy; another is made of the same wood, its construction dated from plantation timbers. The suite has a gas-log fireplace and a walnut-and-rosewood Victorian bed and matching furniture, shipped upriver by steamboat years ago from New Orleans.

For history buffs in particular, Bolivar and its environs make for a pleasant day trip from Memphis, 90 minutes away. Nearby is Shiloh National Military Park, and historians believe Hernando de Soto passed through the area on his epic search for the Mississippi River, a journey noted by various markers.

Address: *418 N. Main, Bolivar, TN 38008, tel. 901/658–6700.*
Accommodations: *3 double rooms share 1 bath, 1 suite.*
Amenities: *Air-conditioning, cable TV in common area.*
Rates: *$55–$65; full breakfast. No credit cards.*
Restrictions: *No smoking, no pets.*

The Wren's Nest Inn

The Wren's Nest Inn is in the sleepy college town of Martin, across the street from a shady municipal park whose main attraction is an old red caboose. The late-Victorian house is unmistakable by its turret, which looms above the trees in the yard. Glen and Sue Byrd are the owner-hosts; he is a former Knoxville restaurateur, and she teaches fashion merchandising at the University of Tennessee campus a few blocks from the inn. Guests are more likely to encounter Glen than Sue.

The Byrds are a well-traveled pair; Glen did a stint as a missionary in Africa, and both have made trips through Europe. They keep a hand in international activities by frequently serving as a host family to foreign students, whom guests have a good chance of meeting from time to time. Glen also works part-time at the university, teaching English to immigrants. Their affection for distant places shows up throughout the house in works of art like handwoven Egyptian rugs and African batik prints.

The 1894 house is in impeccable condition; it was beautifully restored in the early 1980s and is spotlessly maintained. Its high ceilings lend a spacious air to the place, and the windows let sunlight stream in, illuminating carpeted rooms decorated with dark Victorian fabrics and bright, floral wallpaper. The Byrds

are accomplished basket makers, and their handiwork turns up on shelves and in nooks throughout the house. A long stairway leads upstairs from the bright parlor past a zebra hide that hangs on one wall.

One bedroom is outfitted with a four-poster canopy rice bed; another has twin four-poster beds and an adjacent screened-in "sleeping porch"; both have private back entrances. Guests have the run of much of the lower floor, including a high-ceilinged living room and a classic wraparound porch with a swing, near the confluence of two sidewalks where neighbors take evening strolls.

The Byrds' private quarters has a separate entrance, and they are quiet but attentive hosts. One of their habits is to place fresh-baked pastries or a bowl of fruit in the guest rooms each day. The inn is out of the way for Memphis–Nashville travelers, but well worth the diversion, roughly 2½ hours from either city.

Address: *109 Park St., Martin, TN 38237, tel. 901/587–6563.*
Accommodations: *2 double rooms with baths.*
Amenities: *Air-conditioning, cable TV, and soft-drink bars in rooms.*
Rates: *$55; full breakfast. AE.*
Restrictions: *No pets.*

Highland Place

Peggy and Larry Hewgley spent a whole summer looking for a house they could turn into a bed-and-breakfast inn—then found it in their own backyard. The Federal-style brick manor, across from the high school where Peggy taught for 17 years, sits behind a black wrought-iron fence in a historic if somewhat run-down district.

All of its owners seem to have treated the house well since its 1911 construction. Its 6,600 square feet have glossy hardwood floors and sunlight is fractured by leaded-glass windows and bounced off several chandeliers. The kitchen and the breakfast nook are relatively new additions. Other renovations include the library (with a fireplace) and the recreation room (with a billiard table) illuminated by a skylight. The bedrooms are roomy and decorated with antiques and family heirlooms. Two share a bathroom with a 6-foot tub, and a small private nook off the hall is usually available for small guests. One bedroom is furnished in austere oak, the other in walnut with burl inlay.

Address: *519 N. Highland Ave., Jackson, TN 38301, tel. 901/427–1472.*
Accommodations: *1 double room with bath, 2 doubles share 1 bath.*
Amenities: *Air-conditioning, cable TV in common area.*
Rates: *$45–$55; full breakfast. MC, V.*
Restrictions: *No smoking, no pets.*

The Peach Tree Inn

The Peach Tree Inn is on a West Tennessee back road an hour east of Memphis, not far from Interstate 40. Owner-hostess Sharon Anderson, a former Houston restaurant manager, has brought her culinary skills back to her hometown. Much of what her inn kitchen offers is culled from recipes handed down from her mother, whose handicrafts are sold in a gift shop on the premises. The inn's location, on a 200-acre farm, is its biggest draw. The cypress building is a former lodge (built in 1978) that retains its original rustic charm, although the interior has been polished up in recent years. A big plank porch off the sun room sits above a small lake stocked with catfish (guests are welcome to drop in a line), and sports-oriented people will appreciate the adjacent field, a frequent volleyball and softball site, which once served as a driving range for a pair of visiting golfers. Spectators can watch the action from an old-fashioned swing on the wide front porch. The bedrooms are adequately furnished (one has a view of the lake), with beds that are a little soft.

Address: *1551 Skeet Rd., Brownsville, TN 38102, tel. 901/772–5680 or 901/772–9369.*
Accommodations: *4 double rooms with baths.*
Amenities: *Air-conditioning, cable TV in common area, restaurant, gift shop; pool, hot tub.*
Rates: *$45; Continental breakfast. MC, V.*
Restrictions: *Smoking discouraged, no pets.*

Directory 1
Alphabetical

Directory 2
Geographical

Alabama

Anniston
Noble House *167*
Ashville
Roses and Lace *169*
Fairhope
The Guest House *182*
Merschon Court *182*
Florence
Wood Avenue Inn *168*
Franklin
Rutherford Johnson
House *181*
Greensboro
Blue Shadows *177*
Lafayette
Hill-Ware-Dowdell
House *177*
Mentone
Mentone Inn *166*
Montgomery
Red Bluff Cottage *178*
Mt. Meigs
The Colonel's Rest *173*
Prattville
The Plantation House
176
Selma
Grace Hall *174*
Talladega
Oakwood *175*

Georgia

Americus
Merriwood Country
Inn *157*
Morris Manor *158*
Andersonville
A Place Away *158*
Atlanta
Ansley Inn *129*
Brunswick
Brunswick Manor *142*

Rose Manor Guest
House *144*
Calhoun
Stoneleigh Bed and
Breakfast *134*
Chickamauga
The Gordon-Lee
Mansion *132*
Clarkesville
Glen-Ella Springs
Hotel *130*
Commerce
The Pittman House
133
Cumberland Island
Greyfield Inn *140*
Darien
Open Gates *141*
Fort Oglethorpe
Captain's Quarters
Bed & Breakfast
Inn *132*
Hawkinsville
The Black Swan Inn
150
Macon
The 1842 Inn *149*
Victorian Village *151*
Madison
The Brady Inn *150*
Mountain City
The York House *134*
Savannah
Ballastone Inn *142*
The Gastonian *139*
Magnolia Place Inn
143
Olde Harbour Inn *143*
Pulaski Square Inn
144
Senoia
The Veranda *156*
Statesboro
Statesboro Inn *151*

Tate
The Tate House *131*
Thomasville
Evans House Bed &
Breakfast *157*
Susina Plantation Inn
159
Watkinsville
Rivendell *133*

Louisiana

Abbeville
A la Bonne Veillée *258*
Cheneyville
Loyd's Hall *243*
Covington
Plantation Bell *236*
Destrehan
Ormond Plantation
253
Jackson
Milbank *251*
Lafayette
Bois des Chênes *261*
Chrétien Point
Plantation *259*
Mouton Manor Inn
260
Ti' Frère's House *262*
Madisonville
River Run Plantation
236
Napoleonville
Madewood Plantation
250
Natchitoches
Cloutier Townhouse
242
Fleur-de-Lis *244*
Jefferson House *244*
William and Mary
Ackel House *245*
New Orleans
Cornstalk Hotel *234*

Notes

Notes

Notes

Notes

The South

Please help us evaluate B&Bs and country inns for the next edition of this guide. Mail your response to Fodor's Travel Publications, Inc., 201 E. 50th St., New York, NY 10022.

B&B or Inn

City/State

Comments

B&B or Inn

City/state

Comments

General Comments

Your Name *(Optional)*

Number/Street

City/State/Zip

Fodor's Travel Guides

U.S. Guides

Alaska
Arizona
Boston
California
Cape Cod, Martha's
  Vineyard, Nantucket
The Carolinas & the
  Georgia Coast
The Chesapeake
  Region
Chicago
Colorado
Disney World & the
  Orlando Area
Florida
Hawaii

Las Vegas, Reno,
  Tahoe
Los Angeles
Maine, Vermont,
  New Hampshire
Maui
Miami & the
  Keys
National Parks
  of the West
New England
New Mexico
New Orleans
New York City
New York City
  (Pocket Guide)

Pacific North Coast
Philadelphia & the
  Pennsylvania
  Dutch Country
Puerto Rico
  (Pocket Guide)
The Rockies
San Diego
San Francisco
San Francisco
  (Pocket Guide)
The South
Santa Fe, Taos,
  Albuquerque
Seattle &
  Vancouver

Texas
USA
The U. S. & British
  Virgin Islands
The Upper Great
  Lakes Region
Vacations in
  New York State
Vacations on the
  Jersey Shore
Virginia & Maryland
Waikiki
Washington, D.C.
Washington, D.C.
  (Pocket Guide)

Foreign Guides

Acapulco
Amsterdam
Australia
Austria
The Bahamas
The Bahamas
  (Pocket Guide)
Baja & Mexico's Pacific
  Coast Resorts
Barbados
Barcelona, Madrid,
  Seville
Belgium &
  Luxembourg
Berlin
Bermuda
Brazil
Budapest
Budget Europe
Canada
Canada's Atlantic
  Provinces

Cancun, Cozumel,
  Yucatan Peninsula
Caribbean
Central America
China
Czechoslovakia
Eastern Europe
Egypt
Europe
Europe's Great Cities
France
Germany
Great Britain
Greece
The Himalayan
  Countries
Holland
Hong Kong
India
Ireland
Israel
Italy

Italy 's Great Cities
Jamaica
Japan
Kenya, Tanzania,
  Seychelles
Korea
London
London
  (Pocket Guide)
London Companion
Mexico
Mexico City
Montreal &
  Quebec City
Morocco
New Zealand
Norway
Nova Scotia,
  New Brunswick,
  Prince Edward
  Island
Paris

Paris (Pocket Guide)
Portugal
Rome
Scandinavia
Scandinavian Cities
Scotland
Singapore
South America
South Pacific
Southeast Asia
Soviet Union
Spain
Sweden
Switzerland
Sydney
Thailand
Tokyo
Toronto
Turkey
Vienna & the Danube
  Valley
Yugoslavia

Wall Street Journal Guides to Business Travel

Europe

International Cities

Pacific Rim

USA & Canada

Special-Interest Guides

Bed & Breakfast and
  Country Inn Guides:
  Mid-Atlantic Region
New England
The South
The West

Cruises and Ports
  of Call
Healthy Escapes
Fodor's Flashmaps
  New York

Fodor's Flashmaps
  Washington, D.C.
Shopping in Europe
Skiing in the USA &
  Canada

Smart Shopper's
  Guide to London
Sunday in New York
Touring Europe
Touring USA